THE · HISTORY · OF SILVER

THE · HISTORY · OF SILVER

GENERAL EDITOR · CLAUDE BLAIR

BLACK CAT

First published in Great Britain in 1987
by Macdonald & Co (Publishers) Ltd
London & Sydney

Reprinted 1991 by Macdonald & Co (Publishers) Ltd
under the Black Cat imprint

A member of Maxwell Macmillan Pergamon
Publishing Corporation

British Library cataloguing in Publication Data

The History of Silver.
1. Silverware—Collectors and collecting
I. Blair, Claude
739.2'37 NK7230

ISBN 0 7481 0308 2

Filmset by Servis Filmsetting, Manchester

Printed and bound in Czechoslovakia by Aventinum

Editor: Sarah Chapman
Art Editor: Linda Cole
Picture Researcher: Philippa Thomson
Indexer: Helen Baz

The photographs on page 1–6 show items from the silver-gilt twenty-three-piece toilet service of 1670 by Pierre Prévost, which is also illustrated on page 111. (Trustees of the Chatsworth Settlement, Chatsworth, Derbyshire)

Macdonald & Co (Publishers) Ltd
Orbit House
1 New Fetter Lane
London EC4A 1AR
50834

· CONTENTS ·

· INTRODUCTION ·

Silver is one of the most beautiful and versatile of the traditional decorative metals, and therefore also one of the most widely used. A great deal has been published about its many different aspects, and it may reasonably be asked, therefore, what the justification is for producing yet another book on the subject. The answer is that this one does something never attempted in English before: it provides, in a single volume, a survey of the development of silver – and to a lesser extent gold – plate in Europe and European America from the earliest times to the present day. All previous surveys that have attempted international coverage (and they are few) have been much narrower in scope and, because they were written by individuals, less authoritative in overall treatment. The range and authority of this book reflect the fact that it has been written by a team of people who are specialists in their fields.

The main purpose of the book is to provide the interested non-specialist with a general account of silver that will both stimulate interest further and offer a sufficient grasp of the subject to enable further studies to be made with the aid of the bibliographies. Specialists, too, will find that it provides a helpful background survey of their subject.

Since the book deals only with Europe and European America, a brief account of what happened in other parts of the world follows here, and especially of the origins – in the Near East – of the working of silver and gold. Gold is often found naturally in its metallic state ('native gold'), and in this form does not have to be extracted from ore by any technical process, as is the case with most other metals. For this reason, it was perhaps the first of all the metals to be worked, despite the fact that the earliest gold artefacts recorded date only from c.5000 BC (as against c.9500 BC for copper ones). The metal was already being deliberately mined in the Near East at least as early as the fourth millennium BC, and one of the first main sources was the Nubian desert, where numerous mines were exploited by the Egyptians. Gold is rarely found in its pure state, but normally contains a percentage of other metals, notably copper and silver; and a high proportion of the earliest 'gold' or 'silver' artefacts has proved on analysis to be made of electrum, a natural gold-silver alloy. In order to produce pure metal the electrum had to be refined. Native silver is very much rarer than gold, and it could never have been an adequate source of supply for the metalsmiths. Silver ore takes a number of forms, the most important of which in the ancient world was galena (lead sulphide), from which lead is also obtained, and which is widely distributed. Silver-rich lead was smelted from the ore, and the silver was then extracted by the cupellation process described on page 233, which was possibly used as early as the seventh millennium BC in the Near East.

The cupellation process had become widespread by the beginning of the third millennium, both in the Near East and in Greece, and it is at this period that the earliest examples of wrought gold and silver plate, in the modern sense, appear. They include the vessels from the Sumerian royal graves at Ur in Mesopotamia (c.2500 BC), Alaca Hüyük in Cappadocia (c.2400–2200 BC) and Troy in West Anatolia (c.2200 BC). These are of such extraordinarily sophisticated design, including many cup shapes that could pass as twentieth-century ones, and show such a mastery of most of the goldsmithing techniques still used today as to indicate that they are part of a fairly long tradition of metalworking. Earlier pottery versions of one particular form of silver two-handled beaker have been excavated in Anatolia, and the fact that their design is clearly a metalworker's one suggests that an even earlier metal prototype existed, presumably in Anatolia also. It is, in fact, in this area, which was probably the cradle of all metalworking, that the craft of the goldsmith – the term covers workers in both gold and silver – seems first to have developed.

For several thousand more years plate of fine quality continued to be produced in Mesopotamia, by the various nations that established themselves there. Knowledge of the goldsmith's craft spread from there westwards to Europe, eastwards to Persia and possibly to the Indus Valley civilization of India, northwards to the steppe peoples, and perhaps via them to China and eventually Japan, though the last country seems to have had little enthusiasm for gold and silver plate until it came under European influence in modern times.

Gold and silver seem to have been unknown to the inhabitants of North America until the arrival of Europeans, but in South America the precious metals, especially gold, were widely used. Wrought and cast goldwork is first encountered in Peru in c.2000 BC, and silver about a thousand years later in the same region. Knowledge of metal technology then spread slowly over the rest of the subcontinent, but did not reach Mexico until AD c.700–900. All the metalworking techniques used in the Old World were eventually employed there, though with less sophistication, but whether developed independently or under outside influence is uncertain. Since Spanish colonial times, distinctive silver plate has been produced in Central and South America, but except for the products of the earliest colonial goldsmiths of Mexico it has rarely been of high quality.

CLAUDE BLAIR

· 1 · THE ANCIENT WORLD ·

BYZANTINE CUP *(facing page), gold, from near Durazzo, Albania, c.AD 600. It is decorated in repoussé with low-relief female personifications of imperial cities and the metropolitan sees of Constantinople, Cyprus, Rome and Alexandria, identified by Greek inscriptions.*
Height: 16.8 cm (6½ in)
(Metropolitan Museum of Art, New York, Gift of J. Pierpont Morgan)

Throughout the ancient Greek and Roman world, gold and silver plate had an important role to play, both in life and in death. For example, during the Trojan War, in about 1250 BC, Odysseus is said by Homer (*Iliad* xxiii, 741: composed c.750 BC) to have won an athletic prize of a silver wine-mixing bowl during the funeral games for Patroclus. At another funeral, of the Emperor Justinian at Constantinople in AD 565, an essential part of the ceremonial was a great display of gold plate.

The story of silver plate begins in about the middle of the third millennium BC, when the gold and silver deposits of Anatolia first became available. The export of these metals to supply Sumerian craftsmen introduced to Asia Minor Mesopotamian techniques of metalworking. The consequent manufacture of gold and silver vessels in Asia Minor indicated a growing prosperity there, which in turn resulted in trade further west after 2500 BC. Gold and silver vessels reached the mainland of Greece via Troy and the islands of the Cyclades. Silver from Anatolia also reached Crete, where precious metals were not available locally.

From about 2000 BC, as wealth in Crete was concentrated more and more into the hands of royal rulers, gold or silver plate began increasingly to be used. The wealth of Crete from this time until about 1600 BC – for which there is the evidence of the Minoan palaces and Cretan control of maritime trade – had no parallel on mainland Greece. Nevertheless, the flowering of Mycenaean culture, which was later to become pre-eminent in Greece, is represented by the Royal Burials at Mycenae. The gold and silver vessels from the shaft graves at Mycenae, mostly dating from the second half of the sixteenth century BC, demonstrate the considerable wealth of their owners, kings and great men who drank from their own personal cups of precious metal. The decoration on the gold and silver in the shaft graves is predominantly Minoan in character, and it was once thought that the vessels represented loot taken by the Mycenaean lords from Crete. Nevertheless it is now generally believed that in the sixteenth century mainland Greece and Crete were independent, but that there was Cretan influence on shapes, techniques and decoration, probably through Cretan imports and perhaps through the presence on the mainland of Cretan craftsmen.

The Mycenaean culture of Greece was now predominant, politically and economically, especially after the Minoan culture of Crete was destroyed, perhaps by a huge eruption of the volcano of Thera in about 1500 BC, followed by an invasion of mainland conquerors about fifty years later. In Crete from now on there was only one palace, at Knossos, which was finally destroyed in the fourteenth century or the early part of the thirteenth. In Greece, on the other hand, palaces continued to flourish at various places besides Mycenae. At about the turn of the thirteenth and twelfth centuries, the palaces of Mycenae, Tiryns and Pylos were destroyed by fire, marking the onset of an artistic Dark Age. Throughout the Bronze Age gold and silver were in the possession only of the very wealthy and in shrines of the gods; and precious metal vessels were always rare; but finds of the period after 1200 BC have been very few indeed.

· EARLY GREEK SILVER ·

The Mycenaean world finally collapsed in about 1200 BC, and it was not until the eighth century that the expansion of Greek colonization and trade began. This led to a great increase in the wealth and population of the Greek cities. By the seventh century dedications of gold and silver plate were being made at Greek sanctuaries, metalwork was being imported from the eastern Mediterranean, and, when local and foreign supplies of precious metals again became available, gold and silver plate began to be made in the richer Greek city-states.

According to the Greek writer Theopompus, the dedications of Gyges, King of Lydia (c.687–652), were the first to be made at Delphi, the most notable being six golden bowls weighing 'thirty talents'. The fashion for dedications was followed by other rulers, who came into contact with the Greeks, and then by the Greeks themselves. In the second half of the seventh century the Cypselid tyrants of Corinth built a treasury at Delphi in which the treasure of Gyges was housed. In about 580 BC the Greek Glaukos of Chios made a silver crater and iron stand for Alyattes of Lydia which, according to Herodotus, were the most remarkable sight of all the offerings at Delphi. Croesus, Alyattes' son, presented among other gifts two great bowls, or craters, probably the work of Theodorus of Samos, which stood in the temple of Apollo until it was burned down in 548 BC, and were then moved to the treasury of Clazomenae. During the same period, wealthy and powerful cities flourished on the western and southern coasts of Asia Minor, and even the Anatolian kingdoms of Lydia and Phrygia were largely Hellenized. The Persian conquest first of Lydia and then of Greek cities did not eradicate the strong Greek influence in Asia Minor; rather, the skilled Greek artists found employment at the Persian court, and much of Persian art of the late sixth century betrays this indebtedness. Greek and Persian art became fused, and many of the great number of objects now known from the East Greek area are Greek in style rather than in form. Some, however, are among the finest Greek objects of the period, as, for example, the silver *oinochoe* which has a handle in the form of a youth, and which is now in the Metropolitan Museum of Art, New York.

The handleless cup or bowl known as a *phiale mesomphalos* is of eastern origin. It was already in use as a sacrificial vessel in the seventh century, and was quickly adopted by the Greeks as their own most common libation vessel. It is a shallow, flat-bottomed bowl with curving sides and a central boss pushed up on the inside, which was used as a finger-grip when drinking or pouring. Over two hundred bronze examples were found in the sanctuary of Hera Limenia at Perachora in Greece, but only one in plain silver,[1] indicating the rarity of silver vessels at this period. Indeed, only one other plain silver *phiale mesomphalos* has survived, from the rich late-Hallstatt burial at Vix (France), which dates from the later sixth century BC (Musée de Châtillon-sur-Seine).

Decorated forms of the *phiale mesomphalos* also occur. The most remarkable is a deep gold bowl with a series of wide radial flutings and a central *omphalos*, found in Greece, at Olympia (Museum of Fine Arts, Boston). An inscription on the outside near the rim records that the bowl was dedicated by the sons of Kypselos of Corinth from the spoils of Herakleia. The bowl may well have been made and lettered at Corinth at some time between 625 and 550 BC.

There is no direct evidence that other gold and silver vessels existed in Greece itself; but some of the bronze vessels made in Corinth find parallels in precious metal in Etruria in Italy, and it is possible that they too were made in Corinth. One of the few examples of archaic-period plate that has survived in the Greek world is a two-handled silver *kantharos* from Rhodes (Louvre), dating from the first quarter of the sixth century BC.

LIBATION BOWL *(phiale mesomphalos), gold, from Olympia, Greece, early sixth century* BC. *Such bowls were eastern in origin and became the most common form of Greek libation vessel. The inscription on the outer rim says that the bowl was dedicated by the sons of Kypselos of Corinth from the spoils of Herakleia. Diameter: 16.8 cm (6½ in) (Museum of Fine Arts, Boston, Francis Bartlett Fund)*

Some of the earliest Greek examples of precious metalwork were made for wealthy barbarians living on the fringes of the Greek world. The Illyrian burials of the later sixth century BC found at Trebenishte in Yugoslavia include three silver *kantharoi*, considered to be pure Greek works, while vessels made by Greek craftsmen to the order of the local tribesmen include drinking horns and tall, cylindrical beakers.[2]

· ETRUSCAN SILVER ·

A considerable amount of gold and silver plate has survived from early Etruria (now central Italy), especially of the seventh century. The wealth of the Etruscan lords is preserved in several rich burials, including the Regolini-Galassi tomb at Caere (Cerveteri), and the Bernardini and Barberini tombs at Praeneste (Palestrina). Some of the silver vessels in the Etruscan tombs are in shapes characteristic of the area, and it is believed that many of the shapes of the *impasto* and succeeding *bucchero* pottery were made in imitation of precious metal vessels. Thus in the Regolini-Galassi tomb, dating from around 650 BC, there was a little *amphora* with repoussé spiral decoration which is exactly matched in early *bucchero* (Vatican Museums, Rome). Among the drinking vessels, one of the most popular, also purely Etruscan, is a deep, footless bowl, closing slightly at the top, raised rather than cast, and usually decorated below the rim with rows of incised semicircles. Examples have been found in the Regolini-Galassi tomb (Vatican Museums, Rome), in several tombs at Marsiliana d'Albegna, in Vetulonia, and in the Bernardini (Villa Giulia, Rome) and Castellani tombs at Praeneste.

Other drinking cups have Greek, mainly Corinthian, shapes. In the Regolini-Galassi tomb there are four well-preserved examples as well as fragments of a deep cup of this type, which has curving sides, a concave flaring rim, and two upturned loop handles (Vatican Museums, Rome). The Protocorinthian deep cup or *kotyle*, with horizontal loop handles, was one of the most popular shapes in Etruria during this period, occurring in gold, silver, bronze and pottery. Two gilded silver examples, found in the Barberini tomb at Praeneste, were decorated with engraved friezes of animals and silver ornament inspired by decoration such as is found on the 'Phoenician' bowls. A fine gold cup of this form was found in the Bernardini tomb at Praeneste. On each of the handles are perched a pair of sphinxes, some of the details of which are made up of lines of gold granulation. (All three cups are now in the Museo Nazionale di Villa Giulia, Rome.) Granulation was used by the Etruscans mostly for their elaborate jewellery; but it is found also on some surviving gold vessels, such as the deep bowl of about 650 BC in the Victoria and Albert Museum, London, and a little *alabastron* from Palestrina now in the British Museum.

Objects of eastern origin are found in Etruria. Just as bronze versions of 'Phoenician' bowls have

DEEP BOWL *(facing page, above), gold, Etruscan, about 650* BC. *Its granulation ornament was an Etruscan technique usually reserved for elaborate jewellery. Height: 6 cm (2⅜ in) (Victoria and Albert Museum, London)*

CUP, *gold, from the Bernardini tomb, Praeneste, second quarter of the seventh century* BC. *On each handle is perched a pair of sphinxes, some of the details of which are made up of lines of gold granulation. Height: 13.2 cm (5¼ in) (Museo di Villa Giulia, Rome)*

BUCKET, *silver-gilt, from Chiusi, c.650* BC. *Known as the Plicasnas* situla *from the name, either of the owner or maker, inscribed on it twice. The decorated scenes depict an Etruscan religious ceremony with athletes, pipers and dancers; the lower scene shows a shepherd and his flock. Height: 13.8 cm ($5\frac{3}{8}$ in) (Museo Archeologico, Florence)*

been found in Greece at Olympia, so they form the most numerous series of silver bowls found in seventh-century Etruria. Examples found at Caere, Praeneste and elsewhere, for example at Pontecagnano near Salerno (Petit Palais, Paris), are among the best of their kind. It is unlikely that any of the bowls found in Etruria were made there, even though the precise technique, in which gilding was finally scraped away so as to leave gilt frames round the figures, is not found anywhere else. The decorative scheme of the Bernardini bowl, with its mixed oriental style, is typical of these bowls. The central medallion shows a male figure in Egyptian dress – an Egyptian pharaoh – overcoming his enemies. Round this medallion is a frieze of horses and birds perhaps inspired by Greek work. The main frieze illustrates a series of episodes connected with hunting which are Assyrian in derivation, and another Egyptian motif, a coiled snake's body, frames the whole bowl.

Another variety of shallow bowl in seventh-century Etruria, like the Phoenician bowls, is also oriental in origin, having its nearest parallels in Assyria. It has a low foot ring and a series of radial flutings, convex on the outside, framing a flat central zone. It is common in bronze; but there is one silver example, very fragmentary, from the Regolini-Galassi tomb (Vatican Museums, Rome), and fragments of another were found in the Artiaco tomb at Cumae.[3] These bowls were presumably sacrificial in function, like the Greek *phialai mesomphaloi*, though the *phialai* and their derivatives were not known in Etruria until the sixth century.

Besides sacrificial bowls and drinking vessels, there were other vessels including an unusual large bowl from the Bernardini tomb which has a close-fitting lid in the form of a strainer, to which a ladle was attached, forming a kind of table-set for serving wine (Museo Nazionale di Villa Giulia, Rome). Less unusual are a number of jugs, also of eastern origin. One fairly complete example and a fragment of another were found in the Regolini-Galassi tomb (Vatican Museums, Rome). These jugs have a tapering neck with a little trefoil mouth and a handle composed of two tubes set together.

Other examples of this kind of jug have been found at Praeneste, Vetulonia and Cumae, and versions were also made in bronze and in *bucchero* pottery.[4] It seems certain that they are of eastern origin, and a very close parallel for the Regolini-Galassi jug is a fragment of neck and handle with palmette plaque, found at Curium in Cyprus.[5]

The rich tombs of the seventh century preserved good evidence of a small number of types of silver plate. Very few later Etruscan pieces have survived, but one of them is the bucket or *situla* from Chiusi known as the Plicasnas *situla* (Museo Archeologico, Florence), from the name – either that of the owner or the maker – inscribed on it twice. The shape of the *situla* may be inspired by a Corinthian model; but the decoration, while related to the style of the Phoenician bowls, seems to be an independent Etruscan development with scenes from Etruscan life. On the main zone of figured ornament is depicted a religious procession to a sacrificial altar with athletes, pipers, and dancers. The lower scene shows a shepherd and his flock. The *situla* was probably made in Chiusi between 600 and 550 BC.

From the later sixth century in Etruria no vessels of precious metal have survived. Evidence, however, that expensive plate was still being made and used comes from paintings of metal vessels in sixth-century tombs. In seventh-century Etruria the practice of burying gold and silver vessels with the dead preserved them for posterity; but the practice did not outlast the century, and for this reason the finds give only a partial idea of the quantity of Etruscan silver. After 600 BC there is almost no direct evidence for Etruscan plate until the fourth century. One silver beaker with engraved bands of ornament, from Cività Castellana, may date from the fifth century BC (Metropolitan Museum of Art, New York). After that little has survived except from a number of tombs of the third and second centuries, especially at Chiusi. It is rather poor in quality and mostly imitates contemporary Greek fashions.[6] Its manufacture may well have been stimulated by the influx of plate from southern Italy as a result of Roman campaigns in the region.

· LATER GREEK SILVER ·

Because of booty won from the Persians in 479 BC, silver from new veins of ore at Laurion, and gold from Thracian mines controlled by Athens, the quantity of gold and silver plate produced in Greek cities in the fifth century increased. Most of it seems to have been ritual vessels or for use as dedications at sanctuaries of the gods. The evidence for the increase in production and for its use comes from official inventories of temple-treasures, catalogues made by boards of magistrates appointed to take stock. For example, in the Treasure Lists at Delos are sixty kinds of vessel.

Very little classical silver has been found in Greece itself. Our knowledge of it comes largely from finds on the fringes of the Greek world such as Thracian tombs in Bulgaria, Scythian tombs in southern Russia, and tombs in Cyprus. At Duvanli, in southern Bulgaria, for example, the tumulus of Baschova Mogila, dated to the end of the fifth century, contained the burial of a man whose ashes were collected in a *phiale mesomphalos* made by an Attic craftsman (Archaeological Museum, Plovdiv). Other silver vessels in the tomb included a stemless cup, a drinking horn (*rhyton*) ending in the foreparts of a horse, and a little jug with a reeded body, all probably of Athenian workmanship. The *phiale*, jug and *rhyton* have the name of their Thracian owner, Dadaleme, inscribed on them in Greek letters. While the men's burials at Duvanli included helmets and cuirasses, the women's burials included gold jewellery, also made by Greek workshops. All the mounds contained a large number of pottery vases, and the women's, like the men's, also contained silver vessels. The Koukova mound, for example, dating from the very beginning of the fifth century, included a silver *phiale* (Archaeological Museum, Plovdiv) and a silver *amphora* (Archaeological Museum, Sofia).

The treasure from the Koukova mound dates from a period when the Thracian regions were under Persian rule and the Persians were preparing their campaign against the Greeks. The *phiale* and *amphora* are Achaemenid pieces, part of the Persian metalwork which had a strong influence throughout this period. Enormous booty of Persian gold and silver was taken at the Battle of Plataea in 479 BC and divided among the allies. The type of the Achaemenid *phiale* is known in Greece as early as the sixth century BC: a bronze example was found at the Sanctuary of Hera Limenia at Perachora. No silver examples, however, are recorded in Greece itself, and knowledge of them depends on Bulgarian finds such as the Koukova treasure (500–490 BC) and the Moushovitsa treasure (c.500 BC), which was also a Thracian woman's burial (Archaeological Museum, Plovdiv). There is no doubt that they did exist in Greece in silver, however, and by the middle of the century Greek craftsmen were imitating them. Of the three *phialai* of about 450 BC from the Alexandrovo burial, one is gold and two are of silver, and one of the silver *phialai* has a Greek inscription giving the name of its owner, Kotys, King of the Engestai (Archaeological Museum, Plovdiv). The adoption

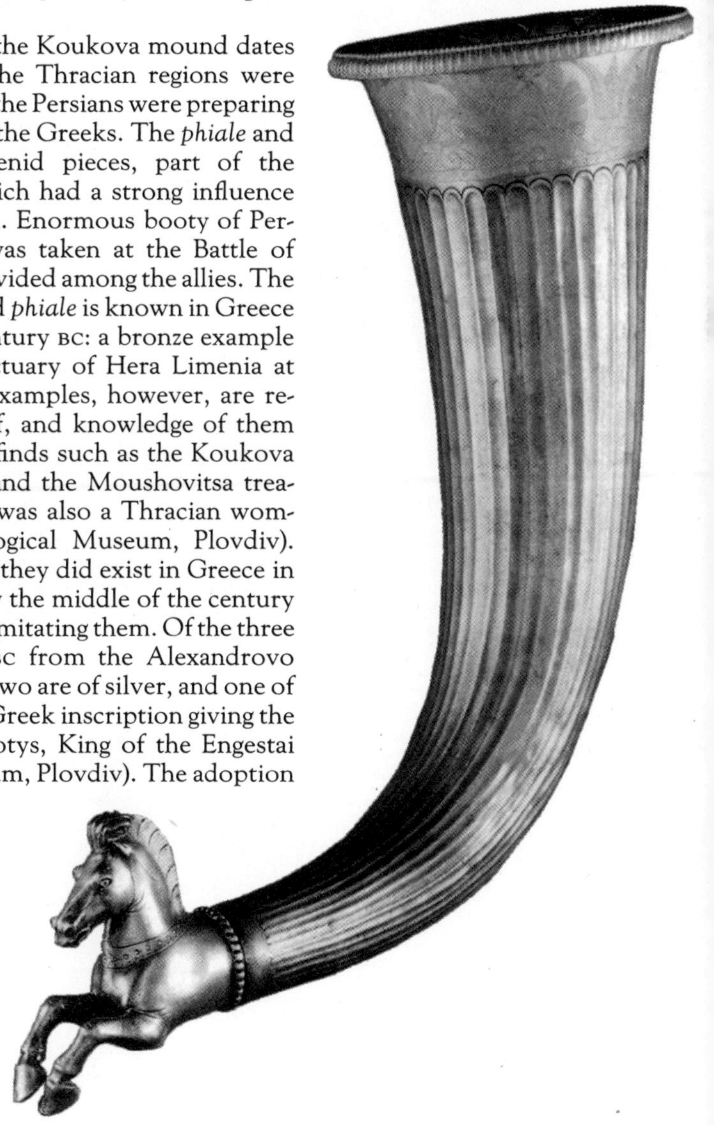

RHYTON, *silver with gilt details, ending in the foreparts of a horse. From the Baschova Mogila mound, Duvanli, Bulgaria, c.400* BC. *Height: 20.6 cm ($8\frac{1}{8}$ in) (Archaeological Museum, Plovdiv)*

of the *rhyton* as a popular form of drinking vessel has a parallel origin in Persian influence and a long subsequent history.

In about the middle of the fifth century Greek silversmiths began to engrave a small number of types of cups, including the *kantharos* and the *kylix*, with figured scenes and ornaments, as counterparts of pottery vessels decorated in the prevailing manner of line drawing in the red-figure technique. The output was not large, and the fashion did not last much longer than fifty years. One of the earliest examples of this kind of silver comes from the second kurgan (tumulus) of the group of burial-mounds known as the Seven Brothers, in the Kuban, USSR. It is a fragmentary *kylix* with a medallion on the inside showing Bellerophon in combat with the chimera, surrounded by a frieze of male figures (Hermitage Museum, Leningrad). The scenes were engraved on the silver and then covered with gold leaf, which was then apparently burnished over the engraving so that the lines of the drawing showed through it. The surplus leaf was then cut away from the outlines of the figures. A stemmed *kantharos* from the tumulus of Golyamata Mogila at Duvanli belongs to about the same period (Archaeological Museum, Plovdiv). Scenes are engraved on opposite sides of the body. On one, a Naiad is bringing a fawn to Dionysos; on the other, a satyr and a maenad are dancing. The *kantharos* is one of five known in silver, of which four are of Greek manufacture (Plovdiv, Leningrad and Baltimore), while the fifth, from

Roscigno near Paestum in Italy, is a copy of a southern Italian pottery *kantharos* (Provincial Museum, Salerno).

One of the finest pieces of engraved plate found at Duvanli is a *phiale mesomphalos* from the tumulus of Baschova Mogila, dating from the last decades of the fifth century BC (Archaeological Museum, Plovdiv). *Phialai* richly decorated with repoussé reliefs also became common in the later fifth century. The fashion had been developing earlier in the century, and by the end of it *phialai* with overall repoussé decoration were popular. A *phiale* with a design of concentric rows of acorns was shown in the hands of the Caryatids from the Erechtheum. A gold *phiale* of about 400 BC, found in South Russia in the tumulus of Kul Oba (not far from Kertch),[7] had as its basic decoration radiating lotus and palmette patterns, overlaid with a profusion of ornamental motifs: a narrow frieze of dolphins round it, and Gorgons' heads superimposed on the elements of the radiating leaf pattern, grotesques, and scrolls and floral motifs.

Towards the end of the fifth century many of the characteristic black-glazed pottery vessels of Attic manufacture were matched in silver, reflecting increased private wealth and the use of gold and silver plate in domestic life. A silver cup from Nymphaeum, near Kertch in South Russia, may be dated by comparison with clay vessels to around 400 BC (Ashmolean Museum, Oxford), while another from the Vouni Treasure in Cyprus, stored in a jar with other vessels in 380 BC, has its closest parallels among the thin-walled black-glazed cup-*kotylai* of the late fifth century in Athens.[8] A plain cup with a ribbed handle, which was found in 1879 at Dalboki, Stara Zagora in Bulgaria, also has exact counterparts in Attic black-glazed pottery. The contents of this find also included two engraved beakers of local design, one of them decorated by a Greek craftsman. (All three vessels are now in the Ashmolean Museum, Oxford.)

Silver vessels with animal heads or *protomai* also show the close relationship between silver and pottery in the fifth century. The two main forms are the animal-head cup, of which pottery examples are known throughout the fifth century, and the horn *rhyton* ending in the foreparts of an animal, which did not appear in any material in the Greek world until the later part of the fifth century. Greek craftsmen of the Black Sea colonies, however, were making this kind of vessel for Scythian patrons earlier in the century, and examples of their work include the two gold horn *rhyta* which were found, together with a purely Persian piece, in the fourth kurgan of the Seven Brothers in the Kuban, a burial of a little before 450 BC.[9] One of these ends in a ram's head and the other in the foreparts of a leaping dog, while the horns are decorated with chased geometric ornament. A Greek version had evolved by the end of the fifth century: the *rhyton* from Baschova Mogila at Duvanli, which probably comes from an Attic or east Greek workshop (Archaeological Museum, Plovdiv), is fluted down its length and ends in the foreparts of a horse, and has a band of engraved lotuses and palmettes on the upper part of the horn and leaf ornament on the lip. A complementary picture is presented by Greek animal-head cups: the earliest in pottery belong to the early fifth century BC; but there are no surviving metal examples occurring before the end of the century.

While some foreign fashions, such as horn *rhyta*, were gradually taken up by Greeks themselves, Greek craftsmen continued to make some vessels solely for non-Greek customers. In about 400–350 BC craftsmen in Panticapaeum (Kertch) made fine silver vessels for Scythians, which were generally decorated in relief with scenes of Scythian life. The shapes of the vessels are often local, but the craftsmanship is Greek. The masterpiece is the Chertomlyk *amphora* (Hermitage Museum, Leningrad), which is 70 cm (27½ in) high and has three outlets in the lower half of its body, each equipped with a strainer. The principal outlet is in the form of a horse's head, while the side outlets have lions' heads. On the shoulder are two bands of relief decoration, the upper band showing animal groups in low relief, and the lower band showing, in high relief, Scythian warriors breaking in a horse. The figures in the latter have been cast separately and soldered on. The body of the vase is covered with an overall design of birds, scroll ornament and palmettes, which on the main side is worked in repoussé relief, while on the back it shades off into engraving.

CASKET, *gold, from Vergina, Greece, Royal Tomb, 350–325* BC. *It contained bones, probably those of Philip II of Macedon. It bears the star emblem of the Macedonian dynasty. Height: 20.7 cm (8 in) (Archaeological Museum, Thessaloníki)*

AMPHORA *(facing page, left), silver-gilt, from Chertomlyk, USSR, c.350* BC. *A masterpiece of Greek craftsmanship, it is decorated with scenes of Scythian life, scrolls and palmettes. Height: 70 cm (27½ in) (Hermitage Museum, Leningrad)*

OINOCHOE *(facing page, right), silver, from Vergina, Royal Tomb, 350–325* BC. *The vessel bears a Silenus-head. Height: 24.5 cm (9½ in) (Archaeological Museum, Thessaloníki)*

· EARLY HELLENISTIC TIMES ·

In spite of written evidence of the existence of wealth in gold and silver, the quantity of plate from early Hellenistic times (330–200 BC) was small until recent years, when very large numbers of vessels have been found , mainly in Macedonian tombs. Their high artistic level indicates that similar contemporary works, discovered in modern Bulgaria, South Russia, Turkey and Egypt, also came from the workshops of Macedonia. The most important treasure is that discovered at Vergina in 1977, in what is probably the tomb of Philip II of Macedon himself (Vergina mound, Royal Tomb II), and now in the Archaeological Museum, Thessaloníki. Two gold caskets in the tomb, each decorated with the star emblem of the Macedonian dynasty, contained the bones respectively of a man and of a woman, probably Philip II and his last wife, Kleopatra. Besides the two caskets, gold objects in the tomb included three wreaths, a royal diadem, a quiver, a pectoral, two Medusas, a pin, little disks and a woman's diadem. There were also horse trappings and weapons – swords, greaves, a cuirass and a shield – and two wooden couches decorated with ivory, gold and glass. In addition, eighteen silver vessels were found, among them *oinochoai*, *skyphoi*, a strainer, two *amphorae* in the shape of lidded *alabastra*, bowls, ladles and spoons. Such a collection of silver vessels of the fourth century BC is unique, not, however, isolated: another unrifled royal tomb (Tomb III) in the same mound at Vergina contained twenty-nine silver vessels. As a whole they cannot be compared with the silver from Tomb II, but some of the pieces are incomparable, such as the *patera* with a ram's head at the end of its handle.

Among domestic plate, silver ladles and strainers become common in this period. Their form does not differ from the Mycenaean and Etruscan examples. Bowls are rather shallow, handles straight or curving slightly backwards and widening to a shoulder from which springs a narrow loop ending in a duck's head. A ladle of this form was part of a find at Prusias in Bithynia, Turkey (Metropolitan Museum of Art, New York). Another comes from a late fourth-century grave in the Sellenskaya Mountains on the Taman peninsular (South Russia), which contained a collection of plate typical of early Hellenistic finds.[10] Besides the ladle there was a strainer with handles terminating in ducks' heads, a fragmentary plain-stemmed *kantharos*, a plain cup-*kotyle* with two loop handles, a *phiale* of Achaemenid type with fluted body and a straight offset rim, a small long-necked flask with scroll decoration and fluting on the body, a jug, a little plain flask and a bucket-shaped container with a lid and loop handle. Another ladle of the same kind was found with several silver vessels at Montefortino in North Italy, dated to before 290 BC (Metropolitan Museum of Art, New York).

The forms of some of the silver drinking cups of this period are derived from classical predecessors. In the Sellenskaya and Prusias finds, for example, there are cup-*kotylai* with loop handles, a high cavetto foot and a flaring rim, which may be compared with Attic clay vases of about the end of the fourth century; and two *kantharoi*, from a tomb of the late fourth century BC at Derveni in Macedonia, may be compared in shape with Attic black-glaze pottery vessels of about 300 BC. Western Greek workshops in Italy or Sicily, also of about 300 BC, seem to be the source of an important group of stemless *kylikes* decorated on the inside with engraved ornament. Examples come from Montefortino (Metropolitan Museum of Art, New York) and Boscoreale in Italy (British Museum) and from Paternò in Sicily (Staatliche Museum, Berlin). A woman's grave of about 200 BC, found beside the Quarantine Road at Kertch, contained silver including two shallow *kylikes*, decorated inside with appliqué medallions representing Helios in his chariot.[11] This form of decoration must have been common on the drinking cups of the period and is imitated in clay vessels. The Quarantine Grave also includes a cup-*kotyle*, engraved on the outside with a chased and gilt necklace stretching between the handles, and the moulding of the foot is also decorated (Hermitage Museum, Leningrad). It was at this time that cups with chased ornament on the outside were beginning to become fashionable, and all the drinking cups with rich repoussé and chased decoration belong to the period after 200 BC.

Vessels for religious use include bowls of various sorts, drinking horns, and 'head vases'. Two of the most magnificent of the bowls are gold *phialai mesomphaloi*. One, from the late fourth-century treasure found at Panagyurishte in Bulgaria, has three concentric rows of negro heads in repoussé relief with a narrow band of ornament and a row of acorns immediately round the *omphalos*; the spaces between the heads and the acorns are filled with palmettes in low relief (Archaeological Museum, Plovdiv). An inscription gives the weight of the *phiale*, expressed in the Attic system and its equivalent in Persian darics (100). The second gold *phiale*, in New York, is ornamented with three concentric rings of acorns diminishing in size towards the centre and a row of beechnuts immediately round the *omphalos*. The spaces between are filled with low-relief ornament of little bees and motifs based on palmette designs. This *phiale* has a weight inscription in Punic characters dating from the third century BC and a short Greek graffito, suggesting that it was made by a Greek for a Carthaginian.

The design of the Panagyurishte and New York *phialai mesomphaloi* had been developed in the late fifth century BC and is Greek. A *phiale* in the

KANTHAROS, *silver, with double handles in the shape of ivy leaves, fourth century* BC. *Height: 8 cm (3⅛ in) (Archaeological Museum, Thessaloníki)*

ALABASTRON *(facing page), silver, from Vergina, Royal Tomb, 350–325* BC. *Appliqué heads of Herakles decorate the points where the handles are attached to the body. Height: 35 cm (13¾ in) (Archaeological Museum, Thessaloníki)*

PHIALE MESOMPHALOS *(right), gold, third century* BC. *The motifs are in circles of acorns and beechnuts round the omphalos. Diameter: 22.4 cm (8¾ in) (Metropolitan Museum of Art, New York, Rogers Fund)*

CUP *(facing page, above), silver, from Alesia, France, probably mid-first century* BC. *It has typical Hellenistic naturalistic ornament. Height: 11 cm (4⅜ in) (Musée des Antiquités Nationales, Saint-Germain-en-Laye)*

AMPHORA-RHYTON *(facing page, below), gold. Panagyurishte, Bulgaria, c.300* BC. *This richly decorated piece was probably made in eastern Greece. Height: 28 cm (11 in) (Archaeological Museum, Plovdiv)*

FOOTLESS BOWLS *(below), silver, from Cività Castellana, Italy, second half of the second century* BC. *Diameter: 18 cm (7 in) (Museo Nazionale, Naples)*

Prusias find, however, also in New York, is one of the so-called leaf *phialai*, a type derived from Achaemenid fluted *phialai* of the fifth century and perhaps known in Greece by the fourth century. In the Hellenistic period there are complicated interactions of this sort between Greek and Achaemenid forms. Another example is the 'Achaemenid deep bowl', a type of little bowl with a hemispherical body and a concave upper part with a flaring rim. Examples of the shape occur in the fifth century in Achaemenid contexts, for example a silver one from Gordion in Turkey and a gold one (in Teheran Museum) inscribed 'Xerxes the Great King'; but the type does not occur in the Greek world until the fourth century. The earlier examples are either plain or decorated very simply, with an ovolo moulding dividing the two parts of the body. In Hellenistic times, however, while the upper part is plain, the lower is ornamented with fluting, ribbing or leaf ornament. A particularly elaborate example of the tall form of these 'deep bowls', a cup from Ithaca in Greece (and now in the British Museum), is not much earlier than 200 BC. It has a calyx of leaves on the lower part combined with egg-shaped bosses, and an engraved and gilded vine wreath on the upper part of the body. This combination of leaves and bosses had been popular in Egypt from early Ptolemaic times. An example from Egypt (Brooklyn Museum, New York) is decorated with a calyx of leaves similar to those found on 'Megarian' pottery bowls of the second century BC.

Particularly spectacular examples of drinking horns (*rhyta*) and head-vases were found in the Panagyurishte Treasure, the source of the *phiale mesomphalos* mentioned above. The treasure includes four gold *rhyta*, three head-vases and a richly decorated *amphora-rhyton* (Archaeological Museum, Plovdiv). It seems likely that these vessels were made in eastern Greece, where Persian influence was particularly strong during the early Hellenistic period, since some of the weight measurements on the vessels are given both in the Persian and in the Attic system.

It is hard to suppose any other use than a ritual one for the vessels in the Panagyurishte Treasure, which suggests that they were the possessions of a religious shrine. For personal use, however, toilet vessels became an important part of silversmiths' work in Hellenistic times. Such vessels include perfume vases, little trinket boxes (*pyxides*), mirrors and strigils. An attractive perfume vase and a *pyxis* were found in a tomb of the late third century BC at Bolsena in Italy (Metropolitan Museum of Art, New York). The perfume vase has leaf ornament on the lower part, a necklace-garland chased and gilded on the body and two handles, giving it the appearance of a little *amphora*. Although it has an Etruscan inscription the vessel was probably made in southern Italy, perhaps Apulia. The little cylindrical *pyxis*, of a type very common in the Hellenistic period, has a pyramidal lid with a moulded finial which is decorated with leaf ornament, and a band of chased scroll ornaments and decorated mouldings on the body.

In the third century the box mirror, with a hinged lid decorated with repoussé relief, replaced the open disc mirror of archaic and classical times. The finest silver example is one with a relief of Selene and Endymion, found in a grave at Demetrias in Greece (National Museum, Athens). A number of small mirrors of this type, probably made in Tarentum, have been found in Apulia, and it may be as a result of the sack of Tarentum in 272 BC that the products of southern Italian silversmiths became known to the Romans and their neighbours. A number of little box-mirrors with rather poor reliefs on their lids, perhaps modelled on the Apulian type, have been found in central Italian tombs of the third and second century BC. A group of silver objects from a tomb at Chiusi includes two such hinged mirrors with poor repoussé relief on the lids showing Dionysos between a Silenus and an Eros (Museum of Fine Arts, Boston).

· THE LATE HELLENISTIC PERIOD ·

After 200 BC the Romans became ardent collectors of silver, and much of the plate produced was made for the Roman market. The 'Hellenistic' style thus merged completely with the 'Roman' at the time of late Republican Rome, and it was during the following two centuries that the fashions were established for the various types of silver plate that were to be popular in the early years of the Roman Empire, both in table plate such as bowls, cups, ladles, strainers and jugs, and in toilet vessels.

Among the most characteristic finds of the period are undecorated footless bowls, probably used as drinking cups. They occur in only two main forms, a deep hemispherical bowl and a deep conical bowl, and are undecorated except occasionally for a turned disc at the bottom and a little convex moulding at the rim, both in the interior. Their distribution ranges from Persia, southern Russia and the Balkans in the east, to Spain in the west.[12]

Although decorated forms of the footless bowl (known in their pottery form as 'Megarian' bowls) came into fashion around 300 BC, the surviving examples in precious metal were almost all made after 200 BC. The two finest pieces formed part of a large find of silver made in Italy at Cività Castellana in 1811 (Museo Nazionale, Naples). The hoard is probably some of the 'Asian' silver which is known to have flooded into Italy after Attalus III of Pergamum in north-west Asia Minor bequeathed his kingdom to Rome in 133 BC, including Croesus' ancient kingdom of Lydia. The Cività Castellana bowls are composed of an outer repoussé case and an inner lining. The scheme of decoration on both is that of the so-called Pergamene bowls, consisting of a rich calyx of leaves radiating from a central rosette. The leaves

PERFUME FLASK *(facing page), silver, parcel-gilt, from Bolsena, Italy, late third century* BC. *It has acanthus-leaf ornament on the base, a necklace-garland chased and gilded on the body and two handles giving it the appearance of a little amphora.*
Height: 14.1 cm (5½ in)
(Metropolitan Museum of Art, New York, Rogers Fund)

THREE CUPS *(below), silver, from a treasure found at Tivoli, Italy, mid-first century* BC. *Each cup in this group is inscribed with the name of Sattia.*
Heights: 3.1 cm (1¼ in)
Diameters: 8.4 cm (3¼ in)
(Field Museum of Natural History, Chicago)

are alternately those of the acanthus and the *nymphaea caerulea*, the latter enriched with finely chased stems and flowers, with little birds and animals in low relief. Little garnets are inserted at the centre of the main rosette and some of the subsidiary rosettes, and the detail is richly gilded.

Bowls and dishes ornamented with relief medallions, or *emblemata*, on the inside were very common in the last two centuries BC; but the *emblemata* were generally soldered on to the vessel, and it is these which have been found all over the Hellenistic world, very few bowls having survived complete. One particular *emblema* seems to show a portait of Antiochus VII Sidetes wearing Parthian headdress and torque, and it might have belonged to a bowl in a set made in commemoration of the King's exploits.[13] A satyr-head in high relief and a portrait of Demosthenes found at Miletopolis, not far from Pergamum, are probably Pergamene work of the second century BC,[14] as might also be the four from the hoard from Nihawand in Iran (Staatliche Antikensammlungen, Munich), while the *emblemata* of the first century are often framed by elaborate floral ornament.

Drinking cups of the period fall into three main types, all of which are represented amongst the plain Hellenistic grave-goods silver in tombs of the first century BC at Ancona in Italy. One type is a deep, straight-sided cup on a tall, turned stem with two handles; another is a cup with a wide, shallow bowl on a low base ring, with either *kylix* handles or ring handles; and another is a deep cup of ovoid shape on a fairly tall foot, and having handles of either type (Ancona Museum). Examples of the deep cups were found in a hoard from Tivoli (Metropolitan Museum of Art, New York) and in a princely Belgic grave in England, at Welwyn in Hertfordshire (British Museum). Both pairs might have been made as early as the first half of the first century BC.

It was as early as the second century BC that the outside of drinking cups began to be decorated with elaborate ornament in repoussé and chasing. A two-handled deep cup of the second half of the second century BC, found in grave 2 of Artiukhov's Barrow (Taman, South Russia), has decoration similar to that found on the 'Pergamene' bowls, a radiating pattern of acanthus and *nymphaea* (Hermitage Museum, Leningrad). The cup stands on a moulded foot enriched with decoration, and the handles are made of stout wire knotted in the middle and surmounted by a long horizontal thumb-grip. The ornament is in low relief and was probably done by chasing from the front.

By the early first century BC it had become fashionable to decorate drinking cups with high-relief figured scenes, as well as floral decoration. As soon as high relief came into fashion cups had to be made in two parts, an outer repoussé case and an inner plain lining. Many of the cups of this kind in the Campanian hoards may be as early as 100 BC;

but the other Hellenistic cups belong to later in the century. One is a silver *kantharos* found in the Delta, Egypt, which has been thought of as Alexandrian work (Walters Art Gallery, Baltimore). The lower part of the vessel is ribbed, and on the concave upper section is represented the Indian Triumph of Bacchus. Another silver *kantharos*, found in the Meuse near Stevensweert in Holland and now in the Library of the Dutch Academy, Amsterdam, has ivy leaves and branches decorating the lower part of the vessel and a frieze of satyr-heads and other Bacchic attributes on the concave section. While a date of around 100 BC is not incompatible with the decoration, the only possible fixed dating-point for these Hellenistic cups is provided by the hypothesis that the cup from Alesia in Gaul (Musée de St-Germain-en-Laye, Paris) was lost at the time of Caesar's siege in 52 BC. The cup has the kind of naturalistic ornament of fruit and flowers which came into fashion in late Hellenistic times; but there are no firm grounds for dating the manufacture of such cups to the first century BC.

Ladles, strainers and jugs are well represented by the Arcisate hoard of around 75 BC, a little drinking set which has one of each and also a shallow bowl or cup (British Museum). The ladle is typically late-Hellenistic, keeping the duck's-head handle of earlier examples, but having a much deeper, almost hemispherical bowl. The handle is curved backwards and at its junction with the bowl are metal coils like the ones flanking the handles on drinking cups of the period. The strainer has a deep, straight-sided bowl with ornamental perforations. The little, round-necked jug is a characteristic vessel of the hoards of the first century BC. This type of jug was still fashionable in the early Roman Empire. Although it is the only type of jug that can be firmly associated with the late Hellenistic period, richly decorated jugs of various kinds, like those found in the Roman hoards, were probably already being made.

Toilet silver became more common in late Hellenistic times, and it too is found in the hoards together with drinking vessels. For example, cylindrical *pyxides*, *unguentaria*, and a strigil, together with a duck's-head ladle were found in a tomb at Goritza in Thessaly.[15] A jug and strainer, like those found at Arcisate, were part of a hoard found near Lake Trasimene in central Italy, together with a pair of strigils on a ring and a combined pin and comb (Metropolitan Museum of Art, New York, and Walters Art Gallery, Baltimore).

The finest surviving toilet vessels of the period are a *pyxis* and an *alabastron*, of about 100 BC, from Palaiokastron in Thessaly. Both these pieces, now in the National Museum, Athens, have repoussé decoration of the kind that was becoming fashionable on drinking vessels. The *alabastron*, rounded at the bottom, tapering towards the top and with a narrow round neck, is ornamented with repoussé and chasing, having a calyx of leaves at the base, a principal scene with figures in high relief representing the childhood of Dionysos, and a narrow frieze of Erotes above that. The cylindrical *pyxis* has a pyramidal lid surmounted by a pomegranate, and the body is decorated with figures of dancing maenads in high relief, and on the lid is a garland of fruit supported by theatrical masks and bukrania. The style and themes of the vessels link them with the work of the neo-Attic school which grew up in Athens during the first century BC. The neo-Attic school was a response to the Roman demand for works of decorative art in Greek style, which had been stimulated initially by the sack of Syracuse in

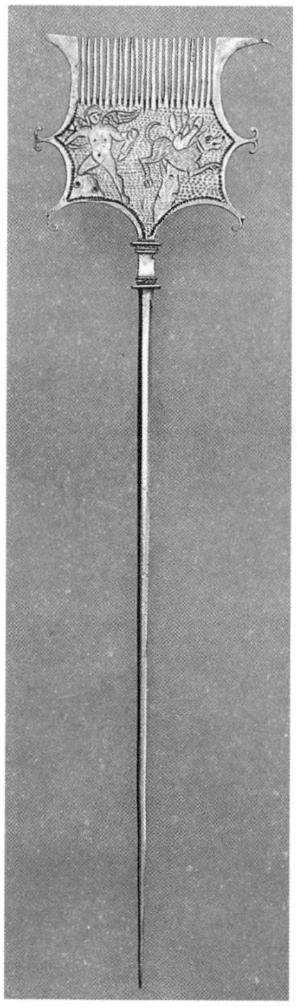

211 and of Tarentum in 209 BC, and then by the bequest of Attalus to the Romans of Pergamum in 133 BC. The influx from these and other military enterprises had a growing influence on taste for silver in the later Roman republic.

· ROMAN SILVER IN THE FIRST · · CENTURY AD ·

Our knowledge of Roman domestic silver of the first century AD is particularly good, because of the finds made at Pompeii and Boscoreale in houses destroyed by the eruption of Vesuvius in AD 79. The earlier discoveries of small collections of plate at Pompeii and Herculaneum were completely overshadowed by the discovery in 1895 of a hoard of 109 pieces of silver plate that had been stored in a wine vat below a villa at Boscoreale (Louvre, Paris). The second outstanding Campanian hoard (Museo Nazionale, Naples) was discovered in 1930 in the House of the Menander in Pompeii itself, wrapped in cloth inside a bronze-bound wooden chest. It consisted of 118 pieces of fine table silver of all kinds.

Chief among finds from sites not buried by Vesuvius is the Augustan silver found in 1868 by soldiers constructing earthworks at Hildesheim near Hanover in Germany. There are more than sixty pieces, ranging in size from multi-gallon mixing bowls to cups only a few centimetres in diameter, and including elaborate centrepieces (Staatliche Museen, Berlin). The findspot lies outside the Empire and the treasure is thought to have belonged to a Roman commander lost on campaign against Germanic tribes, perhaps Varus in AD 9. Silver presented by the Roman government as diplomatic gifts is represented by two Augustan relief-decorated cups of very fine quality (National Museum, Copenhagen), found in a rich chieftain's grave at Hoby in Denmark. Religious shrines contained not only ritual plate, but also dedications, sometimes of domestic plate as at Berthouville in France, or sometimes of special kinds of vessel, like the cylinder-shaped vessels in the British Museum, dedicated at Aquae Apollinares (Bagni di Vicarello), near Bracciano, north of Rome.

Silver drinking cups were in general use at this time, and occur in most of the hoards of the period. The shapes are Greek in origin and developed from late Hellenistic versions. They include deep ovoid or hemispherical cups, generally on a moulded stem and with two handles, and broader, shallower cups also with two handles but standing on a base ring. There are also one-handled, beaker-shaped vessels with straight or slightly concave sides and a flat base. The plainer versions of these cups usually have decorated mouldings on the foot and rim and some chased or engraved ornament. Two pairs of deep, plain cups, from Tivoli and Welwyn (already mentioned), may be late Republican or early Imperial; but dating is difficult within the first century BC and first century AD, as it is for most other such pieces, including a pair of cups from Olbia (USSR) with *kantharos*-shaped bodies set, in this case, on a low foot ring (Wadsworth Athenaeum, Hartford).

Cups richly decorated with repoussé seem to have become fashionable soon after 100 BC. The taste for them seems to have lasted until about the middle of the first century AD but not longer, for Pliny the Elder, who died in the eruption of Vesuvius in AD 79, says that the art of repoussé was very little practised in his own day. Some of the cups can be placed approximately within the period. The detail of the chased floral ornament on the Mars and Venus cups from the Casa del Menandro find at Pompeii (Museo Nazionale, Naples) suggests the mid-first century BC. The form of the handles on the pair of olive cups in the same find is Hellenistic rather than Roman. The big goblet with floral arabesques from the Boscoreale hoard, now in the Louvre, has also been attributed to the mid-first century BC. On two *kantharoi* in the Hildesheim Treasure, however, decorated with Bacchic masks and attributes, the decorated mouldings and the handles in the form of twisted branches seem to be typical of the first century AD, as do the similar handles on the cups from Hockwold in England.[16]

A number of decorated cups can be dated firmly to the Augustan and Julio-Claudian periods by their subject-matter or style, including two famous cups with historical scenes, found at

Boscoreale (Louvre). On one, Augustus is shown in two scenes illustrating his rule in peace and war. The other shows Tiberius in a triumphal procession. The cups were made in the period of Tiberius and are probably officially inspired works of propaganda, perhaps distributed as gifts on a special imperial occasion. Of the same class and period are two cups from the Hoby grave, and four from a painted tomb at Vize in eastern Thrace (Turkey), the latter matched by two similarly decorated pairs from Boscoreale and from Italy.[17] Most cups, however, cannot be dated within the period, even though there was a great difference between the artistic climate of the first century BC and the first century AD.

In spite of the problems of dating, it is clear that the thin repoussé vessels went out of fashion in the last part of the first century AD and were replaced by more solid relief bowls and cups, cast in heavy silver. Good examples are a shallow cup with a Homeric scene from Ingolstadt in Germany, a cup with an Amazonomachy in Turin, and a cup in Belgrade with Dionysos and a maenad on a hippocamp.[18] Storks and water-birds appear on solid cast cups from Calafat (Donau) in Romania and in the British Museum, London.

Plates and dishes of this period are as complex in form and decoration as cups. In the Casa del Menandro find is a complete service of plates all made to the same pattern, consisting of one large serving dish and sixteen smaller plates, four of 16 cm (6⅓ in) diameter, four of 11.1 cm (4⅜ in), four of 10.1 cm (4 in), and four of 7.5 cm (3 in). The plates are all round, of shallow curved section with a pronounced convex rim, and each has a pair of segmental flat handles decorated with cast ornament in low relief. The decoration consists of a head of Silenus flanked by geese, whose necks stretch out to form the arms by which the handle is soldered to the rim of the dish. One of the interesting aspects of this and other finds at Pompeii is their confirmation of the general use of sets of four, of which evidence survives in an inventory on papyrus of the plate of a wealthy Roman in Egypt.

'Ear' handles with reliefs decorate the exceptionally large and richly decorated dish, probably of the second half of the first century AD, dredged up from the sea off Bizerta in Tunisia. Its maximum length including its two handles is 92 cm (36 in), and it weighs 9 kg (20 lb). A central medallion of Apollo and Marsyas has the figures inlaid in gold and electrum, a frieze of putti and animals is engraved on the surface of the dish, and the frieze round the rim shows Bacchanalian scenes in low relief. The handles were cast separately and soldered on (Musée du Bardo, Tunis). The dish's rich decoration thus illustrates several of the techniques used by the silversmiths of the first century AD in the production of show plate, including 'picture' dishes, on which the whole surface of the dish is used as the field for a relief picture. They are a Roman idea, and one of the earliest is the so-called Aquileia *patera*, which belongs to the class of propaganda court silver like the historical cups from Boscoreale (Kunsthistorisches Museum, Vienna). The dish is 29.5 cm (11$\frac{1}{16}$ in) in diameter, and its whole surface is decorated with a scene showing a Roman emperor or prince, perhaps Claudius, as Triptolemus, the bringer of prosperity and fertility to the earth.

Dishes and bowls with figured relief-medallions on the inside also belong to the class of show plate, for the medallion often occupies the larger part of the bowl or dish and makes it useless for any practical purpose. The fashion for *emblema* dishes began in the third century BC, and the Romans of the late Republic collected them enthusiastically. A typical example is a bowl found at Boscoreale and now in the British Museum, which is decorated in the centre with the bust of an elderly man of the time of Augustus, perhaps an ancestor of the final owner. The Africa bowl, from the famous Boscoreale Treasure and now in the Louvre, is one of the finest surviving *emblema* bowls. It is decorated with a high-relief medallion showing a personification of Africa wearing an elephant headdress and carrying a cornucopia. Such medallion dishes were often made in pairs with related subjects. Two in the Hildesheim Treasure have medallions of Attis and Cybele, and two others found at Hermopolis in Egypt have female profile busts facing in opposite directions.

Apart from table silver, toilet silver is the main surviving type of silver. A wealthy lady of the time would have had a wide range of small silver implements – ear picks, cosmetic sets – and she would keep her jewellery and other possessions in silver boxes. The contents of a woman's tomb of the first century AD found at Bursa in Turkey (British Museum) includes a cylindrical *pyxis*, a little straight-sided bowl, a little spoon with a

ALABASTRON AND PYXIS *(facing page, above), silver, from Palaiokastron, Greece, c.100* BC. *Both have figures in high relief – the childhood of Dionysos on the* alabastron *and figures of dancing maenads on the* pyxis. *Height of* alabastron: *18.3 cm (7⅛ in) Height of* pyxis: *19.3 cm (7½ in) (National Archaeological Museum, Athens)*

PIN AND COMB *(facing page, below), silver, from Lake Trasimene, Italy, mid-first century* BC. *The plaque is engraved with a boy and a wolf on one side, a lion on the other. Length: 17.6 cm (6¾ in) (Metropolitan Museum of Art, New York, Fletcher Fund)*

MARS AND VENUS CUP, *silver, from Casa del Menandro, Pompeii, probably mid-first century* BC. *Height: 12.5 cm (5 in) (Museo Nazionale, Naples)*

are rare. The Greek *phiale mesomphalos*, serving as the sacrificial *patera*, appears frequently in this form, sometimes equipped with a horizontal handle. 'Egg' *phialai* have been found in the Boscoreale Treasure and at Pompeii, but may be Hellenistic survivals. A fluted *phiale* from the Berthouville Treasure (Bibliothèque Nationale, Paris), on the other hand, does date from the first century AD. On the outside it looks not unlike a Hellenistic egg *phiale*, while on the inside a central medallion shows Omphale reclining on Hercules' lion skin. The Berthouville Treasure is the contents, or part of the contents, of a religious shrine, the Temple of Mercury at Canetonum, collected over a period of many years. The find of sixty-three pieces of plate represents the ritual and dedicated plate of the sanctuary, and it covers a period from the first century AD to around AD 275, when it was buried. The *patera* is common in bronze but not in silver, while ladles for domestic and religious use cannot be distinguished in surviving finds. Two of the finest decorated jugs, however, from the Berthouville Treasure, do have religious associations. Their reliefs represent Homeric subjects: on one, Achilles mourning and the ransoming of Hector; on the other, the dragging of Hector's corpse and the death of Achilles. The style is Hellenistic and the cups might be as early as the first century BC; but it has also been suggested that the scenes were copied from cups of the late Hellenistic period by a silversmith of the Flavian period. A pair of richly decorated jugs from the Boscoreale Treasure (Louvre) is actually decorated with sacrificial scenes, which hints at their use.

looped handle ending in a swan's head (probably used for cosmetics), a mirror and a spindle. Silver mirrors, too, were widely used. Some plain disc mirrors without handles were in use, as were mirrors with rings for suspension that could be moved from room to room, one such from the Casa del Menandro being 13.6 cm ($5\frac{1}{3}$ in) in diameter. The popular form, however, consists of a disc with the reflecting surface on one side and decorated on the back with concentric circles, and long handles attached to the disc by arms. A baluster handle is the commonest type, though at Pompeii the form of Hercules' club was popular. The backs of several mirrors are decorated with roundels, one of the most striking of them, from the Casa del Menandro hoard, having a relief medallion showing a female head in profile. Two more from the Boscoreale Treasure, in the Musée du Louvre, Paris, are of the same kind: one has a bust of a maenad on the back and is inscribed with the name of its maker, M. Domitius Polygnos; the other has a medallion of Leda and the Swan.

Vessels for religious ritual – *phiale, patera* with handle, ladle and decorated jug – are often shown on monuments of the period, but actual survivals

· ROMAN SILVER OF THE SECOND AND · · THIRD CENTURIES AD ·

In contrast to the wealth of evidence for the first century AD, the finds of second-century silver are disappointing: there are no large hoards and only very few closely dated finds. Most of the third-century hoards contain plate of the period in which they were buried, probably because, since fashions in domestic silver had changed, much older silver had gone into the melting-pot to make pieces in the latest style. Thus, in the Treasure of Chaourse in France which is a collection of domestic plate and the nearest approach to a complete service of silver among the third-century hoards, all the pieces seem to be of this date. A most important exception is the Treasure of Berthouville.

The predominance of finds from the western part of the Roman Empire, especially Gaul, gives a rather one-sided picture of the total production of silver plate in this period; but not all the silver from the Gaulish hoards was made locally. Most of the 'Hellenistic-Roman' silver in the Berthouville hoard presumably comes from Italy, and such a fine piece as the Hunting Dish (no. 15) described later is probably an import. This dish is

AFRICA DISH *(top left), silver, from the Boscoreale Treasure, perhaps first century* BC. *One of the finest* emblema *bowls, it is decorated with a personification of Africa with elephant headdress and cornucopia. Diameter: 22.5 cm ($8\frac{3}{4}$ in) (Musée du Louvre, Paris)*

DISH *(above left), silver, from Aquileia, Italy, first century* AD. *It is decorated with a scene showing a Roman Emperor as bringer of prosperity and fertility. Diameter: 29.5 cm ($11\frac{5}{8}$ in) (Kunsthistorisches Museum, Vienna)*

closely matched by one from the Treasure of Karnak in Egypt (Staatliche Museen, Berlin). Other examples of very similar pieces are found widely scattered over the Empire, and in style and detail of ornament there is a surprising uniformity throughout the Roman world, as a result of the freedom with which plate, designs and models passed about the Empire. It seems that fashions were created mainly in Rome and Italy, though it is likely that the continued popularity of traditional forms like the medallion bowls was due to the influence of Hellenistic centres.

Silver drinking cups were generally less common at this time. There are no plain examples of the traditional Hellenistic goblets and beakers, and it is probable that glass drinking vessels were more favoured. From the Chaourse Treasure are two tall beakers in the British Museum with concave upper parts and shallow bowls on a high foot ring and a set of four silvered bronze cups with a profile ultimately derived from the old Greek *kantharos* form. None of these cups has handles. Many of the smaller conical and hemispherical bowls of the period probably also served as drinking vessels.

A number of drinking cups decorated with reliefs continue the tradition of the early Empire. Unlike earlier cups, examples of the second and third centuries are usually cast solid and not made by repoussé; they do not require the use of an inner lining. This technique of solid casting is one feature that distinguishes the cups of the period; the relief is usually lower, and Bacchanalian themes are used almost exclusively. One of the finest examples, which must have been made some time in the second century is the cup from Ostropataka (Hungary), on which the loopless handles, decorated in relief on their upper surface, consist of horizontal grips soldered by means of arms to the rim; Bacchic masks and animals in low relief decorate the body of the cup (Kunsthistorisches Museum, Vienna).

During the third century decorated cups without handles, of the same shape as some of the plain vessels from Chaourse, were in fashion. One (in the Bibliothèque Nationale, Paris), with reliefs showing groups of fighting animals on the upper part only, is made of heavy cast silver with the highest parts of the relief cast separately and fitted into beds, a technique that has been noted on a number of silver vessels of the time. A cup with

VESSELS, *silver, from the Chaourse Treasure, France, third century* AD. *The jug is plain except for a convex band decorated with guilloche ornament. The deep Hemmoor bucket has a narrow frieze of scroll ornament below the rim.*
Height of jug: 26.5 cm ($10\frac{3}{8}$ in)
Height of bowl: 17 cm ($6\frac{5}{8}$ in)
(British Museum, London)

handles in the National Museum, Copenhagen, from Varpelev in Denmark, found together with a coin of the late third century, consists of an elaborate openwork silver case with vine ornament and a good-luck inscription in Greek, with a cup of blue glass inside it.

Very few jugs have been found in the hoards of the second and third centuries. The three best known are all similar in form. One in the British Museum (from the Chaourse Treasure) is a slim vessel on a low base-ring, with a rather angular handle equipped with a curving thumb-piece at the top; the neck is decorated with a convex band of guilloche ornament. A similar vessel in the Hermitage Museum, Leningrad, was found in the Tomb of the Queen with the Golden Mask at Kertch, together with a little decorated *pyxis* and a large plate with niello ornament. Another jug, similar in general shape to the Chaourse example, was found together with two silver plates and a silver statuette at Daphne by Antioch in Turkey; this jug (in the Dumbarton Oaks Collection, Washington) has a sharply angular handle and stands on a low foot-rim. The form of the handle relates it to the jugs of the fourth century, and it can hardly be earlier than the late third century.

A large number of saucepans of the second and third centuries survive. Most have plain handles, usually straight-ended or waved; examples with disc ends appear occasionally. Of these three forms the handle with waved end was most popular in the third century but occurs in the second, the disc-ended type is probably not later than the second, while the straight-ended variety may occur throughout the period. There is a good deal of variety in the shapes of the bowls, the form with a straight-sided conical bowl being frequently found, for example, at Notre-Dame d'Allençon in France and Marwedel in Germany.[19] Bowls with curved sides tend to be narrower and deeper than those of the earlier period. Three examples in the Archaeological Museum, Turin, illustrate well the main features of the saucepans of this period. On one a bust of Mercury between animal heads decorates the end of the handle; below are masks, vases and a bird and animals, arranged in separate registers. The same decorative theme extends to the arms of attachment. The second is round-ended and decorated with figures of Mercury and the child Bacchus, between rosettes; a ground line separates the figures from a zone with Bacchic masks and animals. On the arms are baskets of fruit and other attributes. The third saucepan is simpler in design, with a figure of Mercury between swans' heads at the end and a rustic shrine and tethered goat in register below; there are baskets of fruit and dolphins' heads on the arms. Sometimes the saucepans' bowls were also decorated. A plain, wave-handled saucepan found at Manching in Germany is vertically fluted on the body,[20] a saucepan from Chatuzange in France with acanthus ornament on the handle has decorated ribbing on the outside of the bowl, and another one, said to come from Syria, has spiral fluting on the body and in the centre of the inside a roundel of the Three Graces.[21]

One of the most interesting vessels in the Chaourse Treasure is a combined strainer and funnel in the British Museum. The strainer fits into the bowl of the funnel and the two are hinged together; the holes are punched in geometric and floral patterns. The piece is unique and bears no relation to the standard bronze forms of strainer in the Roman period. A charming little circular casket found on the site of the Walbrook Mithraeum in London (and now in the Museum of London) contains a cylindrical strainer or filter with patterned holes on the bottom which is lifted out by means of crossing bars at the top. A very similar strainer (Nitra, Czechoslovakia) was found at Stráže in Czechoslovakia. The outside of the Walbrook casket is richly decorated with cast and chased reliefs showing hunting scenes in a style which seems to relate to the medallions on the hunting dishes from Berthouville and Karnak, and the casket was probably made in the early third century. The strainer might have had some special use in Mithraic cult.

Many different kinds of dishes and plates were made in silver during this period, and matching services of plates and bowls were still in fashion. Oval dishes came into general use; dishes with ear handles of the type popular in the early hoards continued to be made and the same type of handle

DISH, *silver, from Berthouville, France, second century* AD. *It has a central medallion showing a hunting scene, and a framing frieze.*
Diameter: 35 cm ($13\frac{3}{8}$ in)
(Cabinet des Médailles, Bibliothèque Nationale, Paris)

was often applied to oval dishes. This handle was losing popularity, however, and probably went out of general use in the third century. Dishes with beaded rims were very popular. Relief decoration was applied to flat or convex friezes round the edges of the dishes and to central medallions; a combination of framing frieze and central medallion was particularly fashionable. Niello came into general use in the decoration of plates, and flat dishes with upright rims decorated with relief on the outside also occur in this period.

A few large and elaborately decorated 'ears' from dishes of this kind may be assigned to the second century. The Birth of Venus is depicted on a fine example (in the Louvre) from Bondonneau in France. The reliefs on these handles are cast, chased and gilt. It is impossible to say whether the handles belonged to round or oval dishes; but the ear handle seems to have been especially popular on oval dishes during this period. One of the finest examples is a dish in the Archaeological Museum, Turin, decorated with a typically second-century border of animals, masks and trees. A very similar dish, now lost, was found – together with a cup and two spoons – in a tomb at Lillebonne (Seine Inférieure), and dated to the Antonine period.

Dishes in practical use were often decorated with low-relief medallions in the centre. A good example is the late second- or third-century dish with a medallion of the goddess Fortuna from Batum (Hermitage Museum, Leningrad). A smaller dish from the Chaourse Treasure, now in the British Museum, shows a figure of Mercury richly gilt. The reliefs were generally cast, or, as in the case of the Mercury dish, cut in the solid metal. Another popular form of decoration in this period was a fairly wide relief border round the outside of the plate; the ornament is generally Bacchic in inspiration but floral designs and other kinds of decoration are found. In the Caubiac Treasure there is a little flat plate, probably part of a large service in the same pattern, decorated with Bacchic masks on a raised border (British Museum).

Some of the finest dishes of the period combine a central medallion and framing frieze. One of the best is the Hunting Dish from the Treasure of Berthouville; the medallion, cast in low relief, shows a hunting scene and the frieze is decorated with animals, Bacchic masks and other attributes. Round the medallion is engraved an inscription to the god Mercury of Canetonum. A very similar dish 43 cm (17 in) in diameter, found in the Egyptian Treasure of Karnak (which consisted of sixteen pieces of plate and 1200 gold coins dated up to the third-century Emperor Elagabalus), has a medallion showing a lion hunt and a border of hunting scenes, animals and masks. The plate, in the Staatliche Museen, Berlin, probably dates from the second century.

The Caubiac Treasure contains one very large dish, 38–75 cm (15–29½ in) in diameter, with an upright curved rim decorated with Bacchic masks and attributes in low relief (British Museum). Large dishes with this kind of rim, perhaps serving dishes, were probably coming into use in the third century. A fine engraved dish found in the late second-century hoard from Lovere in northern Italy, and now in the Castello Sforzesco, has a central roundel showing a fisherman and a surrounding broad band of fish and other sea creatures. A dish from Berthouville is decorated all over with lightly engraved arabesques, and flat chasing is used to make floral and figured designs on another dish in the same treasure. A style of flat chased ornament which became common in the later Roman Empire makes its earliest appearance on two plates found at Daphne by Antioch,[22] together with the silver jug referred to above. One of the plates is decorated with an eight-pointed star in the centre and a border of fluting, and the other has a star and feather design in the middle and overlapping leaves around the rim. These plates are perhaps not earlier than about AD 300.

One of the most popular kinds of dish in the third-century hoards is a flat dish with a beaded rim and a central decorative motif inlaid in niello.

STRAINER AND BOX *(above left), silver, from the Temple of Mithras, London, third century* AD. *The sides and lid are decorated with enigmatic scenes of conflict between men and animals, possibly symbolizing certain rites. The strainer may have served as an infuser for the preparation of a drug used in these rites. Height: 6 cm (2⅜ in) (Museum of London, London)*

PEPPER POT *(above), silver, from Sidon, Lebanon, first half of the third century* AD. *In the shape of a small boy, it has holes in the base and was designed to stand on a table. Pepper was introduced to the Roman world from India in the first century* AD. *Height: 9.5 cm (3¾ in) (Museum of Fine Arts, Boston)*

One of these, 38.3 cm (15 in) in diameter, was found in the Treasure of Chatuzange; the central motif is a swastika (British Museum). The same motif also appeared on one of the lost dishes in the Wettingen Treasure. There are three dishes of this kind from the Chaourse Treasure in the British Museum; one has a swastika, another a rosette, while the third is plain except for the beaded rim. More elaborate niello motifs appear on some examples of the period.

It is difficult to classify the wide variety of bowls made in silver during the second and third centuries. Some were made to the same pattern as the dishes, to form part of the same service. Four hemispherical bowls in the Chaourse Treasure have beaded rims and a central niello motif on the inside matching the dishes found in the same treasure; similar bowls have been found at Graincourt in France (Louvre), Niederbieber on the Rhine, and Nicolaevo in Bulgaria.[23] To judge from the Gaulish finds, for example, the Treasures of Berthouville and Notre-Dame d'Allençon,[24] one of the most popular shapes in the second and third centuries was the conical flat-bottomed bowl, which appears in saucepans.

Bowls with separate cast or repoussé relief *emblemata* in the fashion of the first century AD continued to be made. There are a number of these bowls in the Berthouville Treasure; unlike earlier examples, the *emblema* is usually let into a recess in the bottom of the bowl. The bowl with high-relief busts of Mercury and Maia in the Treasure dates from the Antonine period, and belongs to a tradition that goes back to the second century BC. Fluted bowls were popular throughout the period. Two fine examples in the British Museum, one a large bowl with a star-pattern engraved in the roundel on the bottom, were found at Chaourse. Also in the British Museum are a spirally-fluted bowl with a low-relief central medallion of Aphrodite, one of the pieces from Caubiac, and a remarkable bowl in the form of a lotus flower with a central medallion of the Three Graces, from Chatuzange-le-Goubet.

Flanged bowls seem to have become popular in the second century in Gaul, and examples have been found at Chaourse, at Graincourt and at Mérouville.[25] One of the bowls from Chaourse stands on a foot ring, and the flange which curves downwards is decorated with floral ornament and surmounted by a vertical rim. The bowl from Mérouville has a frieze of masks and animals on the flange. The Graincourt bowl is very similar to one of the Chaourse bowls. The variant form of flanged bowl without the vertical rim is characteristic of fourth- and fifth-century hoards and seems to be a later development.

A type of vessel peculiar to the Gaulish hoards of this period is the so-called Hemmoor bucket, a deep hemispherical bowl on a low foot with single or double bucket-handles swivelling in vertical ring-attachments on opposite sides. This type of bucket is common in bronze between AD 150 and 250; five silver examples are known. Two of these, in the British Museum, come from the Treasure of Chaourse; one is plain and the other decorated with a narrow frieze of scroll ornament below the rim. The bronze examples often have a frieze of animals and Bacchanalian themes between decorated mouldings in this position, and a similar design seems to have been used for a silver bucket in the lost Treasure of Trier (Germany). The body of a bucket of this kind from Tourdan (near Vienne in France) is decorated with low-relief figures of the Four Seasons (British Museum). The fifth example, found in a third-century burial at Zakrzow in Poland, is plain except for a decorated moulding below the rim.[26]

In the Chaourse Treasure a little pepper pot in the form of a squatting negro boy was found; the holes for the pepper are punched in the boy's head. A similar piece found at Nicolaevo, near Pleven in Bulgaria, is in the form of a negro boy holding a puppy (Archaeological Museum, Sofia). This has its holes in the base, as does also an example from Sidon, in the Museum of Fine Arts, Boston. Unlike early Roman pepper pots, these decorative examples would stand neatly on the table.

Not much toilet silver of this period survives. Silver mirrors were certainly still in common use, although mirrors with long handles seem to have gone out of fashion. A mirror from the Backworth hoard (British Museum) consists of a plain disc with turned rings on the back to which a handle seems to have been attached with arms in the form of leaves. Mirrors from Chaourse are simply plain discs with turnings on the back, but other mirrors of the period often had a handle fixed to the back such as the example, probably of the early third century, found at Wroxeter (Central Library, Shrewsbury), while one found near Sofia (British Museum) may have been fitted with a wooden stand. Little silver pots of various kinds were used to keep cosmetics, and various implements for applying them were also made of silver. A popular type of pot which may have been used for cosmetics has a bulbous body and low, concave neck. There is one with punched circles on its body in the Berthouville Treasure.

· ROMAN SILVER OF THE FOURTH AND · · FIFTH CENTURIES ·

A large number of important hoards give a clearer picture of the silver of the fourth and fifth centuries than of any other, except the earlier part of the first century. As in the case of the third-century hoards, the great majority of late Roman finds have been made in Italy and the western provinces, especially Gaul and Britain; but Syria, the Danube provinces and southern Russia have also yielded some interesting and important finds, and a large hoard of silver from Carthage (in the British Museum) is one of several finds from Roman North Africa.

Silver drinking cups are not common in the late hoards, but there are a number of new and attractive shapes. Three cups found at Canoscio in Italy are similar to vessels from Chaourse, though on a rather higher foot, which was a characteristic of the cups, bowls and dishes of the period.[27] Two plain conical beakers on low foot-rings (Römermuseum, Augst) were found in the Treasure of Kaiseraugst, Switzerland, and a silver vessel found in England in a small hoard at Great Horwood (Buckinghamshire County Museum, Aylesbury) is a version of the long-necked beaker common in pottery of the third and fourth centuries. A shallow goblet on a baluster stem and wide base plate (from the Treasure of Traprain in Scotland, and now in the National Museum of Antiquities, Edinburgh) seems to represent a type popular in the period: there were fragments of six such goblets from Traprain, and a pair of similar goblets was found in the Mildenhall Treasure in England. It has been suggested that the wide base plates could be used as miniature dishes or stands, and they are, in fact, decorated underneath with chased leaf ornament. Decorated cups are rare.

Of the three main types of silver jug of this period, one is a tall slim vessel with ovoid body, long tapering neck and flat circular mouth with upright rim. The lower part of the body may either narrow downwards and widen out again for the foot, or there may be a ball stem between body and foot. The foot is sometimes edged with heavy beading. The handle may either arch above the level of the rim or run horizontally from the rim and bend downwards at a sharp angle to join the body of the vessel. A fine gold example of this form, from the Treasure of Petrossa in Romania (National Museum, Bucharest) is decorated on the body with wavy fluting. The second type of jug has a bulbous body, a narrow tapering neck, sometimes with a roll moulding, and a horizontal spout which may be fitted with a hinged lid; there is often a ball stem between the body and the foot and the handle may either arch above the level of the mouth or curve downwards from it to join the body at its widest point. An example from Venticane, south-east of Benevento in Italy, has a hinged lid and the inscription VIVAS IN CHRISTO QUINTA in nielloed letters on the neck

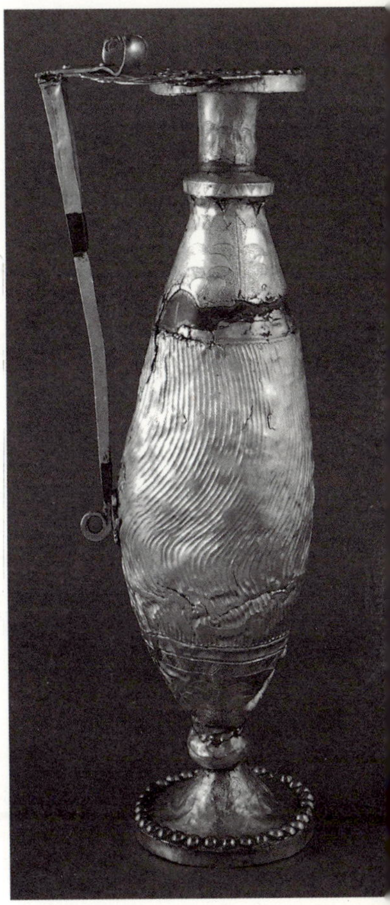

JUG, *gold, from Petrossa, Romania, fourth century* AD. *One of the three main types of jug of this period, it has repoussé and engraved decoration which includes wavy fluting on the body. Height: 36 cm (14⅛ in) (National Museum of Antiquities, Bucharest)*

GREAT DISH *(left), silver, from Mildenhall, Suffolk, fourth century* AD. *It is decorated with a low-relief medallion of Oceanus and a surrounding Bacchic scene. The two are separated by a border of scallop shells. Diameter: 60.5 cm (23¾ in) (British Museum, London)*

OCTAGONAL DISH *(above left), silver, from Kaiseraugst, Switzerland, fourth century* AD. *It has low-relief scenes from the life of Achilles. Cast or hammered relief ornament is used to decorate the roundels and borders. Diameter: 53 cm ($20\frac{7}{8}$ in) (Römermuseum, Augst)*

THEODOSIUS DISH *(above right), silver, from Almendralejo (Badajoz), near Mérida, Spain,* AD *388. The low-relief figures are Theodosius I flanked by Arcadius and Valentinian II. The inscription refers to the Emperor's ten-year anniversary in* AD *388. Diameter: 74 cm ($29\frac{1}{8}$ in) (Real Academia de la Historia, Madrid)*

(Bibliothèque Nationale, Paris). The third type of jug has an ovoid body on a foot-ring, a narrow neck, usually decorated with a roll moulding, and a round mouth with vertical rim. The handle rises vertically from the widest part of the body and is attached to the rim by a horizontal plate with arms closing on the rim. A good example of the shape (a direct development of third-century jugs) was found at Trier and is now in the Rheinisches Landesmuseum there, decorated with niello and gilt geometric ornament on the neck and upper part of the body; a faceted jug of this kind was found at Aquincum in Hungary (Aquincum Museum, Budapest).

Related in shape to the jugs with ovoid body, and a popular vessel of this period, is a flask with no handles usually decorated with rich ornament of some kind. The ovoid body of the flask rests on a low foot-rim, the narrow neck is often decorated with a heavy roll moulding, and the wide round mouth has a vertical rim. One of these flasks (found at Traprain Law in Scotland) is decorated with repoussé scenes from the Old and New Testaments; the foot-rim, as on a number of other flasks, is formed by heavy beading. There were fragments of two other flasks decorated with scenes from classical mythology in the same treasure; one shows the figures of Pan and a hermaphrodite and the other the discovery of Achilles among the daughters of Lycomedes. All three are in the National Museum of Antiquities, Edinburgh.

Saucepans of the traditional form were certainly being made in this period and continued in use much later. A pair found in the Valjevo district, in Yugoslavia, have straightened handles edged with a decorated moulding and leaf ornament on the surface; they probably belong to the fourth century (National Museum, Belgrade). A shallow *patera* from the Esquiline Treasure, Rome, consists of a shallow bowl with a narrow horizontal rim decorated with a series of little scallop shells in relief. The inside of the bowl is treated as a large scallop shell in which Venus appears attended by two putti, one holding a lotus flower and the other a mirror (Petit Palais, Paris). The handle is occupied by the single standing figure of Adonis with a dog at his feet. A smaller *patera* in the British Museum, from the Carthage Treasure (Tunisia), shows the figure of a frog, perhaps a Christian motif, in high relief on the centre of the inside; the horizontal handle is in the form of a knotted branch.

In the late hoards a number of small ladles with horizontal handles was found. The Mildenhall Treasure in the British Museum contains five with handles cast in the form of dolphins and joined to the bowl with arms of attachment terminating in birds' heads; the bowls are similar in shape to the bowls of the saucepans and are plain except for a series of turnings on the bottom of the inside. A similar ladle, with the handle in the form of a dolphin holding the rim of the bowl in its mouth, is in the Traprain Treasure.

The design of the dishes of the period generally follows the fashions of the third century, although the biggest dishes tend to be larger than those of the earlier period. For example, the two dishes found at Cesena in Italy are 62 and 63 cm ($24\frac{1}{2}$ and $24\frac{3}{4}$ in) in diameter, the Oceanus dish from Mildenhall is 60.5 cm ($23\frac{3}{4}$ in), and the diameters of the large dishes in the Treasure of Traprain range from 45 to 60 cm (18–$23\frac{1}{2}$ in). The main innovations of the period were a fashion for angular

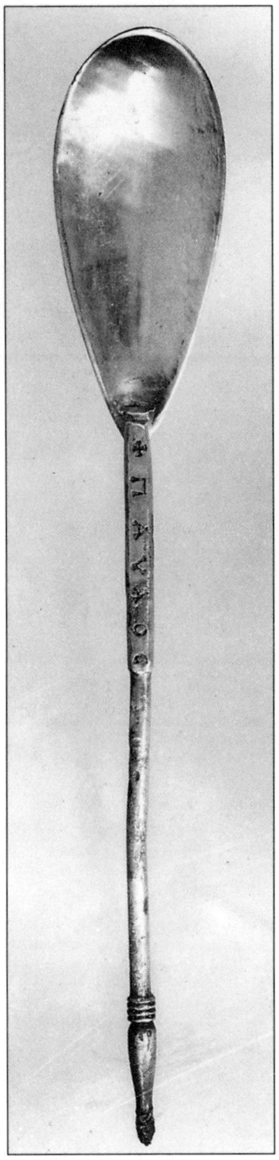

shapes, including rectangular and multangular dishes, for round dishes within a square frame, and for dishes with various openwork borders.

Elaborate use of gilt and niello is characteristic of the period, both for floral geometric ornament and for figured scenes, and plainer dishes were often monogrammed in niello and gilt with the name of their owner. Two sets of small dishes in the Esquiline Treasure, four round with moulded rim and four rectangular with openwork border, had the monogram of Projecta in gilt and niello letters within a gilt and niello wreath (British Museum). Geometric ornament decorates the fine niello dish from the Mildenhall Treasure; this has a central roundel with a complex geometric pattern of circles and squares and similar geometric and floral patterns on the broad, slightly raised, flange round the heavily beaded edge. At Kaiseraugst in Switzerland another dish with geometric niello patterns on the flange and medallion was found, along with a masterpiece of the technique in which the central medallion shows a walled town by the sea with cupids fishing in the foreground, and the flange shows hunting scenes separated by bands of geometric interlace (Römermuseum, Augst). The popularity of this technique is shown by numerous fragments from other sources. The Treasure of Kaiseraugst (Römermuseum, Augst) also contained a most elaborate rectangular dish or tray with a design of openwork scrolls and scallops round the edge. Its surface is richly decorated with relief and gilded and nielloed engraving; in a rectangular panel in the centre, Ariadne is shown enthroned between a satyr and Bacchus, and in the panels round the outside there are cupids playing with animals.

The characteristic chased ornament of this period is very distinctive, and features leaf patterns, diapers and interlace in a technique of chased lines and grooves worked in the soft metal. The Euticius dish from the Kaiseraugst Treasure has a broad flange edged with beading and decorated with chased leaf pattern in this style; the surface of the dish is covered with close-set wavy fluting, another popular motif of the period (found on dishes from the Carthage Treasure, Canoscio and Traprain Law). Other examples of the same style of chasing include three dishes found in Moesia, Hungary (National Museum of Antiquities, Budapest), and a great gold plate from the Treasure of Petrossa, Rumania (National Museum, Bucharest), which is 56 cm (22 in) in diameter and weighs over 7 kg ($15\frac{1}{4}$ lb); its central medallion is decorated with a wave pattern and the border with zigzag leaf ornament. A dish from Mileham in England (British Museum) combines a circular recess with a square flange decorated with chased leaf ornament and edged with beading.

Cast or hammered relief ornament was also much used, especially for picture dishes and for the roundels and borders of dishes. One of the finest examples of this technique, the eight-sided dish from the Treasure of Kaiseraugst, has a central roundel showing the discovery of Achilles among the daughters of King Lycomedes and a wide border divided into panels representing various episodes in the life of Achilles.

Several magnificent picture dishes have been found in the late hoards. The outstanding example is the Oceanus dish from the Mildenhall Treasure (British Museum). This large dish – 60.5 cm ($23\frac{3}{16}$in) in diameter – has a heavy beaded rim decorated in low relief, and a central medallion showing a frontal head of Oceanus which is

PROJECTA CASKET *(above left), silver with gilding, from the Esquiline Hill, Rome, mid-fourth century* AD. *This marriage casket of Secundus and Projecta bears the figures of the husband and wife in the central roundel. Height: 28.6 cm ($11\frac{1}{4}$ in) (British Museum, London)*

SPOON *(above), one of a pair, silver, from Sutton Hoo, England, c.*AD *625. This one is inscribed Paul; the other Saul. Length: 25.5 cm ($9\frac{7}{8}$ in) (British Museum, London)*

DAVID PLATE *(above), silver, from Karavas, Cyprus,* AD *613–30. This dish shows, in low relief, three scenes of the battle between David and Goliath. It is the largest of all the David Plates and one of the finest silver plates in antiquity.*
Diameter: 49.4 cm (19½ in)
(Metropolitan Museum of Art, New York)

ANTIOCH CHALICE *(above right), silver with gilding, from Antioch-on-the-Orontes, Turkey,* C.AD *500. It has openwork decoration including two scenes of Christ, teaching and resurrected.*
Height: 19 cm (7½ in)
(Metropolitan Museum of Art, New York)

immediately surrounded by a narrow frieze of nereids riding on sea-monsters; a broad outer frieze depicts satyrs and maenads in revel. Another picture dish that was found in the Tyne near Corbridge, England, in the eighteenth century, and which seems to be the survivor of a hoard, is rectangular with a raised border decorated with running scroll enclosing a relief scene showing a group of deities worshipped on the island of Delos.[28] It has been suggested that the subject was chosen to commemorate the sacrifice offered to Apollo at Delos by Julian the Apostate in AD 363, and that the dish should be interpreted as a product of the pagan reaction to Christianity under that Emperor. A dish found at Parabiago in Italy (Soprintendenza Archeologica della Lombardia) shows the goddess Cybele with Attis in a chariot drawn by lions and surrounded by symbolic figures of the Sun, Moon, Earth and Ocean, and another picture dish found at Lampsacus on the Hellespont in Turkey (Arkeoloji Müsezi, Istanbul) is decorated in low relief with a magnificent seated figure of India surrounded by beasts and birds, and framed by an ornamental border of geometric pattern inlaid with niello, closely comparable with that on the niello dish from Mildenhall. The Lampsacus plate may have formed one of a set representing Africa, Asia and India. Another characteristic picture dish of the period is the Diana dish in Berlin, which may be compared with the dish from Ballana (Nubia), showing Apollo Alexikakos.[29]

The so-called *largitio* plates, which were distributed on the occasion of imperial anniversaries, form an important class of late Roman silver. The earliest of these are the dishes commemorating the tenth anniversary (Decennalia) of Licinius in AD 317, and there is also a dish of the Emperor Valentinian I, showing him flanked by his soldiers, probably made either for his fifth anniversary (Quinquennalia) in 369 or for his tenth.[30] The best-known of the *largitio* dishes is the Plate of Theodosius I (found in 1847 near Mérida, Spain), which shows the Emperor and his two co-regents Arcadius and Valentinian II seated before a temple or tribunal, together with attendants and soldiers.[31] The inscription reads D(OMI)N(VS) THEODOSIVS PERPET(VVS) AVG(VSTVS) OB DIEM FELICISSIMVM X, referring to the Emperor's ten-year anniversary in AD 388 (Real Academia de la Historia, Madrid).

A number of bowls have close-set fluting on the outside, including one from the Esquiline Treasure. Bowls with fluting on the inside were also common, the fluting often combined with a central decorated medallion. A bowl in the Kaiseraugst Treasure has a series of wide radial flutes around a central medallion; the medallion and the narrow horizontal rim are decorated with chased ornament. Spiral fluting is also found on the interiors of bowls. A large, deepish bowl on a high foot-rim from Traprain is decorated in this way and has a central roundel with a head in relief surrounded by a zone of punched dots.

Characteristic bowls of the period were shallow, usually fairly large, and with a series of alternate broad flutes with rounded ends on the inside and flat, straight-ended panels usually decorated with chased leaf ornament. In the centre there would usually be a roundel, also richly decorated with chased or engraved ornament. The Esquiline Treasure contained a fine example of this kind of bowl, and there is one in the Mildenhall Treasure and another from Weiden, near Cologne. Flanged bowls also continued to be popular: several examples were found in the Mildenhall Treasure, one of them of the same form as bowls of the third century, with a vertical rim and a broad, down-curved flange. The bowl, which may be one of the earliest pieces in the Treasure, was later given a lid with decoration in a different style.

One of the best-known pieces of 'toilet silver' is the large Casket of Projecta in the Esquiline Treasure. This oblong box, with a lid in the form of a truncated pyramid and a body of similar shape, is decorated with repoussé reliefs in panels framed by bands of formal ornament. The casket, a wedding present to Projecta, bears the inscription SECVNDE ET PROIECTA VIVATIS IN CHRISTO preceded by a chi-rho monogram (symbolizing Christ); a roundel on the centre of the lid shows the husband and wife. A second casket in the Treasure is a cylindrical box with a high-domed lid, the dome being formed with alternate flutes and flat panels, a combination of straight lines and curves that is wholly typical of the silver in the late hoards. The sides of the casket are also alternately concave and flat and decorated with repoussé ornament showing figures of Muses beneath arcading. Inside the casket is a thin bronze plate with holes cut in it to contain cylindrical boxes with lids, presumably for cosmetics.

· EARLY BYZANTINE SILVER ·

Although the fourth and fifth centuries marked the end of the spirit of pagan antiquity, pagan traditions in iconography and style lived on in the following two centuries in the decoration and design of vessels made for Christian usage. It is difficult to distinguish plates with pagan subjects known (from their Byzantine control marks) to have been made in the sixth century AD from work of the fourth century such as the Diana dish in Berlin. Classical models continued to serve as a source of inspiration, and the techniques discovered and used under the Roman Empire were still employed when the Roman world had shifted its centre and focus from Rome to Constantinople.

In spite of the continuity of the classical tradition, however, one of the major differences between the silver plates of the fourth and fifth centuries and those of the sixth and seventh is the visible Christian content. This is true even for one of the best-known assemblages of secular silver of the period, buried as part of the grave-goods in the Sutton Hoo Ship-Burial, which is the burial of King Raedwald of the East Anglians who died in AD 625/6. The treasure (now in the British Museum) consisted of arms and armour, gold jewellery and sixteen pieces of silver, and the quantity of silver is one of the most remarkable features of the burial. Particularly striking must have been the large dish with niello decoration, made in the reign of Anastasius (AD 491–518), the fluted bowl of the fourth or early fifth century, and the sixth-century 'Saul' and 'Paul' spoons, which could have been obtained by pilgrims at the church of the Holy Apostles in Constantinople. Of about AD 600 is a set of silver bowls in four or five pairs, each decorated with four cross-arms radiating from a central roundel.

DISH, *silver, from Klimova, Perm, USSR, c.* AD *530, depicting a herdsman with goats and a dog. The border is decorated with curling acanthus leaves and edged with a narrow band of rope pattern. Diameter: 24 cm ($9\frac{1}{2}$ in) (Hermitage Museum, Leningrad)*

There are no sixth- or seventh-century pieces in traditional forms and with classical decoration in the Sutton Hoo treasure, but one category of silver retaining such form and decoration is saucepans and handled *paterae*, an example of which is a saucepan (in the Louvre) from Cap Chenoua, near Cherchel in Algeria, dated by its control stamps to the reign of Justinian (AD 527–65). A single figure of Neptune occupies most of the space on the handle, as on some third-century saucepans, and the wide arms of attachment end in eagle heads. The rest of the space is taken up with two dolphins flanking a shell. The inside of the bowl is plain, the outside has fishing scenes.

Figured circular plates and dishes with classical subjects form a substantial group. One of the finest, a plate probably of AD 542 and found in Perm (Russia), has a relief of a shepherd with two goats and a dog, and on the reverse an ornamented leaf pattern with chalices. Also from Perm, and dated AD 550–65, is a plate 26.5 cm ($10\frac{7}{16}$in) in diameter, with a relief depicting Venus in the tent of Anchises. A plate dated to AD 577, from the region of the River Kama (Russia), now lost, had a relief, worked in repoussé, of a personification of

Abundance. On about the same scale as the previous examples, with a diameter of 28 cm (11 in), but dated to the reign of Heraclius (AD 613–29/30) is a dish probably found in Russia and showing Meleager and Atalanta in relief. The scene is divided into two zones by a horizontal ground-line. In the larger, upper segment Atalanta leads her horse from the left, while Meleager, at the hunt, leans on his spear. On either side stand attendants, and in the lower zone two dogs play near a hunting net. These three plates are in the Hermitage Museum, Leningrad. Of exactly the same date (AD 613–29/30) as the Meleager plate is a bucket found in Kuczurmare, Bukovina (USSR), and decorated with a relief depicting six gods between ornamented wreaths at top and bottom (Kunsthistorisches Museum, Vienna).

Decoration without figures and some other forms of vessel are found in the hoard from Malaia Pereshchepina (Poltava, southern Russia), discovered in 1912. One of the oldest pieces was the 'Plate of Paternus', a paten 61 cm (24 in) in diameter with a chi-rho monogram in the centre of the bowl (Hermitage Museum, Leningrad). It was made in the reign of Anastasius, probably in AD 498. Around the rim is a design of vines, birds and chalices, while a band of inscription in the bowl round the monogram refers to a 'renovation' of the piece by a Bishop Paternus, who may have been Bishop of Tomi in Rumania after AD 500.

Included in the Malaia Pereshchepina hoard were a number of pieces with Christian symbols, as indeed there were also in the Sutton Hoo silver. In the fourth and fifth centuries those who had embraced the Christian faith often had chi-rho monograms and other Christian symbols engraved on their silver, though its decoration might be purely pagan in inspiration, like the silver in the Esquiline hoard. At the same time they collected plate with Christian themes, such as the flask with scenes from the Old and New Testaments in the Traprain Treasure. A good deal of plate was certainly being made for religious use at the time, but very little has survived. The earliest such collections are the remarkable Water Newton Treasure (fourth century) and those from Canoscio in Umbria, Italy, and from Kumluca in south-west Turkey (both probably deposited in the sixth century).[32] In the sixth and seventh centuries Christian silver changed dramatically, both in its decoration and its use for worship. For the first time distinct types of plate were developed for liturgical use – chalices, patens, censers and fans – as well as reliquary caskets, and were more highly regarded than pictures of Christ's life.

The most important liturgical vessels are the chalice and paten. The earliest example from this period of a eucharistic drinking vessel is the Antioch chalice in the Metropolitan Museum of Art, New York. Dating from about AD 500, it has openwork decoration and a very low foot below a roll moulding. Represented on the chalice are two complex scenes, each with Christ among Apostles and with symbolic animals or objects. The scenes probably depict on one side Christ teaching, and on the other the resurrected Lord with the lamb and the eagle. Such elaborate scenes are unusual on surviving chalices.

The most common form of early and middle Byzantine chalice was an undecorated hemispherical bowl with slightly inturned rim, a knop and a flaring base, often, but not always, with an inscription around the rim. There exists, however, a sixth-century chalice from Syria with a decorative band instead of an inscription, which was found along with three inscribed chalices whose bowls are enhanced with busts in roundels of the youthful, beardless Christ holding a codex, the Virgin, St Peter and St Paul (Cleveland Museum of Art). Equally elaborate, dating perhaps from about AD 600, is a gold cup found in the Albanian Treasure (Metropolitan Museum of Art, New York), which has the same form as the silver chalices but on a rather higher flaring foot below the knop. It is decorated in repoussé with four female personifications of imperial cities and metropolitan sees.

Widespread among early Christian patens was a platter with an inscribed flat base with engraved cross, a near-vertical wall and a horizontal rim which may also be decorated. Two such patens, the Riha Paten and the Stuma Paten (the Riha Treasure and the Stuma Treasure[33] were probably a single find from a site south-east of Antioch) were made in about AD 577–578. They both have a dedicating inscription on the rim and the base decorated with a relief of the Communion of the Apostles. Behind the altar depicted on each, two haloed figures of Christ administer the wine on the left and the bread on the right. The representation of two Christ figures during the Communion of the Apostles occurs only in the Eastern Church but is thought to reflect the universal liturgical practice of, originally, two deacons, and later of a priest and a deacon, administering the sacrament. Found with the Riha and Stuma patens were two silver discs, dated by their stamps to the time of Justin II (AD 565–578). These discs, designed to be carried on staffs, have engraved borders with peacock-feather eyes, indicating that they are fans.

In the church service the senses of sight and smell were cultivated deliberately, and the appropriate equipment was made in silver. The treasure found at Lampsacus included a slender, undecorated candlestick and a pendent lamp-holder with pierced decoration consisting of a probable chi-rho monogram and of crosses alternating with palmette design around the rim. The candlestick was made in the reign of Justinian (AD 527–65), the lamp-holder probably in AD 577 (British Museum).

Various kinds of censer are preserved, from undecorated bowls to openwork vessels with lids and figure-decorated incense-burners, which could be set up, hung, or carried and swung. The silver censer from the First Cyprus Treasure (British Museum), made in about 602–10, is one of the few in precious metal. It is a six-sided vessel 10.9 cm (4$\frac{5}{16}$in) in diameter, standing on a low foot-ring, and on each side there is a roundel containing a haloed bust, of Christ, the Virgin, Saints Peter, Paul, John the Evangelist, and James.

Crosses appear as decorative motifs on patens, chalices and other objects, and the altar table assumed significance as a symbol of the salvation-bringing cross; but the cross itself was not at this period placed on the altar. At least two surviving silver crosses with tongues at the foot, those from Phela and Hama, may be taken therefore to be processional crosses, set originally on standards.[34] The Phela cross, 47.6 cm (18$\frac{3}{4}$ in) high, belongs to the late sixth or early seventh century, and is inscribed along the four arms with a dedication: 'In the time of the priest Ioannes. An offering to the church of the Mother of God of the village of Phela.' That from Hama is somewhat smaller, being 35.7 cm (14 in) high, but is of the same form and has a dedication saying: 'Kyriakos has presented the cross after praying to St Sergios.'

The confident attribution of unmarked pieces to a particular workshop is peculiarly possible at this period because a strong chronological and stylistic framework is supplied by the many plates and vessels which carry imperial stamps. These stamps not only date the objects with the ruler's monogram but also permit an attribution to the workshops of the imperial court. The series of stamps begins with the financial reforms of the Emperor Anastasius (AD 491–518), which included a reorganization of the controls in all the traffic in precious metals, and extends to the reign of Constans II (AD 641–68).

The dating system plays a particularly important part in the study of the two linked treasures found in Cyprus in 1899 and 1902. The first (in the British Museum) includes two plates, one with a representation of St Sergius or St Bacchus (and dated to 641–51), a censer, already mentioned, and twenty-four spoons. The second treasure (in the Metropolitan Museum of Art, New York) has a series of plates, some decorated with the life of David, five flasks and a girdle made up from a gold medallion and coins of Maurice Tiberius, Justin, Justinian and Theodosius. One of the plates carries control marks of the Emperor Maurice Tiberius (AD 582–602); but most were stamped in the reign of Heraclius, after AD 610.

The nine David Plates from the second Cyprus treasure are notable for their unique narrative relationship and because they carry deliberate and specific political messages. All of them bear the five control stamps of the Emperor Heraclius (AD 610–41), and date between AD 613 and 629/30. Four of them demonstrate the close connection between the imperial art of the fourth and the seventh centuries, for they show David in a setting of companions and architecture which is immediately reminiscent of the composition of the fourth-century Theodosius Dish. The subjects of this set of four are the marriage of David to Michal, David trying on Saul's armour, the anointing of David, and the introduction of David to Saul.[35] The subjects of all the dishes not only have definite connections with the illuminated Byzantine Psaltery of the ninth to twelfth centuries, but are also a link with the art of the fourth-century church. For example, six out of the nine subjects on the fourth-century carved wooden doors of the church of St Ambrose in Milan correspond with the series on the plates. In addition, there is a direct imperial reference in the plates as a whole, for the stimulus for making the set may well have been a specific event in the life of the Emperor himself. In AD 627 Heraclius, during his campaign against the Persian Emperor Khusro, fought the Persian general Razatis in single combat, beheading his opponent, as David did Goliath. Support for this theory of a contemporary identification of Heraclius with David, and Razatis with Goliath, comes from a description of the battle by a chronicler at the Merovingian court of King Dagobert in AD 629. The stamps show that the David plates were made in the period AD 613/30, while the political interpretation of the content places the manufacture at the end of that period. Of the David Plates, the dish showing the battle between David and Goliath (Metropolitan Museum of Art, New York) is one of the finest surviving silver plates of antiquity, comparable with the Mildenhall Great Dish.

FAN, *silver with gilding, from Riha, south-east of Antioch, Syria,* AD *565–78. It has an engraved tetramorph and was designed to be carried on a staff. The borders are engraved with peacock-feather eyes. Height: 30.9 cm (12 in) (Dumbarton Oaks Collection, Washington DC)*

La·Royne Jehe Deureux·Royne de france·et de Nauarre Compaigne

· 2 · THE MIGRATION PERIOD AND · · THE MIDDLE AGES ·

Far more is known about the jewellery and personal ornaments of the Dark Ages than about its plate, secular or ecclesiastical. The history of early secular plate suffers from a lack both of actual pieces and of inventories and other precise historical records. There is a little more information about church plate, but it, too, is patchy.

· EARLY SECULAR PLATE ·

While little is known of the history of secular plate between AD 500 and AD 800, much of significance certainly occurred in the centuries following the fall of the Roman Empire. For instance, certain types of classical plate, such as the great embossed dishes made for display which are known from a number of late Roman treasures (and which continued to be made in Byzantium) disappeared from the West. Other types of vessel were introduced by the barbarian invaders, including drinking horns mounted in silver or gold, and the two principal state drinking vessels of the Middle Ages, the cup, whose distinguishing feature was a deep vertical bowl, and the *hanap*, whose bowl by contrast was broad and flat. The dignity of these two vessels was indicated by the foot on which they were raised, which in the case of the cup was to develop into an elaborate stem and foot.

The ordinary drinking vessel of post-Roman and medieval times, however, was undoubtedly the small, flat silver bowl usually described in Latin as a *ciphus*. Although these vessels must have been extremely common in the Dark Ages, only a few survive, notably the seven bowls of St Ninian's treasure, found in the Shetland Islands (National Museum, Edinburgh). Decorated in punched dots with interlace, animals and other patterns, they probably date from the late eighth century. Drinking had played an important festive and ceremonial role in the heroic societies from which the Frankish, Anglo-Saxon, Viking, Teutonic and Lombard cultures derived, and it long retained this traditional prestige. Certainly the drinking vessels used at feasts were decorated with becoming richness when intended for great personages, and the drinking horn itself survived as a ceremonial vessel into the later Middle Ages, and in some regions, such as Germany, Holland and Scandinavia, even later, long after it had ceased to be in ordinary use.

Ornament, too, certainly underwent great changes after the triumph of Christianity in the fourth century and the collapse of the Empire. Christian detestation of Greco-Roman paganism accounted for the gradual eradication of subjects from classical mythology, while the barbarians introduced their own techniques and styles of ornament. The Romans seem to have regarded enamelling not as a metropolitan technique but as one practised by barbarians on the northern margins of the Empire. Red enamel made its appearance in Celtic Europe, but blue, yellow and other colours were added in Britain and Gaul under the Romans. These early Celtic and Romano-British or Gallo-Roman enamels were all in the *champlevé* technique (the cells for the enamel are cut out in the plaque of the metal), and as far as is known the designs were rarely figurative. *Champlevé* enamelling was to have a persistent vogue among European goldsmiths until the end of the Middle Ages, reaching its apogee in the twelfth and thirteenth centuries, after which it declined into an ancillary decorative technique. *Cloisonné* enamel, on the other hand, seems to have been an Eastern invention; it became a standard Byzantine technique in the sixth century. Its motifs are created by chasing plates of gold with designs whose component parts are then separated by walls (*cloisons*) of gold; the enamels are then laid and fused within these compartments.

Niello and filigree, by contrast, were classical techniques. Niello is essentially an enrichment of engraving, in which the incised lines of a design are filled with a black sulphide created by mixing silver sulphide with sulphur or, after the eleventh century, by a molten alloy of silver, copper and lead with sulphur. Filigree, a late-classical technique, spread widely among the peoples of the Migration period. Essentially, filigree creates designs by the manipulation of twisted gold wire, which is then soldered to a metal plate. Its

VIRGIN AND CHILD *(facing page), silver-gilt and enamel. France, fourteenth century. This small reliquary statue was presented in 1339 by Queen Jeanne of France to St Denis. Height: 69 cm (27⅛ in) (Musée du Louvre, Paris)*

VASE DE SAINT-MARTIN, *onyx with gold rim and foot set with gems and pearls and decorated with* verroterie cloisonnée. *France, probably eighth century. Height: 22.3 cm ($8\frac{3}{4}$ in) (Treasury of St Maurice d'Agaune, St Maurice, Switzerland)*

attraction lay in its richness of texture combined with play of movement and depth, and it was to remain a popular decorative technique in goldsmiths' work into the early thirteenth century. Barbarian styles of ornament had a much shorter life. Thus *verroterie cloisonnée* (*opus inclusorium*), in which plaques of red glass or garnets are set in metal compartments, disappeared at the end of the seventh century, when classical ornament seems to have reasserted itself, displacing the Celtic, Viking, Anglo-Saxon, Merovingian and Teutonic styles. As late as the eighth century, however, both Northern and Celtic ornament were still to be seen on certain objects from Germany, and in areas outside the Carolingian orbit of power, such as Anglo-Saxon England, Ireland and Scandinavia, they retained a local vitality.

Perhaps the earliest medieval secular vessel to survive is the so-called *Vase de Saint-Martin* in the treasury of Saint-Maurice d'Agaune in the Valais, probably dating from the eighth century. It consists of an onyx bowl, whose handle is now broken, mounted with a rim and foot of gold, set with gems and pearls and decorated in *verroterie cloisonnée*. What is certain is that gold and silver were still lavishly employed in costly and massive pieces of plate. The sixth-century Frankish historian Gregory of Tours writes of precious objects kept in the treasure chambers of Merovingian kings and queens, along with jewellery and rich raiment. When, for example, Gregory visited King Chilperic (d.584) at Nogent in AD 581, the king showed him a massive dish of gold set with gems.

The setting of objects in precious metal, especially of gold, with gems – principally sapphires, balas-rubies, and emeralds – and with crystals and pearls, was to remain a constant feature of the medieval goldsmith's art. Antique cameos were prized for this purpose, and there existed dealers in gems and cameos, known as *gemmarii*, certainly by the Carolingian age. Stones for setting were generally collected by the patron, as we know from Abbot Suger's graphic description of how he collected gems for his works at St Denis in the 1140s. It was often the patron, too, who gave the goldsmith the raw material for a new work – old plate for refashioning, coins, or in the case of religious goldsmiths' work, gifts of jewellery or plate from the devout.

Such pieces as Chilperic's were made for display, not use, which their weight and costliness precluded. This was also true of the large platter (*scutella*) and two basins of gold set with gems which Queen Brunhild of Austrasia sent c.589 as a present to the Visigothic king. This distinction between plate made essentially as treasure and brought out to impress at a feast or, more rarely, for actual use on occasions of great ceremony, and plate made for everyday use, dated from Roman times and remained constant into the nineteenth century, and even beyond. It has produced little or no variation in the types of plate made by the goldsmith: rather the difference has lain sometimes in the scale and always in the lavishness of the materials, and of the decoration and workmanship.

The two silver dishes (*catinae*) which King Guntram of Burgundy and Orléans (d.592) had set on a table for a dinner he gave at Orléans in AD 585 for the bishops of his kingdom were certainly intended for everyday use. They had originally belonged to the traitor Mummolus, and were part of the half-share in his thirty *catinae* that had fallen

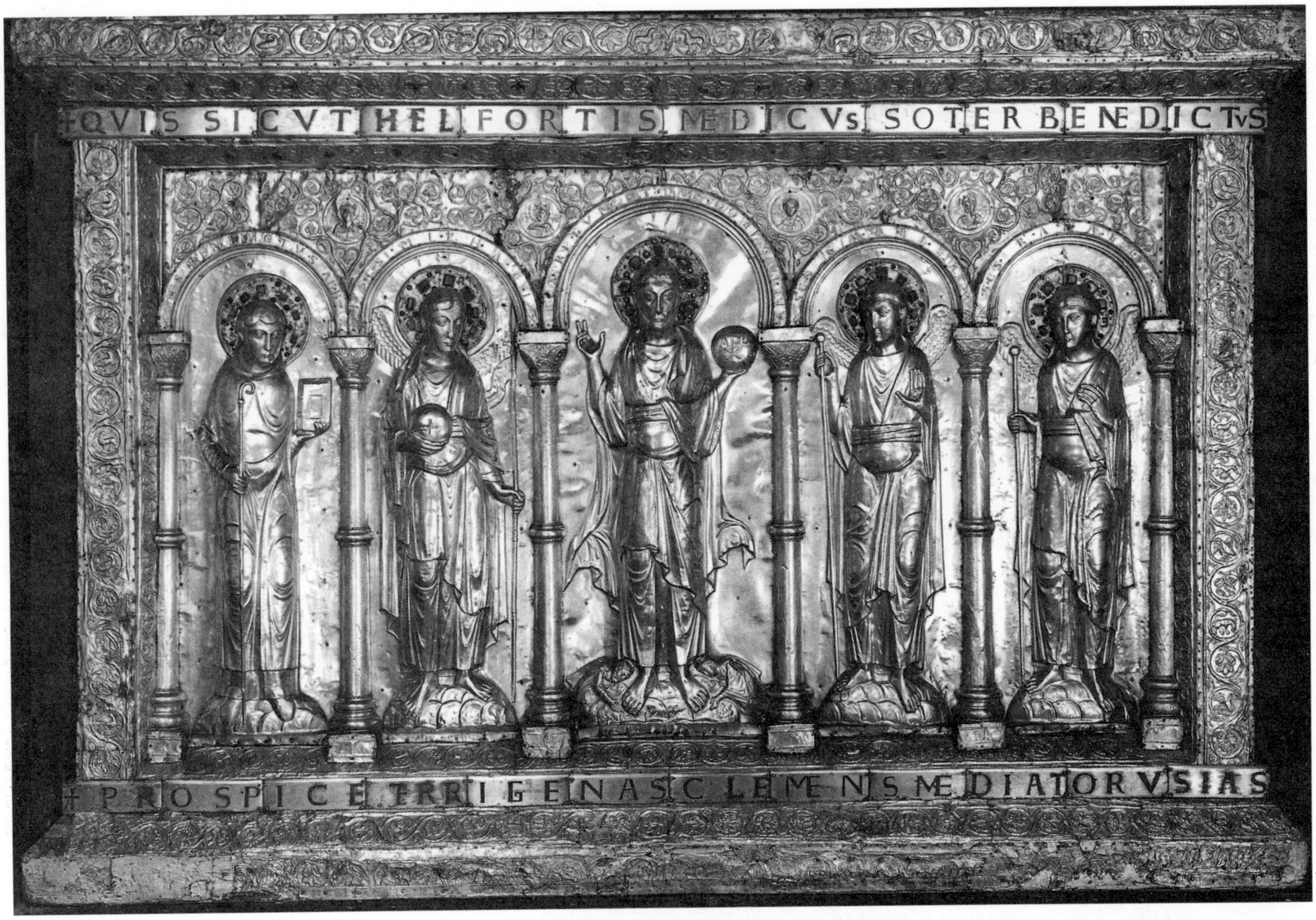

ALTAR *of the frontal of Basle Cathedral, gold. Germanic Empire, early eleventh century. Dimensions: 95 × 178 cm ($37\frac{3}{8} \times 67\frac{1}{4}$ in) (Musée de Cluny, Paris)*

to Guntram, who had kept only these two, feeling that they were all he required for a daily table service. This record of thirty great dishes of silver possessed by Mummolus points to the magnitude of the treasures of plate owned by Frankish dignitaries, and shows that the traditions of late Imperial splendour continued in the West as well as in Byzantium.

We know little of the goldsmiths of these centuries. St Eligius, later to become the patron saint of goldsmiths, made 'very many vessels of gold, silver and gems' for the Frankish king Dagobert (ruled 629–39), as well as shrines for the relics of St Germanus, St Severinus, St Quentin and many other saints. In the 1140s Abbot Suger was proud to think that he had obtained for the altar of his abbey church an incense boat which King Louis VII, his patron, had pawned and been unable to redeem, and which had mounts of *opus inclusorium* (usually thought to be *verroterie cloisonnée*) believed to be from the hand of St Eligius himself, and regarded by the goldsmiths of Suger's time as a most precious treasure.

During the Dark Ages goldsmiths in royal or monastic service usually carried out their tasks in workshops attached to the palace or monastery buildings, which meant that they worked in the country, as this was where most palaces and monasteries were built. There traditions of technique and style were formed, diffused and handed down. In the ninth century, Loup, abbot of Ferrières in northern France, sent two boys to a friend's monastery to be taught the art of goldsmith's work.

Goldsmiths independent of great and wealthy patrons also existed. Gregory of Tours, our chief source of knowledge of sixth-century Gaul, tells of a goldsmith living in the Alps who persuaded a messenger of the Emperor Leo to allow him to make imitations in silver of a gold case for a gospel-book, and of a gold paten which the messenger was bearing as a present from the Emperor to the church of Lyons. From the context it is clear that this goldsmith lived in his own house, in some small town or village on the highroad from Italy to Lyons. Goldsmiths were held in high esteem, both for their skill in working precious metals and for their association with them, and the best goldsmiths ranked among the foremost artists of their day. This remained their status until the end of the Middle Ages, deservedly so given the variety of skills, figurative, decorative and manipulative, that they were required to master: chasing, engraving, embossing, gem-setting, enamelling, niello-

work, to name only the principal techniques, combined with a knowledge of drawing, design, and ornament.

One of our few glimpses from the early Middle Ages of a young goldsmith in training is a literary description of c.1200 of a young apprentice drawing ornaments of 'little flowers' for practice on wax tablets. Medieval goldsmiths differed from their successors in that they worked as freely in the base metals of copper and brass as they did in silver and gold. This is especially true up to the thirteenth century: many monumental pieces were executed in copper enamelled in the *champlevé* technique.

· EARLY CHURCH PLATE ·

It was the Emperor Constantine who, after his conversion to Christianity, set the example of munificent gifts of gold and silver plate to churches. As ornaments wrought in the world's most precious metals and gems, such gifts were an affirmation of piety and dedication to God, and their magnificence was to be imitated by secular rulers and great ecclesiastics until the fall of the *ancien régime*.

Already in sixth-century Gaul, we read of chalices, patens and gospel-books made of gold set

LOTHAIR CROSS *(left), gold set with gems and a cameo of the Emperor Augustus, the reverse engraved with a Crucifixion. Ottonian Empire, c.1000. Height: 50 cm ($19\frac{11}{16}$ in) (Aachen Cathedral Treasury, Aachen)*

with gems, of altars and saints' tombs covered with plaques of gold and silver, and of gold and silver portable reliquaries (*capsae*). No early shrine of a saint sheathed in precious metal survives, but we can still see, from the high altar of the great Church of San Ambrogio in Milan, how altars were clad in gold and silver. Its elaborate casing of embossed precious metal was executed by the goldsmith Wolvinius and his associates for Bishop Angilbert (824–56). The front is of gold, set with *cloisonné* enamels and sapphires, rubies and crystals, the favourite stones of the Middle Ages. Its sides are of silver parcel-gilt, already showing that impeccable taste in contouring and contrasting plain silver with gilt that was to continue until the demise of the Gothic style. The Wolvinius altar was completed under one bishop, but the casing of an altar sometimes took many centuries. Thus Charles the Bald gave a gold antependium (altar frontal) at some date between 823 and 877 to the high altar of St Denis; in the 1140s Abbot Suger commissioned gold side-panels and an even richer rear panel 'so that the whole altar might appear of gold'. Sometimes, as at Peterhausen near Constance, the four columns of the ciborium, or altar-canopy, were also plated with silver (by 1156).

Even if the whole altar was not encased in precious metal, its dossal or retable and its frontal might be executed in silver, silver-gilt or gold. Some impression of the intended effect of such altars with frontals and dossals can be gained from the twelfth-century Golden Altars of Denmark, comparatively provincial works executed in base metal, such as those from Lisbjerg (c.1150) and Odder. Both of these have frontals shaped as a large vertical central panel flanked by three rows of pairs of small panels, which appears to have been a common arrangement. The central panel usually contained a figure of Christ in Majesty, as at Odder, or of the Virgin and Child enthroned to represent the motif of *Sedes Sapientiae* (the Throne of Wisdom). In the smaller panels were other figures, saints, Virtues and the like. The whole formed a representation of Paradise. In the Danish altars the dossal is a low panel, again decorated with figures of Christ and the Apostles. From the centre rises a cross encircled by an arch resting on either side of the panel. The theme of Christ and the Apostles, representing the Gospel and its preaching, seems to have been a usual one for dossals, and is found again on the beautiful Romanesque retable of silver-gilt framed in copper, representing the Pentecost, from the bishopric of Liège, now in the Musée de Cluny, Paris.

The canons of the Church forbade the celebration of Mass over an unconsecrated altar. In the itinerant life led by the great in Carolingian and medieval times, ecclesiastics, whether they belonged to churches, monasteries or the household of a king or lord, were in daily need of some form of consecrated altar that could be carried in their baggage. The portable altar, which enshrined a relic or relics, met this need; it could be laid on any temporary support when mass was to be said. Portable altars were of two main types: a flat slab of stone, usually a precious marble or hardstone, in a metal frame or a flat oblong box with four low feet, generally with a piece of precious marble or stone set in the lid. In keeping with their especially sacred purpose – an altar is central to the sacrifice of the Mass – portable altars were often richly decorated with engraved or enamelled figures, sometimes devised according to an elaborate symbolic or theological programme, like the beautiful enamelled mid-twelfth-century portable altar from the abbey of Stavelot in the Ardennes (now in the Musée du Cinquentenaire, Brussels).

Portable triptychs also came into use on altars that had no dossal, or else on journeys and in private oratories and chapels. The earliest examples known are Byzantine. Indeed, the Triptych

FRONT OF THE WOLVINIUS ALTAR *(facing page, above; detail, facing page, below), gold set with cloisonné enamels and sapphires, rubies and crystals. The sides are of parcel-gilt. It was executed by the goldsmith Wolvinius and his associates for Bishop Angilbert (824–56). The contrasting of plain silver with gilt was to continue until the demise of the Gothic style. Dimensions: 85 × 220 cm ($33\frac{1}{2} \times 86\frac{5}{8}$ in) (Church of San Ambrogio, Milan)*

of the True Cross made for Wibald, Abbot of Stavelot, one of the greatest of mid-twelfth-century patrons of goldsmiths, was commissioned to enshrine two small eleventh-century Byzantine reliquary triptychs of the True Cross in gold and *cloisonné* enamel, which he had brought back from Constantinople in 1154. A number of such twelfth-century triptychs survive from the Mosan region of Belgium: all are in copper-gilt and enamelled, all contain relics of the True Cross and were no doubt set up only on special occasions and feasts for veneration. Thus the Triptych of the Holy Cross, made for the Church of Sainte-Croix in Liège c.1150, contains relics of St Vincent and St John the Baptist, but its principal motif is suggested by the most important relic of all, a fragment of the True Cross said to have been presented to the church by the Emperor Henry II in 1006. It is enclosed in a small case, set in the central panel and held by two angels in relief – a design that was to enjoy a long popularity and to continue its existence in a characteristic Gothic mutation.

The Alton Towers Triptych (Victoria and Albert Museum, London), a brilliant mid-twelfth century work in copper-gilt and enamel, shows that the triptych form was not reserved exclusively for reliquaries of the True Cross as is sometimes claimed, but was also used for objects perhaps best described as portable retables. Occasionally portable altar and retable were combined: a portable

DOLGELLY CHALICE AND PATEN *(bottom), silver. England, c.1240. It bears an inscription referring to Nicholas of Hereford, who may have been the goldsmith. Height of chalice: 19.7 cm ($7\frac{3}{4}$ in) (National Museum of Wales, Cardiff. Reproduced by gracious permission of HM the Queen)*

ARDAGH CHALICE *(below), silver, gold, bronze, enamelled glass. Ireland, c.700–50. Height: 17.8 cm (7 in) (National Museum of Antiquities, Dublin)*

WILTEN CHALICE *(above), silver decorated with niello work. Romanesque, c.1160/70. The simple form of bowl, knop and foot is set off by fine engraving. Height: 16.7 cm (6½ in) (Kunsthistorisches Museum, Vienna)*

folding altar of gold was made for Verdun Cathedral by commission of the city's Count Hermann (c.1000–28), and was contrived 'in the fashion of retables'; that is, when opened it became an altar and also the panels of a retable showing the figures of Moses and Aaron to either side of the Crucifixion.

The monumental crucifixes that hung in the choirs or stood on the rood-beams of eleventh- and twelfth-century churches, of which wood and metal examples survive, were sometimes made or covered with precious metal. Hermann II, Bishop of Münster (d.1168), for example, gave his cathedral a great silver cross which hung over the choir and contained the Host and many precious relics. From the eleventh century onwards the principal ornament of the altar was also a cross. In addition to altar crosses, the rituals of the Church also required processional crosses, generally altar crosses of larger size. The piety of the great in Carolingian and early medieval times clad both types of cross in gold and silver, and the refulgence of their metal, especially in the light cast by the candles on the altar itself or thrown by great hanging coronals of candles, themselves often plated with gold and silver for magnificence and multiplication of light, must often have excited a mystical fervour of devotion in the dark, narrow-windowed churches of the eighth to twelfth centuries.

The finest surviving early medieval crosses are the Ottonian crosses of the old Imperial lands, such as the crosses of the two Mathildas (c.973–82; c.1000) and that of Theophano (c.1039–56) at Essen or the gold cross of Gisela at Munich (c.1006). The so-called Lothair cross at Aachen (c.1000) is perhaps the most beautiful of all, with its front of gold subtly patterned with large and small precious stones, the whole dominated by the great cameo of Augustus set at the crossing, and its reverse engraved with a Crucifixion of simple linear pathos. Even more richly ornamented is the Imperial cross (early eleventh century) now in Vienna, with its formal patterning of precious stones enriched by pearls. In form these earlier crosses are either equal-armed or have an extended lower arm; their ends are square or lightly everted and moulded. Their aspect is majestically weighty and stable, rather than light and upward-mounting like the later crosses of Gothic art. In this they obey the general aesthetic of Carolingian, Ottonian and Romanesque goldsmiths' work. Customarily, these early crosses were set in a rich cross-foot. The finest surviving example of these is the Romanesque cross-foot of enamelled copper from the abbey of St Bertin, in the museum of Saint-Omer. Its elaborate iconographical scheme recalls the lost cross-foot of enamelled gold devised by Suger for the great gold cross set with gems he caused to be made in the 1140s for St Denis. Processional crosses often had staves of silver for carrying.

SAINTE COUPE *(right), silver. France, early thirteenth century. This ciborium was probably a secular cup converted to religious use. Height: 31 cm (12¼ in) (Musées de Sens, Sens)*

Of the vessels used in the Mass the most important are the chalice and paten. The earliest post-medieval chalices to survive are all small, humble vessels in base metal, with plain deep bowls, a central knop and a trumpet foot, varying only in the size of the bowl and its relation to the size of the foot. This is also the form of the Tassilo chalice presented by Duke Tassilo of Bavaria in about 788 to the monastery of Kremsmünster in Austria. Of copper, it is decorated in silver damascening and niello with medallions enclosing figures of Christ and the Evangelists.

EAGLE VASE, *porphyry mounted in silver-gilt. France, mid-twelfth century. Suger obtained this vase for St Denis, and converted it from a ewer into the figure of an eagle by adding the mounts; it was probably intended to serve as a container. Height: 43 cm (17 in) (Musée du Louvre, Paris)*

Large chalices with two handles, known as ministerial chalices, must also have existed from an early date, for until the Church withdrew the cup from the laity such a chalice was an aid in giving wine to communicants from the congregation. The famous Ardagh chalice in Dublin is one of the earliest surviving known examples, probably dating from the first half of the eighth century. Not all large chalices had such a form: the chalice of Doña Urraca in San Isidoro, León, and that of Abbot Domingo of Silos (1041–73) in Burgos, both dating from the eleventh century, are examples of rich chalices without handles.

The chalice of Doña Urraca has a hardstone bowl mounted in precious metal – indeed it may well have been a secular cup converted for use as a chalice, for the great often offered cups to churches and monasteries for just such a purpose. Suger in the 1140s was proud to obtain for the high altar of St Denis a chalice whose bowl was cut from 'a single and solid sardonyx', which he had had mounted in gold set with gems. While some early chalices had bowls of glass or wood or hardstone, the predominant materials were gold and silver. Indeed, from the twelfth century, the Church attempted to ensure that all churches had a silver chalice. In poor churches this ideal was never completely realized; perhaps the most such churches could ever afford was a chalice of pewter or copper-gilt, at best with a silver bowl. But in rich churches, or in ones with pious and wealthy benefactors, the chalice and paten were always of gold or silver. Large ministerial chalices were usually accompanied by a matching paten and a spoon of precious metal for adding a little water to the wine. In reverence for the Holy Blood, the celebrant might also have a Eucharistic reed of precious metal for drinking the wine, though these fell gradually out of general use towards the end of the thirteenth century.

Surviving Ottonian and Romanesque chalices are often extraordinarily splendid and complex in ornamentation. The devout naturally wished to adorn these, of all vessels, with significant motifs and with all the richness of engraving, niello, enamel and gems. Yet their essential design is simple, consisting of a hemispherical bowl on a short or shortish stem, which might not even be more than a knop, and a round foot. This is the design of the late tenth-century gold chalice of St Gauzelin, in the Cathedral of Nancy, where the simple forms of bowl, knop and foot are set off by bands of filigree set with precious stones and panels of *cloisonné* enamel. It is still the design of the late twelfth- and early thirteenth-century chalices that survive, largely in Germany and Austria. One of the finest Romanesque chalices is that of the abbey of Wilten, Innsbruck (now in the Kunsthistorisches Museum, Vienna), decorated in niello. A matching paten accompanies it, as was usual with chalices of any pretension. A common motif engraved on patens was the Lamb of God.

The host was normally reserved in a pyx, a

CHALICE, *sardonyx mounted in gold and silver-gilt set with gems and pearls. France, c.1140. Abbot Suger obtained it for the high altar of St Denis. Height: 19 cm (7½ in) (National Gallery of Art, Washington)*

small silver box or cup, suspended over the altar. Very few examples in precious metal survive, as is also true of the ciborium, or pyx mounted on a foot, which appeared in the late twelfth century and became common from the thirteenth. This sometimes took the form of a tower, symbolizing the tower-shape which was believed to be that of the rock of the Holy Sepulchre. The finest early examples of vessels of this kind in precious metal are the beautiful early thirteenth-century silver *Sainte Coupe* in Sens Cathedral, a similar cup in the treasury of Saint Maurice d'Agaune and the so-called *Coupe de Charlemagne* in the same treasury. It is likely that all three were secular cups converted to religious use. Two beautiful late twelfth-century English ciboria of enamelled copper still survive, the finer of them the superb Burleigh ciborium (Victoria and Albert Museum, London).

Water and wine for the service of the altar were kept in containers of various sorts and sizes, most, but not all, of vase, flagon or jug form. Suger secured for St Denis in the 1140s a *justa* or container of rock-crystal, which had been given as a wedding present c.1137 by Eleanor of Aquitaine to her husband Louis VII of France, and which Suger had specially mounted in gold set with gems. Suger's famous eagle vase, which he converted from a ewer into the figure of an eagle by adding eagle-shaped mounts of gold, again set with gems, was probably also intended to serve as a container. The water and wine were poured into the chalice from ewers. A sardonyx ewer mounted in gold (now in the Louvre), which Suger obtained for the high altar of St Denis, shows a more or less conventional Romanesque form. *Aquamaniles*, or vessels from which water was poured over the hands of the priest to be caught by a basin held beneath, were introduced by the ninth century; but water was commonly poured from one basin into another. *Aquamaniles* were sometimes of silver, and sometimes of delightfully capricious design, like the beautiful twelfth-century griffin, probably German, of silvered and nielloed bronze in the Victoria and Albert Museum, London. Basins for washing, known now only from thirteenth-century examples in enamelled copper made in Limoges, were also frequently of silver.

The altar candlesticks, too, were often of silver and sometimes gold, like the pair presented by Louis VI of France to St Denis between 1108 and 1137. No examples in precious metal survive, but some impression of their intricacy and elaboration of workmanship is given by the famous Gloucester candlestick of copper alloy between 1104 and

RELIQUARY *(above right) of the chains of St Peter, gold with niello inlay. Prague, c.1368–78. This reliquary once belonged to the Emperor Charles IV. Height: 12.5 cm (4¾ in) (Schatzkammer, Vienna)*

RELIQUARY *(right) of the Holy Thorn, foiled crystal, gold and enamelled silver, gems and pearls. France, c.1300. Height: 30 cm (11¾ in) (British Museum, London)*

1113 for Abbot Peter and the monks of Gloucester (Victoria and Albert Museum). Churches themselves were lit by great hanging chandeliers shaped as circles with prickets for candles. These were often of silver or silver-plated, their design richly charged with symbolism. One at Hildesheim, of copper alloy with silver crockets, has a wall with twelve doors symbolizing the twelve Apostles, and twelve towers symbolizing the tribes of Israel.

The censer was also intricately wrought in openwork to allow the incense to escape. In the twelfth century it, too, might be surmounted by towers symbolizing the heavenly Jerusalem, following a tendency towards architectural design which was to be accentuated in Gothic art. The incense for it was contained in a vessel called an incense boat (from its traditional shape). It might be made either of precious metal or of hardstone mounted in precious metal, like a sardonyx incense boat mounted in gold which once belonged to St Denis and is now in the Cabinet des Médailles of the Bibliothèque Nationale in Paris.

RELIQUARY *(left) of St Andrew's foot, gold, enamelled and set with gems, glass and pearls. Trier (Egbert-Werkstatt), 977–93. Height: 31 cm (12¼ in) (Cathedral Treasury, Trier)*

SHRINE OF THE THREE KINGS, *gold, silver-gilt, bronze gilt, gems, pearls and enamel. Cologne, late twelfth century. This Romanesque shrine is fashioned after a church rather than a coffin, a style fully realized by the Gothic goldsmiths of the following century. Height: 153 cm (60 in) Width: 110 cm (43¼ in) Length: 220 cm (86⅝ in) (Cathedral Treasury, Cologne)*

· GOSPEL-BOOKS ·

Together with crosses and chalices, it was the gospel-books and books of Epistles used for the altar which received in these centuries the greatest lavishness and elaboration of ornament. *Textus* in gold and silver cases or covers existed as early as the sixth century. The book itself was not necessarily of the same date as the covers. It seems to have been with exceptional munificence that Heilica (d.1170), wife of Otto von Wittelsbach, had a gospel-book written for the abbey of Ensdorf 'adorned within and without with gold and gems', and added a chalice worked on the model of the gospel-book 'so that the sacraments taught by the book should be figured on the vessel'. The richest of all had both front and back covers in gold and silver: the less magnificent ones had only a front cover in precious metal.

In general, the front covers had a central panel recessed within a broad frame. This was often set with a panel of carved ivory – a number of Carolingian and later ivories of this kind which have been detached from their settings of precious metal still survive. One of the most beautiful to survive complete is the *Évangéliaire de Metz*, dating from c.950–75, and probably made in Metz (Paris Bibliothèque). It has an ivory plaque of the Crucifixion inset in a triple border of gold, set with gems along the outer and inner border and with plaques of *cloisonné* enamel and inscriptions along the central border.

Alternatively the central plaque might be a panel of precious metal embossed with a figure in relief. A favourite motif was Christ in Majesty, as on an eleventh-century silver-gilt cover from Enger, now in the Berlin Kunstgewerbemuseum. The late tenth-century gospel-book of St Gauzelin, in the treasury of Nancy Cathedral, is decorated with a gold cross in relief. The crossing has a circular medallion raised on arcades of filigree, set with glass cabochons alternating with circular ornaments of *cloisonné* enamel and enclosing a medallion of the Virgin in *cloisonné* enamel on gold. In the spandrels of the cross are silver plaques engraved with the Evangelists, an obvious and popular motif for such gospel-books. Some of the principal preoccupations of Carolingian, Ottonian and Romanesque art in the decoration of such books were clearly the enrolment of a variety of techniques to obtain contrasts, of engraving, for instance, with embossing, and to add splendour of colour provided by inset gems and enamels. Richness was enhanced not only by the use of gold and gilding but by the intricacy of surface produced by panels of filigree, figures in relief, gemstones and the raised framework.

· RELIQUARIES, SHRINES AND STATUES ·

The chief spiritual treasures of a medieval church were its relics, and the deep reverence felt for them was expressed by the rich reliquaries and shrines in which they were enclosed. It was not until 867, however, that the Council of Rheims sanctioned their exposition on church altars. Hence some of the earliest reliquaries from pre-Carolingian times are small and purse-shaped with little ring handles for carrying; sometimes they have crude figural decoration, but more often are decorated with ornament – embossed or filigree, or in *verroterie cloisonnée* – and set with gems. At other times reliquaries were in the form of a simple box or casket. Indeed, the commonest type of small early medieval shrine was the box or casket with gabled lid, resembling a miniature coffin or sarcophagus. It is not known when the type was invented, but bone examples survive from the eighth century. The great reliquary shrines of the eleventh and twelfth centuries – indeed, of later medieval centuries – were usually enlarged versions of this design.

No early reliquaries have the transparent crystal containers that permitted the faithful to view the holy bones or blood themselves from the thirteenth century onwards. Accordingly, it became common to give reliquaries a form that indicated the precise nature of the relic they enshrined; for example, bones from the head were enshrined in head-reliquaries. The first recorded head-reliquary dates from c.879–87, when Boso of Burgundy gave one to the Cathedral of Vienne, but the oldest surviving example known is that of St Paul from the eleventh century, in the treasury of Münster Cathedral. In a fashion typical of the period the principal motifs of the costume are emphasized with bands of filigree and gems. A more faithful image of the austerely stylized canons of early medieval portraiture is given by the eleventh-century bust of St Candidus in the

HEAD RELIQUARY *(above) of Pope Alexander, silver mounted on a base of enamelled copper set with gems. Mosan, 1146. It is one of the richest of early reliquary heads.*
Height: 44.5 cm (17½ in)
(Musées Royaux d'Art et d'Histoire, Brussels)

SAINT FOY IN MAJESTY *(above right), gold and gems over a wooden core. France, ninth century, except for the head whose origin is problematical.*
Height: 85 cm (33½ in)
(Conques Abbey Museum, Conques)

treasury of St Maurice d'Agaune. Perhaps the most beautiful and the richest of early reliquary heads is that of St Alexander, a silver head of a holy pope made in 1146 for Abbot Wibald of Stavelot. Mounted on a base of enamelled copper that takes the form of a traditional reliquary casket, the head rather than a bust proper is an emblem of the relics contained within the casket (Musée du Cinquentenaire, Brussels).

This is also true of other early reliquaries, like the late tenth-century St Andrew reliquary from Trier, where a foot is mounted on a reliquary casket in the same way. Bones from the hand or arm were enclosed in arm-shaped reliquaries which sometimes show the hand in the act of blessing, a motif that must have seemed movingly expressive as the priest raised the reliquary to display it on feast days to the crowds of the faithful, eagerly seeking spiritual and physical blessings from the enshrined relics. Reliquaries were sometimes shaped to the actual form of the relic they enclosed, as in the late tenth-century reliquary of the Holy Nail, also in the treasury of Trier. Relics were also placed in small portable reliquaries known as phylacteries, which are recorded from as early as the ninth century, and which were probably in use even earlier. These might be worn by priests or monks, carried by them in procession, hung up for veneration from a bar over an altar, or taken about in the baggage train of a great ecclesiastic or layman. Thus the Emperor Henry III (ruled 1039–56) always carried with him a relic of the Holy Blood of Mantua. So valued were phylacteries as a divine assurance of protection that William the Conqueror was able to bequeath to Battle Abbey in 1087, no less than 300 of gold and silver, mostly suspended from chains of the same precious metals and all of them an inheritance from the Anglo-Saxon kings. In the twelfth and early thirteenth centuries they were usually made in a beautiful quatrefoil or polylobed shape, and towards the end of this period they might even be mounted on a foot for display on the altar. Relics were also placed in crosses, probably from early times, and from the period of the Crusades the scrapings brought by pious pilgrims from the various holy places of Palestine were frequently enshrined in crosses.

In contrast with these small reliquaries were the shrines made to hold the bodies of saints, often the size of the sarcophagi they represented. The earliest seem to date from the tenth or eleventh centuries. The inner casings were customarily of wood, to which the metal sheets and strips were fastened. The figure of Christ in Majesty would usually be at one of the narrow ends with the figure of the saint whose relics lay within at the other. Figures of saints and prophets were set in arcades on the long sides. The culmination of surviving Romanesque shrines is probably the late twelfth-century shrine of the Three Kings in Cologne Cathedral. It shows the tendency of that time to give the shrine the form of a church rather than of a coffin, a tendency fully realized by the Gothic goldsmiths of the thirteenth century.

Such shrines were among the more ambitious works whose design was usually devised by a cleric, and whose allegories were often intended, as Suger proudly says of the programme he invented for the rear panel of the high altar of St Denis, to be open only to the eyes of the lettered. When a shrine was made for the relics of St Foillon in the church of Fosse in Brabant between 1075 and 1091, the work was actually paid for by a devout and wealthy laywoman, but the programme was devised by Berengar, provost of the church, while the design was devised by the goldsmith who made 'a sculptured and precious work . . . with the saint's passion on the upper sides of the shrine, and the Four Rivers of Paradise and the Twelve Apostles with inscriptions signifying who they were'. On the front end was Christ in Majesty, trampling on the asp and basilisk (a motif also found on an eleventh-century panel of the shrine of St Hadelin at Visé, in the Meuse Valley). On the other end, angels received the saint's soul with the hand of God extended above in protection and welcome.

One of the most famous works of the early medieval period is the statue of Sainte Foy in the abbey church at Conques in central France. At once a reliquary and a statue for veneration on an altar, it consists of a sheathing of gold attached to a wooden central core, and in its original form dates from the late ninth century, except for the head whose origin is problematical. The figure was first made to house a relic from the head of the saint, a young Christian girl martyred at Agen in AD 303. At some date between 864 and 875 the body was stolen from a church there and brought to Conques, where the saint's cult immediately became popular with pilgrims. About 985, the statue wrought a miracle by restoring the sight of a certain Guibert, and in consequence was enriched by a closed crown and bands of filigree set with gems which represent the borders of the saint's robe, and by an enlarged throne. The compelling gaze of Sainte Foy gives the statue a curious barbaric power. An equally alarming vitality of gaze emanates from the enamelled eyes of the late tenth-century Virgin and Child, known as the Golden Madonna, in the treasury of Essen Cathedral. Sculptures of this kind often appeared on the medieval altar, most frequently portraying the Virgin and Child enthroned, representing the *Sedes Sapientiae*. There are records of such sculptures as early as the ninth century, and they continued to be made throughout the Middle Ages, especially in Spain and southern France. The Golden Madonna, however, is perhaps the most beautiful surviving example. Like Sainte Foy, it has a wooden core, and sheets of gold have been applied to the figures, while the seat is largely sheathed in copper-gilt. With its motif of the Virgin holding up an apple, it is a curiously touching work in the contrast of a homely and human theme with the formalized, almost primitive simplicity of the figure style and such rich motifs of decoration as the bands of filigree on the apple.

GOLDEN MADONNA, *gold and copper-gilt over a wooden core. Bavaria, late tenth century. Height: 74 cm (29⅛ in) (Cathedral Treasury, Essen)*

In Anglo-Saxon England, where sculptural tradition persisted more continuously than in the Carolingian Empire, prejudiced against sculpture by influences from the Iconoclastic movement in Constantinople, we also hear of figures of saints appearing in goldsmiths' work. In the 970s Brithnoth, first abbot of Ely, commissioned images of wood plated with gold and silver of his abbey's two saints, Etheldreda and Sexburga, to be set on either side of the high altar, while between c.981 and 1019 Leofwin, a rich layman, gave Ely in penance for killing his mother a large enthroned Virgin and Child of silver-gilt set with gems to be placed on an altar he had founded to the Virgin.

· CHAPEL PLATE ·

The great laymen of the Middle Ages, emperors, kings and nobles, kept chapel plate as well as secular plate for use in their households. Chapel plate was already of great richness and value by the ninth century when our first real records of it begin, and its owners sometimes presented pieces of it to a favourite monastery or church. For example, the Ciborium of King Arnulf of Carinthia (c.890), now in the Munich Schatzkammer, is a portable altar of gold surmounted by the arches of a ciborium (canopy) and is a miniature version of a real altar. One tradition says that it was Arnulf who presented to the abbey of St Emmeran the gospel-book or *Codex Aureus* with its famous golden cover (now in the Munich Staatsbibliothek); again it may originally have been part of his own chapel plate.

GOSPEL-BOOK OF *St Emmeran (the front cover), gold set with gems. Ninth century. Dimensions: 42 × 33 cm (16½ × 13 in) (Staatsbibliothek, Munich)*

Something of the chapel plate of a Carolingian lord is known from the will of Count Everard of Friuli in north-eastern Italy, made in 867. It consisted of a gold *tabula* or altar-frontal; a gold ciborium topped by a gold and silver cross; a gold reliquary casket; two gospel-books, one with a gold and one with a silver cover; a missal with a cover of gold and silver-gilt; a gold chalice and paten; a glass chalice mounted in gold; a walnut chalice mounted in gold; two silver chalices; two silver candlesticks; a ewer and *aquamanile* of silver; two silver censers; and a crystal casket containing relics.

It was probably his own chapel plate that King Athelstan (925–59) gave to Lindisfarne: a cross mounted with gold and ivory (possibly a larger version of the beautiful small Anglo-Saxon cross of gold and enamel with ivory crucifix figure which is now in the Victoria and Albert Museum); two *tabulae* of silver-gilt; two patens, one of Byzantine workmanship; two candlesticks of silver-gilt; and three horns of silver-gilt. To Croyland, Abbot Thorketill (d.975) gave a gold chalice, two cruets of silver-gilt 'made in the fashion of two angels', two silver basins of 'wondrous size and workmanship' – evidently secular in origin, for they were decorated with armed knights. All had been given to him when he was serving as royal chancellor by the Emperor Henry I as gifts from his own chapel. Bishops, too, might give their own private chapel plate to a favourite monastery, as did Siward, Bishop of Rochester, who in 1075 left his to Abingdon – a relic-shrine, two gospel-books with silver-gilt covers and a great chalice 'of excellent workmanship'.

Athelstan's horns and Henry's silver basins show how easily precious objects intended for secular use entered the service of the Church. The horns were probably given so that they could be filled with relics, and so converted into reliquaries. Similarly, kings and noblemen would often offer their most precious drinking vessel to serve as a vessel to hold the host, or to be remade into a chalice, or for other purposes. As early as 917, for example, Alalolphus, the lay abbot of St Bertin in Flanders, gave the abbey his gold drinking cup to make a chalice, offering his armlets at the same time to be converted into a paten. A singular instance of this custom is the head-reliquary of St Elizabeth of Thuringia, now in the State Historical Museum, Stockholm. Its lower part consists of

Emperor Frederick II's two-handled state drinking cup mounted in gold and gems, which he gave in 1236 as an offering when Elizabeth's body was translated. It was then converted into a reliquary for a fragment of her head by the addition of a crown, which the Emperor also gave to the saint, who was his kinswoman.

· MEDIEVAL CHURCH PLATE ·

So great has been the destruction of Carolingian and early medieval church plate that we can scarcely conceive of the number and splendour of the altar frontals of silver and gold, of the great crosses, the rich shrines and lesser reliquaries, the gold and silver chalices, candlesticks, cruets and censers that ornamented the great abbeys and churches of western Europe from Durham to Cassino, from Exeter to Magdeburg. The great ambo, or pulpit, of Aachen Cathedral, sheathed by command of the Emperor Henry II in plates of silver-gilt, testifies to the even more exceptional lavishness which the pious eagerness of patrons, anxious to glorify God and save their own souls, could occasionally prompt. All this magnificence must have been in sharp contrast with the comparative poverty of the seventh century; it appears to reflect a great revival of prosperity after the rise of the Carolingian Empire. Between 823 and 833 Ansegisus, abbot of Fontanelles, gave the abbey of Luxeuil in Burgundy 'a wondrously fashioned cross of gold, adorned with precious gems, on a silver-covered stave which was that on which it had been his wont to support his steps', a gold chalice with its paten also 'of marvellous fashion', three chalices of silver-gilt decorated with embossed work, and an *aquamanile* and ewer, also of 'wondrous work'. To the altar of the Virgin he gave a *tabula* of wood, covered with silver figures, and to his own abbey of Fontanelles a two-handled chalice of gold set with gems and another of silver, beautifully embossed. A frontal of silver and ten silver chalices and candlesticks were his gift to the abbey of Flavigny.

A burst of comparable magnificence manifested itself during the tenth- and eleventh-century religious revival in Anglo-Saxon England. We know that German goldsmiths' work was admired by eleventh-century English patrons, for Aldred, Archbishop of York from 1060 to 1069, gave Beverly Minster a pulpit above the door of the choir made 'with incomparable workmanship' of bronze, gold and silver. Over it curved an arch from which rose a lofty cross of the same materials, and the whole was *opus theutonicum*, or German work. Anglo-Saxon goldsmiths' work in turn was admired on the Continent: the chronicler of Monte-Cassino records the 'wondrous casket, sent by a certain English noble, in which is now placed a fragment of the Holy Shroud, most beautifully and subtly ornamented with English work in silver, gold and gems'.

AMBO, *sheathed in plates of silver-gilt, by command of Emperor Henry II (1039–56). This great pulpit testifies to the lavishness of its pious patron. Height: 146 cm (57½ in) Width: 115 cm (45½ in) (Cathedral, Aachen)*

At Abingdon, Abbot Aethelwold (c.950–75) gave the church a great corona, or circular ring of lights, of wood or metal covered with plates of silver-gilt, which bore twelve lights and was hung with innumerable bells. He adorned the high altar with a dossal of silver-gilt which showed the Twelve Apostles, and had wrought three great crosses of the same, each four feet tall. For the high altar he provided a gold chalice of immense weight, service books of gold set with gems and silver, and silver candlesticks. King Edgar (959–79) gave to Glastonbury a silver-gilt cross for the high altar and a silver-gilt shrine mounted with ivory figures, enclosing relics of St Vincent and the head of St Apollinaris. For the high altar of Ramsey Abbey Earl Ailwin (d.992) commissioned a frontal covered with large and massive plates of silver set with stones of various sorts, and his munificence

CHALICE, *silver. Oignies, near Namur, c.1228–30. Maker: Hugo d'Oignies. The new sobriety of the late Transitional and early Gothic styles appears in the restrained contrasts of this piece, with its exquisitely natural scrollwork of vine leaves and grapes. Height: 17.8 cm (7 in) (Trésor d'Oignies, Soeurs de Notre-Dame, Namur)*

was emulated at Durham between about 1051 and 1066 by Earl Tostig of Northumberland and his wife Judith. They had a cross made for the cathedral with figures of the Virgin and St John 'and clad in gold and silver', while Tostig with other nobles gave gifts of gold, silver and gems from which were made a gold cross and a gold cover for a gospel-book. By 1079 the Anglo-Saxon treasure of Ely numbered three altars with silver *tabulae* (frontals or dossals), thirteen gold and silver shrines, a gold chalice, twenty chalices largely of silver-gilt with patens and four without, three silver Eucharistic reeds, fourteen gospel-books with silver-gilt covers, three silver censers, two silver candlesticks, two reliquary caskets of silver and nine phylacteries. At Evesham, Abbot Mannius (1044–66) made a shrine for St Egwin of silver, gold and gems set with three stones 'whose splendour lit up a great part of the church at night'.

The magnificence of Ottonian and early medieval Germany was even greater. About 1017 the Emperor Henry II, perhaps the most piously lavish of all early imperial patrons of goldsmiths, gave to Merseburg Cathedral a gospel-book with a gold and ivory cover, two chalices of gold and silver, each with a paten and reed, and two silver crosses and cruets. Shortly afterwards he added three tabulae and a silver ewer, and then, with increasing munificence, an altar frontal and a reliquary casket, both of gold set with gems, and a collectorium decorated at the joint expense of himself and the church; then came offerings of three missals, one with covers of gold and ivory, one with covers of gold and ivory set with gems, while the third, most precious of all, had covers of gold, *electrum* (amber?) and gems. In addition he presented other gifts, including three crosses of silver-gilt and two of silver, two silver cruets and three chalices, one of massy silver, one of gold, and all three 'most wondrously worked with art and all sorts of gems and they are still commonly said to be the price of his soul's redemption'.

To the abbey of Berg outside Magdeburg, Bishop Siegfried (1009–20) gave a gold cross set with precious stones 'for the remedy of his soul', and a gold altar set with gems which cost fourteen talents, all of which he paid except for two-and-a-half talents that he took from the church. To St Stephen in Magdeburg Bishop Arnulf gave c.1020 a *tabula* of gold and gems for the high altar, a gold censer and a gold box for the incense, and a gold chalice and paten. In Westphalia Meinwerk, the Bishop of Paderborn (1009–36) gave the abbey of Abdinghof magnificent furnishings: a silver altar frontal, a gold chalice weighing eight marks and adorned with seventy-two gems, a chalice of cast silver adorned with the martyrdom of St Stephen, together with seven other smaller chalices, two silver processional crosses with staves, two silver candlesticks, a silver cup for the Host, five silver cruets, a silver coronal light with twelve candles signifying the Twelve Apostles to hang before the high altar and another to hang in the middle of the church, with seventy-two lights symbolizing Christ's disciples, who no doubt were also signified by the seventy-two gems on the gold chalice. Herduwick, third abbot of Komburg (1103–38) in Baden-Württemberg, had made 'two tables in which were represented the figures of Christ, of the Last Judgment and of the Twelve Apostles'. One of these he gave to the Church of St Giles in Komburg, reserving the other, which still exists and which was larger and of enamelled copper set with gems, 'for his own abbey church'. He also commissioned 'a gold cross which was a cubit high and four fingers wide, radiant with many gems, of which the chiefest was a cameo as big as a hen's egg, with the face and chest of an Aethiop: this gem was valued at 1000 florins by a certain *gemmarius*.'

While the fashion for studding plate with gems

remained so strong, patrons were careful to collect them before commissioning a work of especial magnificence. Suger describes how he collected the gems for the gold frontal of the choir altar in which St Denis lay enshrined. He lists the variety of stones he assembled with pride: jacinths, rubies, sapphires, emeralds, topazes and a great diversity of pearls. Some of these came from rings which kings and great nobles, archbishops and bishops, moved by devotion, offered to the work when they visited the church. Others came from the *gemmarii*, many of them no doubt Italian, who flocked to St Denis on hearing that Suger was collecting gems for his frontal.

· MEDIEVAL SECULAR PLATE ·

The importance of secular plate is often forgotten by medievalists, wedded since the nineteenth century to too ecclesiastical a view of their period. Documents from Carolingian times, however, make it plain that secular plate was often sumptuous. Between 823 and 833 Ansegisus, abbot of Fontanelles, gave the abbey of Luxeuil 'a silver *hanap*, excellently made, resting on four gold feet shaped as snails' and to Fontanelles itself two cups of glass mounted in gold. In 867 Count Everard of Friuli died possessed of a gold drinking bowl, a drinking vessel of hardstone mounted in gold and silver, two drinking bowls of horn mounted in silver and gold, and another of silver, four silver *scutellae* (shallow bowls for eating), five silver *garales* (cups or goblets) and seven silver spoons, two of them matching. We have here already the principal table vessels of the Middle Ages. Vessels of hardstone, often antique themselves, were mounted on a foot to make stately drinking vessels.

The most remarkable surviving piece of early secular plate is the so-called ewer of Charlemagne in the treasury of St Maurice d'Agaune. A flat, flask-shaped vessel of gold set with sapphires with a curved handle and shallow spout, its sides, neck, and edges are set with panels of the finest *cloisonné* enamel. The designs of the enamelled discs on the sides, one showing two griffins, the other two lions affronted, are of oriental inspiration, but the rest of the vessel is certainly western in execution, and probably Carolingian.

By the thirteenth century the types of secular plate used in western Europe seem to have become established. Plate was principally for the toilet and table. The great washed in deep silver basins, and before meals rinsed their hands in water poured over them from a silver basin or ewer and caught in a second silver basin. They also shaved in silver basins. They were lit by silver candlesticks, and at table they drank from cups, beakers, goblets and drinking bowls of silver, and ate from low silver bowls (*écuelles*) or trenchers. Food was served from silver platters, and to test it for poison, 'serpents' tongues' were hung either on the salt or from the tree-shaped vessels known as *languiers* in French and as *Natterbaum* in German. Drink, too, might be assayed from a little goblet or bowl into which the chamberlain poured some of his master's wine or water before allowing him to taste it. Liquid to be served in the dining-hall was held in silver flasks, bottles and vessels of jug or pitcher form. A principal ornament of noble tables was the salt, the state salt being treated with great richness of design and materials. Sweetmeats were served from low bowls on feet, known as *drageoirs* in French, as spice plates in English. Small forks

EWER OF CHARLEMAGNE, *gold set with sapphires and cloisonné enamel. Carolingian, ninth century. The fine enamel panels are of oriental inspiration. Height: 30.3 cm (12 in) (Treasury of St Maurice d'Agaune, St Maurice, Switzerland)*

SHRINE OF ST ELEUTHÈRE *(right), silver, gilded copper and enamel. France, 1247. But for the trilobed Gothic arches enclosing the niches, it is essentially Romanesque. Height: 87 cm (34¼ in) (Cathedral Treasury, Tournai)*

RELIQUARY *(below) of the Seamless Robe, silver. France, late thirteenth century. It was probably sent to St Francis of Assisi by Queen Jeanne of France in 1285. In the central niche Christ raises his stigmatized hands; in the other two St Clare and St Francis invite the kneeling nuns below to adoration. Height: 28.5 cm (11¼ in) (Treasury of San Francesco, Assisi)*

were sometimes used for taking such sweetmeats, but the principal medieval aids to eating were the fingers, spoon and knife. In great houses the service of meals was a solemn ceremony, and one for displaying family wealth. The containers of drink and the platters of food were set on special dressers, and hence the custom of making rich plate solely for display on dressers as a sign of rank.

Early medieval secular plate clearly continued past traditions of sumptuousness. In 1023 King Robert of France and the Emperor Henry II exchanged presents of gold nefs, boat-shaped vessels for holding spoons, napkins and other personal articles; throughout the Middle Ages, nefs seem to have been reserved for princely personages and great nobles. William the Conqueror, holding court at Fécamp in Normandy in 1067, amazed the French nobles with 'his gold and silver vessels, of whose number and beauty things incredible could be related. The immense company drank only from such vessels, or from oxhorns adorned with the same metal at either end.' Godefroy de Huy, one of the greatest of twelfth-century goldsmiths, spent much of his working life moving from court to court fashioning plate for kings. It was the custom, too, for presents of plate to be given for political reasons, as for example, in 1153, when the citizens of Milan offered the Emperor Frederick Barbarossa a gold cup filled with gold coins. The plate owned by Count Sigboto III of Hadmarsperch shows what a twelfth-century Imperial nobleman might possess: in all he

ÉVANGÉLAIRE, *(left), silver. Oignies, near Namur, c.1228–30. Maker: Hugo d'Oignies. Height: 32.5 cm (12¾ in) (Trésor d'Oignies, Soeurs de Notre-Dame, Namur)*

PORTABLE SHRINE *(right), enamelled silver-gilt set with gems and pearls. Paris, 1320–40. Franco-Flemish, bequeathed in 1491 by Thomas Bazin to the Church of St-Jean d'Utrecht. Height: 25.4 cm (10 in), including cross. (Pierpont Morgan Library, New York)*

SHRINE OF ST TAURIN *(below), silver. France, c.1240–55. Height: 76.2 cm (30 in) (St-Taurin, Evreux)*

had twenty-eight silver vessels distributed between two castles. There were five silver cups with lids and four without, six drinking bowls, ten pitchers (six with lids), three silver *scutellae* (eating bowls) and four silver spoons. Abbots, too, had silver vessels for eating: in 1167 Heinrich, Abbot of Laurensheim, created feeling among his monks by bequeathing a silver drinking bowl to his uncle Otto and two silver *scutellae* to two knights of his household. Apart from the noble classes, only merchants of the thriving towns of the twelfth century had vessels of silver, or sometimes even of gold.

The few surviving silver drinking vessels of the tenth to twelfth centuries are almost all from Scandinavian hoards. A small mid-eleventh-century bowl from Lilla Valla, in Gotland, must be Scandinavian, if only from the interlaced dragons engraved round its rim, but the gadroons, or boss-like ornaments, into which its bowl is fluted went back to classical antiquity and were a generally used medieval motif. Sometimes such bowls were mounted on trumpet-shaped feet, though the plain bowl without foot was more common. Simple and unpretending, these vessels do not really give us an image of those more elaborate Romanesque drinking vessels whose workmanship was often just as rich and refined as that of religious plate. Fortunately a few such vessels, or fragments of them, survive from the later twelfth century, notably three cups on feet and a beautiful large silver drinking bowl, exquisitely patterned with gilt ornament, from the Gotland treasure of Dune,

RELIQUARY *(right) of the veil of St Aldegonde, silver-gilt and enamel. Valenciennes, 1469. It was made for the abbey of Maubeuge. Height: 52.5 cm (20½ in) (Church of Maubeuge, France)*

and a bowl from a cup now in the Cloisters Museum, New York. All the cups have or had broad, swelling bowls and short trumpet feet; they are richly ornamented with bold designs in strongly defined frameworks, executed in relief and enhanced by engraving, gilding and niello. In one of these cups the heads of the decorative figures have been executed in relief, a device also found in Limoges enamel and so presumably fairly widespread in the late twelfth and early thirteenth centuries. Such vessels are still true to the spirit of Romanesque art in a certain heavy stateliness, with none of the upward thrust that the Gothic style was later to communicate to goldsmiths' work.

· THE GOLDSMITHS AND THEIR CRAFT ·

In the early medieval period it is difficult in some cases to tell who were the patrons and who the actual goldsmiths. This is the case, for example, with Bishop Bernward of Hildesheim (993–1022), who filled the churches of Hildesheim with fine metalwork. Professional goldsmiths were attached to the households of kings, great lords and ecclesiastics, and also worked in towns. Those of greatest skill were often internationally famous and in great demand. Thus Anketill, the early twelfth-century English goldsmith, was sent to Denmark at the urgent request of the Danish king, and spent seven years there in charge of the king's goldsmiths' work as head of his mint and chief money-changer.

A leading goldsmiths' centre for much of the twelfth century was the region known as Lotharingia, comprising modern Lorraine, Liège, Cologne and the surrounding Rhineland. In 1147 Suger summoned seven Lotharingian goldsmiths to St Denis to make his great cross and other works. The great goldsmiths of the bishopric of Liège, Renier de Huy and Godefroy de Huy, survive only by reputation or in works in base metal, and almost all the smaller surviving works from the entire region are in enamelled copper. This is not true of course of the great silver-gilt shrines, like that of St Heribert at Deutz or the Three Kings in Cologne, the latter of which has been attributed to the greatest of late twelfth-century goldsmiths, Nicolas of Verdun (in northern Lorraine), whose certain works are an enamelled copper ambo completed in 1181 for the abbey of Klosterneuburg, near Vienna, and the rich silver-gilt shrine of Notre Dame, completed in 1205 for Tournai Cathedral.

In a sense the work of Nicolas of Verdun marked the end of an era. From Merovingian times the aesthetic of goldsmiths' work at its richest had been a polyphony of masive chords of decoration: glowing colour from bright enamel and shining stones, broad bands of filigree with their rich scrollwork and play of depth and shade, applied to the solemn ordonnance of altar frontal or book-cover, or to vessels in which stateliness and massiveness of effect were the leading principles of design. Figure-style, so far as is known, was austere and stylized with an emphasis on linear rhythms and simplified volumes, for all its power to represent with dramatic liveliness and force, as well as with hieratic majesty. The figures of Nicolas of Verdun are in the style now known as Transitional, whose keys are naturalism and a new classicism. Figures are softened and humanized, moving with ease and grace, in a fashion that heralds thirteenth-century Gothic art.

A new style of ornament also appears, in which the stately classical motifs and stiff *rinceaux* of the Romanesque are replaced by an exquisitely natural scrollwork of vine leaves and grapes. The place of origin of this ornamental style is unknown, but its most famous exponent is Hugo d'Oignies, who retired in the 1220s to the small monastery of Oignies, near Namur, where he executed the cover of a gospel-book, a chalice and a reliquary of the rib of St Peter, all in silver. The new sobriety of the late Transitional and early Gothic styles appears in the restrained contrasts of these three works. The rich colour of enamel is eschewed in favour of niello, and gilt and ungilt surfaces are set in refined contrast. There is a loss of power and a gain in elegance. The same style was practised in northern France, Flanders, Brabant and Hainault into the middle of the thirteenth century.

The increased popularity of niello is a feature of thirteenth-century work. The age was one of great artistic sophistication, and the succinct elegance of niello and its sharpness of outline on plain surfaces of silver and gold seem to have been particularly appreciated throughout all western Europe. Its popularity sems to have declined in the fourteenth century except in Italy, though it is

EWER *(facing page), silver-gilt and enamel. Paris, 1333. It shows that the principles of Gothic design were applied to secular as well as ecclesiastical plate. Height: 22.5 cm (8¾ in) (Nationalmuseet, Copenhagen)*

found on some of the finest pieces of the later fourteenth century, the crosses and reliquaries made in Prague for the Emperor Charles IV of Luxembourg. On these, however, niello is used pictorially, announcing Italian niellos of the fifteenth century, rather than in the more purely linear manner of earlier times. *Cloisonné* enamel, too, came into fashion in thirteenth-century France, perhaps influenced by fresh contacts with Byzantium in the course of the Crusades. *Champlevé* enamel, by contrast became restricted to light ornamental motifs and heraldry.

· THE GOTHIC PERIOD ·

It was in the early decades of the thirteenth century that the Gothic style was gradually introduced into goldsmiths' work, both religious and secular. Thus on Nicolas of Verdun's shrine of Notre Dame, completed in 1205, the three arches of the long sides are cusped and pointed. Pointed arches also appear on the shrine of the Virgin in the treasury of Aachen Cathedral, executed between 1215 and 1247, while the shrine itself has projecting transept gables, suggesting a church rather than a sarcophagus. Again on the shrine of St Eleuthère in the treasury of Tournai Cathedral, completed in 1247, and essentially a shrine of traditional Romanesque design, trilobed Gothic arches enclose the niches.

At first, then, Gothic alters only single architectural motifs. All the more outstanding then is the change that appears in the shrine of St Taurin at Evreux in Normandy. Executed c.1240–55, it resembles not a gabled sarcophagus but a church. The ends are sharp-pointed gables, flanked by towers composed of pinnacles surmounting openwork niches. From the sides project similar gabled transepts, and the vertical thrust of the whole design, so characteristic of Gothic, culminates in the openwork central tower. Pointed arches replace the rounded niches of the earlier style, and a new effect of recession in depth is sought by setting tricusped arches within their openings. All in all there is a much more dramatic movement of surface, with contrast and richness of effect sought by the use of the same devices in miniature as in full-scale Gothic architecture. Within their niches the figures have not only the slender lightness of High Gothic sculpture but also something of its freedom of movement.

We do not know the origins or early evolution of this new style, but the shrine of St Taurin is already so thoroughly Gothic that it must have been preceded by other works. Most probably the style was invented in the Paris of St Louis, perhaps in the milieu of the Sainte Chapelle. It spread not only into Normandy, where it is found in the late thirteenth-century Chasse de St Romain at Rouen, but had reached Flanders and Hainault by 1272, when the goldsmiths Colars de Douai and Jacquemon de Nivelles contracted to make a

shrine for the relics of St Gertrude for the abbey of Nivelles after a design provided by Jacques d'Anchin, a Benedictine monk. Although clerics often gave the iconographic programme for such important works, we now know that Jacques also possessed qualifications as a designer, for in secular life he had been a goldsmith, plainly of standing. Completed by 1298, this magnificent shrine was destroyed by bombs in 1940, but it is nonetheless known to have carried the imitation of Gothic architecture in miniature still further. Thus the ends were transformed into church façades of two storeys, the upper one pierced with a rose-window, while the arch of the doorway was decorated with canopied voussoirs (wedge-shaped stones) containing statues.

The Gothic style also modified the design of smaller types of church plate. For reliquaries a particularly beautiful design was evolved, probably in Paris, in which two angels standing on a base hold a horizontal transparent crystal container. An early fourteenth-century Parisian example is in the treasury of San Domenico, Bologna; the symbolism of the design, with its angelic bearers of holy relics, as well as its elegance, made it popular until the end of the Middle Ages, as can be seen in the beautiful reliquary of the veil of St Aldegonde, in silver-gilt and enamel, made at Valenciennes in 1469 for the abbey of Maubeuge. The tabernacles and triptych – reliquaries set on altars for public or private worship – seem to have been among the first objects to receive a Gothic form. The great silver-gilt *Polyptyque* of the abbey of Floreffe, in Hainault, executed in 1254, is a composition of large and small canopied panels, the central one containing a relic of the True Cross supported by two angels, while the side-panels are set with statues representing scenes of the Passion. The casket-reliquary was also 'Gothicized', often by giving it a superficial structure of buttresses and canopies, and architectural compositions were devised for objects that the Romanesque goldsmith would have treated conventionally. Thus in the reliquary of the Seamless Robe in the treasury of San Francesco, Assisi, which seems to have been sent there by Queen Jeanne of France c.1285, the front is formed as three canopied niches, with the side ones angled to the centre one. In this, Christ raises his stigmatized hands, while in the other two niches St Clare and St Francis invite the kneeling nuns below to adoration.

The form of the cross was also affected by the Gothic style. The squared ends of Romanesque crosses had already been replaced by lobed ends, then by ends formed of cusped and pointed lobes, as in the beautiful processional cross of about 1200 from Clairmarais in Picardy (Museum of St Omer). These rapidly evolved into a truly Gothic, elegant trefoil cusping, as in the refined processional cross from Nailly, now in Sens Cathedral, which must reflect Parisian court style.

From the mid-thirteenth century the principles of Gothic design were applied with ever greater thoroughness to both secular and religious plate. The bowl of the chalice was made deep and tapering, while tall polygonal stems, often known in France as 'pilliers', replaced short round ones. Circular feet were broken into pointed or rounded lobes, or into polygonal forms with incurving sides. Censers become miniature architectural compositions, sometimes reflecting recent changes in Gothic architectural style, like the beautiful mid-fourteenth-century English censer from Ramsey Abbey, whose companion incense boat has sharply pointed ends and a foot with incurved sides (both London, Victoria and Albert Museum). These tendencies were carried just as far in secular plate. Thus the early fourteenth-century King's Lynn Cup, probably English, has rich Gothic leaf-cresting round the lid, a polygonal bowl, and a foot which is an elaborate variation on a sexfoil, the trefoil-shaped lobes being linked by

MERODE CUP, *silver-gilt and enamel. Burgundy, c.1400. The enamels are set in bands round the cup and cover. The arched panels, tracery and crocket embellishments are characteristic of the Gothic architectural style.*
Height: 17.5 cm (6⅞ in)
(Victoria and Albert Museum, London)

inverted trefoil cusps. Even in ewers, which might seem to need no fundamental redesigning, polygonal bodies were often substituted for round, as in the beautiful Paris ewer of about 1330, now in the National Museum, Copenhagen.

Gothic forms and ornament prevailed in Germany by the 1270s, having spread there from France. They had also reached Italy by the late thirteenth century, when we find the first dated example of a new decorative technique, translucent enamel. This is on a Gothic chalice made c.1290 for Pope Nicholas IV by a goldsmith of Siena, Guccio di Mannaia, for presentation to the San Francesco in Assisi. In this type of enamelling a ground was sunk by chasing and engraving the silver or gold and then coated with translucent enamels, the differing degrees of depression of the ground producing a delicate play of light and shade. It is not yet fully developed on Guccio's chalice, suggesting that it had only recently been invented. There has been much dispute as to its place of origin, but the technique is essentially pictorial, and as the fourteenth century was a great age both of painting and of goldsmiths' work in Siena, the city has some claim to its invention.

The most beautiful surviving work of the Sienese goldsmiths is the Reliquary of the Corporal of Bolsena, executed in 1337–8 for the Bishop and Chapter of Orvieto by Ugolino di Vieri, in partnership with other goldsmiths. It is in the form of a soaring tabernacle of three pointed canopies flanked by pinnacles and topped by a cross and resting on a broad base with everted sides. The whole might be best described as a reliquary in the form of an altar-retable. The inspiration of Gothic architectural forms is perhaps most striking in the introduction of such motifs as gargoyles and buttresses, functional in real architecture, as ornaments. Sculptural eloquence is added by the small figures of angels, of Joseph of Arimathea and Nicodemus, of the Virgin and St John on the pinnacles and cross, and by the figures of Prophets and Evangelists set on the feet of the base. The refined glow of the gilded framework throws up the intense, celestial blue which is the dominant colour of the translucent enamel panels it encloses. These relate the principal scenes of Christ's birth, childhood and Passion and of the miracle of the Corporal in compositions of great narrative accomplishment and ambitious perspective effects.

Translucent enamel spread with remarkable swiftness throughout western Europe and remained the most popular form of enamelling on precious metal until the end of the Middle Ages, allowing the goldsmith to emulate the miniaturist in treating subjects pictorially. The mastery of the scenes on the Corporal of Bolsena indicates that the finest medieval goldsmiths were finished artists in their own right, uniting the talents of the architectural designer, miniaturist and sculptor. The best works of the Gothic goldsmith have an assured elegance of taste and perfection of workmanship, together with the ethereal lightness and radiance of colour found in the architecture and stained glass of the great Gothic cathedrals.

There were of course many goldsmiths occupied at a humbler level, making simple drinking vessels, humble chalices and jewellery, and their work could be crude in form and decoration. In larger towns goldsmiths began to organize themselves in guilds to protect their corporate interests, among which was the assurance of satisfactory standards by the system of apprenticeship and self-supervision. Guilds also provided a means whereby royal, feudal and civic authority could regulate the craft. By the thirteenth century guilds existed in many of the flourishing communes of Italy, including Siena, Perugia, Bologna and Venice; they also appear in Montpellier, Tours and Paris. In London the Goldsmith's Company was in unofficial existence by 1180.

CHALICE *Pope Nicholas IV, silver and translucent enamel. Siena, c.1290. Maker: Guccio di Mannaia. This Gothic piece, made for presentation to the Church of San Francesco, Assisi, is the first dated example of the technique of coating chased and engraved metal with translucent enamels. Height: 22.4 cm (8¾ in) (Treasury of San Francesco, Assisi)*

One of the special difficulties in regulating the craft is the high intrinsic value of the precious metals. All early goldsmiths' statutes enacted measures to protect the customer from fraud, especially in the form of vessels wrought in silver below the prescribed standard. The stamping of silver vessels had been practised in Byzantium as late as the seventh century, but as no later Byzantine secular plate is known, it is not clear whether the practice was continued. When it appears in the West it is in thirteenth-century France, where the practice of striking a town-mark appears to have been an established custom in Tours by 1275. A royal ordinance of that year ordered all towns with silversmiths to institute a town-mark; maker's marks are recorded, also in France, from the early years of the fourteenth century, and it was in Montpellier, in 1427, that the year-letter mark was instituted. The French system was imitated in England, but medieval use of marks was sporadic, and much church plate and many special commissions (as opposed to goods for general sale) escaped marking altogether.

Exaggerated significance has been attached to the plate produced in fourteenth-century Avignon, while the city was the residence of the Popes. Goldsmiths were attracted to the city and its wealthy ecclesiastical patrons from Siena and other Italian cities, France and Germany, but they worked there in their own styles. In northern Europe the two great centres of the art were Paris and Cologne, but whereas the goldsmiths of Cologne were purely German, the royal court of Paris attracted not only French goldsmiths, but goldsmiths from the Netherlands and Cologne as well. There was a long-established international trade in goldsmiths' work: as early as 1127 Lombard merchants were selling plate at the great fair

RELIQUARY *(facing page) of the Corporal of Bolsena, silver, enamel and precious stones. Siena, 1337–8. Executed for the Bishop and Chapter of Orvieto by Ugolino di Vieri and others. The panels relate to the principal scenes of Christ's birth, childhood and Passion and of the miracle of the Corporal. Height: 1.39 m (55 in) Museo dell' Opera del Duomo, Orvieto)*

ROYAL GOLD CUP *(below), gold, gems and pearls and enamel. France, c.1390. Made for Jean, Duke of Berry. Purely for display, it is enamelled with the history of St Agnes. Height: 23.5 cm (9¼ in) (British Museum, London)*

RETABLE AND FRONTAL *of the altar of St James the Apostle, silver. Pistoia, late thirteenth century. These were successively refashioned or reshaped and enlarged until 1456, when the whole was finally finished. (Cathedral, Pistoia)*

of Ypres, and Italian merchants were still tempting princes with choice pieces in the fourteenth and fifteenth centuries. This circulation of objects as well as of goldsmiths no doubt assisted the international diffusion of styles, most of which of course promptly acquired strong local idiosyncracies.

Only one new type of church plate was introduced in the late thirteenth and fourteenth centuries. This was the monstrance, a vessel intended for the permanent exposition of the Host. Its introduction sprang from the fervent cult of the Host which spread from the diocese of Liège in the first half of the thirteenth century and led to the formal institution of the feast of Corpus Christi in 1264. The earliest dated monstrance was made in Paris in 1286 for the Flemish monastery of Herkenrode. Only in the fourteenth century did the monstrance acquire its characteristic form of an upright transparent cylinder containing a holder for the Host, adorned with buttresses and pinnacle work, the whole resting on a stem and foot.

Small reliquary statues of the Virgin and saints became increasingly popular in the late thirteenth and fourteenth centuries. Some might be given to churches, like the beautiful figure of the Virgin and Child on an enamelled casket-shaped base presented in 1339 by Queen Jeanne of France to St Denis (now in the Louvre), together with a pendant-statue, now lost, of St John the Baptist. Others were made in large numbers for the private chapels of patrons and as votive offerings: in 1466 the Czech Tetzel saw in the church of St Catherine de Fierbois, a pilgrimage church in Touraine, 'silver figures weighty as themselves' dedicated by kings, dukes and noblemen.

There was one great change in patronage in the fourteenth and fifteenth centuries. The shift in wealth and economic power to the bankers and merchants of Italy and Catalonia meant that new silver altars were no longer made in northern Europe, but in cities like Gerona, north of Barcelona, and in the oligarchic Italian republics of Tuscany and Venice. In Italy they were an expression of civic patronage rather than of the wealth and devotion of a single great lord or churchman. Venetian civic pride was concentrated on the completion of the Pala d'Oro, the great retable of the high altar of San Marco. Begun in 976–8, when Doge Pietro Orseolo ordered a retable of silver and gold from Constantinople for the then newly built church, it was renewed in the early twelfth century, and refashioned once more in 1209. From a purely Byzantine work it was altered again in 1345 by setting the panels of *cloisonné* enamel of the earlier retable into a Gothic framework. The civic urge to glorify a patron saint found expression in the wealthy Pistoia of the late thirteenth century in a silver retable and frontal for the altar of St James the Apostle in the cathedral, which enshrined a relic obtained from Compostella in 1145. These were successively refashioned or

reshaped and enlarged until 1456, when the whole was finally finished. Similarly, Florence in emulation made from 1366 to 1452 a silver dossal of St John the Baptist, the city's patron, on which many artists, including Michelozzo, worked at intervals until its completion.

By contrast, seigneurial patronage was all-important in late fourteenth-century France, where the splendour of the court of Charles V was fostered by his prudent government and where the ambitions of his brothers, Louis, Duke of Orléans, and Jean, Duke of Berry, were sustained by ample feudal lands. All three brothers accumulated vast collections of chapel and secular plate – some 2500 pieces in the case of Charles, some 4000 in the case of Louis – not only as an expression of their wealth and power and as a reserve of treasure, but because of their real affection for the art. Charles used to relax in the late afternoons from the cares of state by examining with friends '*joyaux* and other rich works', while Louis either compiled, or supervised the compilation of, a great descriptive inventory of his plate. The great numbers of pieces owned by these royal patrons do not mean a great increase in the types of plate that were made: they simply possessed exceptional numbers and exceptionally elaborate examples of every type. Thus they owned large quantities of gold plate, whereas usually one or two vessels of gold were all that even very great lords and ladies possessed. And many of the pieces made for them offered great fancifulness of design and elaboration of motif. Fortunately, one secular object of gold made c.1390 for Jean, Duke of Berry, still survives, the Royal Gold Cup now in the British Museum. Like most gold plate, it was made purely for display, and was orna-

THE BELÉM MONSTRANCE *(facing page), gold and enamel. Lisbon, 1506. Attributed to Gil Vicente. Height: 83 cm (32⅔ in) (Museu Nacional De Arte Antiga, Lisbon)*

PRUNKPOKAL *(far left), silver and silver-gilt, richly enamelled. Burgundian (?), c.1440–50. Height: 28.5 cm (11¼ in) (Kunsthistorisches Museum, Vienna)*

LACOCK ABBEY CUP *(left), silver. Fifteenth century. Height: 35 cm (13¾ in) (On loan to the British Museum, London)*

BEAKER *(above), gold, gems, pearls and enamel mounted with crystal. Burgundian, c.1453–67. This great beaker shows a sumptuous naturalism of fancy that enriches the clear outlines of the Gothic design. Height: 46 cm (18⅛ in) (Schatzkammer, Vienna)*

GOLDENES RÖSSEL *(right), gold and enamel. Made in Paris for Charles VI, c.1404. This Gothic reliquary depicting the Adoration of the Virgin is the most famous surviving example of the technique of* émail en ronde bosse *for colouring features on gold. Height: 58.4 cm (23 in) (Treasury, Altötting)*

mented with sapphires and balas-rubies on the knob and pearls on the cresting, some of which remain. It is enamelled 'well and richly' with the history of St Agnes, largely in translucent enamel, with one or two details in opaque enamel.

Hardstones continued to make prized elements in plate, especially in salts. Crystal retained its old popularity and vessels were also made of jasper, chalcedony, alabaster and beryl. There was also a custom, dating back to early medieval times, of mounting exotic shells, eggs and nuts in gold or silver-gilt which continued well into the seventeenth century. Nautilus shells, ostrich eggs and coconuts were all favourite choices for mounting: essentially, of course, such pieces were for display, not use.

The trend of the later fourteenth century was away from the stylized forms of earlier Gothic art towards greater naturalism, not only in ornament and the representation of detail, but in the portrayal of man and beast. Many of the works described in the royal French inventories must have resembled tableaux in their effect, though no doubt their style was that of the gay and poetical International Gothic rather than the more harshly realistic style of the fifteenth century. To suit this taste for naturalism, new techniques emerged. It was already the custom to pigment portions of figures in certain more elaborate pieces, and during the last decades of the century the technique of *émail en ronde bosse* (in which the enamel was applied like ceramic glaze to contoured surfaces) was invented in France for colouring features on gold plate naturalistically. As it was used only on gold, it was confined to plate made for royal patrons, though its use on a small scale in jewellery was more widespread. The most famous surviving example of the technique is the *Goldenes Rössel* of Altötting, made in Paris c.1404. It is also the only example of the large-scale tableaux known as *joyaux* made for French royal patrons, here as a devotional work. The tradition of such tableaux continued into the early sixteenth century, as can be seen on the reliquary of St Ursula in the treasury of Rheims Cathedral.

The magnificence of French goldsmiths' work foundered under the renewed English assault of the early fifteenth century. But one last technique, which led enamelling to become wholly pictorial in its conception, was evolved in France. This was painted enamel, in which motifs and scenes are painted in enamel with brush and spatula on an enamel ground. The foot of the reliquary of the Holy Thorn in Rheims Cathedral is the only surviving early French example, but the technique flourished under the Dukes of Burgundy in the Netherlands. Here the technique of painting in white *en camaïeu* (monochrome) on a blue background seems to have been evolved. By the 1460s it had reached considerable sophistication, and we still have a number of beakers and spoons decorated in it with playful motifs of wild men and animals from the medieval repertory of the wildwood, the bestiary, and Reynard the Fox. Later this courtly Netherlandish technique was coarsely imitated in Venice. The southern Netherlands and the Rhineland retained their old importance in the fifteenth century. The great Burgundian beaker of the Imperial treasury in Vienna shows crystal mounted with a sumptuous naturalism of fancy that enriches the clear outlines of Gothic design. So, too, the famous gold votive figure given by Charles the Bold in 1471 to the Cathedral of Liège shows the degree to which naturalism was now influencing goldsmiths' work, both in its portraiture and in its gay but realistic enamelling. Made between 1468 and 1471 by the court goldsmith Gérard Loyet, it borrows its principal motif of St George presenting the Duke from a painting by Van Eyck.

A new phenomenon at this time was the rise to European importance of the goldsmiths of southern Germany, and especially of Nuremberg. Their work combines the rough, broad, rather dry naturalism of late Gothic ornament with the extreme precision of line and complexity of German architectural design, quickened by liveliness and caprice of motif. The most majestic of their secular vessels was the cup, in single or monumental double form, the latter a peculiarly German type in which the lid of a cup is itself a cup. A feature of German plate was the setting of little sculptures on the lids of stately drinking vessels as the climax of the design, a tradition which was to spread to the goldsmiths of the Renaissance elsewhere in Europe. German engraving was also of singularly high quality and expressiveness: interestingly, the father of Albrecht Dürer was a Nuremberg goldsmith.

German influence was felt in both Venice and Spain, where the greatest dynasty of sixteenth-century goldsmiths, that of the Arfes, was founded by Enrique (Heinrich), originally from Harff, near Cologne. The Spanish Gothic style flourished first in the kingdom of Aragon, which included the wealthy regions of Catalonia and Valencia. At the height of Aragonese power in the fourteenth and fifteenth centuries, Gerona, Barcelona and Valencia were particularly important centres for goldsmiths, and a style influenced by France, Italy and Germany, but peculiarly Spanish in its florid vigour and much use of rich embossed work, evolved. The cult of the Host found a significant expression in Spain in the custodia, in which the slender, spiring fantasies of the Gothic goldsmith reach their most monumental form.

So strong was the hold of Gothic on patrons and craftsmen alike that even in Renaissance Florence it was not abandoned till the 1470s. In Venice it persisted till the end of the century, while in France, England, Spain and Germany it retained a hold into the 1520s. In the Low Countries Gothic was not abandoned in church plate till the end of the sixteenth century, while in Anglican England Gothic experienced its first revival under High Church patronage in the seventeenth century.

SALT AND COVER, *known as the 'Giant' Salt, silver, parcel-gilt and pigmented, fifteenth century. It has no marks.*
Height: 45 cm (17⅝ in)
(All Souls College, Oxford)

· 3 · THE RENAISSANCE AND MANNERISM··

The Renaissance and Mannerist styles prevailed during much of the fifteenth and sixteenth centuries in Italy and almost the whole of the sixteenth century in northern Europe. This was an important period in the history of silver, and one in which designs tended to be closely linked to mainstream artistic and architectural developments. The now commonplace distinction between 'fine' and 'decorative' arts had no place in the Renaissance mind, and patrons chose to express their taste and wealth as much through their plate as through their pictures and buildings. Goldsmiths enjoyed a prestige greater than at any time since, and many of the most famous artists of the day, such as Brunelleschi, Dürer and Cellini, were trained initially in the craft. But while such an environment gave the period a sense of continuity, its two styles were based on different principles and had a completely different character. During the Renaissance, design was guided by a logical approach similar to that which conditioned architecture; decoration tended to emphasize form and would have been judged by such criteria as proportion and clarity. Mannerism, on the other hand, favoured elaborate and exaggerated forms, recondite allusions and symbolism in ornament and a constant spirit of experimentation. The driving forces behind it were virtuosity, complexity and cleverness, and these were reflected in the range of techniques that were used, resulting in turn in a diversity of objects that is unmatched by subsequent periods.

As with earlier periods, only a tiny proportion of the silver made in the sixteenth century actually survives. Objects were seldom regarded as valuable merely on account of their age, and it was still usual to melt down plate that was out of fashion or when funds were needed. While this is true of later periods too, the destruction of plate from the sixteenth century (and earlier) has been so complete that it is impossible to form a clear view of its overall character and range from surviving pieces. This is particularly true of ordinary domestic plate – the type that would have been most common at the time – and the quantities that survive are minute compared with ornamental pieces. For the former there would have been no incentives to counter the pressures of fashion, wear and financial necessity that ensured its periodic replacement, while ornamental and commemorative pieces would have been more likely to be preserved on grounds of artistic merit or for sentimental reasons. The survival of much of the earliest plate of Oxford and Cambridge colleges, for example, is on account of its association with their founders.

Other than actual plate, there are three main sources of information on sixteenth-century silver, all of which need in various ways to be treated with caution. Inventories of the period provide important and often tantalizing information about the distribution and quantities of plate in use, but they are almost invariably descriptive rather than illustrative, and so from an art-historical point of view at best imprecise. Drawings and printed pattern books survive in large numbers, and are generally more reliable than other sources. However, it cannot be inferred from their existence that they were necessarily executed, since many of them represent projects that might have been submitted to a patron for approval, but such drawings do at least give incontrovertible evidence of the artistic climate of the time. Likewise, paintings can help fill the gaps left by the lack of surviving pieces, although such subjects as the Adoration of the Magi frequently show vessels that better represent the flights of the artist's fantasy than the style of plate actually made, and many of the objects found in such designs and paintings would in practice have been impossible to carry out.

More reliable information may sometimes be gleaned from paintings which show plate being used. This can often provide evidence of the function of objects whose use would otherwise be unclear. For example, a painting of the mid-century by Claeissens shows a group of noblemen or civil servants feasting, with servants in attendance. Before each of the diners is a small, plain plate; fruit and sweetmeats are on a variety of stemmed dishes around the table, and vessels of surprisingly similar shape, with broad brims and

HOLY-WATER BUCKET *(facing page), silver-gilt and enamel. Spain: Valladolid, c.1525. It bears Valladolid hallmarks, and its embossed decoration combines Gothic and Renaissance details. The coat-of-arms dates from the late sixteenth century. Height: 25 cm (10 in) (Private collection)*

Sandro Botticelli, The Wedding Feast of Nastagio degli Onesti and the Daughter of Paulo Traversaro, *Florence, 1483. The buffet of plate is typical of the applied arts of the Italian Renaissance, rationally proportioned and with ornament derived from architectural sources. Dimensions: 80 × 140 cm (32 × 55 in) (Private collection)*

shallow bowls, serve as wine cups. What is particularly interesting, however, is that the fruit dishes tend to be plain and white, while the wine cups are more ornate and gilded. There are no bottles or flagons on the table; each cup would have been refilled as needed from large flagons kept in cisterns on the floor. Since all the objects shown in the picture are known from other sources to be accurate representations of standard forms, it seems reasonable to accept this evidence of their function.

· THE EARLY RENAISSANCE ·

The early Renaissance in Italy was quite distinct from that in the rest of Europe. As in painting and architecture, in goldsmiths' work the break with the Gothic style was both earlier and more dramatic than elsewhere. But even in Italy it was only the most radically original artists who made an entirely clean break with the earlier tradition. The sort of uneasy compromise that frequently resulted from designs submitted to a committee is suggested in the composition of the great altar cross of 1457 by Pollaiuolo: the whole of the stem is handled architecturally and is entirely Renaissance in character, while the base and the arrangement of the figures flanking the crucifix are much more Gothic (Museo dell' Opera del Duomo, Florence).

Unlike the altar cross, a silver-gilt and enamel-mounted jasper vase of about 1460 (Museo degli Argenti, Florence) was commissioned for a single patron, Lorenzo the Magnificent, but it again shows a transitional character. The foot is distinctly Gothic while the stem alludes to current architecture, although its overall design is more clearly Renaissance even than Pollaiuolo's cross. Its decorative restraint, strong horizontality and careful articulation all suggest a 'logical' approach to design that is in a different world from the Gothic.

The wholesale destruction of sixteenth-century domestic silver was particularly devastating in Italy, and almost none of its secular plate from the first half of the century survives. What little knowledge is available comes almost entirely from secondary sources. Botticelli's painting of the wedding feast of Nastagio degli Onesti (private collection), painted in 1483, shows in some detail a buffet of contemporary plate. All the vessels display similar clarity of organization, carefully worked-out proportions and a dependence on architecturally inspired decoration. However, unlike that of the Claeissens painting, the setting here suggests that this was an imaginary vision of a wedding feast rather than a factual record, with an artist's idealization of what plate should look like. In any event, it shows fashionable display plate; of the appearance of ordinary domestic silver in fifteenth- and sixteenth-century Italy virtually nothing is known.

Elsewhere in Europe the transition from Gothic to Renaissance took a different course. Whereas in Italy Renaissance ideas were widely accepted by the middle of the fifteenth century, it was not until well into the sixteenth that they began to make a major impact north of the Alps. In countries ruled by central government and with a powerful and wealthy court, such as England and France, the intellectual and cultural influence of the new fashions was widespread. In German-speaking and Scandinavian countries the Renaissance was slower to win general acceptance. There the transition was expressed by a gradual imposition of restraint and discipline on design and modification, rather than the radical transformation, of shape and decoration. For example, though the proportions of a Swiss silver-gilt beaker of 1541 (private collection) are subtle, they owe little to Renaissance ideas, while the naturalistically engraved foliage, the ogee form of the cover and the wildman finial are all entirely Gothic. In one important respect, however, it has moved away from the Gothic: whereas in most decorated Gothic plate form and ornament are so merged together that it is impossible to consider one in isolation from the other (the series of cups designed by Dürer in 1507 in the Sächsische Landesbibliothek, Dresden, for example, are essentially stylized plant forms) here form and decoration have been conceived quite separately. A different aspect of the transition is illustrated by a silver-gilt cup and cover of about 1520 (Santo Treasury, Padua), which is unmarked but attributed to the workshop of Ludwig Krug of Nuremberg. The bands of classicizing cameos set into the bowl and cover show a rather uneasy awareness of the antique, while their powerful horizontal arrangement checks the otherwise predominant verticality of the bowl's design and the complex, even confused, outline of the cup.

Although important differences existed between German-speaking and other northern European countries, these two pieces highlight the way in which the region's goldsmiths first took up the challenge of the Italian Renaissance. The physical isolation of the Iberian peninsular, on the other hand, has always resulted in a rather different line of artistic development and this was as true for silver as for other branches of the arts. The Spanish and Portuguese transition seems to have been less from a well-defined Gothic tradition as from a sort of amorphous medievalism. The decorative programmes of Portuguese dishes from the early sixteenth century, such as one in the Kunsthistorisches Museum, Vienna, are typically concerned with subjects such as chivalry, courtly love and the Last Judgment, all of which were preoccupations of the northern European mind a hundred years earlier.

Practically no Spanish secular plate from the early sixteenth century is known, and religious silver tends to be conservative. A silver-gilt holy-water bucket bearing Valladolid hallmarks for about 1525 (private collection) is Gothic in form, but it is of particular interest because its decoration combines medieval foliage with distinctly Renaissance features, such as fluted vases and cherubs. Such details are evidence that printed pattern books were almost certainly in circulation in Spain at this time, as indeed they were elsewhere. But in this case they seem to have been used by the goldsmith purely as a source of ornament, without in any way influencing form.

CUP AND COVER, *silver-gilt with cameos, c.1520. It is unmarked but attributed to the workshop of Ludwig Krug of Nuremberg. The cameos set into the bowl and cover are classical in style and offset the strong vertical effect of the overall design. Height: 39 cm ($15\frac{1}{4}$ in) (Santo Treasury, Padua)*

· SECULAR RENAISSANCE PLATE ·

The secular Renaissance plate of northern Europe may be divided into three categories: plain domestic, decorated and court. Domestic plate was the least susceptible to the influence of fashion and tended to retain more regionally characteristic form and detail. Court plate was the most fashion-conscious of all, and decorated secular plate was, to varying degrees, a synthesis of the two other types.

As in Italy, ordinary domestic silver of other countries has been almost totally destroyed, and only in Germany does anything approaching a representative sample survive. Although inventories contain valuable information about the range of objects in daily use, knowledge of their actual appearance is restricted in most cases to a few chance survivals. On the basis of these a few general observations can be attempted, but any conclusions drawn must be tentative.

While some seventeenth- and much eighteenth-century silver is entirely plain, little from the sixteenth century, however ordinary, seems to have been left totally undecorated. In Germany or Switzerland decoration might be limited to a little gilding or to some restrained engraving; in England frequent use was made of die-stamped ornament, such as around the base of a beaker of 1525 (Gilbert Collection, Los Angeles). While decoration increased the cost of a finished article, it was frequently of a rudimentary and repetitive nature and must have made only a marginal difference to the price. For example, virtually all Elizabethan communion-cups, which generally had to be as cheap as possible, are decorated with die-stamping around the foot and engraved foliage around the bowl. Even spoons, the most common and functional items of sixteenth-century plate, usually have a decorative finial that was cast separately and soldered to the stem.

Of at least as much interest as types of ornament, however, is the variety of forms that predominated in different countries. The history of silver is in a sense the history of a gradually expanding catalogue of objects, and during the sixteenth century various novelties such as forks, tazzas and casters all began to come into general use. Apart from spoons, the most common items of domestic plate during the early part of the century in England seem to have been mazers, font-shaped cups and drinking vessels of various materials mounted with silver. Goblets formed from coconut shells were popular early in the period, but by the middle of the century these had been largely superseded by imported German stoneware. Most surviving silver cups of the time, such as the Campion Cup of 1500 (Victoria and

Antoon Claeissens, Feast, *1574. This Flemish painting depicts a banquet of Bruges civil servants and illustrates a range of fashionable plate in use, including tazzas, wine-cups and flagons. Oak panel. Dimensions: 130 × 155 cm (51 × 61 in) (Groeningemuseum, Bruges)*

VASE *(right), jasper, silver-gilt and enamel. Florence, c.1460. Commissioned for Lorenzo the Magnificent and made in the Medici workshops, it illustrates the transition from the Gothic to the Renaissance style. Height: 21 cm ($8\frac{1}{4}$ in) (Museo degli Argenti, Florence)*

BEAKER AND COVER, *silver-gilt and enamel. Basle, 1541. It bears the maker's mark of Johann Rudolf Faesch-Glaser. The plain tapering cylindrical body has a flared lip and two bands of engraved scrolling foliage. The cover is of ogee form and surmounted by the naked figure of a wild man with a club and shield with enamelled coat-of-arms. Height: 33 cm (13 in) (Private collection)*

Albert Museum, London) or the Cressner Cup of 1503 (Goldsmiths' Company Collection, London), are of surprisingly heavy-gauge metal. Plain plates and dishes were made in large numbers and are recorded in many inventories. None from the early part of the century survives, but there is little reason to suppose that they differed significantly in form from the service of 1581–1601 that still exists in a private collection in Scotland, or from the dishes shown in Hans Eworth's portrait of 1567 of the Cobham Family at Longleat. The former are all circular, parcel-gilt and with fairly deep, rounded bottoms.

In France, as in England, most ordinary plate seems also to have been made in connection with drinking. Beer was less popular in France than in England or the German-speaking countries, and there is no plate that can be associated with its consumption. The most common French drinking vessels were shallow silver bowls described as 'hanaps'. Like the mazer, this was essentially a medieval vessel that survived into the sixteenth century. Hanaps were usually plain but sometimes decorated with repoussé ornament or a coat-of-arms in the centre. By the middle of the century they had been replaced by shallow-stemmed wine cups, which as the century progressed generally became taller. This was partly fashion, partly a result of the increasing supply of bullion into Europe from the New World which made more silver available for making into plate. In addition to hanaps, beakers and cups with wooden bowls and short silver stems were also widely used.

The German predilection for ornament made totally plain silver of this period particularly scarce. Most domestic silver of the early years of the century takes the form of beakers (which were usually raised on feet of some kind and chased with lobe decoration) and mounted vessels. Early sixteenth-century German silver seems usually to

DISH, *silver-gilt. Portuguese, first quarter of the sixteenth century. It is embossed with the biblical story of Judith and other subjects. Diameter: 60 cm ($23\frac{1}{2}$ in) (Kunsthistorisches Museum, Vienna)*

have been of a thinner gauge than English, and this was conducive to raised decoration which also made the object more rigid. A popular version of the mazer in German-speaking lands was a shallow covered vessel with bulbous sides and a side-mounted handle, either in solid silver or in wood with silver mounts. In the Low Countries the repertoire of domestic silver was broadly similar to that of Germany. As in England, evidence exists of large quantities of purely functional silver, such as plates and dishes, but very little of this survives although there is little reason to suppose that it differed much from that made later in the century.

Although it was ordinary domestic silver that was produced in the greatest quantities, the real interest of sixteenth-century silver lies in more ambitious plate; and in matters of taste the lead usually came from the court. The court style that flourished in England and France during the reigns of Henry VIII and Francis I can probably best be defined by reference to a particular drawing, the design for a gold cup and cover supplied by Hans

Holbein to commemorate the marriage of the King and Jane Seymour in 1536 (Ashmolean Museum, Oxford). It contains all the characteristics of the style, most importantly a balance between its horizontal and vertical elements and a strong sense of physical stability. In the drawing the subtle proportions which control the movement of the eye up the cup testify to the hand of a great master. Other characteristics of the style are its rhythmic decoration whereby, for example, each section of the design is punctuated by a repeated band of flutes, a restrained use of classical architectural motifs and an *horror vacui* that leaves no part of the surface undecorated. Within the constraints of the style, the aim was to create an impression of wealth and grandeur, and this was achieved by the use of extravagant materials and as wide a range of techniques as possible. Despite its great delicacy and richness, however, the Seymour Cup is essentially usable, and its basic proportions and shape are not very different from those of an ordinary drinking cup. This is what distinguishes the Renaissance from the fully developed Mannerist style.

The court style practised by goldsmiths in England, France and the Low Countries was remarkably similar during the second quarter of the century. In common with almost all the Tudor royal plate, the Seymour Cup was melted down during the reign of Charles I. Two pieces in very similar style do, however, survive. One, the so-called Michael Cup (Kunsthistorisches Museum, Vienna), is unmarked but almost certainly made in Antwerp, and is one of the few examples of Flemish gold from the period. It was a gift from Charles IX of France to Archduke Ferdinand II in 1570. Its proportions are rather more attenuated than the Seymour Cup, but otherwise it is close to Holbein's drawing. The other, from the Paris court workshop, is a silver-gilt ciborium of about 1530–40 made for Francis I, now in the Louvre. Comparison of the two pieces demonstrates the internationalism of the style in that part of Europe. An important feature of the style was the use of polychromy to enhance the effect and richness of vessels. In the case of the ciborium this is achieved through gilding and the use of precious stones and cameos, but was sometimes taken to extremes by the extensive use of polychrome enamel. An even more elaborate object, again attributed to a design by Holbein and one of only three identified pieces from the Tudor Jewel House, is a rock-crystal and enamel bowl and cover in the Schatzkammer at Munich. This object is still in its original state, but for the finial which was originally some three times its present height and set with further precious stones and pendent pearls. Such decoration was by no means an innovation: jewelled and enamelled cups and reliquaries had been made throughout medieval Europe and the character of these sumptuous pieces was something between plate and jewellery. Objects in the court style at this level of sophistication were intended to be admired for their magnificent craftsmanship and the value and rarity of their materials, and not intended for use.

There are a number of reasons for the stylistic

BEAKER, *silver. London, 1525. This is a unique survival of what was probably a common form in the sixteenth century. Diameter: 10.2 cm (4 in) (Gilbert Collection, Los Angeles)*

DESIGN FOR A CUP *(left), by Hans Holbein. The gold cup, embellished with enamel and precious stones, was made to commemorate the marriage of Henry VIII to Jane Seymour in 1536, and melted down in 1629. (Ashmolean Museum, Oxford)*

CIBORIUM *(far left), silver-gilt, rock-crystal, precious stones and cameos. Made for Francis I in the court workshop in Paris, c.1530. Height: 33 cm (13 in) (Musée du Louvre, Paris)*

unity of northern Europe at this time. One was the increasingly international outlook of princes and other wealthy patrons, and another the circulation of printed pattern books which helped disseminate new fashions. The movement of artists themselves also became increasingly important as princes competed for the services of the most outstanding artists. Hans Holbein travelled from Switzerland to the court of Henry VIII in London, and Benvenuto Cellini from Florence to Paris, while the Emperor Rudolf II attracted many of the most talented artists and intellectuals to his court at Prague. At a lower but broader level, the guild system also played an important part in the universalizing of style. Throughout Europe it was difficult to work as a craftsman except under the aegis of a local guild. The authority of the guilds, however, varied from country to country. In Nuremberg, the leading centre of the craft in Germany during the early sixteenth century, the apprenticeship of a goldsmith lasted seven years, and included a *Wanderjahr* in which the apprentice was required to travel abroad for a year to gain experience in other workshops. Similar practices were common throughout the craft guilds of continental Europe and ensured a constant exchange of decorative and technical innovations.

Flemish and English decorated plate of the mid-century is stylistically very similar, with English styles tending to follow those of Flanders. The two countries had long enjoyed close commercial links through the wool trade and in 1540 these were briefly endorsed by the marriage of Henry VIII to Anne of Cleves. Henry's inventories make frequent mention of Flemish plate and it is known that Flemish goldsmiths were working in London, especially during the Spanish occupation of the southern provinces and the subsequent religious persecution that drove many protestant

COVER TO BOWL, *rock-crystal, gold, enamel and precious stones. English court workshop c.1540, possibly from a design by Holbein. Height: 16 cm (6¼ in) (Residenzmuseum, Munich)*

craftsmen abroad. In these circumstances it was inevitable that Flemish plate should have had a strong influence on English work. Comparison of a London-made ewer and basin of 1545 at Corpus Christi College, Cambridge, with another set made in Bruges at about the same date demonstrates the Flemish superiority. Their forms are in all important respects identical, but the Flemish example is chased and engraved with the latest ornament while the English one is decorated with comparatively old-fashioned foliage and tear-shaped lobes reminiscent of medieval ornament.

With so prominent an item of display plate, every effort would have been made to reflect the latest fashions. It was at a slightly lower level that national characteristics could be expected to emerge, but again, with such limited survivals it is impossible to be definitive about these traits. The Rochester tazzas of 1528 and 1530 (British Museum), are among the first known English pieces fully to have escaped the Gothic idiom. They are not sophisticated, but their ornament is entirely abstract and rigidly organized in a peculiarly English manner, and compares closely with

THE MOSTYN EWER AND BASIN *(above), silver, parcel-gilt and enamel. Bruges, c.1550. It is chased around the centre and engraved around the border with fashionable strapwork and arabesques. The arms of Mostyn applied to the centre are slightly later.*
Height of ewer: 22 cm ($8\frac{1}{2}$ in)
(National Museum of Wales, Cardiff)

WINE-CUP *(left), parcel-gilt. London, 1551. Its short, thick stem is an English characteristic.*
Height: 12.7 cm (5 in)
(Southampton Museum)

the Charlecote Cup of 1524 (National Trust, Charlecote Park). The short, thick stem is also an English characteristic and is still in evidence on a shallow wine cup of 1551 (Southampton Museum) and another of 1557 in the Kremlin. The latter is an example of restrained English decoration at its best. This is in some contrast to an Antwerp tazza of 1548 (Provinciaal Museum Sterckshof, Antwerp) which, although no less purely Renaissance, has a greater sense of elegance by virtue of its slender fluted stem and flatter proportions. The little evidence we have (such as the Claeissens painting) does suggest that such a shape is more characteristic of Flanders than England.

The engraved and chased decoration of the Bruges ewer and basin represents a new repertoire of ornament that seems to have originated in France but which was soon universal throughout northern Europe, especially in France, England and the Low Countries. Strapwork, which is thought to have been invented by the Italian architect Rosso Fiorentino, first appears in the plasterwork ceilings commissioned for the palace of Francis I at Fontainebleau. It is used there in bold three-dimensional forms that resemble cut and curling straps of leather. Although it subsequently became one of the main decorative motifs of Mannerist plate, its potential as abstract ornament for all kinds of objects, whether plate, woodwork or ceramic, was quickly realized, and the speed with which it was disseminated was due largely to the fact that it was made popular through the printed pattern books of Jacques Du Cerceau and René Boyvin. On the Bruges basin it is used three-dimensionally and in a two-dimensional variety combined with moresques or arabesques, a style of ornament that had been introduced slightly earlier.

This type of tightly scrolling linear foliage is first found on Spanish and Saracenic metalwork of the early sixteenth century; by the mid-century, artists such as the Antwerp-based Balthasar Sylvius popularized a version of the arabesque contained within a framework of flat strapwork that made ideal frieze ornament. The moresque occurs on English plate of the 1540s, such as the Corpus basin, and its earliest recorded occurrence is in Holbein's drawing of 1536. But one of the first instances of the combined strapwork and arabesque that became so ubiquitous a feature of northern plate is on a cup and cover bearing London marks for 1554 (private collection). The engraved decoration around the lip is very close indeed to ornament published by Sylvius in the same year. The longevity of this particular device, especially in Flanders and England, is exceptional. Popularization, however, almost invariably leads to a decline in standards and in England a slavish use of old pattern books, continuing until late in the century and even into the next, resulted in such a decline. In southern Germany the device was used over a shorter period, and was usually of a higher standard.

· THE RENAISSANCE IN GERMANY ·

The main centres of German goldsmithing were Augsburg and Nuremberg in the south and Lübeck and Lüneburg in the north. But in Germany, lacking as it did the political cohesion of France and England, the craft was far more evenly distributed throughout the country than elsewhere. Whereas it is unusual in England to find an object of any importance made outside London, important plate survives from a wide variety of German towns, such as Cologne, Strasbourg, Brunswick, Frankfurt and Hamburg.

Among the earliest surviving German silver in completely Renaissance taste is a pair of standing cups which are unmarked but attributed to Erasmus Krug, probably made while he was in Strasbourg in around 1530 (private collections). They are decorated with a series of classical coins let into the body in several tiers, but equally important are the carefully proportioned design and the disciplined way in which the ornament is organized. Such a radical break with the Gothic tradition is unusual for German silver of this date and is probably explained by the advanced taste of Wilhelm Honstein, Bishop of Strasbourg, for whom the cups were made. Erasmus and Ludwig

TAZZA AND COVER, *one of a pair, silver-gilt. London, 1528 (the cover 1532). Its simple design and abstract ornament are peculiarly English. Height: 19 cm (7½ in) (British Museum, London)*

CUP AND COVER *(above left), silver-gilt and rock-crystal. London, 1554. The mounts were made in England, but the rock-crystal was imported and was possibly carved in Freiburg im Breisgau in Germany. Height: 28 cm (11⅛ in) (Private collection)*

CUP AND COVER *(above right), gold, agate and precious stones. Nuremberg, 1536. Attributed to Melchior Baier. The cover is embossed with scenes relating to Justice. Although the design of the stem is conservative, the conceit of carving the agate body in the form of a shell is characteristically Mannerist. Height: 31 cm (12¼ in) (Residenzmuseum, Munich)*

CUP AND COVER *(far right), gold and enamel. Nuremberg, 1534–6. Maker: Melchior Baier. It was made in memory of Melchior Pfinzing, Provost of St Sebald's Church in Nuremberg. Height: 17 cm (6¾ in) (Germanisches Nationalmuseum, Nuremberg)*

Krug and Melchior Baier were among the most important goldsmiths working in Nuremberg during the second quarter of the sixteenth century, and they played an important role in the formation of the South German Renaissance style. Even these goldsmiths tended on occasion to resort to familiar Gothic ornament, and German goldsmiths were generally reluctant to abandon this repertoire, even after Gothic form had been abandoned.

Of the three, Ludwig Krug was perhaps the most technically accomplished, yet despite his attempts to introduce modern Renaissance details into his designs they still retain a strong Gothic character. Melchior Baier's work was rather different: his gold and enamel cup of 1535 (Germanisches National Museum, Nuremberg) must have been one of the most important commissions of its time, and its survival is remarkable. The careful organization of its parts, the use of portrait

THE JANUS CUP *(right), silver-gilt with inset coins. Lüneburg, 1536. Maker: Joachim Gripeswoldt. Known as the Janus cup because of its finial, it formed part of the civic plate of the city of Lüneburg. It is typical of the German interpretation of the Renaissance. Height: 48 cm (18¾ in) (Kunstgewerbemuseum, Berlin)*

ALTAR CANDLESTICK *(far right), one of a pair, silver. Rome, 1581. Maker: Antonio Gentile. The design is highly architectural and sculptural, and strongly influenced by Michelangelo's Medici tomb figures. Height: 100 cm (39 in) (Vatican Sacristy, Rome)*

medallions and Latin inscriptions are all in Renaissance taste, but at the same time the reluctance to leave any space undecorated and the exuberance of the enamel foliage are distinctly Germanic traits.

A rather different style is represented by a remarkable group of Lüneburg civic plate (Kunstgewerbemuseum, Berlin), which is among the most monumental of all surviving sixteenth-century plate, and typified by the so-called Janus cup of 1536. Whereas the South German goldsmiths concentrated on organizing even quite large surfaces with a mass of closely worked detail, the Lüneburg style sought to express the monumentality of the object through very broadly handled, stylized surface decoration. Although this has all the typical characteristics of Renaissance design – stability, marked horizontality and a clear sense of structure – it has not wholly escaped the Gothic idiom: the foliage, both chased

ALDOBRANDINI TAZZA, *silver-gilt. Italy, mid-sixteenth century. One of a set of twelve, each is surmounted by the figure of one of the twelve Caesars and the bowl embossed with four scenes from his life. Each is also pricked with the arms of Cardinal Aldobrandini, later Pope Clement VIII. Height: 43 cm (17 in) (The Minneapolis Institute of Arts, Minneapolis)*

and cast, has a naturalism that looks just slightly too real for comfort. In a cup of 1562 (Kunstgewerbemuseum, Berlin) Renaissance proportions have been retained, but its overall conception has reverted to Gothic inspiration. The stem is formed as a naturalistic Tree of Jesse, the finial as a Virgin and Child emerging from a bursting bud of leaves, and the whole cup is chased in high relief with scrolling foliage.

· MANNERISM IN ITALY ·

By the mid-century developments in Italy had placed the art in a very different state from that elsewhere in Europe. The dominance of architecture and sculpture in Italy and in particular the powerful influence exerted by a number of individual artists created conditions very different from those in other countries, and inevitably had an impact on many of the most important commissions. Cellini's famous gold salt-cellar made for Francis I of France (Kunsthistorisches Museum, Vienna), though embossed and not cast, is in effect pure sculpture. Designs for plate of an equally sculptural nature were produced by Giulio Romano for his patron the Duke of Mantua. The pair of monumental altar candlesticks of 1582 by Antonio Gentile (Vatican Sacristy, Rome) are strongly influenced by Michelangelo, who may have been responsible for their design. These are more architectural than almost any other surviving silver of the period. Comparable architectural and sculptural qualities characterize what is probably the most impressive monument of Italian secular silver of the sixteenth century, the set of twelve tazzas made around 1550–60, known as the Aldobrandini tazzas (Minneapolis Institute of

Arts, etc.). The circumstances of this commission are not recorded, but careful comparison with other pieces of known origin suggests these were the result of workshop collaboration, the stem and surmounting figure being made by an Italian master and the chased scenes around the bowl by an itinerant Flemish craftsman.

Such collaboration was usual in sixteenth-century workshops, where numerous specialists would have been employed on major commissions for specific tasks such as casting, chasing and engraving. Benvenuto Cellini's autobiography describes the organization of his Parisian workshop when he was working on the gold salt-cellar for Francis I:

> I had hired a large number of workmen to help with the goldsmith work. They included Frenchmen, Italians and Germans . . . Some of the Germans who were more expert than the others could not stand the strain of keeping up to my standard . . . [Since] it was the sort of work I had never tackled before . . . I asked the advice of some of those fine old Parisian craftsmen. I told them all the methods employed in Italy for that sort of work. They said they had never used such methods, but that if I let them do it their own way they would return it to me, finished and cast.

The clarity of organization that typifies the design of the Aldobrandini tazzas has no trace of the Mannerism that was already becoming fashionable for the finest plate and was soon to spread to northern Europe. With the work of Michelangelo the line of classically inspired development that had begun with Brunelleschi came to a natural conclusion. This, anyway, is how it was interpreted by Giorgio Vasari (1511–74), whose *Lives of the Artists* propounds a line of development that began with Giotto and exhausted itself with Michelangelo ('the benign ruler of heaven graciously . . . decided to send into the world an artist . . . whose work alone would teach us how to attain perfection in design . . .'). Clearly a new direction had to be found, and the first indications of this are in Italian painting and architecture of the second quarter of the sixteenth century.

The term Mannerism has its origins in *maniera*, a word used by Vasari to describe a certain type of pictorial representation practised by his contemporaries. This he had identified first in the work of artists such as Pontormo, whose pictures contain a strong schematic quality whereby emotion is expressed by the manipulation of construction and colour and exaggeration of the human form. Mannerist painting and architecture rejected the rules of proper construction established during the Renaissance. For example, a doorway in the Uffizi, Florence, designed by Vasari himself, makes use of the particularly bizarre device of reversing the broken pediment above; but in deliberately breaking the rules he presupposes a knowledge of them in order that the gesture might be understood. In this sense, the style is intellectualizing and esoteric.

In goldsmiths' work the first manifestations of the style were inspired by the three-dimensional plaster decoration of Francis I's palace at Fontainebleau, in which figures are shown in exaggerated poses and arrangements within complex strapwork settings. Designs for various kinds of vessels by Rosso were published, and the style was soon taken up by goldsmiths and designers in the Netherlands and South Germany. Other aspects of the style are more closely related to those characteristics already noted in painting and architecture: an exaggeration of form to the detriment of function, a constant search for originality and a rejection of architectural construction. In place of the balanced, stable vessels of the Renaissance, elongated forms of complex profile on precariously diminutive feet became fashionable. A significant development was a growing predilection for subtle and often obscure allusions to philosophical or learned subjects, which, together with a tendency towards ever-increasing complexity of ornament, was connected with another key element of Mannerism, known as *difficultà*. This notion embraced both technical and intellectual virtuosity, and was designed to express both the taste and sophistication of the patron and the skills of the goldsmith. In this constant search for novelty, programmes of theological or philosophical significance became hopelessly confused, while figurative details became entangled with sexual innuendo.

Characterized like this, the foundations of the Mannerist style could hardly be more different from those of its Renaissance precursor, and yet the differences are not always so obvious. This is partly because the vocabulary of ornament is essentially the same and partly because it was a style that admitted of many degrees, and comparatively few surviving pieces take the possibilities of the style to its extremes.

Some of the most exuberant embossed strapwork decoration is to be found on plate, especially ewers and basins, attributed to the Fontainebleau school, but not all fine plate followed this new fashion. Although too little French plate survives for a proper view to be formed, a small group of ceramic wares highly suggestive of metalwork and attributed to the St-Porchaire pottery gives some idea of the appearance of some fashionable plate of the mid-century: dignified and architecturally constructed objects such as salt-cellars and tazzas with an emphasis on cast and engraved rather than embossed ornament.

An Italian ewer and basin of about 1600 (private collection) in the Mannerist style make an interesting comparison with the Aldobrandini tazzas of about fifty years earlier. Whereas the tazzas are both ostensibly and actually objects of display only, the ewer and basin are ostensibly

EWER AND BASIN *(facing page), silver-gilt. North Italian, c.1600. It is embossed with eight episodes from the story of Susanna and the Elders. The form of the ewer, with its long neck, small foot and sculptural handle is typically Mannerist. Height of ewer: 39 cm (15⅛ in) (Private collection)*

functional and yet in fact could hardly have been intended for use at all: the basin is too shallow and the ewer is equipped with a foot so small that it would have been unstable in use, while the construction of the handle pays closer attention to its sculptural aspects than to its practicality.

· MANNERISM IN NORTHERN EUROPE ·

Italy had a much stronger classical tradition than countries north of the Alps, and consequently the classical rules of construction were less easily abandoned there. In the North no such scruples, indeed no such traditions, existed. The potential extravagances of Mannerism were, in a sense, allied to the attitudes that fostered the Gothic. It was therefore quite natural that many of the most elaborate examples of Mannerist goldsmiths' work should have emanated from South German workshops, since it was there that the late Gothic style had flowered most brilliantly. But the most successful goldsmiths of the day looked for a wider market than their immediate locality. This was essential, given the high cost of working substantial objects, the frequent delays in receiving payment and the necessarily small market for such luxury goods. This again made it inevitable that the most sophisticated plate came from centres of international trade which in northern Europe were primarily Augsburg, Nuremberg and Antwerp.

The commercial importance of Antwerp was unchallenged until the 1570s and 1580s, when violent rioting by occupying Spanish and then French troops and finally the siege and capture of the city by the Duke of Alba in 1585 effectively destroyed it as a financial centre. Antwerp had previously been one of the richest cities in Europe and a major centre of the art market. It was also the home of a number of leading exponents of the Mannerist style, such as Erasmus Hornick, Adriaen Collaert and Hans Vredeman de Vries, all of whom produced influential designs for plate. It is therefore hardly surprising that some of the earliest silver in the new style should have been made by Antwerp goldsmiths. The transition, however, was by no means dramatic; for example, in most respects a shallow covered cup from Antwerp of 1541 (Emmanuel College, Cambridge) is a typical example of Renaissance rather than Mannerist design. The stem, however, has a new complexity incorporating precariously perched figures that appear to support the bowl above. Such playfulness and exaggeration became an important feature of Mannerism.

Two further pieces from Antwerp show other Mannerist features, namely a predilection for the grotesque and for recondite allusions. Both the handle of a ewer, made in about 1558 (British Museum) and the strapwork on the bowl of the approximately contemporary rock-crystal cup (private collection) distort the human form to little more than a decorative cypher. On the ewer, a faun's body has been stretched out like elastic, while on the bowl of the cup it has been 'encased' in strapwork. On both pieces the decoration is intended to appeal to the learning of the observer. The cover of the cup is chased with the Four Elements, and the ewer and basin are decorated with scenes of the Rape of Helen, the Judgment of Paris and the Triumph of Neptune.

The Mannerist fondness for the grotesque was actually taken far further than these pieces suggest. Drawings, in particular by Erasmus Hornick, show ewers in the form of writhing monsters that would have appealed more to a sense of morbid sensuality than to one of beauty. Among the most

EWER *(below) of silver-gilt, made in Antwerp in 1558. It is embossed around the body with the Rape of Helen, after Raphael. Height: 35.5 cm (14 in) (British Museum, London)*

extreme examples of surviving Netherlandish Mannerism, and one of the most captivating objects of fantasy of the period, is a nautilus cup made in Delft in 1598 (private collection), probably based on drawings by Adriaen Collaert of Antwerp. Although formally a cup, its intricate construction virtually precludes use altogether. This would have appealed for two reasons: the majority of the mounts are cast rather than raised and technically extremely accomplished; secondly, the main elements of the design allude to current philosophical ideas in a way that is typical of the period. Neo-platonic philosophers such as Pico della Mirandella gave currency to a sort of secularized theology in which the triumph of good over evil was sublimated into an aesthetic version depicting the triumph of beauty over ugliness. This is exactly what is represented by the beautiful maiden astride the molluscan monster on the Delft cup.

Mannerist silver was given its most prolific expression in South Germany. Antwerp's commercial links with Augsburg and Nuremberg and the wealthy merchant classes that dominated all three towns combined to create a comparable demand and taste in silver. Migrant artists, too, reinforced contacts. Erasmus Hornick, for example, who had been born and trained in Antwerp, moved to Nuremberg in 1559 and worked there until his death in 1583. South German Mannerist silver, however, has a character of its own, epitomized by the work of one

CENTREPIECE, *(above left; detail above right), silver-gilt and enamel, made by Wenzel Jamnitzer c.1549 and purchased by the Nuremberg City Council. A technical tour de force, it is one of the most remarkable of Jamnitzer's surviving works. Height: 100 cm (39⅜ in) (Rijksmuseum, Amsterdam)*

particular craftsman, Wenzel Jamnitzer, arguably the greatest of all sixteenth-century goldsmiths.

Jamnitzer's career lasted from about 1535 to 1585 and embraced not only goldsmithing but draughtsmanship, sculpture and mathematics. Born in Vienna, he moved to Nuremberg where he became a master of the goldsmiths' guild and then the city mint. He showed a technical command that, with rare exceptions, exceeded that of his contemporaries. Although many of his works are lost, one of his earliest and most ambitious surviving pieces is the famous Merckel centrepiece of 1549 (Rijksmuseum, Amsterdam). Technically it is a *tour de force*, incorporating casting, chasing and enamelling, and also a technique that Jamnitzer made very much his own, the casting in minute detail of real insects and plants. This centrepiece was purchased from Jamnitzer by the Nuremberg City Council which at around the same time also commissioned from him a small silver-gilt and enamel salt-cellar (private collection). This contains all the characteristics of the centrepiece on a much smaller scale. The receptacle for the salt is concealed beneath a Cavalry scene and the octagonal sides contain drawers that could be used as an inkstand. The panels around the base, which come from Jamnitzer's stock of ornament and consist of strapwork and architectural devices in the latest styles, are used with complete assurance at a time when they had barely begun to make an impression in England. This piece represents the German equivalent of the court style promoted by both Henry VIII and Francis I: while having an ostensible function, it is almost too delicate to be handled, more akin to jewellery than to plate. Such objects would have been admired more for their intricacy and detail than for their overall conception. It is indicative of the different social structure of Germany that such patronage should have come from a civic rather than a princely source.

EWER *(right), silver-gilt and trochus shell. Nuremberg, c.1570. Maker: Wenzel Jamnitzer. This is one of the goldsmith's most brilliant Mannerist works. Height: 33 cm (13 in) (Residenzmuseum, Munich)*

On occasions Jamnitzer could show a sense of order and restraint that, compared with these pieces, is almost austere. For example, a jewel casket of 1562 (Green Vaults, Dresden) is constructed with mathematical precision, with rectangular enamelled panels in exactly the same proportion (1:3) as the entire front; the upper band is in effect a classical entablature supported by three pilasters, and all the details are finished to an extraordinary high standard. But a typically Mannerist conceit is the way in which this careful construction is totally abandoned in the treatment of the figure above, which reclines on a naturalistic ground. The figure represents Philosophy, and the eulogy to Science inscribed on her tablet is typical of the somewhat confused, all-embracing view of philosophy held during the sixteenth century: 'Science with the help of memory recalls to life what is ephemeral, erects lasting monuments to the arts and resurrects what has fallen into darkness.'

All these pieces incorporate an aspect of Mannerism known as the *style rustique*. This style involved not only the casting of real insects and plants, but the introduction of crude silver or gold-bearing ore into finely finished silver settings. J. F. Hayward, in *Virtuoso Goldsmiths* (1976), p.125, wrote:'The philosophical principle lying behind the *style rustique* was that of the earthly source of all things . . . the base of a silver vessel was intended to suggest the living material from which the precious metal was won.' Although there is possibly a connection between Jamnitzer's naturalistic casting and the curious products of the French potter Bernard Palissy, its symbolic application seems largely to have been confined to Germany.

Among Jamnitzer's most brilliant Mannerist works is a trochus shell ewer of 1570 in the Schatzkammer, Munich. This exemplifies many of the characteristics of the style, in that the woman's body appears to emerge from the shell, and any true sense of scale between the eagle and the snail has been abandoned. It is Mannerist, too, in details such as the spout's transformation into a kind of bizarre headdress. The piece is not only a definitive example of Mannerism, but is also a work of art of great imagination and subtlety.

The most fashionable ornamental German silver fell somewhere between sculpture and jewellery, with the same tendencies to exoticism and quasi-philosophical allusions as in Jamnitzer's work. These were not objects intended to be used but were commissioned for the treasuries, or *Schatzkammern*, of such patrons as the Emperor Rudolf II, the Dukes of Bavaria and the Electors of Saxony. In 1565 Duke Albrecht V of Bavaria designated certain objects in his collections as 'inalienable heirlooms', while in 1560 the Elector Augustus I of Saxony founded his *Kunstkammer*, or Cabinet of Curiosities, in Dresden. Many of these collections consisted of rare and valuable natural objects mounted in precious metal. The fact that they were deliberately held apart from more mundane plate and valued more as works of art than as objects of intrinsic worth accounts for their survival in relatively large numbers.

Typical of this taste is a silver-gilt mounted quartz cup made in Augsburg in the second half of the century, and now in the British Museum. Ostensibly a drinking vessel, in practice it could only have been intended as an object of curiosity and a vehicle by which the goldsmith could display his skill. Such anti-functionalism is another most important characteristic of Mannerism. The great parade helmets and shields from the Paris court armoury and the workshops of Giorgio Ghisi in Mantua or Luccio Piccinino in Milan are meant purely as symbols of power and prestige and have nothing to do with defence in the field of battle. Likewise, nothing could be a neater rejection of function than the jewelled weapons produced in

SALT-CELLAR, *silver-gilt and enamel. Nuremberg, 1550. It is attributed to Wenzel Jamnitzer and was made for the City Council of Nuremberg. The Calvary scene lifts off to reveal the salt-cellar beneath, and the drawers in the base contain an inkstand. Height: 23 cm (9 in) (Private collection)*

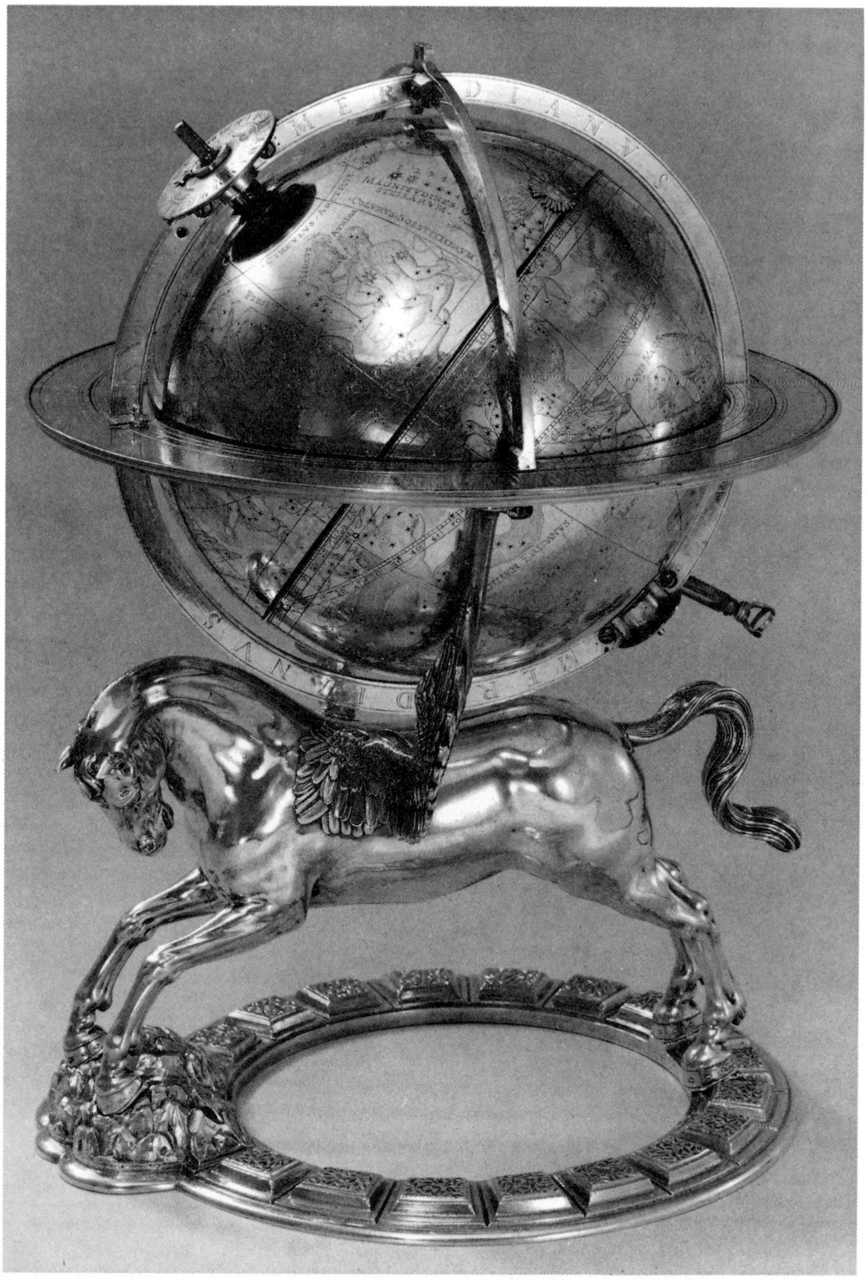

CELESTIAL GLOBE *with clockwork, silver and parcel-gilt. Vienna, 1579. Maker: Gerhard Emmoser. It was made for the Emperor Rudolph II whose court in Prague was one of the most brilliant centres of artistic patronage during the late sixteenth century.*
Height: 27 cm ($10\frac{3}{4}$ in) (Metropolitan Museum of Art, New York, Gift of J. Pierpont Morgan)

Germany during the second half of the century. A gold and enamelled dagger handle made in Augsburg by Hans Mielich, for example, and now in the Louvre, is among the most richly decorated pieces of surviving goldwork.

Other aspects of Mannerism reflected in the German *Schatzkammer* collections are a fascination with science and mechanics, a love of ostentatious wealth and a wide variety of colour and materials. While the strict separation of art and science was a phenomenon of the seventeenth century, associated with the development of Newtonian physics and Cartesian philosophy, science in the sixteenth century was more an entertaining princely pursuit. The court of Rudolf II at Prague, for example, encouraged the serious study of astronomy, but Rudolf's patronage of Tycho Brahe and Johannes Kepler coincided with that of astrologers, and the two elements were not seen as contradictory. The same rather mixed curiosity revealed itself in many of the brilliantly contrived mechanical globes and clocks of the period, which are as much works of art as useful instruments. A celestial globe now in the Metropolitan Museum, New York, made in Vienna by Gerhard Emmoser in 1579 and once in Rudolf's collection, epitomizes this somewhat ambivalent attitude towards science: time can be accurately measured, but is also borne by a winged horse.

The potential of gilding to enhance silver had long been recognized and had the practical function of protecting the silver from contact with substances such as salt, with which it reacts chemically. The decorative possibilities of 'parcel', or partial, gilding had also been known since the Middle Ages and are seen to great advantage, for example, on the Bruges ewer and basin. Another means of enhancing silver was through enamel. The potential of this had been exploited by Jamnitzer, but perhaps its greatest practitioner was David Altenstetter, who moved to Augsburg from Colmar in about 1570 and continued to work there until he became court jeweller to Rudolf II in 1610. One of his most spectacular pieces is a clock case dated 1610, in the Kunsthistorisches Museum, Vienna. Altenstetter seems to have worked in much the same style throughout his career, and continued to produce delightful designs of arabesques populated by colourful birds and monkeys. Equally ambitious, if less pictorial, enamelling was produced in other workshops, such as a gold bowl, probably made in Prague in around 1590 and now in Munich. This is attributed to Hans Karl, a Nuremberg goldsmith who worked for a period under the Emperor's patronage.

The silver and gold objects made for the princely collections belong in the category of the court style. Decorated secular silver of a rather different character was supplied to the guilds, city councils and private patrons. Usually lacking the jewelled intricacy of the *Schatzkammer* pieces, it was generally made for display on important occasions, to be seen from afar and *en masse*. Most of the civic and guild collections in Germany were destroyed during the Thirty Years' War (1618–48) and further depleted during the nineteenth century. The most significant surviving group is the Lüneburg plate, which consists mainly of massive, highly ornate cups that depend largely on a broad impression rather than on detail for their effect. Similarly, a huge silver-gilt cup (private collection) made for the Hamburg City council in about 1600 relies more on size – it stands little short of 80 cm (3 feet) high – and an impression of lavishness than on fine detail. The vocabulary of its ornament is Mannerist, but compared with Jamnitzer's casket or Mielich's dagger it is very broadly handled.

Because of the importance attached to decoration in Germany, form was frequently given less attention than in other countries. This is particularly apparent in domestic plate, where ornament is comparatively restricted. In the late sixteenth century, as earlier, the most usual types of plate were connected with eating and drinking, especially the latter. Tankards and beakers, which survive in considerable numbers, are usually of tapering cylindrical form, but are subject to a variety of decorative techniques including gilding, engraving, chasing and inset coins and medallions. Their decorative schemes are usually products of an eclectic use of the standard pattern books of the period. During the latter part of the century Augsburg began to take the lead over Nuremberg, and from then on much of the best domestic plate was made there. Augsburg goldsmiths seem also to have been responsible for many decorative innovations such as an etched variety of strapwork and moresques, a speciality of Ulrich Möringer, which gave the surface a greater sense of depth than engraving. Other South German innovations included the revival of niello and the application of bands of filigree ornament. The latter is found mainly on glass-bodied tankards with Augsburg or Ulm hallmarks. The use of these techniques in widely varying patterns and combinations gave German sixteenth-century silver a diversity that is unmatched elsewhere.

Prolific though English goldsmiths were throughout the second half of the century, English silver is of limited artistic importance in relation to the achievements of Antwerp and southern Germany. Stylistically, the English goldsmiths relied heavily on Continental, notably Flemish, inspiration, both from printed pattern books and from imported objects. Many pieces in the inventories of Henry VIII's and Queen Elizabeth's plate were of Flemish or German manufacture, and there were frequent cases of the illegal sale of German plate in London, while in 1613 a visiting German reported that a little while earlier 'the goldsmiths in London were nearly all Germans' (quoted by R. W. Lightbown, *Tudor Domestic Silver*, p.3).

While almost nothing survives in France and Italy, and in Germany a sufficient number of pieces exists for a fairly meaningful survey of the entire range of goldsmiths' work to be attempted, in England survivals seem to be of a much more random nature. This has led to a somewhat distorted view of English silver during the late sixteenth century. No collections of any size remain intact, and institutions such as livery companies and colleges have retained only a few items of special significance from their once-considerable sixteenth-century holdings. Nonetheless, the actual number of survivals is far greater than for any previous period, and this has led historians to make categorical statements that would only have been appropriate if the chance survivals were representative. There are grounds for believing this not to be the case, since it is reasonable to assume that the finest objects were commissioned for royal and other aristocratic clients, and the amount of English plate known to have such provenances is negligible.

Even making allowance for this, the general standard of English goldsmiths was not as high as that of the German and Flemish masters. For example, although the Mostyn Salt of 1586 (Victoria and Albert Museum, London) would have been regarded as an important item of plate taking pride of place on the table, by Continental standards the quality of the embossed decoration is unimpressive and the design uninspired. The reason for this is the relative unconcern of the Goldsmiths' Company for the quality of craftsmanship compared with the purity of the metal. Whereas the guilds of Augsburg and Nuremberg went to considerable lengths to impose and supervise exacting

THE WYNDHAM EWER, *silver. London, 1554. It is a unique example of English workmanship at this period. Height: 35 cm (13¾ in) (British Museum, London)*

FLAGON *(above), silver-gilt and one of a pair made in London, 1604. Height: 60 cm (23½ in) (Kremlin Museum, Moscow)*

tests of an aspiring master's skills before he was admitted to full membership of the guild, the Goldsmiths' Company seems to have been somewhat lax in this. The *Order for the Masterpiece* made by the Company in 1607 states that 'very few workmen are able to finish and perfect a piece of plate singularly . . . without the help of many and several hands' (quoted from J.F. Hayward, *Virtuoso Goldsmiths*, p.39).

Nevertheless, plate of the finest quality was made in England, and English goldsmiths did make a significant contribution, particularly in types of objects not generally produced on the Continent, such as the standing salt. Among the finest of these is one of 1572 in the Tower of London, known as Queen Elizabeth's Salt. This bears the same maker's mark as a very fine rock-crystal cup of 1554 (see page 78), and comparison of the two helps to define the change in style from Renaissance to Mannerism in English silver. In the case of the salt, the balance between the vertical and horizontal elements of the design has given way to an emphasis entirely on the vertical. The outline of the salt is restless by comparison, and the range of techniques – chasing, stamping, casting, and engraving – has been used to richer effect. Moreover, whereas the cup uses abstract decorative motifs such as flutes and scrolls, the salt incorporates a series of classical allusions designed to appeal to the learning of the patron.

The close links between English and Flemish silver continued into the second half of the century, as Flemish craftsmen fled to England from religious persecution. A Flemish rock-crystal and silver-gilt cup (private collection) is almost identical to the English Bowes Cup of 1554 (Goldsmiths' Company Collection). The Wyndham ewer (British Museum), also of 1554, is reminiscent of Flemish designs such as those of Cornelis Floris, published in 1548. The grotesque spout and handle are in the height of fashion but, in spite of its Flemish inspiration, details such as the high domed foot leave little doubt that it was made by an English craftsman.

After the mid-century a certain insularity of taste became apparent in English silver. This was partly the result of a serious retrenching of patronage at the highest level after the death of Henry VIII. During Elizabeth's reign the chief problem facing the government from an artistic point of view was how to preserve the appearance of a powerful and civilized court on a financial shoestring. For example, the diplomatic gifts presented by the various embassies to Russia in the early seventeenth century (and still preserved in the Kremlin Museum, Moscow) were mainly made some years earlier, suggesting that rather than commission new objects, the court would plunder the Royal Jewel house for the purpose. Such items also illustrate the somewhat erratic standards of even the most important commissions towards the end of the century. The famous silver-gilt leopards of 1600 in the Kremlin Museum are of the very finest quality, whether judged as sculpture or as examples of casting and chasing techniques, but a flagon of 1604 in the same collection, although highly ambitious, shows a poor sense of form and an inadequate command of decoration.

The relative insularity of English silver is also

CUP AND COVER *(left), silver-gilt and cold enamel, by Dirich Utermarcke, Hamburg, c.1600. Formerly part of the Lüneburg civic plate, this piece is decorated with portraits of Hanseatic rulers and personifications of Prudence, Fortitude, Temperance and Justice. Height: 70 cm (27½ in) (Private collection)*

EWER AND BASIN *(below), silver-gilt and enamel. Spanish, late sixteenth century. This is a typical example of the austere restraint of Spanish plate in the Herrara style. Height of ewer: 25 cm (9⅞ in) Depth of basin: 42 cm (16½ in) (Private collection)*

LEOPARD FLAGON *(right), silver-gilt. London, 1600. This was part of the Royal plate sold to the Emperor of Russia in 1627. Height: 70 cm (27½ in) (Kremlin Museum, Moscow)*

CUP AND COVER *(far right), silver-gilt. Nuremberg, about 1610. Maker: Hans Petzold. Petzold played a leading part in the revival of the Gothic style which became an important aspect of South German silver around the turn of the century. Height: 79.5 cm (31¼ in) (Kunstgewerbemuseum, Berlin)*

BOWL *(below), silver-gilt and Chinese porcelain of the Wan-Li period. The mounts were made in London in 1599. Mounted vessels were very popular during the sixteenth century and made in large numbers. Diameter: 23.5 cm (9¼ in) (Victoria and Albert Museum, London)*

illustrated by the development of certain new kinds of plate that were without parallel in other countries. Unlike the standing salt, which had been a traditional article of English plate since the Middle Ages, the steeple cup was an innovation of the last years of the century. This was a tall cup with baluster stem and ovoid bowl and cover surmounted by a steeple-shaped finial. The form became standardized at an early stage, and its decoration was usually restricted to flat-chased foliage and strapwork of schematic repoussé ornament. In most cases the quality is not distinguished. Likewise, the ewer and tankard forms became standardized by the end of the century, unlike their continental equivalents, and were subject to the same restricted range of ornament. Occasionally, some totally novel solution to design would emerge, such as a ewer of 1610–11 in the shape of a mermaid (Victoria and Albert Museum, London) but generally, English silver did not exhibit the range and variety of form and decoration of German silver.

Although it is difficult to offer a fair assessment of English sixteenth-century silver as a whole, a fairly reliable survey can be made of mounted pieces. These were made throughout Europe but seem to have been particularly favoured in England. Because their bullion content is low, they survive in disproportionate numbers compared with other categories of plate. The most commonly found silver-mounted vessels in England are Rhenish stoneware jugs which were imported in vast quantities. Around the middle of the century, when these jugs first appeared in England, the mounts could be of the finest quality but the standard tended to decline later in the century, presumably because the stoneware was no longer considered worthy of such lavish treatment. Other types of mounted vessel included silver-gilt mounted *façon de Venise* jugs, at least two of which are known from around the middle of the century; later Isnik pottery and Chinese porcelain were also enriched with mounts when such wares became available. The Continental taste for nautilus cups, coconut shells and other natural exotica never achieved the same popularity in England.

EWER, *silver. Toledo or Cuenca, c.1560. The grotesque handle is more extravagant than usual on Spanish plate, and shows possible influence from Italian artists or the Netherlands. Height: 26 cm ($10\frac{1}{4}$ in) (Victoria and Albert Museum, London)*

· MANNERISM IN SPAIN AND · PORTUGAL ·

The silver of Spain and Portugal was less influenced by Mannerism than other countries and continued to develop in relative isolation. This was in part the result of their expansionist policies, which forced them to look to their empires overseas rather than to Europe, and also partly because of the conservatism of Spain as a whole. Under Philip II there was a short-lived period of Italian influence, largely owing to Philip's importation of Italian artists to decorate the Escorial Palace in Madrid. This is perhaps evident in the grotesque handle on a helmet-shaped ewer of about 1560 (Victoria and Albert Museum, London).

To a lesser extent, Flemish decorative ideas also reached Spain and are occasionally to be seen in the grotesques which decorate plate and which are derived from printed sources. But the style did not take root. By the end of the century a more monumental and austere style known as the Herrera style after the Spanish architect, Juan de Herrera, had established itself. This is typified by a ewer of about 1600 (private collection), which has applied panels of cast ornament and a restricted use of enamel.

· MANNERISM IN DECLINE ·

By the end of the century there was a general sense of unease with Mannerist solutions to form and decoration. The pursuit of variety and exaggeration had run the gamut of all conceivable variations and distortions. In England, the Low Countries and northern Germany, decoration tended towards a decadent Mannerism that used the same vocabulary as before but in a looser and less controlled way; while in France the few surviving pieces of the period, such as a small group of flagons and cups in the Louvre and a ewer at Brodick Castle, suggest a virtual rejection of all decoration.

In Germany the vacuum was filled briefly by the style developed by the most prolific and gifted goldsmith of the period, Hans Petzold. Petzold began working in the Mannerist style, but at the end of the century he led a brief but brilliant phase that amounted to a full-scale Gothic revival. The Diana Cup of about 1610 (Kunstgewerbemuseum, Berlin) could never be mistaken for a genuine Gothic object, but the basic inspiration of the form is the late Gothic designs of Albrecht Dürer of about a hundred years earlier. In a sense, this revival was symptomatic of a search for an alternative source of inspiration. While Germany was still searching, Holland found that inspiration in the form of the new auricular style invented by the van Vianen family of Utrecht.

· 4 · BAROQUE SILVER, 1610–1725 ·

The term baroque, in its modern, neutral sense, includes broad, sweeping ornamentation, bold and pronounced outlines, a kind of heavy neoclassicism, and complex play, both formal and decorative, with elements derived from architecture, often combined with sculpture. In its old, rather opprobrious sense of misshapen, irregular or grotesque, however, it might almost have been coined to describe the work of the van Vianens, with its dissolution of Mannerist detail into the auricular.

Adam and Paul van Vianen were both born in Utrecht, Adam in 1569 and Paul in or shortly after 1570. While Adam stayed in Utrecht all his life, Paul travelled widely in France, Italy and southern Germany. His skills were such that he was recruited successively to work for three courts, Munich between 1596 and 1601, Salzburg, where his patron was Bishop Wolf Dietrich von Raitenau, and finally Prague – where he was goldsmith to Emperor Rudolf II – from 1603 onwards. He died in 1614. His art was sophisticated and intended for the collector's cabinet rather than for practical use. Sandrart, the German Vasari of the baroque, says that he was a talented draughtsman, wax modeller and embosser; that he loved doing pictorial embossing, such as is on a beautiful basin with 'the bath of Diana, numerous naked women, animals, landscapes most perfectly delineated, decorated, and with spirit, so that not without reason he was respected and famed as an originator of all such art.'[1] This ewer and basin (Rijksmuseum, Amsterdam) are his most important surviving work, the figures drawn and grouped with great elegance, the detailed landscape embossed in subtle and shallow relief. They were made just before he died, for the Emperor Mathias. While parallels for his pictorial style can be found in the painting of Ytewael and Joseph Heintz the Older, the manner of the basin's border and the body, foot and handle of the ewer were peculiar to Paul and his brother at that date, echoing the cartouches and C-scrolls of late Mannerist ornament but melted into monstrous, cartilaginous, flowing, fleshy forms. There are premonitions of this manner in some Italian graphic designs such as those by Enea Vico (1523–67) and Federigo Zuccaro (1540–1609), and in the grotesques of the Netherlandish engraver Cornelis Floris (1514–75), but Paul seems to have invented the full-blown version of the style, which appears first on his tazza of 1607.

In 1610 Paul paid a visit to Utrecht: it is possible either that Adam was developing the style simultaneously and more or less independently, except perhaps exchanging ideas on paper, or that Paul taught it to him then. Certainly, the earliest known piece by him with this ornament, a tazza with Odysseus and Circe (on loan to the Rijksmuseum, Amsterdam), was made in that year. Four years later, Adam made an extraordinarily bizarre ewer (Rijksmuseum, Amsterdam) which Sandrart also mentions. It was commissioned by the Amsterdam Silversmiths' Guild in memory of Paul, and Sandrart says that it was embossed out of one piece of silver: 'Everything thereon is depicted in grotesque or "Schnackerey", as they call such things, and it was held to be a very strange piece.'[2] Adam continued in this vein until his death in 1627, pushing the malleability of silver to its limits with his three-dimensional embossing, usually of a single sheet of metal, this being the technique which impressed Sandrart so much.

The work of both van Vianen brothers was famous among the cognoscenti, and seized upon by painters who wanted to incorporate an extravagant form in their still-lifes. The ewer made by Adam was repeatedly depicted by Lastman and other painters in Rembrandt's circle, and the basin by Paul already described appears in Claes Moyaert's *Apotheosis of the Christian Faith* (St James's R.C. Church, The Hague) of 1651.

Adam's son, Christian (c.1600–67), who was apprenticed to his father, continued to work in the same manner, and indeed the pieces he made in Holland were all stamped with Adam's mark, even after the latter's death. Much of his work was for the courts, first of Charles I of England and then for Charles II (see below), but during the Civil War and Commonwealth, however, he was back in Utrecht, where in 1650 he published a book illustrating his father's creations under the title

CLOCK *(facing page), with silver and parcel-gilt face and veneered tortoise-shell base. German: Augsburg, c.1700. Maker: Johann Andreas Thelott; clockwork by Franz Xavier Gegenreiner. Height: 80.7 cm (31¼ in) (Metropolitan Museum of Art, New York, Rogers Fund)*

BASIN AND EWER *(above and above right), silver. Prague, 1613. Maker: Paul van Vianen. The central plaquette on the basin is embossed with the figures of Diana and Actaeon and nymphs.It belongs en suite with the ewer, which is embossed with the story of the seduction of Callisto by Jove and her discovery by Diana. They were made for Emperor Mathias. Width of basin: 52 cm ($20\frac{1}{2}$ in) Height of ewer: 34 cm ($13\frac{1}{4}$ in) (Rijksmuseum, Amsterdam)*

Constighe Modellen. Seven of these are of surviving pieces by Adam, such as the ewer of about 1620 with four sunken medallions (Rijksmuseum, Amsterdam). In no other case do known objects of this period exactly match published designs, and here the designs are after the objects themselves.

Christian brought the auricular style to England, and it also spread throughout the Germanic territories. In Italy and France, while the influence of the auricular is evident in the architecture and in designs, the surviving silver hardly seems to have been affected by it. Spain and Portugal seem to have been wholly unaffected.

In England and Germany the auricular became relatively formalized (as is usually the case when a style is being imitated), forming cartouches and the framework for embossed scenes, so taking the place of the strapwork and C-scroll cartouches of Mannerism. The style was also used for cast elements such as tankard handles, and the same model was often employed by different goldsmiths. These casting models continued to be used after the style was no longer fashionable for the

1 contrasting degress of low relief were a typical form at this period.
2 embossing in the Dutch style created a swirling movement suggesting a turbulent sea.
3 flat chasing, executed after the embossed work was completed.

body of a vessel, as with a lobed Augsburg tankard of 1680–89 by Philipp Küsel (Victoria and Albert Museum, London).[3] A pair of 1680 candlesticks (Frisian Museum, Leeuwarden) retains an auricular cartouche with snout and eyes on stalks around the cartouches of the foot, but the rest is covered with flowers, the most popular motif of the seventeenth century.

EWER *(above right), silver-gilt. Utrecht, 1614. Maker: Adam van Vianen. This piece in the auricular style was embossed out of one piece of silver. The van Vianen brothers were Utrecht's supreme contribution to baroque silver smithing. Height: 25.5 cm (10 in) (Rijksmuseum, Amsterdam)*

PAIR OF CANDLESTICKS *(right), silver. Netherlandish, with the town mark of Leeuwarden, 1670. Maker: Nicolaas Mensma. They are finely embossed and chased with flowers and scenes from Ovid's* Metamorphoses. *Height: 30.5 cm (12 in) (Frisian Museum, Leeuwarden)*

In the 1620s and 1630s a formalized floral style known as *cosse de pois*, 'pea-pod' style, with flame-shaped petal forms, developed in France. There was also a floral style that was naturalistic, drawing upon the same scientific desire to record accurately specimens of the natural world that led the Bolognese naturalist Ulisse Aldrovandi to publish his seven books on animals and insects in 1602, and Jan van Kessel (1626–79) to paint his naturalistic picture of flowers and insects. The earliest published designs of this kind seem to have been devised by Nicolas Robert from Lorraine, executed in Rome but published in Paris by Pierre Mariette in 1638. These were quickly copied by a Roman publisher, and described as a *Giardino di Fiori Naturalissimi*. In 1645 Nicolas Cochin's *Livre Nouveau de Fleurs Très-Util Pour l'Art D'Orfèvrerie* appeared in Paris.

The earliest German designs in the floral style did not appear until the 1660s, and this large time-lag suggests that the initial creative impulse for the style came from France. Possibly the earliest surviving example of the style is an unmarked gold coffer in the Louvre, which probably belonged to Anne of Austria, Louis XIV's mother (it was inventoried among the French crown jewels in 1791). By the 1650s the floral style was well established in Europe north of the Alps, and there is no doubt that the most exquisite surviving examples of it are Dutch: for example, an octofoil dish of 1681 by the Bolsward goldsmith Claes Baardt (fl.1654–97) has each segment embossed with a different single flower and with music-making cherubs in the centre (Frisian Museum, Leeuwarden); like the auricular, this style depended upon great embossing skill. Often, as on the Louvre coffer, the flowers are combined with acanthus leaves. Mastery of the acanthus scroll, sometimes called 'Roman leaf', sometimes 'French', was essential for craftsmen in all materials during the second half of the seventeenth century. Numerous designs for it were published, some of the earliest by Polifilo Giancarli in Rome in 1628, and then, as in so many cases, republished in other countries: the Netherlands in 1636 and in Paris and England in 1674. The scrolls also include boys, animals and monsters.

The floral-foliate style was at its most realistic when executed in enamel. Not only vessels but watch-cases, jewellery, bookcases and knife handles were decorated in this way. Painted enamel details and shading make the effect even more tactile and realistic.

ENGLISH ROYAL FONT *(above), silver-gilt. London, 1660-61. The royal arms of Charles II are engraved inside the bowl. The maker's mark, RF between two pellets, is unidentified. Height: 93 cm (36½ in) (The Jewel House, Tower of London)*

COFFER *(left), gold, probably made in Paris c.1645. Supposedly given by Cardinal Mazarin to Anne of Austria, it is one of the earliest examples of the floral-foliate style. Length: 45 cm (17¾ in) (Musée du Louvre, Paris)*

· BAROQUE ARCHITECTURAL · · INFLUENCE ·

Changes in the overall forms of silver during the seventeenth century were the result of applying baroque architectural thinking to silver design. Inevitably, this process began in Italy, but was adopted by French artists working at the court of Louis XIV (1643–1715), and for political and economic reasons its influence emanated from there. The style is architectonic, in the sense that it is formed of architectural elements: friezes, volutes, tripod altars, caryatid figures, and so on. It combines these elements with sculpture and pictorial embossed panels, just as the interior architecture of the day was combined with painting and sculpture. As the newspaper *Mercure Galant* of November 1679 said, 'There is no scrap of silverware [at Versailles] which does not tell a story. Some chandeliers represent the twelve months of the year. Others show the Seasons, and the Labours of Hercules compose another twelve. It is the same for the rest of the silverware . . .' The subject-matter was usually allegorical, often glorifying the King, as on two great silver sconces chased in the middle with the figure of the King as Apollo driving four horses, framed by the palms of Victory, with the Labours of Hercules at the sides; above, two figures of Fame and the King's device, *nec pluribus impar*.[4] At the time the style was thought to be very strictly classical: hundreds of designs by Jean le Pautre (1618–82) for interior architecture and vases often include idyllic classical landscapes and togaed figures, and he refers to two of his series interchangeably as 'À la Romaine' and 'À la Moderne'. While not classical in the sense that they look like true classical objects, or even that their mouldings are in any correct or realistic relationship to each other, the objects are very boldly and clearly delineated. In the late eighteenth century, neoclassicists felt a natural sympathy for French design of this period and, indeed, some designs, such as those of Jacques Stella (before 1657) were used 120 years later by the Wedgwood factory.

Very little survives of the tons of plate made for Louis XIV and his family, and nothing remains of the truly grand early objects produced at the Gobelins manufactory in the late 1660s and early 1670s – the furniture, the candlesticks, the great buffets of vases. But a superb if slightly old-fashioned piece, made in Sweden between 1696 and 1707 by the Parisian Jean-François Cousinet for the Swedish Crown, shows how massive, how superbly chased, how sophisticated in design those objects were. It is a baptismal font 106 cm (41¾ in) high, with a tripod base composed of putto herms, each with his arms and torso in a different graceful position; these support a huge scallop shell, fluted on the outside, with 'basketwork' on the inside (Collection HM the King of Sweden).

To trace the origin of the style on the evidence of actual objects is impossible, but published designs do exist. The ideas produced by a Giacomo Laurentian and the Neapolitan Orazio Scoppa, in around 1630 and 1640, show the bold sweeping S-scroll outline, and openwork scrolls which are so essentially baroque, combined with fully sculptural or half-relief figures. These were unlike anything produced elsewhere in Europe, including France, at this time, firmly indicating the Italian origins of the baroque style in goldsmithing. The influential designers of the day, Charles Le Brun (1619–90) and Jean le Pautre, both spent some years during the 1640s in Rome, Le Brun with Poussin from 1642 to 1645. In their designs the Italian style is made more weighty, more dense. It was Le Brun, Louis' *premier peintre*, Director of the royal workshops at the Gobelins (founded in 1667), and finally even Director of the Académie Royale de Peinture et Sculpture, who was responsible for the totality of the decorations at Versailles. Louis had decided to make his court there, and from 1669 onwards the palace was extended and transformed into an unprecedentedly sumptuous setting for glorifying the monar-

BAPTISMAL FONT, *silver by Jean-François Cousinet, made for the Swedish Crown between 1696 and 1707. Its tripod base is composed of putto herms which support a fluted scallop shell with 'basketwork' interior.*
Height: 106 cm (41¾ in) (The Royal Collections, Stockholm)

TUREEN AND PLATE, *silver. Paris, 1714–15. Maker: probably Claude Ballin the younger. This is a good example of the Berainesque style. The essentially flat surface ornament consists of interlacing bands interspersed with medallions. Height of tureen: 20 cm (8 in) (Residenzmuseum, Munich)*

chy. It was what the Germans call a *Gesamtkunstwerk*, everything including the tapestries, furniture and silver in the same style and often *en suite*.

Most of the silver furnishings were only briefly on view at Versailles, to which the King moved in 1682, because in 1689 all silver above a certain weight was melted down to finance his foreign policy. However, many of these objects were depicted in a set of tapestries (designed by Le Brun, of course) called *L'Histoire du Roi*, woven between 1673 and 1679. One (on page 103) shows Louis XIV visiting the Gobelins, with works of art being offered to him for inspection, many of which can be identified in the royal accounts and inventory, such as the stand (*brancard*) in the right-hand foreground, a form of silver unique to Louis' court. Twenty-four of these were made in the late 1660s, of which four, by Claude Ballin, were supported by satyrs, as here. Twenty-four round silver trays with the King's arms were also supplied to be used on top of them, and one of them is shown on top of the *brancard*. Large decorative vases between 76 and 90 cm (30 and 36 in) high were made to go with them, and dishes, some round, some oval; one of the oval ones embossed with the life of Louis XIV is being carried in behind.

Some of Le Brun's own designs and some by members of his own team survive; another record of what their creations looked like is the collection of drawings in the Print Room at the Nationalmuseum, Stockholm, begun by the Swedish court architect, Nicodemus Tessin the Younger (1654–1728). Tessin was in France himself in 1687, and in the years afterwards continued to have information and drawings sent to him from Paris. A less reliable source, but still a useful one, are the still lifes by artists such as Meiffren Conte (c.1639–1705) and François Desportes (1661–1743) who painted silver of the kind seen at court; but the former sometimes combines in one object details from different objects to please himself.

Jean le Pautre's hundreds of designs, which appeared in small sets from 1645 onwards, are not a record of existing pieces but a powerful stream of ideas from the same stylistic source. Most of them are undated, but the majority of his output lies around the 1660s: he gives ideas for bed alcoves, fireplaces, furniture altars, pulpits, landscapes, historical and biblical scenes, candlestands, vases, firedogs, and even teapots. His style owes a great deal to Charles Le Brun, but he was an inventive genius in his own right, some of his wilder sculptural ewers being extremely close to the rococo. These were not intended as models to be copied exactly but as ideas to fire the imagination, and travellers to France made use of the abundance of prints being produced in Paris at that time. Christopher Wren wrote to a friend that he would bring him 'all France in Paper', and that what he was taking home would 'give our Country-men Examples of Ornaments and Grotesks in which the Italians confess the French to excel.'[5]

· BERAIN AND HIS FOLLOWERS ·

By the late 1670s a new style was emerging which made the heavy sculptural baroque of Le Brun seem ponderous and old-fashioned. This was an essentially flat pattern of grotesques – in contrast to the previous heavily three-dimensional style – with roundels, cartouches, terms, figures, masks, birds, husks and lambrequins, scallop shells and swags, all suspended within a framework of scrolling bands. The artist behind this new style was Jean Berain (1640–1711). (Interestingly, nearly all the elements of this style and much of the same overall effect can be seen in the grotesques of another French designer, Jacques Androuet Ducerceau, but produced a century earlier, in the 1550s and 1560s.) The old style was supplanted very quickly, fickle fashion being assisted by the death in 1683 of Colbert, Minister to Louis XIV, which brought to power Le Brun's sworn enemy, the Marquis de Louvois (1641–91). The grand old man of the French baroque kept his titles but lost nearly all his power to Berain, who at first held the title of royal garden designer. He produced designs for textiles, furniture, carriages, silver clocks and interior decoration. His silver designs include a toilet service for the Dauphine (1680) and silver for Versailles (1700), but his influence in silversmithing went far beyond court circles. He satisfied the need for a lighter, airier style; as Louis XIV himself said to his architect, Mansard, in 1698, 'Il faut qu'il y ait de la jeunesse mêlée dans ce que l'on fera.' ('One must have youthfulness combined with everything one does.')[6] Other designers, like Claude Audran (1658–1734), made the style yet lighter and more youthful, but always following in

Berain's footsteps. Again, prints spread the style: about 350 by Berain were engraved, and copies were produced by the Augsburg publisher Jeremias Wolff from as early as 1703. Berain's most influential follower was Daniel Marot (1663–1752), who entered the service of William of Orange, William III of England, after the Revocation of the Edict of Nantes in 1685. He was another overseeing architect in the manner of Le Brun, and his designs for everything from furniture to ironwork to goldsmiths' work to embroidery were collected and published in The Hague in 1703, and a further 126 plates in Amsterdam in 1713. He worked on and off in England at Hampton Court, Petworth and Montagu House between 1689 and 1706, and his greatest achievement was the decoration of Prince William's palace at Het Loo in the Netherlands. Both his physical presence in England and the Netherlands and his prints did a great deal to spread the Berainesque style in those countries.

As said earlier, the Berainesque was essentially a flat style with a multiplicity of small decorative motifs derived from grotesques and held together by bandwork, but another characteristic often seen on Berainesque plate was that the various parts of the ornament were clearly separate. Engraved designs were soon being published in Germany, popularizing the new French style there. Examples of such publications are *Neues Zierathen Buch von Schlingen und Bandelwerk . . .* (Augsburg) by Johann Jakob Biller (d.1723) and suites of ornament by Paul Decker (1677–1713), beginning with *Groteschgen Werk* (Nuremberg) which consists of fifty plates of interlace patterns, interlace being the element from the Berainesque grotesque which found most favour with German goldsmiths.

While Berain and Marot were enjoying success in northern Europe, Italy remained true to the baroque of Bernini. The most important book of designs to be published in Italy in the early eighteenth century was *Disegni Diversi* (Rome, 1714) by Giovanni Giardini (1646–1721). These designs are quite untouched by the Berainesque and retain the massive, sculptural quality of the high baroque. The only development is that the forms are more tightly waisted and often have

EWER AND BASIN, *silver-gilt, made in Augsburg, c.1730, by Gottlieb Menzel. Its flat surface ornament and medallions are typical elements of the Berainesque style. Height of ewer: 24 cm ($9\frac{1}{2}$ in) (Thyssen-Bornemisza Collection, Lugano)*

angular profiles alternating with rounded ones. Some are very architectural and austere, others are overgrown by acanthus or swags of flowers; one holy-water stoup of shells, dolphins and mermaids anticipates the rococo. Although obviously a compendium of Giardini's designs over some decades, the underlying forms were sufficiently in tune with continuing eighteenth-century taste for the series to be republished in 1750, and it may be assumed that it was quite influential.

· CHINOISERIE AND THE PLAIN STYLE ·

Outside the mainstream of the baroque proper was chinoiserie, the European adaptation of Chinese and Japanese ornament and form. This style was particularly fashionable in England and the Netherlands in the last third of the century, partly because of the Chinese lacquer and porcelain being imported at that time, and partly because of the Dutch embassy to Peking in 1656, which was described and depicted in engravings by Jan Nieuhof (first published in Dutch in 1665, and in English in 1669). The illustrations from this publication, as well as details from the imported objects, were copied in England by goldsmiths who in the 1670s and 1680s devised a style of flat-chasing the surface of the metal with them (an example is the Gubbay toilet service in the Victoria and Albert Museum, London). The style was later exported to North America. The fashion affected form as well as decoration; for example, the silver garnitures of vases, which appear in both England and the Netherlands, were derived from oriental porcelain. A further aspect of the style is the ornamentation of objects with cast sunken panels on which very small oriental figures and motifs such as cherry branches stand out against a matted ground. This derives from Japanese *shakudo* ware, and one Netherlandish designer, C. de Moelder, included an example of it in a straight-sided French-style perfume bottle, among his designs of 1694[7] which are otherwise completely in the French manner but published in London.

The last style to be discussed may actually not be a style at all: it is plain, undecorated silver, of which quite a large amount survives from the period, mostly made in the Netherlands or England, or to a lesser extent in provincial France. (It includes the famous and much-admired 'Queen Anne' style.) The first point to consider is whether this is not just an accident of survival, nearly all the plain plate from previous centuries having been melted down for obvious reasons. The famous Lobkowitz pictorial inventory of 1650 (formerly Schloss Raudnitz, near Prague), for example, includes quantities of absolutely plain silver which must date from the sixteenth or early seventeenth century. Secondly, even in the seventeenth century the cost of working plate elaborately added enormously to the cost of the metal. As Charles Perrault said, the silver at Versailles was of 'A sumptuousness of chasing so admirable that the material, all of silver and heavy as it was, hardly constituted one tenth of its value.'[8] If this sounds hyperbolic, there is also Samuel Pepys complaining (on 19 October 1664) that he took two silver flagons to be valued, the verdict being £50 at 5s. per ounce, 'and they judge the fashion [workmanship] to be worth 5s. per ounce more [that is, as much again] . . . but yet am sorry to see that the fashion is so much and the silver come to no more.'[9]

However, there are a number of instances from this period where the cost of an object cannot have been a consideration, and yet a plain piece was chosen: a case in point is the ewer and basin which Johannes Lutma (1587–1669) made for Amsterdam Town Hall in 1655, and which has only the most subtle shallow lobing to articulate its clear shiny surface. Another example is the almost totally plain toilet service made by Benjamin Pyne (fl.1676–1732) in 1708, and acquired by the Duke of Norfolk. This service is among the English plate made by Huguenot craftsmen who fled from France after the Revocation of the Edict of Nantes in 1685. They made use of heavy-gauge silver and many cast and therefore heavy elements. The style became very popular in England, indicating that when an Englishman bought a heavy, but plain, item of silver it was an aesthetic choice. It is difficult to judge whether, had he been prepared to spend yet more, the buyer would have liked it ornamented as well as heavy.

· TABLE SERVICES AND DRINKING · · VESSELS ·

A great revolution in table manners, led by the French court, took place during the seventeenth century. While it was a hundred years before it affected the bourgeoisie, even in France, it nonetheless had an immediate effect on the types of silver being manufactured, as plate was principally for the aristocratic market. The utensils made as a result of this change belong to the modern world and are recognizable today, while those of an earlier date are more alien. A friend of the group of noble intelligentsia known as the '*Précieuses*', the Marquis de Coulanges, wrote one of his *Chansons* about these changes between the 1640s and the 1680s. He says that formerly the soup was eaten out of a communal bowl without ceremony, and one dipped one's fingers and bread into the *fricassée*, but now everyone ate soup from their own plate; one served oneself politely with a spoon and fork, and from time to time a servant went to wash them at the buffet; the same plate was never used for different foods, but was changed frequently.[10] The general trend was towards greater individual comfort: just as people now sat in chairs rather than on benches around a table, so they came to expect their own cutlery and plate.

The other trend during this period was to-

GOBELINS TAPESTRY, *1673–9. It illustrates Louis XIV's visit to the Gobelins factory on 15 October 1667. It comes from* L'Histoire du Roi, *a series of tapestries executed after designs by Charles Le Brun. Height: 370 cm (147 in) (Musée National du Château de Versailles, Versailles)*

wards homogeneity of ornament, with services of matching plate, cutlery and dishes. The services made for Louis XIV from the 1670s onwards are well documented: in 1680, for example, Nicolas Delaunay (fl. 1672–1709) was paid for the greater part of a white silver service for the Dauphine. This consisted of 380 plates and dishes of various sizes, twelve *assiettes potagiers*, that is, bowls without covers for serving soup, eight dozen spoons and forks, three dozen knives, seven basins, eight ewers, twenty candlesticks, five pilgrim flasks, thirteen tasters, fourteen salts, two *pots à bouillon*, six *marmites*, a covered *écuelle* (porringer), a grater, a heater, four vinegar bottles, three sugar casters, two snuffers, two perfume burners, nine *poisles à confiture*, two salvers and four dish rings. This was obviously for large public occasions; the minimum required for polite dining is shown by her private service for six which was delivered at the same time: twenty-four plates, four *assiettes potagiers*, a *nef à cadenas* (on which more later), two salts, four salvers, two covered cups, a vinegar bottle and sugar caster, six cases containing a knife, fork and spoon, six dish rings, two carving knives and forks, three tasters, a *pot à bouillon* and six large candlesticks *de chambre*, presumably to put on the table.[11]

The large number of plates in both services reflects the need to change them with every course; the tasters were needed because an important part of royal eating ritual was the tasting of food, as was also the practice of bringing food to royalty in covered plates, both customs existing in order to prevent poisoning. The covers used to be simply inverted plates, but by later in the seventeenth century the bowl with cover *en suite* had evolved. The salts were small, the great standing salts of the sixteenth century no longer being fashionable; dish rings were a recent introduction and were quickly copied in England. The casters may have been lighthouse-shaped – a form also standard in England at the time – or they may have been pear-shaped beneath their conical lids, which was how all eighteenth-century casters were to develop. The most important serving dish on the table was the *pot à l'oille* which contained a spicy liquid stew of assorted meats, the main dish of the first course.

This, and the other covered dishes which stood on the table, became part of the display and were more and more sumptuously ornamented, until the elaboration of Meissonier's rococo tureens, his *sculptures de table*, was reached (see chapter five). Elaborate plans, like those for garden *parterres*, were published to show how to ornament a table with dishes, and this new emphasis on what stood on the table led to the development in the 1690s of the centrepiece. There was the *surtout*, a tray on which stood pepper pots, sugar casters, salts, vinegar and oil bottles, often with a raised covered bowl in the centre. No silver examples survive from this early period, but there is a good French gilt-bronze and marble one of about 1700

in the Toledo Museum of Art, USA. Sometimes the *surtout* stood in the middle of the table throughout the meal, but it might be replaced for the dessert course by a *fruitier*, a tiered construction with various small bowls for fruit or sweetmeats, perhaps with holders for sugar casters. The eighteenth-century epergne developed from both of these, as did the German *plat-ménage* (both terms pay tribute to France but do not actually occur in French).

Enough cutlery was supplied with the Dauphine's second service of plate for everyone to have their own knife, spoons and fork. This was a recent idea for, until the mid-seventeenth century at least, one would have brought one's own private set to a meal. The earliest multiple sets of cutlery date from the later part of the century, and forks were by now commonplace at court (if not among the bourgeoisie), although Louis XIV himself never used one.

The *nef à cadenas* was another attribute of rank to which, in France at any rate, only the royal family, the dukes and the most elevated nobility could aspire. It was a tray with an upright double compartment at the end. On this went the napkin, the cutlery and the bread, and the end compartments were for salt. Their use was copied at both the English and German courts.

At the sideboard where the cutlery was washed between courses there were one or more cisterns of water of enormous size. The one in the Hermitage, Leningrad, made in London in 1699 for the Duke of Kingston, weighs 3500oz (99,223g). These cisterns could serve as bottle-coolers, but there is no doubt from contemporary descriptions that they were also used for washing up. Massive fountains provided clean water and in some instances were used for wine. The earliest surviving one (J.P. Getty Museum, Malibu) was made in Paris, and nearly all the others to have escaped melting down are English but imitate French forms; the latest date from the 1770s. The type died out, partly because the proliferation of individual eating implements made washing at the sideboard unnecessary, and also because the fashion for a huge display of plate at the sideboard declined from the 1720s onwards; the outsize pilgrim bottles, ostensibly for wine, disappeared at the same time.

A concomitant of this change was the development, in the very late seventeenth century, of the individual ice-bucket which stood on the table. This followed from a change in drinking habits: throughout the century it had been the practice for a servant to bring a glass on demand, for this to be drained and then handed back to the servant. While the custom continued well into the eighteenth century on the Continent for formal occasions, comfort and more relaxed manners began to be esteemed for more intimate meals, and so it became permissible for the glass, and also the bottle, to remain on the table, close at hand.

The footed salver, of which there are many examples from the second half of the seventeenth century, was used for presenting drink and food, as the trumpet stem could easily be held in the hand. During the Carolean period in England it sometimes came with a porringer[12] or tankard *en suite*. Gradually, from the 1720s onwards, the trumpet foot was replaced by small scrolling feet which provided a more stable base for what is in effect a tray on a table rather than a presenting tray.

The salver's associations with the flourishes of polite society made it a fit candidate for ceremonialization, a process also applied to various other forms of plate, such as ewers and basins and drinking cups. This meant that examples were produced which were scarcely functional, such as the engraved seal tazzas executed in England from the time of William III. These were made from the silver matrices of the seals of office awarded to a postholder when these became obsolete through the death of the sovereign, or a change in his title. One such was made for Henry Boyle who was Chancellor of the Irish Exchequer from 1701 to 1708; he received the matrices on the death of William III in 1702. The absence of wear on the engraving shows that it was purely for display (the Trustees of the Chatsworth Settlement).

The ceremonialization of plate also had the effect of keeping obsolete patterns of silver in use long after they were employed domestically. A case in point is the standing cup, which was so essential a part of the welcoming ritual, and of which so many lavish examples were made in the fifteenth, sixteenth and seventeenth centuries. By 1700, however, it survived only as gifts to bodies which even then were traditionally minded, such as the Livery Companies of the City of London. In France and Italy the type disappeared completely early in the seventeenth century, but in Germany it had a last fantastic flowering, nurtured by the *Kunstkabinett* – the taste of collectors – or by traditionalism. The form was also preserved in England, America and occasionally the Netherlands, for Protestant Communion cups, which had been based on the grander secular drinking vessel.

In England and the American colonies the successor to the standing cup was the two-handled cup and cover which co-existed with it for a while. This evolved out of the two-handled porringers and caudle cups, the sides of which gradually became higher and the foot more defined in relationship to the body, until there emerged in the 1680s a shape which was recognizably the two-handled cup, fashionable from about 1700 to 1750.

Small silver tumblers and plain beakers continued to be produced throughout this period, but glass was gradually replacing plate. The main exception to this was beer drinking: large numbers of silver tankards and mugs survive from all the northern European countries and from America, and are often highly ornamented and therefore expensive items. They are the finest plate to come out of Scandinavia at this time.

The fashion in England and its American colonies for a new drink, punch, led to the creation of a new form. This was a large bowl, often with handles and cover because the punch was drunk hot. In the 1680s the monteith appeared; this was similar to the punch bowl but in the lip were notches on which the stems of glasses could rest while their bowls cooled in the water within. One of the most splendid surviving punch bowls is that of about 1685 belonging to Stamford Corporation; it has massive cast dolphin feet, and a capacity of three-and-a-half gallons (16 litres).

TANKARD *(facing page, above), silver and parcel-gilt set with silver coins. Arböga, Sweden, 1727–35. Maker: Johan Dragman.*
Height: 20 cm (8 in)
(Victoria and Albert Museum London)

SALVER *(facing page, below), silver-gilt. London, c.1702. Unmarked.*
Diameter: 31.7 cm ($12\frac{1}{2}$ in)
(Trustees of the Chatsworth Settlement, Chatsworth, Derbyshire)

ICE PAIL *(below left), silver-gilt. London, 1698. Maker: David Willaume.*
Height: 24.7 cm ($9\frac{3}{4}$ in)
(As above)

CADDINET *(below right), silver-gilt. London, 1683–4. Unidentified maker's mark, WE, and the arms of William III and Mary.*
Length: 32 cm ($12\frac{3}{4}$ in)
Height: 26.75 cm ($10\frac{1}{4}$ in)
(The Jewel House, Tower of London)

Coffee, tea and chocolate were all introduced during this period. The first botanical reference to coffee was in 1592, but it was not imported on a regular basis until the mid-seventeenth century. The English East India Company dominated the trade: in 1664 the total quantity listed in its account books was 44,912lb, while in 1690 it was over six times as much. In that same year the Dutch East India Company was only just beginning to import coffee regularly. In the first half of the following century average annual imports into England were well over half a million pounds.[13]

This pattern of consumption is reflected in the quantity of coffee pots produced. Only English examples survive from the seventeenth century, the earliest, by George Garthorne,[14] dating from 1681. It is exceedingly plain and ungainly, 24.8 cm ($9\frac{3}{4}$ in) tall, a tapering cylinder with a narrow straight spout and incurved conical cover. This basic shape was refined in the early eighteenth century, the spout given an elegant curve and the sides sometimes angled. The French seventeenth-century coffee pot (known only from pictorial sources) had a pear-shaped body on three legs, and its form was copied by the rest of Europe.

Chocolate was introduced into England from the West Indies in the 1650s, but the earliest known pot was not made until 1685, again by George Garthorne. The same form as a coffee pot was normally used, the only difference being that there was a hole in the top through which the stirrer could be twiddled in order to mix in the sediment. There are, however, some early variants: a pear-shaped form, probably derived from France, such as Pierre Platel's example of 1705 in the Assheton Bennett collection, England, and a shape derived from the oriental ginger jar, with a low-set curved spout, such as that made in Boston by John Coney in 1701 (Museum of Fine Arts, Boston).

Tea was available in London before the Restoration, but the earliest surviving teapot dates from 1670 and has the same tall conical shape as the earliest coffee pot. As with coffee drinking, England led Europe, with Holland close behind, so the innovations came from there. The next shape to appear was small and gourd-like, copied from a Chinese wine-pot.[15] In the early eighteenth century many teapots were low and pear-shaped, and this was the form which became most popular on the Continent. A spherical form copied in France and Germany also developed. This was ultimately derived from China, and other variants on Chinese prototypes also appear briefly. A suitable exoticism found on many continental examples is the bird's-head spout.

Generally, however, coffee was more popular than tea at this period in all countries except England and Holland, so teapots are less common than coffee pots. Metal teacups are a great rarity, and they nearly always copy the handleless oriental prototype; tea caddies were either rectangular or vase-shaped and sugar was still kept in caskets rather than bowls.

TEA SERVICE *(below), agate and silver-gilt. Augsburg, 1695–1706. Maker: Tobias Baur. Height of teapot: 16 cm ($6\frac{1}{4}$ in) (Staatliche Kunstsammlungen, Kassel)*

· SILVER FURNITURE ·

Silver or silver-mounted furniture did already exist in the later sixteenth and early seventeenth centuries, but it was in the later seventeenth and early eighteenth centuries that it was most widespread and popular. As mentioned earlier, there was a great deal of it in the *grands appartements* at Versailles including candlestands. In 1670 Ballin delivered some that were over 2.5 m (8 ft 6 in) tall. They were probably *en suite* with tables and mirrors, to stand against the window piers. There were also chandeliers, sconces, firedogs, armchairs, folding chairs, relief plaques (perhaps mounted on furniture), and vases for orange trees. Their weight recorded in the inventory of the day shows that most of them were made of solid silver rather than thin sheet mounted on wood.

In England the earliest surviving furniture is a suite comprising a table mirror and candlestands with the cypher of Charles II, and a pair of andirons, all unmarked, still in the Royal Collection. They are embossed in high relief with acanthus and floral swags, and with putti on the mirror, and must date from about 1665. Charles II's mistress, the French-born Duchess of Portsmouth, also saw to it that she kept up the standards of her native country; John Evelyn noted in his diary (4 October 1683) that she had 'great vases of wrought plate, tables, stands, chimney furniture, sconces, branches, braseras [braziers] and all of massive silver and out of number.' The fashion spread to those among the nobility who could afford it, and at Knole in Kent there remain a silver table and two candlestands, unmarked, but presumably English.

The most splendid surviving set of English silver furniture, now missing its candlestands, is the table and mirror made by Andrew Moore in about 1690 and presented by the Corporation of the City of London to William III (Royal Collection). They are nearly all of solid silver, the caryatid legs being cast, and when complete the set weighed 2071.2kg (7306oz). The edge of the table and the mirror frame are decorated with a running garland of naturalistic flowers and fruit in high relief. The table-top is engraved by another craftsman with heraldic emblems and the royal coat-of-arms over a military trophy surrounded by scrolling acanthus. There is also a pair of andirons dating from 1696, crowned by statuettes of putti with baskets of fruit on their heads.

This suite seems to have been the last set acquired by the English monarchy until 1731, when George II brought over from Germany a pair of tables, a mirror with candlestands and five high-backed chairs made in about 1720 for August Wilhelm of Brunswick. Made by Philipp Jakob VI Drentwett (1686–1754) and Johann Ludwig II Biller (c.1692–1746) of Augsburg, these returned to Germany in the nineteenth century when the two monarchies separated.

Nearly all German silver furniture comes from Augsburg and consists of silver sheet pinned to a wooden frame. The earliest surviving set, belonging to HM the Queen of the Netherlands and now in the palace of Het Loo, was made in the early eighteenth century by Johann I Bartermann (1661–1732), who specialized in such work. The table-top is finely engraved with the story of Endymion. The reason that more silver furniture with Augsburg marks survives than from any other place is because it was exported to courts all over Germany, Denmark and Sweden, and to Russia, and this wide distribution increased its chances of survival. The power of individual patronage, however, was such that very 'metropolitan' works were produced in unexpected places. For example, the Hohenlohe family of Weikesheim in Franconia employed a 'Silberkistler', a silver cabinet-maker, called Johann Heinrich Vogt, at their castle. He was Augsburg-trained and made not only the ebonized furniture so popular in Germany at the time but also a clock, candlestands and the frame of a fire-screen, all covered with silver sheet.

Germany, and Augsburg in particular, also had a tradition of producing clocks and automata in an

TABLE, MIRROR AND CANDLESTANDS, *silver. Augsburg, c.1700. Maker: Johan I Bartermann. The table top was made by Johan Heinrich Mannlich and is engraved with the story of Endymion and Ismene. Width of table: 95.5 cm* $(37\frac{1}{2}$ *in) Height of mirror: 45.5 cm (57 in) Height of candlestands: 92 cm (36 in) (Collection of HRH Princess Juliana of the Netherlands, on loan to the Rijksmuseum Paleis Het Loo, Apeldoorn)*

ingenious variety of forms, and during the seventeenth century and into the early eighteenth the collaboration between clockmakers and goldsmiths continued. While Augsburg clocks of this period were not technically innovative, they did reach an acme of elaboration in design and set the style for all German metal clock-cases. There were four types: the 'mirror' clock which held the clock face on a stem; the table clock which was a series of variations on a casket or aedicule (house-shaped container); the 'altar' clock with a vertical, tiered construction and columns, like a high-altar; and the *Teller* (plate) clock with a flat, often circular but sometimes shaped face, which was usually hung on the wall but occasionally on a stand. The goldsmiths' contribution to these clocks was the embossed silver, sometimes combined with cast statuary or filigree, and often studded with jewels or encrusted with enamel.

ANGEL RELIQUARY, *silver-gilt and copper-gilt, made in Rome in the mid-seventeenth century after a sculpture by Alessandro Algardi in the Sacristy of the Chiesa Nuova, Rome. Height: 27.5 cm (10¾ in) (The London Oratory)*

Outside Germany precious metal clock-cases are much rarer, but a massive filigree table clock dating from the 1660s, and now in the Victoria and Albert Museum, London,[16] was made by the Nuremberg goldsmith Hans Conraet Brechtel (fl. in the Hague 1640–75).

· TOILET SERVICES ·

Another service of plate to evolve in the seventeenth century was the toilet service. By 1650 in France the term *toilette* had come to mean the assemblage of utensils used in the act of dressing and beautifying oneself (it had previously meant the cloth in which they were wrapped). Like table plate, the utensils were made *en suite* and the composition of the sets became standardized. The larger and more precious belonged to the category of display plate, performing the same function in the bedroom (the inner sanctum of baroque court ceremonial) as did a display buffet at a banquet. This purely ceremonial function is confirmed by the lack of wear on the most elaborate surviving pieces. The cult of the toilette was part of the whole ritualization of life, the same process which had courtiers standing by at Louis XIV's *coucher*. Thus, the possession of elaborate toilet services was not confined to women: Louis had two, one in seventeen parts, perhaps his private one, and another in fifty parts, perhaps for the public *coucher* and *lever*.

A toilet service was often acquired on the occasion of a marriage; an example exists which was almost certainly bought in 1677 when William, Prince of Orange, married Princess Mary. Their arms and monogram are on each of the twenty-three pieces: the mirror, pair of candlesticks, ewer and basin for washing the face and hands, a pair of scent bottles, a pair of caskets (almost certainly for powder), another casket for combs, a snuffer tray and snuffer, a small bowl and cover, a mug, a pair of oval salvers, a circular salver, a pair of octagonal boxes and two small oval boxes, all for make-up and beauty spots. This service is only of medium size as it does not include writing implements or eating equipment (in the seventeenth and eighteenth century breakfast was always eaten in one's private apartments); other toilet services would also contain an *écuelle*, an egg-cup, a knife, fork and spoon, marrow-spoon, a coffee and chocolate service including a hot-water kettle, tea-caddy, spice box and *trembleuse* (a small tray with an attached frame into which a small cup or glass fitted). With minor variations this whole assemblage of utensils became the standard German toilet service from the late seventeenth century until the end of the rococo period. Augsburg was the source of most of these sets, the eighteenth-century ones being of silver-gilt or, exceptionally, of gold. Some very splendid ones of the late seventeenth century by Tobias Baur (fl.1685–1735), include agate parts.

Two very important seventeenth-century English examples, in the Victoria and Albert Museum, London, are the Calverley toilet service of 1683,[17] in thirteen parts and set with cast plaques after Gugliemo della Porta, and the Gubbay toilet service of c.1680,[18] in sixteen parts and flat-chased with chinoiserie decoration.

· ITALY ·

Little comprehensive research on Italian silversmithing during the baroque period has been undertaken. For example, while Genoa was one of the most prosperous towns of Italy during the seventeenth century and probably had a flourishing craft of silversmiths, little is known about it. Furthermore, relatively little silver seems to survive: not only did the Napoleonic period and the secularization of religious institutions lead to much wholesale destruction, but a shortage of money in the eighteenth century caused many of the most important treasuries, such as that of the Florentine grand duke, to be sent to the mint. Nonetheless, a few generalizations can be made. Rome was predominant until the early eighteenth century, not only stylistically but also in the quality and probably the quantity of objects made. It was the source of the baroque style for the whole of Europe; the great Bernini, prime mover of the style in architecture, even designed goldsmiths' work, such as the gift from the Barberinis to Queen Henrietta Maria of England in 1636: this was an oval reliquary of St Helena executed by Francesco Spagna, a palm and a half high, of gold and 'christalli di Venetia' with an imperial crown on top set with rubies, the whole on silver-gilt feet.[19]

Work was commissioned by the Papacy, the cardinals and nobility of Rome, the many churches and religious institutions, important visitors to the city, and the town Magistrature. It was traditional for the Magistrature to give chalices to the churches of the city on their patronal feast day, and between 1656 and 1701 most of these commissions (up to forty a year) went to Bartolomeo Colleoni (fl.1656–1701), his uncle and his nephew preceding and succeeding him in this task.

Commissions came from outside Rome as well: of the large presentation dishes given annually to the grand dukes of Tuscany from 1680 to 1737, in fulfilment of a bequest by Cardinal Lazzaro Pallavicini, at least one was made in Rome, by Lodovico Barchi (fl.1711–31) 'sculptor in silver', in 1725. Plaster casts of these dishes survive in the Pitti Palace, Florence and show that Berainesque bandwork was not adopted until the 1720s.[20]

The Roman guild or *Universitá* had a very liberal attitude towards foreigners, requiring only that they work in Rome for three years before being allowed to apply for mastership. The largest number of non-Italians came from Flanders, including one Balduino Blavier from Liège (fl.1645–69), who in 1661 made a large number of plates and salvers for the Grandduke of Tuscany. The famous Parisian goldsmith, Thomas Germain, spent the years 1695 to 1701 in Rome, and there were also a few Germans, mostly from the south.

A goldsmith known to have produced a great deal of work is Fantino Taglietti (fl.1574–c.1650), who made a large shell-shaped basin to a design by Bernini for Cardinal Antonio Barberini, and who worked for the town Magistrature. He also made a metre-high equestrian statue of St Ambrose in 1641 for the Cathedral of S. Giovanni at Ferentino, where it remains today. Of the Colleoni family already mentioned, Carlo Spagna (fl.1669–80) worked for Cardinal Francesco Barberini the older, and among many other things made four great silver-gilt candlesticks in 1669; these were presented to the Treasury of St Peter's (where they remain) to go with the famous sixteenth-century cross and candlesticks by Antonio Gentili. Urbano Bartalesi (fl.1670–1726) was papal silversmith from 1689 to 1700.

A certain papal commission is a gold paten given by Alexander VII (1655–67) to the Chapel of his family, the Chigi, in Siena Cathedral. The central plaque with *basse-taille* (bas-relief) translucent enamelling probably dates from the fifteenth century, and the rich naturalistic flowers on the rim have, exceptionally for the seventeenth century, been executed in the same technique. A vast presentation dish now in a private collection was made in Rome in 1670 by Giovanni Francesco Travani (1640– after 1702) and given by Pope Clement X to the Marquis Luis Manuel de Tavora.

Giovanni Giardini (fl.1675–1722), already mentioned, was not only a goldsmith but also a bronze-founder, appointed officially as such to the Camera Apostolica in 1698. In 1700 he was ordered by Clement XI to complete the tomb of Queen Christina of Sweden, on which the sculptor Carlo Fontana was working too slowly; Giardini had already made the funerary mask, crown and sceptre in 1689, and these were recently found in the tomb (Vatican Museum). He worked with semi-precious stones as well as bronze and silver, and on an architectural scale: for example, he made a tabernacle of porphyry, gilt-brass and rock-crystal (Geistliche Schatzkammer, Vienna), a set of candlesticks and altar-cross of malachite and silver (private collection), and a large double-headed eagle forming part of a lamp (Todi Cathedral). There is no doubt that he was highly esteemed for his goldsmithing and sculptural skills as well as for his designs.

Goldsmiths depended considerably on the work of painters and sculptors for designs, particularly as so much of their important work was pictorial or sculptural. For example, Sebastiano Conca (1680–1764) supplied the drawing for the

PAPAL MACE, *silver and parcel-gilt. Rome, 1696–1710. Maker: Giovanni Giardini da Forlì. The design retains the massive sculptural quality of the high baroque. It bears the arms of Benedict XIV (1740–58) and a shield with the initials of Pius VII (1800–23). Height: 101.5 cm (40 in) (Victoria and Albert Museum, London)*

PATEN, *enamelled gold. The central plaque probably dates from the fifteenth century. This paten was given by Pope Alexander VII (1655–67) to the Chigi Chapel, Siena Cathedral. Diameter: 19.6 cm ($7\frac{1}{2}$ in) (Museo dell'Opera del Duomo, Siena)*

scene in the middle of one of the dishes in the series given to the Granddukes of Tuscany, and an angel reliquary of silver-gilt and copper-gilt (London Oratory) is a miniature version of the angel supporting the book for St Philip Neri in the 1635–38 sculptural group by Alessandro Algardi (1595–1654) in the sacristy of the Chiesa Nuova, Rome.

A particularly close relationship between sculptor and goldsmith existed in the Grandducal workshops in Florence, the Uffizi, where, from 1687, Giovanni Battista Foggini (1658–1725) occupied a Le Brun-like position at the head of the Florentine artistic hierarchy as architect in charge of the hundred-strong team of jewellers, silversmiths, painters, miniaturists, hardstone carvers, sculptors, medallists and porcelain workers. Foggini designed and, in some cases, personally made some very important work in silver and mixed materials. An early work was a silver tabernacle for Pisa Cathedral (1676–86); he also designed the altar frontal for SS. Annunziata in Florence with its three pictorial scenes, executed in 1680–82 by H. Brunswick, a Lübeck silversmith. A typical product of the multiple skills of the Uffizi is the reliquary of St Daniel (1705) in S. Lorenzo, Florence. In the centre is a hardstone

PART OF A TOILET SERVICE, *silver-gilt. Paris, 1670. Maker: Pierre Prévost. The applied coat-of-arms and monogram of William III and Queen Mary are on each of the pieces of the twenty-three-piece set. Height of ewer: 20.3 cm (8 in) Width of basin: 46 cm (18 in) Height of candlestick: 18 cm (7¼ in) Width of boxes: 17 cm (6¾ in) Width of square caskets: 23 cm (9¼ in) Width of glove tray: 21.8 cm (8½ in) (Trustees of the Chatsworth Settlement, Chatsworth, Derbyshire)*

carving of Daniel and the lions, framed by swelling gilt-bronze scrolls richly ornamented with acanthus leaves and festoons of luscious hardstone fruit, and crowned by floating silver-gilt angels holding a crystal receptacle, which were by Cosimo Merlin, the head silversmith and gilder of the workshops. The style is heavy Roman baroque – Foggini had been sent to train in Rome – but the richness of material is characteristic of Florentine court work at this time.[21]

In Venice, specialization was very marked by the end of the century, the goldsmith/jeweller being separate from the silversmith and there being further categorization within these groups. This is shown clearly by the masterpieces required by the Venetian Guild, the Scuola di Oresi, in its decree of 1693. It lists the categories and the appropriate masterpiece for each: those who make *bagatelle*, which in England would have been called 'toys' (spoons with a toothpick which unscrewed); the chasers (a pax with the dead Christ and flowers); the makers of silver *digrosso*, in England 'large workers' (the foot of a cup); chalice makers (a chalice and paten); engravers (a box *a Rabesco*, that is, with arabesques, birds and leaves, or else a coat-of-arms); the founders (a model of Christ which then had to be cast); and the enamellers (a painted enamel flower). This list also includes the various types of gem-cutters, setters, and filigree makers, so that of the 107 members present at the guild meeting, perhaps half of them would have been silversmiths proper.[22]

In Milan, the guild presented a pitiful image of itself during the seventeenth century, complaining that it could not get enough precious metal, that the plague of 1630 had gravely affected it, and, in 1677, that foreign imports, especially French ones of lower-grade silverwares, were under-cutting its trade. Some of these complaints may be looked at sceptically, but the fact that in 1700 members were petitioning to be allowed to sell imported wares does indeed suggest that the craft had declined there. There is, however, at least one remarkable piece surviving from the late seventeenth century: the over-life-size silver statue of St Ambrose with jewelled mitre and book in the Treasury of Milan Cathedral, on which a large team of craftsmen worked between 1681 and 1695. A sculptor provided the model for the head, various painters the designs for the scenes from the servant's life, and four silversmiths assisted Policarpo Sparoletti in the making of it.[23]

Turin, where so much silver in the French style and worthy almost of Parisian goldsmiths was made in the rococo period, was just beginning to organize its silversmiths during the baroque period. In 1678 the Regent, Maria Giovanna Battista, Duchess of Savoy, decreed that a guild be

ALTAR CANDLESTICKS, *one each of two pairs, silver. The one on the left, dating from 1663, is by Tymen van Leeuwen of Utrecht who registered his mark in 1652. The one on the right was also made in Utrecht, in 1698, but the maker is unidentified. Both pairs almost certainly formed part of the plate of the hidden church of St Catherine, Utrecht. Heights: 41.5 cm (16¼ in) and 68 cm (27 in) (The London Oratory)*

set up, together with all the usual assaying and marking regulations, which were in practice by the time a very fine monstrance in the Italian baroque style with an open scrolling stem and foot was presented to the sanctuary at Oroppa by the Regent.[24]

Naples, under Spanish rule until 1707 when the Austrians took over, had in 1620 a large and active goldsmiths' guild with about 350 members. There, as in Rome, Augsburg and elsewhere, certain families of goldsmiths dominated. Of the Treglia family, Aniello made the 60 cm (2 ft) wide sanctuary lamp with the arms of Aragon given by Philip IV of Spain to Amalfi Cathedral, and Nicola made the man-size tabernacle of 1700 in Troia Cathedral. A member of another goldsmithing family, Michele Patuogno, executed a superb four-tiered centrepiece of a type standard in Italy, with three sea-horses and *rocaille* supporting a lapis lazuli sea from which dolphins rise supporting the shell superstructure (private collection). One of the surviving altar frontals in Naples, made between 1692 and 1695 by Giandomenico Vinaccia (and in the treasury of the Church of San Gennaro) is in the wildest southern baroque style. It is architectural, with caryatid nymphs turning in every direction, broken pediments, tightly twisted salomonic columns, bas-relief scenes, a fully three-dimensional cavalcade of Alessandro Carafa and retinue bearing the relic, his horse treading on Heresy, while a floating St Januarius above protects the city. But shortly after such a sublime invention, austere plate of almost Huguenot appearance was being made, such as the helmet-shaped ewer by Andrea de Blasio, with cut-card work, gadrooned foot and plain basin, in Otranto Cathedral, indicating that the craft in Naples was aware of what was being made elsewhere in Europe. Despite the Spanish connection, however, there was no discernible Spanish influence on work from Naples throughout the seventeenth century, the local tradition being artistically more sophisticated and therefore predominant.

· FRANCE ·

Paris dominated French goldsmithing, not only because of Paris's pre-eminent position in the country, but because of quite extraordinary patronage by Louis XIV. Louis founded the Gobelins manufactory in 1667 in order to establish a yet more intensive centre of artistic production than the old Louvre workshops, where, hitherto, the royal artists had worked.

The most active period of silver production at the Gobelins was the late 1660s and 1670s, when the massive silver furnishing pieces were being executed. The names which recur most often in the accounts of Louis XIV, the *Comptes des Bâtiments*, are Jean de Viaucourt (fl.1657–c.1675), Girard Debonnaire (fl.c.1657–c.1681), René Cousinet (fl.1657–c.1681) (the father of Jean-François who made the Stockholm font), Nicolas Delaunay (fl.1672–1705), Claude Ballin (fl.1672–1709), Claude de Villers (mentioned archivally 1665–1703), Jacques Dutel (fl.1668–at least 1683), Tomas Merlin (1672–at least 1684), Alexis Loir (fl.1673–1713).

Production for the court fell off sharply after 1689, when Louis sent all his large plate to the Mint. Sumptuary laws, drastically limiting the size of silver and, more especially, gold objects which could be made, were repeatedly promulgated. It seems likely that the King was the only person restricting himself seriously in comparison with earlier expenditure, since permission to disregard these laws could be bought if one was of a law-abiding nature; nonetheless, they did have a depressing effect on the trade as a whole. The number of goldsmiths allowed to be full masters at any time was supposed to be 300, and earlier there had been pressure to add to this number, but in 1689 there were only 280 goldsmiths, and 273 in

1702. However, by 1715, the year of Louis' death, there were 400, so the setback was only temporary.

The Revocation of the Edict of Nantes in 1685, which withdrew the rights granted to French Protestants, did not affect the Parisian scene. The exodus of craftsmen to England, the Netherlands and to Germany was instead from the provincial towns: for example, the goldsmiths who went to work for the Margrave of Brandenburg came mainly from Metz, Nîmes and Grenoble, and a few from Rouen.

Of the provincial towns, only three had fifty or more goldsmiths in the first third of the eighteenth century: Lyons, Lille (captured by Louis XIV in 1667), and Strasburg (united with France in 1681). Metz, joined to France in 1648, had between thirty and forty, but the numbers in the other towns were much smaller: Dijon and Besançon both had twenty, Poitiers, Tours and Valenciennes about fifteen each, and Caen, La Rochelle, Chatellerault, Troyes, Limoges, Rheims and Auxerre about ten each. The great nobility always had its plate made in Paris, but the local nobility, the clergy and bourgeoisie tended still to buy locally. It is no coincidence that the towns which until recently had been politically independent of France – Lille, Strasburg and Metz – all had large numbers of goldsmiths. Strasburg held a special position in being allowed to work silver of the German standard, thirteen *Lot* = .812, compared to the Paris standard of .958. This not only made it cheaper, but was considered at the time to take gilding particularly well. Strasburg kept a Germanic flavour to its style right into the 1730s, with a form of Berainesque bandwork decoration against a matted ground which was French in origin but very popular in Germany. Its economic connections with Germany remained strong, with German princes ordering work from the leading goldsmiths, no doubt, ironically enough, because they thought it looked very French.

· THE NETHERLANDS ·

In 1579, with the Treaty of Utrecht, the seven northern provinces of the Netherlands declared themselves against their ruler, Spain. Although this struggle was not concluded until the Peace of Westphalia in 1648, it was the beginning of the process which made the United Provinces a powerful force in seventeenth-century politics, and ushered in an extraordinary period for Dutch art. The country produced not only great painters such as Rembrandt, Frans Hals and Vermeer, but was also outstanding in the field of the applied arts. Although the population numbered fewer than a million people, there were twenty-three goldsmithing centres, and while some were more important than others this led to variety and quantity of production; and fortunately, a high proportion of what was made in the seventeenth century survives.

PRESENTATION DISH, *silver. Rome, 1670. Maker: Giovanni Francesco Travani (1640–after 1702). It is embossed with the story of the Rape of Europa. This dish was given by Pope Clement X to the Marques Luis Manuel de Tavora, a member of the 1670 embassy from Portugal. The border incorporates the Tavora coat-of-arms over the cross of the Order of Malta, and the dolphins allude to the Tavora crest. Diameter: 100 cm (39¼ in) (Private collection)*

The richest and most densely populated province was Holland, with its cluster of prosperous towns of which Amsterdam was by far the wealthiest. It was an artistic centre of European importance, and in 1664 supported 300 goldsmiths, as many as Paris. Both commissions and goldsmiths from all over the United Provinces came to the town, which also attracted skilled craftsmen from Germany, such as Johannes Lutma (1587–1669) from Emden who was the greatest follower of the van Vianens' style.

The Hague, the seat of central government and the Stadholder's Court, had eighty goldsmiths in 1664 and a slightly different clientele: instead of wealthy burghers and the guilds, it was the House of Orange, the nobility and the many visitors to the town that were the main customers. Predictably, the goldsmiths here were the ones most affected by the French Court style which had so much influence all over Europe from about 1670 onwards. Friesland had a tradition of cultural independence, with its own Stadholder's Court at Leeuwarden, where some outstanding engraving and chasing was done. In 1664 fourteen goldsmiths were working there, among them Nicolaas Mensma (fl.1669–98) whose work includes a pair of finely embossed and chased candlesticks with scenes from Ovid's *Metamorphoses*; he had been to Amsterdam to perfect his training. The local specialities of Leeuwarden were little silver caskets which were given (filled with coins) at weddings, and brandy bowls, also used at weddings, with prominent 'ears' and angled sides. Also in Friesland, Bolsward had seven goldsmiths in 1664. The town also had outstanding chasers, most famous of whom was probably Claes Baardt (fl.1654–97), whose floral style has already been described.

The van Vianens were Utrecht's supreme contribution to European baroque silversmithing, but the city remained a very productive centre thereafter. In the years between 1616 and 1639

CIBORIUM, *silver-gilt. Brussels, 1657. The cross on the lid is set with rock-crystal. The inscription indicates that the vessel was made for the church of the Béguines (a religious community of women not bound by vows) at Hasselt, Limburg. Height: 61.7 cm (24 in) (Victoria and Albert Museum, London)*

eighty-three masters registered their marks, while in the next twenty-nine years sixty-seven new names were recorded. A high proportion of their work was for churches, Protestant and Catholic (even though the latter were officially banned).

The town of Groningen was the source of two particularly distinctive items: a brandy bowl, usually with lobed sides, scroll handles and a high-waisted foot; and tall flaring beakers, often for Protestant churches, with a rope or spiky moulding around them about one-fifth of the way up their smooth sides, which were usually engraved. Together with spoons, these were the commonest items of production there in the seventeenth century. There was also a large number of lesser centres producing silver, including Leiden, Gouda, Sneek and Dokkum.

The Netherlands' most original contribution to the stylistic repertoire of the baroque period was the auricular; two other masters besides the van Vianens excelled at it: Johannes Lutma (1587–1669) and Thomas Bogaert (1597–1653), both working in Amsterdam. As mentioned earlier, Dutch goldsmiths were also at ease with the floral style which, like the auricular, depended on skill in chasing and embossing. There were far fewer painters designing specifically for goldsmiths than in Italy; instead the goldsmith drew in a more general way on published designs. For the technique of engraved decoration which was so popular an adornment of plain surfaces, however, they often copied work by published artists. The natural connection between graphic art and engraving in metal meant that an outstanding engraver on silver such as Michel le Blon (1587–1656) for example, was also an engraver of ornamental prints. Thus, a beaker made in Sneek in 1648 (Boymans-van-Beuningen Museum) is engraved all around with a map showing the Siege of Breda in 1637, after a print by Claes Jansz Visscher. (The Dutch were especially fond of maps at this time, and they are often shown hung on the walls of rooms in paintings.) Engraved decoration, of course, predicates silver with a plain surface, and a great deal of seventeenth-century Dutch silver is indeed completely smooth and unornamented, or just gently lobed. It is difficult to know whether or not it is the result of a purely aesthetic choice.

The southern Netherlands remained in the control of Spain, and were being strangled economically by their neighbours France and the United Provinces. They were a Catholic society dominated by the Church. France, under Louis XIV, repeatedly tried to gain control over them by diplomatic or military means.

At the beginning of the seventeenth century, goldsmiths' work of European importance was being made here, particularly in Antwerp: Rubens for example, designed a ewer and basin which were made, but which now, sadly are lost. Later in the century, however, the province ceased to be innovative, although its goldsmiths must have enjoyed a good reputation because a number of them, particularly from Liège (the capital of an independent bishopric) found work in Italy and elsewhere, a fact that also suggests that there was not enough work at home to keep them busy. The phenomenon of Flemish goldsmiths abroad deserves more research.

A great many commissions within the Province came from religious institutions, where much plate still survives. The major centres of production were Antwerp, Liège, Brussels, Bruges and Ghent. There was never any Spanish influence: rather, an old-fashioned Mannerism tended to linger as late as the 1650s, when nearly all goldsmiths began to make heavily embossed work in the floral/foliate style, the influences coming as much from France as from the United Provinces.

French influence is also evident on some silver produced in the United Provinces: embossed acanthus ornament, and heavy architectural forms with top-heavy horizontal mouldings in the Louis XIV style, appear most often in the silver made in The Hague. With Daniel Marot Berainesque ornament came to the Dutch court, and the French Huguenot style also came via London because the Stadholder, William, was King of England from 1689 to 1694. Adam Loofs (fl.1682–1710), official goldsmith and 'Keeper of the Plate' to William III, was the most important exponent of the Huguenot style. In 1707 he made a covered bowl with harp-shaped handles, cut-card work, gadrooned border and medallions in low relief on top (Gemeente Museum, The Hague), which could just as well have originated in London as The Hague. A

FOUNTAIN AND CISTERN, *silver. London, 1701–2. Maker: David Willaume. Fountains usually provided clean water and were not often used for wine. Height: 57 cm (22½ in) (Collection of the Duke of Buccleuch and Queensbury, K.T., Boughton House, Kettering)*

fashion for shallow-embossed narrow vertical fluting on the sides of vessels appeared simultaneously in London and the Netherlands in around 1700, and survived in the Netherlands until the 1730s.

The court style was taken up quickly by lesser towns in Holland, including Arnhem, Nijmegen, Zutphen, Middelburg and Maastricht, and by Leeuwarden in Friesland, whose small court looked to The Hague.

· ENGLAND ·

It is often thought that it was the English Civil War (1642–51) and the Commonwealth succeeding it that led to the production in England of very plain, 'puritan' silver. In fact, plain silver reflected an economic slump that had begun as early as the 1620s, brought about by reverses in Europe such as the Thirty Years' War, the decline of the Muscovy Company and the English war against Spain and then France. Plate was already being converted into money well before the Civil War, although not necessarily because of penury: for example, Goldsmiths' Hall was selling plate in the 1630s because it was rebuilding itself.

Throughout Charles I's reign (1625–49), highly sophisticated silver was made for the King and Court: Christian van Vianen (1600–65/7) was in England on a regular basis from 1633 onwards and from 1634 was making the chapel plate for St George's, Windsor. This was one of the greatest losses of the Civil War, looted and melted down by one Captain Fogg in 1642. Although Christian was back in Utrecht by 1645, the upheavals of the following years did not prevent some silver of

TWO-HANDLED CUP AND COVER, *silver-gilt. London, 1717–18. Maker: Pierre Platel. Engraved with the Cavendish arms impaling those of Boyle. Height: 24 cm (9½ in) (Trustees of the Chatsworth Settlement, Chatsworth, Derbyshire)*

TWO-HANDLED CUP, *(facing page) silver. London 1672–3. The maker's mark, TK above a rosette, is unidentified. This early example of the two-handled cup already shows the relatively straight sides and S-shaped handles which were to become standard. It is, however, squatter than later versions (see page 115) and has small feet on its flat lid which could serve as a stand for the cup, a reminder of the earlier practice of making porringers with salvers* en suite. *Height: 20.2 cm (8 in) (Okehampton Town Council, Okehampton)*

outstanding quality from being made. For example, throughout the war an unidentified goldsmith whose mark was a *hound sejant* was producing work in heavy-gauge silver, sometimes with elaborate auricular embossing, usually to order, and therefore only with his maker's mark (an example is a porringer at Wadham College, Oxford). His patrons were royalists and the Anglican Church for which he made much liturgical plate. At the lower end of the market the styles of English silver had become very unfashionable and unadorned by the 1630s, and this was particularly apparent in the provinces, which were reduced to making spoons and the odd plain drinking cup or communion cup.

While the decline was gradual, the recovery in silver production after 1660 was dramatic: the restoration of the monarchy brought in a new period of prosperity as the heavy taxes and fines levied by Cromwell to pay for his standing army ceased, and a new feeling of stability encouraged commercial activity. Charles II (1660–85) returned from France with an eye for French splendour; the time was ripe for foreigners to move in and supply the demand. A royal silversmith Claude de Villers, who in December 1665 received 375 *livres* from Louis XIV to reimburse him for his move back to Paris from London (but of whom there is no record in England), had possibly gone over with Charles II.[25] Christian van Vianen returned to England to be 'Silversmith in ordinary to his Matie for Chasework . . .', a position in which he was succeeded by his son-in-law, the Liègeois Jean-Gérard Cooques (d.1697).[26]

Royal support enabled foreigners to work in London despite the protests of the Goldsmiths' Company. In 1664 Jacob Bodendick of Limburg presented a royal letter to the Warden of the Company requiring it to assay and mark his work. He had a large workshop employing aliens, and the size of his output is reflected in the quantity of surviving pieces by him (such as a clustered column candlestick in the Victoria and Albert Museum, London).[27]

Foreign stylistic influences were very strong: the auricular continued in the work by Cooques; floral embossed work was adopted by many, and there were already notable, if slightly out-of-date indications of the French baroque style. For example, a candlestick in the Ashmolean Museum, Oxford, has a caryatid female on volute feet, supporting acanthus branches (unmarked, c.1680), which must have been inspired by Jean Lepautre's caryatid designs; and the suite of silver furniture made in around 1665, and in the Royal Collection (already described), also shows French influence.

English taste was thus already susceptible to the latest French fashion when, in 1688, the Glorious Revolution brought the Stadholder William to the British throne as William III. As said earlier, the Dutch court followed French fashion particularly closely, especially since the Revocation of the Edict of Nantes in 1685 drove French Protestant goldsmiths into exile from the provincial towns. In fact, the first Huguenot to seek admittance to the London Goldsmiths' Company was Pierre Harache, in 1682, and the English goldsmiths began a long process of complaining about this, as on 11 November 1683, when, incidentally it was revealed that there were over eight hundred working goldsmiths in London.[28] However, whether or not the Company granted the immigrants the right to have their pieces assayed and hallmarked they still managed to work, either as journeymen to an English goldsmith, or by paying one to submit their work in his name for assay (so that one cannot assume that the mark on a piece is that of the maker). Ultimately, many aliens, such as David Willaume, Pierre Platel, Philip Rollos and David Garnier did obtain their freedom of the Goldsmiths' Company, and their marks are well known.

The technical change brought about by these French goldsmiths was that they cast much more of their silver than they wrought, and many of their decorative effects were achieved by applying cast details to a heavy-gauge wrought body. For example, in a silver-gilt ice pail (made in 1698) by David Willaume (Chatsworth Settlement) the body is raised and the gadroons, the rim and foot, the straps around the lower part, the lions' masks and wave pattern beneath the lip are all cast. This is in no way lagging behind French fashion of the day: in 1701 a Parisian goldsmith was to make a closely similar ice bucket (private collection).[29] Indeed, the majority of surviving French goldsmiths' work of the late seventeenth and early eighteenth century is that made by the Huguenots in England, truly French pieces of this period being rare. But the immigrant craftsmen were from the provinces, and their patrons were not as sophisticated as their French counterparts.

The quantity of silver being made in London after the accession of William and Mary was such that it led to a shortage of specie (coin), the sterling standard being the same as the coinage. As a result, in 1697, an Act was passed ruling that in future the standard for plate should be eight dwt. (pennyweight) in the pound troy finer than the sterling standard (i.e. .9583 instead of .925), discouraging goldsmiths from melting coinage of the realm. This should have had the effect of reducing the size and weight of pieces of plate, but the period during which the Act was in force, that is, until 1719, coincided with that of the production of many of the largest surviving pieces of plate, such as wine coolers and fountains, so the principle that fashion is more important than financial consideration where the luxury markets are concerned must be accepted. Throughout the early eighteenth century, Huguenot goldsmiths were heavily patronized by the nobility, and leading English goldsmiths including Benjamin Pyne (fl. 1676–1732) and Thomas Jenkins (fl. 1697–?1708), worked completely in their manner.

· GERMANY ·

As an area of stylistic influence, Germany in this period meant the whole of central Europe – modern Poland, Czechoslovakia, Austria, Transylvania (now in Rumania) and Switzerland. The effect of the Thirty Years' War on silver production in the region was very marked: the number of goldsmiths in Augsburg went down from 186 in 1619 to 139 in 1646, and the town lost two-thirds of its population. Above all, the war interrupted the supply of silver, which led at times to work being produced in sub-standard metal, or even in gilt copper, and this probably also explains why much German silver of about 1640 to 1700 is rather thin in gauge, depending for its effect on elaborate embossing and chasing.

Augsburg recovered as the principal goldsmithing town in Germany remarkably quickly, however, and by the early eighteenth century its position was unassailable: in 1696 there were 204 goldsmiths working there, and in 1722 another fifty. This was for three reasons, the first being that the protracted apprenticeship and journeyman period enforced by the guild assured the competence of the individual goldsmiths. The second was that a system of goldsmith-dealers, already growing up at the end of the sixteenth century, provided a well-capitalized industry, these middlemen bearing the interim costs of large commissions, and farming the work out to specialist craftsmen. Large orders could thus be executed quickly. The third was that the goldsmithing trade was quick to collaborate with members of other crafts – painters, sculptors, clockmakers, furniture-makers and braziers – in the production of exceptional items. Braziers for example, would raise exceptionally large vessels such as wine-coolers for the goldsmiths to finish. Commissions came from patrons both secular and ecclesiastical all over Germany, and from Sweden, Denmark, and the Empire. For example, in 1647 David I Schwestermüller (fl.1628–78) made a ewer and basin for Queen Christina of Sweden to be presented to the Tsar. A display buffet of plate was made for Frederick, Elector of Brandenburg (who

DRINKING CUP *(right) in the shape of a horse, silver-gilt. Zurich, 1712. Maker: Hans Conrad Keller (fl.1691–1730). It was given to the cavalry officer Eschmann by his troops after his successes in the Toggenburg War. Height: 30 cm ($11\frac{3}{4}$ in) (Schweizerisches Landesmuseum, Zurich)*

TANKARD *(facing page, below), silver and parcel-gilt. Halle-an-der-Saale near Leipzig, late seventeenth century. The maker's mark, AH, is unidentified. Its silver decorations include a finely embossed and fretted silver sleeve. Among the foliage of the sleeve is Dido about to throw herself on the pyre. Height: 24.6 cm ($9\frac{3}{4}$ in) (Thyssen-Bornemisza Collection, Lugano)*

in 1701 became King of Prussia); it reached from floor to ceiling of the so-called Knights' Hall (the *Rittersaal*) in Berlin Castle, and some pieces of it, including two 76-cm (30-in) high pilgrim-bottles completed in 1698, are in Schloss Köpenick, East Berlin; its complete appearance is recorded in Merian's *Theatrum Europaeum* of 1703. In 1718 Augustus the Strong of Saxony commissioned a vast heavy service of double-gilt silver; and the fire-screen in Rosenborg Castle, Copenhagen, made between 1720 and 1725 by Philipp Jakob VI Drentwett (1686–1754), is just one of the many pieces supplied to the Danish court.

In the eighteenth century the commissions were remarkable for their great size, often involving tens of pieces at one time, as in table and toilet services. In the previous century they might have been of mixed materials, combining techniques in a way which satisfied the *Schatzkammer* mentality, the desire for collecting precious but non-functional objects: tankards (a very popular form during the seventeenth century) might have carved ivory bodies; table-clocks and display vessels might have enamelled and gem-set decoration; hardstone vessels were also made, as were pieces incorporating hardstones such as a tea-service by Tobias Baur (c.1660–1735) which belonged to the Landgraf of Hesse-Kassel (Staatliche Kunstsammlungen, Kassel). The enamellists, technically members of the goldsmiths' guild but in fact usually specialists in their skill, painted ornamental plaques and foliage for mounting on silver, and after 1720 also ornamented Meissen porcelain. In turn, Meissen porcelain plaques were occasionally used to ornament silver, as with the candlestands of about 1730 by Johann Engelbrecht (1673–1748) in the Residenz, Munich. Augsburg goldsmiths were also capable of producing outstanding sculptural work in silver, some of it three-dimensional and drawing on more monumental work, such as the Hercules fighting the Hydra by Albrecht Biller (1653–1720) (Städtische Kunstsammlungen, Augsburg), and some in the form of plaques, table-tops, clocks or parts of vessels. The most famous master of embossed scenes was Johann Andreas Thelott (1655–1734) who had been a journeyman in Italy. Two of his many reliefs, dated 1684 and 1685[30] respectively, and in the Victoria and Albert Museum, London, were executed while he was still apprenticed to his father.

German goldsmiths of the second half of the seventeenth century generally made much use of embossing, adapting it to a wide range of forms – zoomorphic and anthropomorphic standing cups, small flat-bottomed lobed fruit bowls with S-scroll handles, dishes, tankards, beakers and so on – but only Augsburg could have produced such an extravagant piece as the monstrance in St Maria de la Victoria, Ingolstadt, which shows the whole battle of Lepanto (1571), masts, rigging and all, around the container for the host. Also in Augsburg were skilled engravers whose work was

CANDELABRUM, *one of a pair, silver. Paris, 1709–10. Makers: Noel Duquesnoy and Louis Loir the younger. Height: 29 cm (11½ in) (Musée du Louvre, Paris)*

particularly in demand between 1680 and 1700; not surprisingly, the town continued its sixteenth-century trade of producing engraved pattern-books which spread all over Germany and, coupled with the influence of the journeymen on their travels, helped to ensure that fashions were spread quickly.

Since 'Germany' at that time was composed of many kingdoms, principalities and autonomous towns, there were dozens of goldsmithing centres, some of which made little other than spoons, cups and simple jewellery, and others of which were of real significance. Zurich, for example, produced first-rate work during the baroque period, especially drinking cups in a great variety of forms. In 1640 there were over fifty goldsmiths in the city, working for the guilds, societies and for individual patrons. Even the relatively small town of Halle near Leipzig was capable of producing work of which a London goldsmith would have been proud. Much Catholic liturgical silver of the second half of the seventeenth century was made in Cologne, Aachen, Düsseldorf and the smaller Rhenish towns, and survives in local churches. Secular silver, though rarer, was produced as well.

Munich was a major centre for goldsmiths: Marc Rosenberg, author of the primary German mark-books, lists thirty-eight marks of goldsmiths working there during the baroque period, and much of the city's production, for the churches of Bavaria and the ducal Court, was of the highest level. For Danzig, now Gdansk in Poland, he lists fifty-three masters,[31] a high proportion of whose work went to Russia. Large tankards with finely embossed sleeves were a speciality of this town. In northern Germany, Hamburg was by far the most important goldsmithing centre, its craftsmen supplying both the local, extremely prosperous market and the Danish Court, not only for its own consumption but also for presentation pieces for the Tsars. Some leading names are Dirich Utermarcke (1565–1644), who worked for Christian IV in this context in 1643, Dirich ter Moye (fl.1633–53?) who worked for Queen Christina in 1647, Heinrich Lambrecht II (fl.1649–after 1622) for Charles X in 1655; and Jürgen Richels (fl.1664–1770) for Charles XI. The best place to study Hamburg silver of the seventeenth century is in the Kremlin treasury, but pieces were also executed for the more local nobility such as the dukes of Mecklenburg-Schwerin, the Counts of Braunschweig-Lüneburg and the Electors of Saxony. The churches were important patrons as well. The most famous master of baroque liturgical silver was Jürgen Richels, who made the wonderful busts of Liborius and Meinolphus, dated 1681, in Paderborn Cathedral.

Another notable source of goldsmiths' work was Dresden: only one outstanding patron of great wealth and discrimination was necessary to elicit work of the highest quality from an exceptional artist, even though the city was not an important centre for goldsmiths in general. There Johann Melchior Dinglinger (1664–1731) was court goldsmith to Augustus the Strong of Saxony. He made the exquisite bejewelled and enamelled gold set-pieces for the Grüne Gewölbe (Green Vaults) Treasury, which were direct descendants of the Mannerist *Schatzkammer* works, but these do not really fall within the terms of this book: by the second half of the seventeenth century specialization had become so common in the goldsmithing trades of Europe that a distinction was beginning to be made between silver-workers and those who produced gold *objets-de-vertu*.

· RUSSIA, IBERIA AND NORTH · · AMERICA ·

In the seventeenth century the Russian centre of the goldsmithing trade was Moscow, where there were not only the town goldsmiths but also an association of goldsmiths working in the Armoury of the Kremlin, subject to the Tsar's court. A particularly distinguished boyar, Matveyevich Khitrovo, directed them between 1665 and 1680, and during this period attracted some very fine craftsmen. After St Petersburg was founded in 1703, many German goldsmiths moved there, bringing with them their guild traditions and soon organizing themselves into a professional body. In 1720 Peter the Great made their system mandatory for all towns in Russia. Besides Moscow and St Petersburg, lesser centres including Novgorod and Solvychegodsk also produced goldsmiths' work.

From the first, St Petersburg silver was very similar to that made in Europe, especially Germany, although often rather old-fashioned in style: for example, the seventeenth-century German pineapple-cup survived there into the mid-eighteenth century. Moscow, on the other hand, had its own style. Peculiarly Russian forms of drinking vessel were the *kovsh*, a boat-shaped dipper with a rising handle; the *bratina*, a 'welcome' cup with swelling sides, narrow neck, short foot and, sometimes, a domed cover; and the *charka*, a shallow bowl for vodka, usually on ball feet.

The Byzantine traditions of decoration were still alive: niello, a centuries-old technique of fine inlay with pulverized silver blackened by sulphur, was very popular, and so was filigree enamel in which the enamelling was applied within wire cells soldered to the surface of the metal. This was also practised in Hungary and along the Adriatic. The Orthodox Church played its part in keeping goldsmiths' work traditional, particularly as far as liturgical objects were concerned, but during the seventeenth century the Kremlin workshops, being full of immigrants, made use of every technique and some of the styles fashionable in the West, the products nevertheless being sumptuously exotic. The pea-pod style was adopted only a little later than the time of its development in France, and later in the century the naturalistic

GOSPEL COVER, *enamelled gold set with precious stones. Russia, Kremlin workshops, late seventeenth century. Makers: Mikail Vassiliev, Iona Simidel, Yuri and Stepan Nyrin, Goliach, Christian Kreimer, the diamond-cutter Dimitri Terentiev and the enamellist Yuri Froboss. It was given by Tsar Fedor Alexeivich to the Church Voskressenye Slovonrichtee in 1678. Height: 47 cm (18½ in) (Kremlin Museum, Moscow)*

floral style also flourished, either embossed, nielloed or enamelled. Most of the surviving pieces in the Kremlin were intended for the Treasury and are of gold, brilliantly enamelled and jewelled, demonstrating what an important centre Moscow was at this period, despite its isolation.

Distinctive if more humble groups of objects decorated with baroque flowers in painted enamel on silver-gilt with filigree enamel came from Solvychegodsk. This town lay on the Archangel-Siberia trade route and became a wealthy mercantile centre. The vessels (both secular and ecclesiastical) and the boxes, cutlery and buttons sometimes have large filigree compartments on them, but in any case they are covered with white enamel on which flowers and sometimes a few animals or scenes are painted in bright enamels. In the early eighteenth century the trade route moved away from Solvychegodsk, with a consequent decline in its goldsmiths' craft.

Spanish silver of this period, despite a large number of centres of production, each catering for its respective province (for example Barcelona for Catalonia), is less varied and of lesser quality than that of any other major European country. In the first half of the seventeenth century the simple massive shapes of the Herrera style (called after Philip II's architect of the Escorial) were predominant, decorated usually with engraved, flat-chased or very shallow-relief paired C-scrolls. After 1650 the floral and acanthus style began to make an impression on the decoration of objects and, indeed, became the essential ingredient of a very repetitive, all-over embossed effect which survived well into the following century: the altar frontal of the Capilla Real in Seville Cathedral, dated 1759, is in this manner. The style was exported to the New World to become the staple ornament of church silver from Peru to Mexico; a chalice in the Victoria and Albert Museum, London, made in Mexico City in the second half of the seventeenth century, combines this kind of decoration with an Herrera-style form.[32] It is not known how much Spanish secular plate survives, and very little idea of its average quality can be gained; if it was like the liturgical plate one can assume that it was hardly influenced by the European mainstream of ornament, in contrast with Spanish plate of the previous century.

More information is available about Portugal, where the leading centres of production were Lisbon and Oporto. In particular, a quantity of large circular dishes dating from the last part of the seventeenth century onwards has survived, all with heavily embossed work whose characteristic is a hard chased line around the pattern. Some have continuously scrolling floral and acanthus ornament, often combined with pecking birds; others are divided segmentally or spirally, and isolate each flower from the next with slightly childish effect. Just as the Indies (that is, India and the Far East) influenced styles in furniture and faience, so also was silverware affected, and small, savage, primitively drawn animals and dragons of Eastern form occur. Portugal adopted many more of the styles fashionable in the rest of Europe than did Spain: small deep bowls with cast S-scroll handles, lobing at the top and conventional acanthus and floral embossing beneath correspond closely to English brandy-bowls (it is uncertain which way the influence went in this case), and early eighteenth-century dishes, ewers and basins which differ little from Huguenot forms.

In North America, while there were silversmiths in Boston in the 1630s, and in Philadelphia and New York by the 1680s, the earliest surviving work by truly North American goldsmiths dates from the 1650s; it is by John Hull (1624–83) and Robert Sanderson (1608–93) and is preserved mostly in New England churches. Their work could easily be taken for that by silversmiths working in England, and indeed during the baroque period English styles were generally dominant in the colonies except in New York (called New Amsterdam until it became an English royal province in 1685), where some Netherlandish forms were followed by the mainly Netherlandish silversmithing community there. For example, while a pair of candlesticks and snuffer-stand by Cornelius Kierstede, are, apart from the double-headed eagle on the snuffers, in a style which is as much English as Netherlandish, he also made a teapot with a broad flat bottom and elaborate bird's-head spout which is very much in the Netherlandish style (both Metropolitan Museum of Art, New York). Other specifically Netherlandish forms are a tall flaring beaker with engraved sides, such as the Communion beaker with Faith, Hope and Charity by Jakob Boelen (c.1645–1728) in the New Utrecht Reformed Church, Brooklyn, which looks like pieces fashionable in Europe in the 1640s. Low, gently panelled or lobed two-handled bowls with cast S-scroll handles, often embossed or engraved with single flowers on each lobe, were also made in New York at the end of the seventeenth and in the early eighteenth century; these may well derive from the Groningen brandy bowl. A hybrid English and Dutch influence can be seen in New York tankards, which in form are typically English but often have a narrow base-band of stiff, upstanding acanthus leaves, and which are also sometimes inset with coins, which was not an English practice.

Overall, very little American silver with elaborate embossing survives, perhaps reflecting the silversmiths' level of skill, perhaps the parsimony and tastes of their patrons. A great deal of it is engraved, however, often drawing on European printed sources, as with a tankard of about 1725, again by Cornelius Kierstede (Winterthur Museum), engraved with arms borrowed from Guillim's *Display of Heraldry* (London, 1724). It was made for the Still family, who filched the arms belonging to the Dowager Lady Jane Still, but used them in a lozenge (which was only appropriate for a woman).

The grandest surviving piece, both from the point of view of size and of sophistication, is a monteith 28 cm (11 in) in diameter made in about 1710 by the Boston silversmith John Coney (1655–1722), in the Yale University Art Gallery. This bowl reflects the pre-eminent position of Boston as a centre of silversmithing: its lower half has the narrow flutes fashionable in England from around 1700, while the top is decorated with finely chased cast ornamentation consisting of scrolling pediments, masks, vases and rosettes on a background embossed with acanthus leaves. It is a highly skilled piece of work. Such large-scale plate was, however, very rare in America at this time; candlesticks are also rare, but this may be an accident of survival. Otherwise the forms of American plate surviving are beakers, two-handled bowls or porringers, spoons, tankards, sugar boxes, casters, salts, coffee-, tea- and chocolate-pots, salvers, sugar bowls, standing cups, baptismal bowls and two-handled covered cups.

RELIQUARY *(facing page), silver and silver-gilt. Spain, Saragossa, c.1665. Maker's mark, a lion with CES, unidentified. Height: 62.5 cm (25 in) (Victoria and Albert Museum, London)*

COMMUNION CUP *(above), silver. New England, c.1674. Makers: John Hull and Robert Sanderson. A very early surviving work by North American goldsmiths. Height: 18.5 cm ($7\frac{1}{4}$ in) (Yale University Art Gallery, New Haven)*

· 5 · THE ROCOCO ·

At the beginning of the eighteenth century, France, the arbiter of fashion, was witness to a growing disillusion with the intellectual and artistic tenets of the *grand siècle*. Louis XIV outlived the art and society he created, and his subjects, tired of the monumental splendour of the baroque, turned to art forms calculated to delight rather than to awe. The first stirrings of a new style in France coincided with the death of the Regent, Philippe d'Orléans, in 1723. The style was new in the sense that it abandoned the solid and often ponderous baroque and introduced lightness and freedom, hitherto scarcely seen in the decorative arts.

The term 'rococo', by which the style is now universally known, was not used in France where it was called *le genre pittoresque*, even though the word 'rococo' derives from the French *rocaille*. A strictly literal translation of that word would limit it to rocks and stones whereas, in the context of the new style, it also embraced a watery world of caves and grottoes and their strange denizens. Caves were the earliest shrines of the gods of antiquity and fountains were associated with the sacred springs of the Greeks and Romans immortalized by the Latin poets. The swirling movement of water is the essence of the rococo style, a movement expressed not only in decoration but in the very form of objects. This latter aspect of the rococo was somewhat revolutionary, being at variance with the established rule that shape should be based strictly on function; practical considerations were in fact sometimes compromised in the pursuit of the new ethos.

· MEISSONNIER ·

Although such a drastic departure from well-tried forms is unlikely to have been the work of one person, the accolade for the introduction of the rococo is usually reserved for Juste-Aurèle Meissonnier. The son of Etienne (Stefano) Meissonnier, a goldsmith of Provençal origin living in Italy, Juste-Aurèle was born in Turin in 1695. He was apprenticed, it is believed, to his father who presumably taught him the basic principles of drawing and design. He may have benefited from a family contact with the painter Jean-Baptiste van Loo, though it is unlikely that they were fellow apprentices. Less tenuous is the possibility of a link with the great Italian architect Filippo Juvarra, who also came from a family of goldsmiths and received his earliest training in that craft. Juvarra was the director of all artistic enterprises at the Piedmontese Court from 1714 until 1735, and it is probable that Meissonnier met him in Turin.

Meissonnier's decision to leave Italy and work in France may have been influenced by an order received from the French government in 1715 for a medal (his first recorded commission was for the cutting of steel dies for coins for the Kingdom of Savoy). By 1720, possibly earlier, he was settled in Paris and by 1723 he was sufficiently well established to receive a prestigious order for a silver wine-cooler (no longer extant) from Louis-Henri de Bourbon, Prince de Condé, or Monsieur le Duc as he was known at the French Court. An engraving by Huquier shows the wine-cooler to have been very close in style to the designs for late baroque silver by Filippo Juvarra. There is, however, a hint of a rococo spiral in the bodies of the nereids which form the handles, and their many-planed surface reflects the light in such a way as to suggest movement.

On 28 September 1724 Meissonnier became a master goldsmith by a special brevet of Louis XV. Although in the King's service, he made very few pieces himself and most of them have vanished and are known only from contemporary engravings. He was essentially a designer as opposed to an all-round craftsman; he is also described in French documents as a *ciseleur*, or chaser. The art of modelling is closely allied to designing and chasing and it is likely that he excelled in all three. As a designer – a designer of genius – he was a source of inspiration for two generations of goldsmiths. In 1726 he was appointed *Dessinateur de la Chambre et du Cabinet du Roi*, a post he was to keep until his death. He was required to design settings for Court festivities and such diverse articles for the Royal Family as silver plate and decorative panels. His duties were not so onerous as to prevent him

CUP AND COVER *(facing page), silver-gilt. London, 1745–6. Maker: Paul de Lamerie. The London goldsmith Paul de Lamerie, with his Huguenot background, was ideally equipped to interpret Meissonnier's innovations. French rococo influence is visible in his work as early as the 1720s. Here his complete mastery of the rococo style is apparent in the chased decoration. The fantastical helmets so often worn by his putti here take the form of shells; these children have gossamer wings and, clutching bunches of grapes, they emerge from a frame, part scroll, part cartouche. Grapes form the finial, which is surmounted by a small reptile, and the vine motif is repeated on the body of the cup, interspersed with naturalistic flowers. Lion and cherub masks adorn the lid. The scrolled handles are capped with shells. Height: 36 cm (14 in) (Sotheby Parke Bernet, London)*

SATIRICAL PRINT, *London, 1759. It is remarkable for English familiarity with French designers and goldsmiths: the names of Meissonier and Germain appear on objects, presumably instantly recognizable by those buying the satire. (British Museum, London)*

pursuing his ambition to gain a reputation as an architect. The concept of the all-round artist, the Renaissance man, was still alive in France and, moreover, the status of an architect was superior to that of a goldsmith, however gifted.

It is as 'J. Maissonnier [sic] Architecte' that he signed a triple design for a candlestick, the *Chandeliers de Sculptures en Argent* (engraved by Desplaces), dated 1728. This candlestick represents the beginning of a complete departure from the *Régence* style. The broken rococo scrolls are there, encircling two putti who are themselves part of a very definite spiral curve which rises from a base made asymmetrical by cascading water. A hint of the twisted stem had in fact appeared a year earlier in a monstrance made for the Carmelites at Poitiers, which Meissonnier described, aptly, as a *soleil* (a synonym for the French word for a monstrance, *ostensoir*). As with so much of his work, this piece is known only from engravings.

The most inspired of all his creations has, however, miraculously survived – a pair of tureens commissioned by an English nobleman, the Duke of Kingston, in 1735. (One is now in the collection of Baron Thyssen, the other in the Cleveland Museum of Art, Ohio.) Asymmetry is the keynote, and Meissonnier's use of it is completely new and original. The tureens are cast in the shape of large shells over which the sea swirls restlessly. Even the ornament – an incongruous *mélange* of crustacea, game and vegetables – appears to be tossed upwards and caught in vestiges of sea foam as the wave recedes. This constant state of movement is essential to the rococo style, and it either delights or appals. In 1734, when Meissonnier's designs first began to be published, a brief but complimentary review appeared in the *Mercure de France*. Such prints, according to the writer, ought to stimulate the curiosity of the public and all those interested in 'the best taste':

> They include fountains, cascades, ruins, Rocailles and Coquillages, examples of architecture which have effects that are bizarre, unusual and pittoresque, by their piquant and extraordinary forms, in which often one part does not correspond to the other, though the subject appears no less rich and agreeable.

This was by no means the consensus, and derogatory views began to appear in print from the 1740s onward. The discrepancy in scale between the ornamental motifs was a constant affront to logic as well as to the French respect for order; its emotional impact was disturbing, for it surprised and delighted, unlike the baroque style which was reassuringly monumental and predictable; and exception was taken to the use of mundane rather than exalted motifs for ornaments. So indoctrinated was the French intelligentsia with the principles of rationalism that the full-blown rococo on its own terms was unacceptable for many. It is significant that Meissonnier never became a member of the French Academy, and after his death on 31 July 1750 the notice that appeared in the

Mercure de France in October that year was not so much an obituary as a diatribe against his pursuit of novelty. No one saw fit to comment on the originality of his thought nor his gifts as a designer.

· BESNIER, BALLIN AND THE GERMAINS ·

Meissonnier's critics were proved wrong: the rococo was not a transient pursuit of novelty but an expression of a fundamental aesthetic need which has stood the test of time. In the 1720s two of the finest goldsmiths of the Louis XIV and *Régence* periods were already prepared to embrace the new style: Nicolas Besnier and Claude II Ballin, both in the service of the young king Louis XV. Few of their rococo pieces have survived the infamous melting of plate ordered by Louis XV in 1759 to pay for the Seven Years' War, but a superb *pot-à-oille* made by Besnier for Horace Walpole, English ambassador to Paris from 1723 to 1729, still exists in a private collection; although traditional and architectural in form, the tentative emergence of the new style is clearly visible. Claude II Ballin was sixty-six years old in 1726 when he fashioned his celebrated rococo *surtout à table* for the Russian Court, now in the Hermitage Museum in Leningrad. His mastery of the style is also evident in his candelabra of 1739 in the Cooper-Hewitt Museum, New York. While his readiness to adopt the lightness and fluid curves of the rococo is apparent in these prestigious pieces, Ballin did not subscribe wholeheartedly to the new ornamental motifs. According to the writer of his obituary in the *Mercure* in 1754, 'he was often heard to complain that good taste would be lost and beautiful forms spoiled by substituting for the sensible ornaments of the ancients lobsters and rabbits which, he said, were not suitable for the decoration of silver'.

Thomas Germain, the greatest French rococo goldsmith, immortalized by Voltaire in *Les Vous et les Tu*, was not of this opinion. The ornament on the lids of many of his tureens owes much to Meissonnier; one notable example (in a private collection), a tureen with boar's-head handles made in 1734, appears in several still-life paintings by Desportes.

Although, like Meissonnier, Germain came from a family of goldsmiths, he first studied painting. While still young he went to Rome, where he worked under a goldsmith. During his years in Italy he was mainly employed on ecclesiastical commissions in the late baroque style, and he continued to work on church plate after his return to France in 1706: among his most important pieces were a silver-gilt monstrance and a gilt copper altar-set consisting of a crucifix and six candlesticks for Notre Dame in Paris. In 1720 he was received as a master goldsmith; three years later he was granted apartments in the Louvre and listed, with Nicolas Besnier and Claude II Ballin, as *Orfèvre du Roi*. From then until his death in 1748 Germain was employed in making a large variety of splendid objects in gold and silver for the King and the Royal Family. With a few exceptions, these pieces are known only from contemporary engravings and entries in the royal inventories which fortunately describe the rococo decoration in some detail. The *Journal du Garde-Meuble* left for posterity a graphic and loving description of the legendary gold sunflower candelabra which Germain completed just before his death. Encapsulated in the description are many of the main elements of the rococo: asymmetry, naturalistic flowers, putti, spiral movement and broken scrolls.

Small creatures also appear on many of Germain's pieces: a snail emerges from the grapes and vine leaves decorating a pair of wine-coolers of 1727 in the Louvre; a salt cellar of 1734–6 (also in the Louvre) is composed of a tortoise, a crab and a scallop fashioned so realistically that they might have been cast from the actual shell and carapaces. These latter are hinged and cover receptacles for salt and spices. Two wide scrolls – a legacy of the baroque – form the base, adding to a certain heaviness in the composition. A very similar tortoise appears on the title page of Jacques de Lajoue's *Second Livre de Cartouches* published in Paris in about 1734. It is probable, however, that the tortoise motif was original to Germain who had used it in a more light-hearted vein on an earlier occasion: several of these engaging small reptiles peer out from the base of the famous hunting *surtout* of 1729–31. This magnificent centrepiece was commissioned by the Duke of Aveiro but following his execution was sequestrated by the King of Portugal in 1759; it is now in the Museu Nacional de Arte Antigua in Lisbon.

Thomas Germain, like Meissonnier, also practised as an architect, but it was as a goldsmith that he had long been held in great esteem by the Portuguese monarch who commissioned from him large quantities of fine table silver and church plate. On Germain's death in 1748 the King ordered a requiem mass to be celebrated for him.

Thomas Germain was succeeded by his son François-Thomas who, at the age of twenty-two, not only inherited his father's models together with his huge atelier and workforce, but also his royal and aristocratic clients. Appointed goldsmith to Louis XV in 1748, François-Thomas followed the Germain tradition of fashioning high rococo silver. He has been criticized for putting his name to work bearing his father's maker's mark and for using models designed by Thomas, but the pieces indisputably from his hand are fine enough to secure him a great and lasting reputation.

During the decade following the disastrous Lisbon earthquake of 1755, he was hard at work on pieces commissioned by the Portuguese Court to replace its lost treasures (many of them masterpieces fashioned by his father). The famous salts of 1760 in the form of small boys clad in diminutive feather skirts and head-dresses were meant to

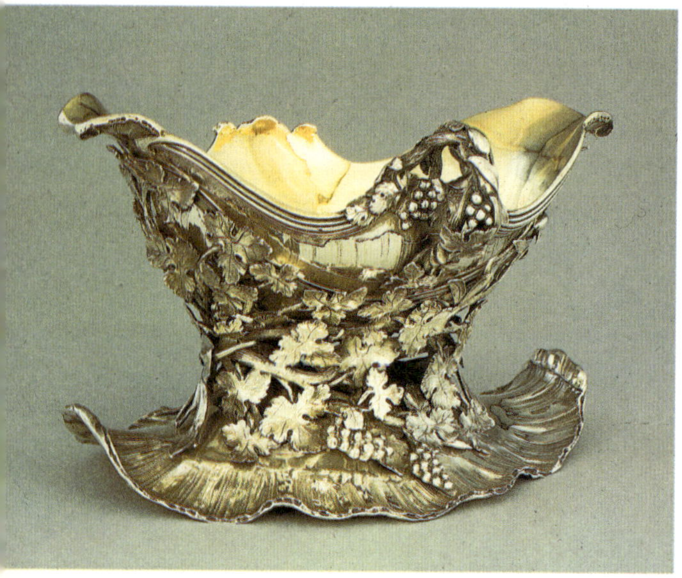

SAUCEBOAT AND STAND, *silver, Paris, 1762. Maker: Jean-Baptiste-François Chéret. The gondola outline and vine decoration recall the sauceboats made by François Joubert for Madame de Pompadour in 1754. Chéret has introduced naturalism with gnarled vine-branch handles. Height: 12.1 cm (4¾ in) (J. Paul Getty Museum, Malibu)*

TUREEN, COVER AND STAND, *one of a pair, silver. Paris, 1734–40. Designer: Juste-Aurèle Meissonnier, 1734–6; makers: Henry Adnet and Pierre-François Bonnestrenne. This well-documented tureen, designed by the great innovator Meissonnier, was commissioned by the second Duke of Kingston in 1735. It epitomizes the essential elements of a high rococo object. The sheer audacity of such works invoked a storm of protest from some French critics accustomed to the solidity and logic of the Baroque. Even so, avant-garde patrons and goldsmiths of the calibre of Thomas Germain and Jacques Roettiers enthusiastically espoused the new ideas. Height: 37.9 cm (15 in) (The Cleveland Museum of Art, Cleveland, Ohio)*

evoke the King's Indian subjects in Brazil. The rococo's insistence on swirling lines can be seen in three elegant coffee jugs made between 1758 and 1760, and now in the Museu Nacional de Arte Antigua in Lisbon; a similar but not identical jug is in the Metropolitan Museum of New York. It is as though François-Thomas Germain swathed the jugs in elegant fluting drawn out in a spiral movement from base to neck. The spouts and handles, formed of coffee leaves and berries, have a rare charm. Only the rococo could have made acceptable a dish-cover in the form of overlapping cabbage leaves, their etiolated stems shaped into a finial. In François-Thomas Germain's hands it became an object worthy of a royal table (Museu Nacional de Arte Antigua, Lisbon).

Germain's reputation brought him orders from Russia. The francophile Czarina Elisabeth commissioned a great dinner service, as well as three putti centrepieces, to celebrate, it is said, a Russian victory over Frederick the Great at Kunesdorf in 1759. The service is now in the Hermitage Museum and one centrepiece is in the Gulbenkian Collection in Lisbon (the other two are believed to be still in Russian hands).

Thomas Germain's reputation for integrity was known far and wide, but his son seems to have been a far less stable character. Apart from his extravagance, he lacked the good sense of his father in business dealings. In 1765 he was declared bankrupt and dismissed from his post as royal goldsmith. At the age of thirty-nine his brilliant career was over: he died in obscurity in 1791.

· THE COUSINETS, DURAND, JOUBERT · · AND THEIR FELLOW GOLDSMITHS ·

The other rococo goldsmiths working in Paris were not eclipsed by the Germains. Although much of their *oeuvre* was consigned to the melting pot by royal decree in 1759 and most of the remaining pieces destroyed at the time of the French Revolution, enough has somehow survived to prove their mastery. Henri-Nicolas Cousinet is remembered for the sumptuous *nécessaire* or toilet set in silver-gilt which he made for Queen Marie Leczinska in 1729 to celebrate the birth of the Dauphin. The dolphin – *dauphin* in French – symbolized the heir to the French throne and appears as a decorative motif on silver associated with him. The feet and spout on the chocolate pot in this travelling toilet set are fashioned as dolphins. In 1757 Cousinet's brother, Ambroise-Nicolas, made sixteen enchanting rococo statuettes which once belonged to the ill-fated Duke of Aveiro. Looking just like silver-gilt Meissen figurines, their outstretched arms may well have been designed to hold festoons of real flowers. This delicate alternative to the *surtout à table* was sequestrated by the Portuguese king, and it is now in the Museu Nacional de Arte Antigua, Lisbon.

Antoine-Sébastien Durand was one of the goldsmiths patronized by Madame de Pompadour. In 1750 he made for her a graceful pair of mustard containers, each in the shape of a barrel set upon a wheelbarrow guided by a winged boy. This set, with its original case, is in the Gulbenkian

TUREEN AND STAND, *one of a pair, silver. Paris, 1744–50. Maker: Thomas Germain. Much of the work of the great French eighteenth-century goldsmith Thomas Germain perished in the Lisbon earthquake of 1755 or was lost through the infamous melting down of plate to finance the Seven Years War, and is known to us only through contemporary documents. These surviving pieces bear testimony not only to the excellence of Thomas Germain's work, but also to his debt to Meissonnier whose influence is visible in the tureen finial formed as a cast and chased lobster and crab surmounted by a cauliflower. Diameters: tureen 27 cm (10½ in); stand 46 cm (18 in) (Christies, Geneva)*

Foundation, Lisbon; an almost identical single group is in the Musée des Arts Décoratifs in Paris The same sulky little boy, in the guise of an infant triton, forms the handle of the silver-gilt ewer which Durand made in 1752. The bulrushes from which the triton emerges symbolize water and were a favourite motif of artists and designers in the rococo period. Their presence on ewers was almost mandatory, underlining the purpose of the vessel. The irregular border of the matching shaving basin ripples with wavelets, giving the impression of constant movement. The winged cartouche, part of the baroque repertoire, seems strangely out of place in this rococo setting. (Both pieces form part of the collection of the Museu Nacional de Arte Antigua in Lisbon.) In 1754 Antoine-Sébastien Durand fashioned an extraordinary dish-cover, with no less than seven recognizable species of fish, eel and crustacea decorating the top, as though some fisherman has emptied his catch over it. This, too, can be seen in Lisbon, at the Gulbenkian Foundation. A salt made by Durand in 1757 is static in comparison: a reclining putto watches sedately over two shell salt and pepper containers, the upper halves of the shells hinged to form lids: it is in the possession of the Philadelphia Museum of Art.

François Joubert also received commissions from Madame de Pompadour. The pair of gondola-shaped sauceboats he made for her in 1754 (now in the Musée des Arts décoratifs, Paris) must be counted among the masterpieces of French

TUREEN, *one of a pair, silver. Rome, 1766–8. Maker: Vincenzo I Belli. Belli was born in Turin in 1710. Situated close to the border between France and Italy, Turin was strongly influenced by French trends. Belli's feeling for French* rocaille *was combined with the taste for Italian baroque which he acquired after his move to Rome in 1741. This* bombé-*shaped tureen is chased with bacchanalian and grotesque masks and surmounted by a finial in the form of a chantecler and hen. Diameter: 27 cm ($10\frac{5}{8}$ in) (Christies, Geneva)*

rococo for their exuberance and decorative audacity. The rocky bases are sharply modelled – *rocaille* in the literal sense – and the chasing is particularly fine. The choice of grapes and olives as decorative motifs suggests that these pieces were used for serving a vinaigrette sauce. A fine tureen by Joubert (now in the Louvre) has a lid decorated with an artichoke, pea-pods, mushrooms, a crayfish and a lizard, an indication that Meissonnier's designs were still in fashion and being used as late as 1761.

To these names should be added that of Louis Regnard, who appears to have made a speciality of the helix form as early as 1733, and Guillaume Egée, who also favoured this fashion, judging by his mustard-pot of 1748 in the Metropolitan Museum of Art, New York. Charles Spire has left to posterity a particularly fine shell-bowl soup-ladle of 1753 and an elegant ewer with a handle formed as a nereid. The chased bulrushes and the grapes held by the nereid indicate the vessel's dual role as a container for water as well as wine. Both these pieces were lately in the Collection of Madame A. Lopez-Willshaw. Louis Joseph Lenhendrick, who was apprenticed to Thomas Germain, made some fine pieces, as did Alexis III Loir, Guillaume le Doux, Jean Fauche, Edmé-Pierre Balzac (who excelled in animal dish-covers of a ferocious naturalism), Antoine Bailly, Etienne-Jacques Marcq and Eloi Guerin, the latter named possibly after St Eloi, the patron saint of French goldsmiths.

As in most countries, some time elapsed before the new style was adopted in the provinces. Among the earliest pieces is a duck-spout teapot with helix decoration and a flower finial made in Bordeaux in 1739–41 by Gabriel Tillet. Adrien Dachery of St Quentin made a similar one in 1754–6. Mustard-pots have survived in some numbers: there is one of helix form with a certain hint of the rococo in its decoration in the Metropolitan Museum of Art in New York, made by Ennemond Ruynat of Grenoble in 1753, as well as a small *chef d'oeuvre* by Mathieu Bouvier of Trévoux, Lyons, dating from 1748, which has a merry little lid in the form of a sleeping-cap complete with tassel. *Ecuelles* with matching dishes were particularly popular in Strasbourg in the late 1760s and throughout the next decade; decorated with finials shaped as artichokes, pomegranates and roses, they were made by Jacques Henri Alberti, Fritz, Jean-Jacques Kirstein and Ludwig III Imlin, all working in Strasbourg. Philippe Laforgue of Toulouse was also making rococo *écuelles* in 1759, as was Louis Landes as late as 1774 (an *écuelle* of that date is now in the Metropolitan Museum, New York). Pepper boxes with shell lids were also produced in Toulouse, notably by Jean Affre and Etienne Barrau.

So little church plate has survived the French Revolution that it is difficult to assess the influence of the rococo upon it. Altar silver was usually supplied by such specialist makers as Guillaume Jacob, Alexis Porcher and Guillaume Loir. The Abbey Church of Saint Sever (Landes) chose, however, to commission its altar vessels from a secular goldsmith, Michel II Delapierre, and the pieces he fashioned were unmistakably rococo. The ewer-shaped cruets, which could easily have graced an elegant toilet set, are differentiated by their decorative motifs: bulrushes for water, grapes for wine. Bulrushes are also chased on an ornate bowl while the chalice is entwined with vine leaves, tendrils and grapes.

· PIERRE GERMAIN AND JACQUES · · ROETTIERS ·

Another important goldsmith of the period was Pierre Germain. He does not appear to have been related to Thomas and François-Thomas Germain although, after an apprenticeship with Nicolas Besnier, he worked in his time for both of them. One of the few surviving pieces bearing his mark is a handsome cruet of 1774 in the Louvre. His *Eléments d'Orfèvrerie*, published in Paris in 1748, and for which he is best remembered, consisted of a hundred rococo designs for goldsmiths. They were not all original to him but were gathered from the leading goldsmiths of the day. A few of them reached such heights of fantasy that it is unlikely that they were ever translated into silver without some modification. Except for important commissions requiring detailed sketches, goldsmiths do not appear to have worked rigidly to patterns or published designs. They chose instead to adapt them to their individual requirements, bending them to their own style and thereby producing a series of variations on a theme. Pierre Germain's book is important because it shows the kinds of pieces being fashioned in France at the height of the rococo period, and which no longer exist, since they were melted down by royal decree in 1759 or destroyed during the French Revolution.

In his preface to the *Eléments d'Orfèvrerie* Pierre Germain pointed out that some of the designs (seven in all) were the work of Jacques Roettiers, pieces commissioned by the Dauphin on which the goldsmith was actually working at the time of publication. Roettiers, born in France in 1707, came of a well-known and unusually well-documented Antwerp family of medallists, and his father had worked for the English Court. The young Roettiers travelled to England in 1731, but was back in Paris by 1733, when he was admitted to the Goldsmiths' Corporation even though he appears not to have served a formal apprenticeship. He did, however, spend some time in the ateliers of both Thomas Germain and Nicolas Besnier, whose daughter he married in 1734. That same year Besnier was appointed director of the Beauvais tapestry factory; this left him little time to devote to the manufacture of silver, so, in 1737, his mantle fell on his son-in-law the goldsmith Jacques Roettiers.

Few pieces from the latter's hand have survived, but his superb 168-piece dinner service, commissioned in 1735 by the Berkeley family, was safely housed in England at Berkeley Castle and remained there for more than two centuries. The decision to place such an important order with a French rather than an English goldsmith was almost certainly influenced by the fact that the Berkeley family had strong ties with France: the third earl's wife Louise was the grand-daughter of Charles II's mistress Louise de Kéroual, duchesse d'Aubigny.

The service, now in the Stavros Niarchos Collection, was made between 1735 and 1738. It is not yet full-blown rococo: the exuberant crayfish and vegetables which decorate the lids of the tureens and *pots-à-oille* are clearly based on Meissonnier's *Livre de Légumes*, but the outlines are still transitional; the candlesticks are, in fact, *Régence* in style. The finely wrought trefoil spice containers, however, are undoubtedly rococo, with sea waves rippling round their bowls and revolving covers formed as intricate exquisitely chased shells. Roettiers went on to make pieces that were clearly high-rococo masterpieces, judging by the description of one of his centrepieces in the *Mercure de France* in July 1749.

The time was fast approaching when Paris would espouse a new fashion and abandon *le genre pittoresque* in favour of *le goût grec*, or neoclassicism. Roettiers, with his fellow goldsmiths, turned with the tide.

WINE-COOLER, *one of a pair, silver-gilt. London, 1733–4. Maker: Paul Crespin. French* Régence *influence is clear in the architectural form of this wine-cooler, but an early awareness of rococo ornament is apparent in Crespin's use of marine and floral decorative motifs and the asymmetrical cartouche supported by amorini. A characteristic rococo spiral movement is already present in the satyr handles presenting a many-planed surface suggesting movement through the interplay of light.*
Height: 32 cm ($12\frac{1}{2}$ in) (Blenheim Palace, Woodstock, Oxon.)

· THE ROCOCO IN ENGLAND ·

Silver in England in the first quarter of the eighteenth century appeared set to continue in the tranquil serenity of the plain, elegant style known colloquially today as 'Queen Anne'. It seemed peculiarly English in its restraint and unlikely to be superseded by anything so foreign, wayward or fantastical as the rococo, but, paradoxically, the rococo took England by storm. English goldsmiths adopted the new style with great enthusiasm. Accustomed to following French trends and quite uninhibited about borrowing, they set about collecting French prints and pattern books to furnish the forms and decorative motifs essential to the new fashion, and then proceeded to adapt them to their own needs, at the same time investing their pieces with a vitality often lacking in French work.

Engravings of Meissonnier's designs were available in Paris from 1734 and would have reached London very soon afterwards, but by the early 1720s the first hint of the rococo in England could be seen in the work of the great Huguenot innovator Paul de Lamerie. De Lamerie's parents had fled France as a result of the religious persecution of Protestants which followed the revocation of the Edict of Nantes in 1685. Paul was born in 's Hertogenbosch in the Low Countries in 1688, but was brought to London when his parents decided to settle in England in 1691. The Huguenot goldsmiths, though removed from France, remained instinctively attuned to all things French; their traditional use of casting techniques, moreover, lent itself to the exigencies of the new style and gave them an advantage over English craftsmen.

By 1732 de Lamerie's advancing grasp of the rococo idiom is demonstrated in a remarkable cup and cover.[1] Its extraordinary handles, each surmounted by a putto leaning backwards, one foot poised in mid-air, flow into grotesque masks reminiscent of the grisly ornament, known as auricular, favoured by the van Vianens and other seventeenth-century Dutch goldsmiths. With that fine disdain for congruity which typifies the exponent of the rococo style, de Lamerie has mingled here many of its main elements: marine motifs in the form of shells and fish scales, masks, festoons of naturalistic fruit and flowers, grapes and vine leaves, terms and putti. The last two are so modelled that they present many planes to the light, giving the illusion of constant movement which is the essence of the rococo.

De Lamerie was closely followed by his fellow Huguenot Paul Crespin. Although the silver-gilt wine-coolers he made for the Duke of Marlborough in 1733, now in the collection of the present duke, are still architectural in form, the satyr handles already show a definite suggestion of a spiral. The waves swirling beneath the feet of the satyrs, the masks above the floral festoons and the asymmetrical cartouche supported by amorini are also wholly rococo. Crespin's use of marine motifs is highly individual. His inkstand of 1739 in the Duke of Devonshire's collection is composed of realistic shells to hold ink and pounce – the fine powder used to prevent ink from spreading on unsized paper – set on a shell-strewn tray resting on dolphin feet. It is interesting to compare it with one made by de Lamerie in 1738 for the Duke of Marlborough. Despite the artistic assurance of the latter, Crespin's inkstand is visually more exciting; his stark coral branch in the centre makes the pouting boy in de Lamerie's piece look positively insipid.

The goldsmiths mostly followed the orders of those patrons who kept a close eye on the latest

EWER AND BASIN *(right and far right), silver-gilt. London, 1735–6 (Basin only; ewer: maker's mark struck four times). Maker: George Wickes. Two of the most original and historically important pieces of early English full-blown rococo silver, this ewer and basin were commissioned by the Common Council of the Corporation of Bristol for presentation to the City's Recorder John Scrope; records of manufacture and donation survive. Wickes's awareness of French designs is evident, particularly in the left-hand cartouche in the centre of the basin, which derives from a print of Jacques de Lajoue published in about 1734, and in the male mask on the body of the ewer, which owes much to Gaetano Brunetti. Diameter of basin: 55.2 cm (21¾ in); height of ewer: 36.2 cm (14¼ in) (Private collection)*

trends, keeping pace with flights of fancy which at times bordered on the nightmarish. The snakes that writhe around the covered cups made by Paul de Lamerie in 1737 and 1739 (the former now in the possession of the Worshipful Company of Fishmongers) pale beside the grotesque dragon which forms the handle of an unmarked sauce-boat, circa 1740 (possibly earlier), in the Ashmolean Museum at Oxford, or Kandler's triple dragon brazier of 1741 in the Metropolitan Museum of Art, New York. Such chimerae can be found in the designs of Gaetano Brunetti whose *Sixty Different Sorts of Ornaments Very Usefull to Painters, Sculptors, Stone-Carvers, Silversmiths Etc.* was published in Paris in 1736. They are in fact part of the marine repertoire of the rococo, denizens of caves and grottoes; they appear to have been seldom adopted as motifs by the French goldsmiths. Frederick Kandler, working in London, also excelled in handles cast as fierce sea birds; they peer down into his sauceboats of 1737 and 1742, also in the Ashmolean Museum.

· THE CARTOUCHE AND OTHER · · MOTIFS ·

The cartouche, which had served merely to enclose armorials in previous centuries, became in the rococo period not only a decorative motif in its own right but also a frame for classical vignettes. Its importance is reflected in the large number of eighteenth-century French pattern books devoted exclusively to the cartouche. Cartouche designs by Watteau, Boucher, Brunetti and de Lajoue were available to the English goldsmiths. They also had easy access to *A New Book of Sheilds usefull for all sorts of Artificers*, published in London in the 1750s by the Augsburg goldsmith Augustin Heckel, who was considered one of the finest chasers of eighteenth-century London.

George Wickes made effective use of the cartouches designed by the Frenchman Jacques de Lajoue. In 1735 Wickes availed himself of one of the cartouche designs in de Lajoue's *Second Livre de Cartouches*, published in Paris a year earlier, to decorate a silver-gilt ewer and basin commissioned by the City of Bristol (private collection). This particular cartouche was to remain in the repertoire of Wickes's firm for many years; his Works Manager Edward Wakelin had it engraved on his tray of 1750, now at Colonial Williamsburg, and on a tea caddy of 1751. His fellow goldsmith James Shruder found inspiration in the title page of de Lajoue's *Second Livre de Cartouches*, using the rearing sea horse as a spout for a high rococo coffee pot of 1749 and a matching tea-kettle. He also made effective use of a boat cartouche and dolphins from de Lajoue's *Recueil Nouveau de Differens Cartouches*. Shruder was himself a designer – his trade-card bears his signature: the batwing ornament above it appears in the feathering on the feet of the coffee pot.

The borrowed designs, when engraved on silver, are occasionally found to be reversed images of the original print (possibly because they were issued in that form). The goldsmiths were not alone in recognizing the decorative value of the cartouche – it appears in architecture, furniture and ceramics, and was widely used by the craftsmen of the period for their trade-cards.

COFFEE POT, *silver. London, 1749–50. Maker: James Shruder. Crests and heraldic devices were occasionally incorporated in the design of a piece of silver, often as finials or handles. Here the sea horse, which figures prominently in the armorials of its original owner Leake Okeover, forms the spout. Jacques de Lajoue's designs provided the inspiration for the spout, the boat cartouche and the sportive dolphins. Unlike many rococo pieces which carry a plethora of incongruous conceits, the inspiration here is wholly marine. Height: 28 cm (11 in) (Victoria and Albert Museum, London)*

DESIGN FOR A CARTOUCHE *(below), etching and engraving, 1734. François Joullain after Jacques de Lajoue. James Shruder used this cartouche design in the form of a sailing boat to great effect on his coffee pot of 1749 (left). Dimensions: 22 × 18.7 cm ($8\frac{3}{4} \times 7\frac{1}{2}$ in) Victoria and Albert Museum, London)*

TUREEN *(facing page), silver, by John Parker and Edward Wakelin, London, c.1760 (maker's mark only). In both form and ornament this tureen illustrates French influence on London goldsmiths. Meissonnier's* Livre de Légumes *inspired the turnip finial and celery feet, which clearly echo Edmé-Pierre Balzac's tureen in the Metropolitan Museum, New York. The shape appeared in Pierre Germain's* Eléments d'Orfèvrerie, *known in England by 1757. A similar finial decorates a tureen made by Parker and Wakelin in 1765, now at Anglesey Abbey (National Trust). Length: 40 cm ($15\frac{3}{4}$ in) (Victoria and Albert Museum, London)*

Meissonnier's *Livre de Légumes*, published in Paris in 1734, was a constant source of inspiration. The finely modelled vegetables, including cauliflowers, artichokes, broccoli, turnips and celery which adorn so many rococo tureens, owe their being to Meissonnier. His crayfish support the handles of two of Paul de Lamerie's tureens made in 1739; one is now in a private collection, the other, formerly in the Swaythling Collection, is now in the Metropolitan Museum of Art in New York.

The importance of Meissonnier was recognized by G. M. Moser, a Swiss working in England and one of the greatest chasers and enamellers of the eighteenth century. When, after his death, the contents of his library were auctioned in 1783, Meissonnier, Brunetti and Le Brun were well represented; and Moser was no doubt equally familiar with the work of Watteau, Toro, Babel, Pineau, Mondon, Boucher and Oppenord.

Moser had close contacts with goldsmiths (six of his designs for watch cases are in the Victoria and Albert Museum) and it is possible that many received tuition from him and from his French colleague Hubert Gravelot at the St Martin's Lane Academy in London. The Academy was founded by the artist William Hogarth in 1735 and exercised a profound influence on contemporary taste. Hogarth, in revolt against the calm classicism of Burlington and his followers, espoused the rococo movement and devoted much thought and energy to disseminating it. In his *Analysis of Beauty* published in London in 1753 he praised the graceful curve and 'the beauty of a composed intricacy of form, and how it may be said, with propriety, to lead the eye a kind of chace'.

Vertue in 1741 vouches in his Notebooks[2] for Gravelot's designs for silversmiths, but they were never published and may simply have been handed down from master to pupil. A high rococo ornamental drawing signed by Gravelot has, however, survived and is now in the British Museum. Its baying hound emerging from a reversed C-scroll owes much to the grotesque designs of Cornelis Bos (c.1510–56) – it was surely the inspiration for the canine masks which decorate four salvers made by Peter Archambo I between 1744 and 1746.

Apart from teaching at the St Martin's Lane Academy, Moser and Gravelot had drawing schools of their own. They would have appreciated Pierre Germain's *Eléments d'Orfèvrerie* (1748) which made available to goldsmiths a hundred plates of designs fashionable on the Continent at the time, seven of them signed by the celebrated Parisian goldsmith Jacques Roettiers. This work had a great influence on the English goldsmiths of the period such as Thomas Heming, whose indebtedness to Germain is clear in many of his pieces, and in the objects adorning his trade-card.

SALT (*left*), *one of a pair, silver-gilt. London, 1742–3. Maker: Nicholas Sprimont. One of Meissonnier's designs in the* Livre de Légumes, *this crayfish appears on many rococo pieces. Sprimont's version is so naturalistic that it may well have been cast from a real shell. The stark rocks on the base are the inspired contribution of Sprimont himself: their fresh modelling is without parallel in rococo silver. A pair of crab salts was made* en suite. *These pieces form part of an important marine service which belonged originally to Frederick, Prince of Wales, a discerning patron of the arts.*
Width: 12.7 cm (4½ in) (Royal Collection, London, reproduced by gracious permission of HM the Queen)

There were, however, other design sources, and they are most apparent in the work of Nicholas Sprimont. A native of Liège, Sprimont was brought up with the baroque fountain sculptures of Faydherbe, van Bossuit and Grupello, and their influence can be seen in the fresh modelling of the stark rocks of his crayfish salts of 1742 and of the male and female figures on the sauceboats of the following year in the Service of Frederick, Prince of Wales, in the Royal Collection, London. The shells and crustacea on these and pieces by other rococo goldsmiths may well have been cast from nature. No documentary evidence of such casting is as yet available for the eighteenth century, but from a discovery made by Sir Geoffrey de Bellaigue in Vulliamy's silver book for 1810–15[3] it is clear that shells were bought specifically for this purpose early in the nineteenth century.

The exact date of Sprimont's arrival in England is unknown, but he was certainly settled in London by January 1743 when he registered his maker's mark at Goldsmiths' Hall. He could only have been in his twenties. A prestigious commission from such a discerning patron as Prince Frederick Louis is a measure of his standing as a rococo goldsmith; as a designer and modeller Sprimont has few peers. His reputation is based on the relatively few pieces he made between 1743 and early 1749 when, forsaking silver, he became manager of the Chelsea Porcelain Factory. Sprimont was a close friend of the Huguenot sculptor Roubiliac. According to George Vertue, writing in August 1749[4], Roubiliac 'went to Liège where he learnt his art' and it is possible that he met Sprimont on the Continent before the Walloon goldsmith emigrated to England. In 1744 Sprimont stood godfather to Roubiliac's daughter Sophie. The sculptor is known to have supplied the Chelsea Porcelain Factory with at least one model – Hogarth's pug dog Trump – and he may also have collaborated with Sprimont and the Huguenot goldsmiths of London in the production of works in silver.

Until comparatively recently the credit for a fine piece of silver went automatically to the goldsmith whose maker's mark was struck on the object. However, the actual manufacture was often done by competent well-trained workmen who may not have had the benefit of highly developed artistic gifts but who were provided initially with a design and a good model from which to cast. Unfortunately, little is known of the modellers and their *modus operandi*. A big firm such as that of de Lamerie or Wickes with a large clientèle might have employed a full-time modeller, but it is more likely that the modellers were freelance specialists, each with his own repertoire. This theory is supported by the widespread use of identical, easily recognizable cast ornament on pieces emanating from many different workshops, though it could be argued that goldsmiths either lent or hired their models to their fellow craftsmen. There is a growing belief that the highly skilled chasers of the eighteenth century were often also designers and modellers. G. M. Moser certainly falls into this category. A pair of Apollo and Daphne caryatid candlesticks, unfortunately unmarked, was undoubtedly based on an extant drawing signed by Moser. He may also have provided models, and it is possible that the chasing was carried out by him. The drawing and the candlesticks are in the Victoria and Albert Museum, London.

Chasers occasionally signed their work, particularly gold boxes and watch cases. Some twenty such signatures are known, among them those of George Daniel Gaab, John Gastrell, Augustin Heckel, John Valentine Haidt, Henry Manley and Ishmael Parbury. Parbury's son George, also a skilled chaser, worked on at least two occasions for the firm of John Wakelin and William Tayler. Their Workmen's Ledger[5] records his repair of a silver figure of Apollo in 1794 (which probably involved chasing) and, more importantly, the supply of 'a pattern'. This could only have been a model in wood or metal from which a mould would have been made for a casting. The importance placed by Wakelin and Tayler on good models led them to commission work from Edmund Coffin whose busts and wax portraits were exhibited at the Royal Academy from 1783 to 1803. His name appears in the Workmen's Ledgers[6] in the period 1796–1803, during which time he supplied sketches, copied drawings and provided models for a variety of ornament (including monkeys and dolphins). A cast of a sphinx is mentioned, reflecting the public interest in Egypt following Nelson's victory at the Battle of the Nile, as well as 'three casts of mask heads'. As Coffin was a specialist modeller there is no mention of chasing.

The heightened interest of silver scholars in the modellers and chasers has led inevitably to theories on the authorship of certain pieces. For example, the remarkable silver-gilt Poseidon centrepiece in the Royal Collection – part of the Service of Frederick, Prince of Wales – bears the maker's mark of the Huguenot goldsmith Paul Crespin, but the Liègois character of the modelling led Charles Oman, the doyen of English silver scholars, to conjecture that it might have been the work of Nicholas Sprimont who at the time of assay had yet to register a mark. Continental influence is particularly apparent in the bowed head of the merman, in the four great stylized dolphins (which owe much to the fountain sculptures of Liège) and in the broad S-scrolls, heavily baroque, which are found in the work of many Continental goldsmiths including Thomas Germain. Since no preliminary sketches for this object have so far come to light, Sprimont's involvement cannot be proved.

There is no mention either of the centrepiece or of the marked Sprimont salts and sauceboats of the Prince's Service in the records of the third

INKSTAND OR STANDISH, *silver-gilt. London, 1738–9. Maker: Paul de Lamerie. Snakes are frequently found on pieces by Paul de Lamerie, their sinuous writhing contributing to the illusion of movement. This asymmetrical inkstand is also decorated with a cornucopia as well as a caduceus and cock, the attributes of Hermes the Messenger, proclaiming its function. The sulky boy on the bell handle was much favoured by French rococo goldsmiths, notably by Antoine-Sébastien Durand in the 1750s. Length: 30 cm ($11\frac{3}{4}$ in) (Blenheim Palace, Woodstock, Oxon)*

Earl of Scarbrough, his Treasurer and Receiver-General; they are similarly absent from the Prince's Household Accounts in the Duchy of Cornwall Office. Frederick's major purchases of plate usually appear in the ledgers of his goldsmith George Wickes (now in the Victoria and Albert Museum), but these particular pieces are not recorded unless the Crespin centrepiece was the mysterious – and costly – 'surtout compleat' entered by Wickes on 24 June 1742, a few weeks after the change of assay date letter. It was transferred the same day from Frederick's account to that of Ritzau, a minor member of his household, and immediately shipped abroad (possibly to Liège for finishing). The absence of a troy weight in the ledger – in itself strange – thwarts any attempt to compare it with the marine masterpiece bearing Crespin's mark and dated 1741.

The rococo preoccupation with the sea embraced form as well as decoration. The shell lent itself not only to tureens, salts and inkstands, but also to baskets. A delicate pierced-shell basket of 1747 by Paul de Lamerie (one of two in the Ashmolean Museum, Oxford) has a handle cast as a female term and rests on three dolphin feet. The same design was also used by Edward Wakelin. The vogue for organic forms was not confined to the sea: teapots and tea-kettles assumed the shape of melons and gourds; sauceboats were fashioned as overlapping vine leaves (the Victoria and Albert Museum has a particularly fine pair of 1755 by Philip Bruguier). This latter fashion is also to be found in contemporary ceramics.

English designers, while less prolific than Pierre Germain, were every bit as fantastical. Thomas Johnson, a teacher of drawing and modelling, first published his *One Hundred and Fifty New Designs* in 1758, but only five of them were intended for the goldsmiths, who would have been hard put to reproduce them exactly in silver. At about the same time John Linnell, son of the cabinet-maker William Linnell, published ten designs for high rococo condiment vases and cream jugs. Three of them are known to have been realized in silver in a slightly modified form by Edward Wakelin, Aymé Videau and Arthur Annesley; all three are now in the Victoria and Albert Museum.

In several of these designs, particularly those of Thomas Johnson, the rococo taste for chinoiserie is apparent. In the 1750s, not content with marine fantasies, masks human, leonine and auricular, Greek myths and a sylvan world of flower-garlanded putti and amorini clutching grapes and frolicking amid butterflies, lizards and small insects, the goldsmiths turned with unabated enthu-

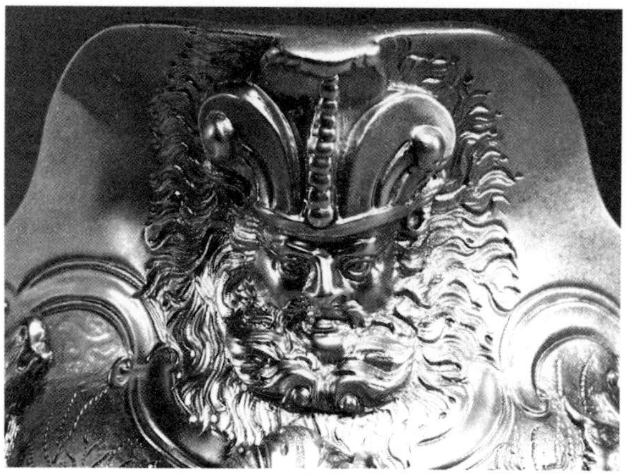

CREAM BOAT *(right; detail below), silver. London, 1740. Maker: Christian Hillan. Greek myths were a favourite source of inspiration. A grazing cow often appears as a decorative motif on a cream boat: here the majestic bearded mask beneath the lip invokes the legend of Zeus and Io. Zeus ravished Io, a priestess of Hera, his wife. To protect her from Hera's wrath he turned Io into a heifer. The head on the handle probably portrays Hera. Length: 12.5 cm (5 in) (Private collection)*

TEA KETTLE, LAMP AND STAND *(facing page, left), silver. London, 1747–8. Maker: Thomas Whipham. The four chased allegorical panels represent a curious design combination based on three of the Four Elements and fragments from Aesop's fables. Height: 39.5 cm (15½ in) (Brand Inglis Limited)*

THREE FANCY-FRONT TEASPOONS *(facing page, right), silver and silver-gilt. English, mid-eighteenth century. Various makers. The putto (centre) is reminiscent of the delicate* amorini *of Boucher. Apollo with lyre and bow (left) personifies the preoccupation with Greek myths. The Gilles figure (right) is possibly after Watteau's* Pierrot Debout*.*
Length of putto: 11.2 cm ($4\frac{1}{2}$ in)
Length of Apollo: 11.9 cm ($4\frac{11}{16}$ in)
Length of Gilles: 12.1 cm ($4\frac{13}{16}$ in)
(Private collections)

siasm to chinoiserie, an enthusiasm shared by cabinet-makers, manufacturers of porcelain, textiles and wallpaper, and by landscape gardeners. The English love of chinoiserie was long-standing, but now the delicately engraved human figures, birds and flowers of Caroline times were replaced by bolder casting and chasing. While undeniably charming, many of these rococo pieces betray great ignorance of the Orient and its art: Paul de Lamerie was a prime offender, with tea caddies depicting coolies labouring under palm trees. Sprimont mixed chinoiserie with every other rococo conceit in 1745 on his fantastic kettle (now in the Hermitage Museum). Its cast finial takes the form of a fat Chinaman, a tea ceremony is chased on the body of the kettle, the spout is modelled as a grotesque beast and the base, for good measure, is decorated with human masks representing the four continents. This piece embodies the essence of the rococo at its most extreme: it is audacious and unpredictable; boredom is impossible since the eyes and mind make strange and fresh encounters at every turn. Its detractors may hate it, but they can hardly ignore it or fail to be impressed by its sheer virtuosity. In contrast, the epergnes fashioned as pagodas which were *à la mode* in the 1750s and 1760s have a delicate restraint. Such a one, made in 1760 by Thomas Pitts, a specialist maker of epergnes (and formerly in the Ionides Collection), achieved a certain artistic unity with a canopy shaped like a temple roof hung with bells and surmounted by a Chinaman carrying a parasol.

Horace Walpole was appalled by this vogue for chinoiserie, and wrote scathingly about it in his anonymous contributions to the magazine *The World* in the early 1750s. 'According to the present prevailing whim,' he wrote, 'everything is Chinese, or in the Chinese taste . . . even our most vulgar utensils are all reduced to this new-fangled standard.' He ended with a perceptive comment: 'our Chinese ornaments are not only of our own manufacture . . . but what has seldom been attributed to the English, of our own invention'. He might well have been referring to the silver of the period.

Only the very wealthy could afford the chinoiserie epergnes and other large and prestigious pieces, but those of modest means could bring the rococo into their homes, then as now, with the charming decorated spoons known today as fancy backs and fancy fronts. The die-stamped ornamen-

tal motifs range from shells, scrolls and flowers, to putti, amorini and Greek gods, and represent the rococo period in microcosm.

In England, as in France, the rococo was by no means universally acclaimed. As early as 1738 the *London Magazine* had commented acidly that 'the ridiculous imitation of the French has now become the epidemical distemper of the Kingdom'. By 1755, according to André Rouquet in *L'Etat des Arts en Angleterre*, published in Paris in that year, 'the taste called contrast, a taste so ridiculous and whimsical, when applied to objects susceptible of symmetrey, has reached as far as England, where it every day produces, as it does elsewhere, some new monster'. Many English people shared this opinion and insisted on plate that was both symmetrical and restrained. Unable to sustain its momentum, the rococo finally began to falter, in England as in France, and in a very short time the frenzied shell forms lost their appeal and were replaced by calm Attic shapes.

In other countries a time lag, similar to that existing between the two main protagonists and their provincial centres, delayed the transition to neoclassicism. Silver in the rococo taste continued to be made in the rest of Europe and America long after it had become outmoded in Paris and London. Changes in form and decoration occurred gradually, the two styles in some cases in strange juxtaposition. For this reason the rococo and neoclassical periods in countries other than France and England have been treated as an entity at the end of the chapter on neoclassicism.

· 6 · NEOCLASSICISM ·

In France the rococo, which owed its being to a reaction against the ponderous baroque favoured during the reign of Louis XIV and the short interregnum of Philippe d'Orléans, was ousted in its turn by a nostalgia for the values of the *grand siècle*. The French, with their innate respect for reason and logic, felt at home with their seventeenth-century edifices on the Roman plan, and their brief flirtation with the rococo began to assume the proportions of a positive *mésalliance*.

The rococo is now generally regarded as one of France's most original and delightful contributions to the Arts, and it is difficult to believe the antagonism it provoked in contemporary critics.

The Abbé Le Blanc was one of the most vituperative, and his sense of outrage was expressed in a series of diatribes written between 1737 and 1744. The taste of the day, he wrote, is 'so depraved that I do not think it can continue much longer'. He was joined in 1754 – and again in 1755 (*Mercure de France*, February 1755) – by the engraver-critic Charles-Nicolas Cochin, who made an impassioned plea to goldsmiths, chasers and carvers in the *Mercure de France* of December 1754. With more than a glancing blow at Meissonnier, he begged them not to set beside a full-scale artichoke 'a hare as big as a finger, a lark as large as life' and 'children the same size as a vine leaf'. He went on to inveigh against inventions 'so marvellous that they are beyond the province of reason'. The petition was clearly no more than a tirade against the rococo, but in later years Cochin persuaded himself that this and a subsequent article in the same publication had been instrumental in ushering in neoclassicism. 'The truly decisive epoch', he wrote in his *Mémoires Inédits*, 'was the return [in 1751] of M. de Marigny and his company from Italy'. The Marquis de Marigny was not so styled when he was sent to Italy in December 1749 by his sister Madame de Pompadour, in order to prepare him for his cultural responsibilities as future *Directeur général des Bâtiments*. Cochin, the Abbé Le Blanc and the architect Jacques-Germain Soufflot, who accompanied Marigny on the Grand Tour, enjoyed a certain eminence in artistic circles in Paris, as did the Comte de Caylus. De Caylus, the son of a niece of Madame de Maintenon, had sufficient private means to indulge his passion for collecting classical antiquities which he drew and described in his famous *Recueil d'Antiquités*, published in seven volumes between 1752 and 1767. He was regarded by some as the French counterpart of the distinguished German scholar Winckelmann, an opinion not shared by Diderot who is said to have penned this epitaph on de Caylus:

'Ci-gist un antiquaire acariâtre et brusque,
Ah! qu'il est bien logé dans cette cruche étrusque.
(Here lies an antiquary crotchety and brusque,
How well is he lodged in this Etruscan vase!)

Although the anti-rococo lobby was vociferous, it did not hasten the demise of the rococo, nor did it bring about an overnight return to sanity in the guise of neoclassicism: until the 1770s the curves and scrolls continued to co-exist alongside the clean, severe lines of the antique.

The new style first became evident in architecture, spread quickly to furniture and then to silver. It was taken up so enthusiastically by the fashionable world that some of its more learned protagonists, including Cochin, found themselves bewailing the general lack of discernment. According to Baron de Grimm in his *Correspondance Littéraire* of 1763, the coxcombs of Paris considered it beneath their dignity to carry snuffboxes not in the latest Greek mode. The snuffbox was but a beginning; fashion decreed that every silver object should be fashioned in the Greek manner. The goldsmiths, not at all abashed by such a radical change in style, set about familiarizing themselves with new patterns, untroubled by the fact that the designs owed more to Rome than to Athens.

The French had long maintained an academy in Rome, housed in the Palazzo Mancini, where young architects, sculptors and artists were sent to further their training by studying the works of antiquity. Many returned to France with portfolios of drawings which included Attic vase shapes. The sculptor Jacques Saly published his vase sketches, which he engraved himself, in Paris in 1746, and the architect Jean-François de Neufforge also made a significant contribution with his vase

NARCISSUS EWER *(facing page), silver. Paris, 1784–5. Maker: Jean-Baptiste-François Chéret. This incomparable ewer, fashioned on the eve of the French Revolution, is a masterpiece of elegant restraint. A finely modelled term figure of Narcissus forms the handle, his face mirrored in a shell-pool concave lid. The architectural line, bearded mask and scrolling frieze are reminiscent of late seventeenth-century ewers. Bulrushes interspersed with water-leaf decoration emphasize the function of the vessel. Height: 33 cm (13 in) (The Metropolitan Museum of Art, New York)*

VASE DESIGNS *from* Raccolta di Vasi diversi *by Stefano della Bella, published in Paris, c.1646. Della Bella's designs appealed to eighteenth-century taste. Robert Adam owned a scrapbook containing 180 della Bella prints. Although they were regarded in some quarters as genuine reproductions of the antique, their whimsical forms are far closer to the fantastical designs of the Florentine Mannerists. (Victoria and Albert Museum, London)*

designs, as did Joseph-Marie Vien and Charles de Wailly; all these designs were produced before excavations began in earnest at Pompeii. Not all the forms, however, were based directly on Attic models. The designs of Renaissance, Mannerist and late seventeenth-century artists often proved more acceptable. For example, Stefano della Bella's *Raccolta di Vasi diversi*, published in Paris in about 1646, was based on the work of Florentine Mannerists such as Buontalenti and Parigi, but it nevertheless served the goldsmiths as a useful source of 'neoclassical' vase designs.

The vase and the urn represented a victory of form over fantasy: unlike the shells of the rococo they were architectural and made expressly as containers, even if, as was frequently the case with the urn, they were originally intended for mortal remains. The discovery of the site of Pompeii in 1748 and its excavation, started in 1755, added greatly to the general interest in the artefacts of Greece and Rome. 'Etruscan' antiquities were equally venerated, their devotees unaware that many of them had originally been imported from Greece. Greek, Etruscan, Roman, all were classical as far as fashion was concerned, and in Paris fashion was paramount.

While the urns and vases afforded admirable shapes for tureens and ewers, the column was the obvious form for candlesticks and candelabra. The early examples are, however, far removed from the elegant pillars of Greece and Rome: it is as though the French designers and goldsmiths were unable to recognize the importance of entasis, the slight convexity given to the shaft of a column to correct the illusion of concavity produced by a straight shaft. Delafosse's designs for richly ornamented monumental candlesticks in his book *Nouvelle Iconologie historique* (1768) are undeniably squat. The fashioned objects of the early years of neoclassicism fare no better: not even the genius of François-Thomas Germain can redeem the unpleasing proportions of his silver-gilt pair of 1762 (Musée Nissim de Camondo, Paris), nor those of 1765 (Museu Nacional de Arte Antigua in Lisbon).

Germain had, in fact, been quick to appreciate the importance of the new fashion. His grotesque Chinaman tea-kettle (one of a pair) of 1763, in the Portuguese Royal Collection, rests on an elegant neoclassical stand, made seven years earlier and decorated with cast rams' heads and laurel festoons. Two more disparate objects can scarcely be imagined: while the kettle is late rococo, the stand shows a confident mastery of neoclassical form and decoration at a time when François-Thomas Germain's fellow goldsmiths were making their first tentative essays in the style.

The study of French silver is bedevilled by the paucity of surviving examples, not least of this period. Not only were great quantities of fine plate melted down in 1759 and 1760 to finance the Seven Years' War, but during the hostilities the Court orders to the goldsmiths were greatly reduced. Their reputations, however, stood high in the courts of Europe and Imperial Russia, and some of their work has fortunately survived in foreign collections. The six soup tureens and six *pots-à-oille* which François-Thomas Germain despatched to Russia in 1761 were clearly neoclassical in form, judging by an account in *L'Avantcoureur* which described them as having 'the shape of those oval classical urns intended for sacrificial ceremonies'. His gold egg-cup of 1764 in the Museu Nacional de Arte Antigua in Lisbon is remarkable for the Vitruvian scroll round the rim.

François-Thomas Germain was succeeded at the French Court by Jacques Roettiers, whose work was clearly influenced by the new classical style by the 1760s. Roettiers was joined in 1765 by his son Jacques-Nicolas, formerly his apprentice, who succeeded him as *Orfèvre du Roi* in 1772. Jacques-Nicolas was the goldsmith chosen by Catherine II of Russia to make the large and sumptuous neoclassical dinner service which she presented to her favourite, Prince Orlov. It was made in 1770 in a massively architectural style, and although it was largely executed by Jacques-Nicolas, he was assisted by his father and Edmé-Pierre Balzac, Louis-Joseph Lenhendrick and Claude-Pierre Deville. Supplanted in the Tsarina's affections by Potemkin, Orlov died insane in

VASE *(facing page, left), silver-gilt. Paris, 1765. Maker: Antoine-Sébastien Durand. Laurel and palm leaves were much favoured as design motifs in the neoclassical period. In this important Louis XV vase the finial is formed as a stylized laurel bud above a broad chased band of laurel leaves which is repeated on the plinth. A bold swag of laurel leaves is applied to the partly fluted body of the vase above the calyx of palm leaves. Beading decorates lid and handles, and the plinth rests on well-modelled paw feet. Height: 53 cm ($20\frac{7}{8}$ in) (Private collection)*

1783, and Catherine took the opportunity of buying the service back from his heirs. With the exception of certain important pieces which have found their way to private collections and museums in the West, the service remains intact in the Kremlin and the Hermitage. Jacques-Nicolas Roettiers retired with a considerable fortune in about 1777, leaving the stage to Robert-Joseph Auguste, one of the greatest exponents of the neoclassical style.

Auguste in his turn was also commissioned to supply splendid dinner services to the Russian Empress. He worked in the neoclassical style to the manner born; eschewing the ponderous effects of a too slavish adherence to architectural forms, he fashioned pieces of extraordinary elegance and felicity. In 1775 he made a magnificent twenty-piece silver dinner service for the Count de Creutz, Swedish Ambassador to the Court of Louis XV. The tureens, set with gold plaques in low relief, are the purest expression of the neoclassical style. The same tureens, lacking only the gold plaques, enhance a dinner service made between 1776 and 1785 for George III, King of England and Elector of Hanover. Retained at Herrenhausen, it passed eventually to George III's son Ernest Augustus, King of Hanover and Duke of Cumberland. Until 1979 a large part of this service was in the Louis Cartier Collection.

Auguste extended his mastery of proportion to candlesticks and candelabra. A pair of candelabra of 1766 has columns decorated with laurel swags and finials formed as cassolettes. The cassolette (perfume burner) was a favourite neoclassical shape which lent itself particularly well to candelabra. In Auguste's famous triple term candelabra of 1767 (Metropolitan Museum, New York), the cassolette rests on the heads of three women of a rare classical beauty. This female term design was obviously an artistic success, for he used it again on several occasions, notably for a set of twelve identical candlesticks of 1775 (Swedish Royal Collection).

The pieces Auguste fashioned for the French Court have long since vanished, including his gold statuettes of a sailor and a child, made in 1755, which served Madame de Pompadour as pepper pot and salt cellar: they are said to have been modelled by the sculptor Etienne-Maurice Falconet whose designs for vases, intended for porcelain, were displayed at Versailles in 1762. Auguste's versatility is demonstrated by his work on the gold crown and chalice made in 1774 for the coronation of Louis XVI in collaboration with the court jeweller Ange-Joseph Aubert. Auguste also worked in bronze: his marble column with gilded bronze mounts, made to the design of Charles de Wailly, was exhibited at the 1761 Salon. While nothing remains of his prestigious early work, two gold boxes from the 1760s have survived: one of 1762 is in the Musée du Louvre and the other, bought in Paris in 1769 by the first Earl Spencer, is now in the collection of the present Earl.

The only Auguste pieces in the English Royal Collection are two silver-gilt *pots-à-oille* made in 1788 by Robert-Joseph's son Henry; they are based on his father's design for the Creutz service but without the charming putti handles. Engraved with the armorials of George IV as Prince Regent, the pair was purchased in the early nineteenth century from a Neapolitan ambassador.

It is a measure of Auguste's achievement that his work was highly appreciated in his lifetime; in contemporary French sale catalogues, pieces bear-

POT-À-OILLE *(below right), silver. Paris, 1770–71. Maker: Jacques-Nicolas Roettiers. This pot-à-oille was one of twenty-two tureens in the 842-piece dinner service commissioned by the Empress Catherine II of Russia for Prince Grigoriy Grigorevitch Orlov. Architectural in style, the ponderous magnificence of the Orlov service owes much to Delafosse whose influence was marked in France in the 1770s. Part of this masterpiece remains in Russia; some pieces are now in Paris (Musée Nissim de Camondo and the Louvre), in New York (Metropolitan Museum), and in private collections. Total height (pot and stand): 35 cm (13⅘ in) (Musée Nissim de Camondo, Paris)*

SOUP TUREEN *(right), silver. Ghent, 1786. Maker: Johannes Bapt. Paulus. Many of the decorative motifs made fashionable by French goldsmiths can be seen in this tureen. The shallow fluting, the band of scrolling foliage and the beading below it all proclaim the influence of neoclassicism. Rococo elements are, however, still visible in the finial and handles. Stand: 35 cm (13¾ in) Width: 46.8 cm (18⅜ in)*

ing his mark are described as 'perfectly executed by Monsieur Auguste'. Like Thomas Germain and Jacques Roettiers, Auguste employed a large number of workmen, and like them he was able to avail himself of the services of a goldsmith son, his erstwhile apprentice. Henry Auguste succeeded to Robert-Joseph's court appointment in 1785. His work after the French Revolution presages the

TUREEN, *silver with gold plaques. Paris 1775. Maker: Robert-Joseph Auguste. This tureen formed part of a dinner service commissioned by Count de Creutz: it was acquired by Gustavus III of Sweden in 1781. Chased acanthus leaves decorate the tureen; the laurel band below the lid is repeated on the fluted stand. Height: 32 cm (12½ in) (The Royal Collections, Stockholm)*

Empire fashion, and his most distinguished pieces are in that style.

As Swedish Ambassador at the Court of Louis XVI the Count de Creutz, a distinguished diplomat and man of letters, was ideally placed to observe the latest neoclassical trends. The service he commissioned from Auguste consisted of two tureens, two *pots-à-oille*, twelve female term candlesticks, two sauceboats and two oil-cruets. The remarkable gold plaques in low relief which decorate the tureens and *pots-à-oille* are thought to have been made from models by Augustin Pajou. They commemorate important events in the reign of King Gustavus III, subjects certainly chosen by the Count de Creutz, a close friend of the King. The service is notable for the perfection of its proportions, the quality of the rich chasing and the rare charm of the putti which form the handles.

Although French silver in the neoclassical period was dominated by François-Thomas Germain, Jacques Roettiers and his son Jacques-Nicolas and by the Augustes, father and son, much fine work was produced in other ateliers in Paris and the provinces. Louis-Joseph Lenhendrick is represented in the Russian Imperial Collection by his tureen of 1769 with putti handles and finial similar to those on the vessels François-Thomas Germain delivered to St Petersburg in 1758 and to the Court of Portugal in 1756. Lenhendrick has taken the putti out of their original rococo setting and added them, not entirely satisfactorily, to a quasi-neoclassical outline, architectural in form, complete with laurel swags and ribbons tied in bows.

Lenhendrick was not alone in this inability to renounce old and familiar forms. As late as 1772 Jean-Baptiste-François Chéret succumbed to the temptation: his tureen in the Bensimon Collection, has all the fashionable motifs – goats' heads, festoons of leaves (in this case oak and acorns instead of the ubiquitous bay), ribbon bows and pine-cone finial – applied to a shape that is very far removed from an antique urn. By 1789, judging by a superbly proportioned vase-shaped tureen in the Espirito Santo Foundation, Lisbon, made by his son and collaborator, Louis-Jean-Baptiste, the Chéret works had mastered the new style. Here the vessel is set on a pedestal foot (in itself an innovation) which rests on an underdish which is more plinth than plateau. Apart from a wide chased acanthus-leaf frieze, the polished surface of the tureen is completely plain. This style enjoyed a great success which lasted throughout the Empire period.

The excavation of Pompeii, which began in 1755, had made familiar not only the forms most widely used in classical times, but also the decorative motifs. The goldsmiths chose patterns which could be effectively translated into silver (and occasionally gold) until they had amassed a sizeable repertoire of neoclassical ornament. Ovolo and guilloche borders and acanthus leaves had been familiar for centuries, but the Greek key pattern was something of a novelty to their generation. Also new to them were *paterae* (circular classical ornaments based on the saucer used in sacrificial libations), goat and ram heads with long, gracefully curving horns, palmettes (a legacy from the ancient Egyptians), anthemions (stylized honeysuckle often confused with palmettes), water-leaves, oval medallions and the ribbon bows used to secure drapes of cloth and swags of laurel or bay. Running scrolls and spirals of foliage (*rinceaux*) took on new and interesting forms, and the fluting which was part of the goldsmiths' stock-in-trade became more shallow and delicate. Silver pearls were used on rims instead of gadrooning; a garland of bay bound with ribbon provided an ideal alternative finish. The publication of the collection of antiquities belonging to the Comte de

Caylus[3] provided the goldsmiths with illustrations of classical borders. The wave of the sea pattern, sometimes called the Vitruvian scroll, became very popular.

The classical forms and motifs were not reserved for large pieces, but appeared on salts and egg cups. The tripod form was particularly adaptable: the elegant pepper container on three console feet made by Vincent Bréant (a specialist maker) in 1768 has a pierced cover of laurel leaves; it now forms part of the Collection of the Musée des Arts décoratifs in Paris. A rock-crystal vase set in a tripod of silver-gilt resting on a plinth was used by Jean-Nicolas Bastin in 1780 for a set of egg cups (now in a private collection). Decorated with perfectly proportioned goats' heads and hooves, Bastin's egg cups have an architectural quality no less monumental for being in miniature.

The Palais-Royal in Paris is said to have inspired the fashion for arcaded silver – usually of a light gauge which lent itself to stamping – which provided an attractive foil for blue glass containers designed to hold sugar, salt and mustard. The alliance of silver and blue glass was popular in the last quarter of the eighteenth century. Marc-Etienne Janety, François Picard and Etienne Modenx specialized in this field (a *sucrier* of 1786 by Modenx is in the possession of the Metropolitan Museum in New York). News of this ephemeral fashion for arcaded silver must have reached Catherine II in Russia: in 1783 she commissioned a blue glass tureen set in a silver frame from Antoine Boullier. It has a delicate scrolling frieze of acanthus leaves similar to those seen on Boullier's earlier work, notably the magnificent twenty-three piece toilet set he fashioned in 1778 for a member of the Potocki family. Far from being stamped out of thin metal, like so much arcaded silver, this toilet set has all the grandeur of deeply chased and embellished raised silver of heavy gauge. Boullier received part of his training at the Ecole Gratuite de Dessin in Paris where he was awarded a first prize. The school was run by Jean-Jacques Bachelier, one of the three artistic directors of the Sèvres Porcelain Manufactory, who espoused the 'noble symmetry' of neoclassicism and insisted that his pupils should be taught geometry.

The quest for regularity of form can be clearly seen in the small boxes of the period; usually of gold and oval or rectangular in shape, they are now generally classified as snuff boxes. A plethora of neoclassical ornament is crowded into these small objects, but the borders and motifs are so skilfully chosen that they heighten the effect of richness instead of detracting from it. The goldsmiths most associated with the production of these boxes are Robert-Joseph Auguste, Jean-Joseph Barrière, Jean Frémin, Charles Le Bastier, Mathieu Coiny, Jean George, Pierre-François Drais, Jean Formey, J.-M. Tiron and Louis Roucel. There are some fine examples in the Musée du Louvre, the Victoria and Albert Museum (Jones Collection), Waddesdon Manor, Buckinghamshire, and the Wrightsman Collection, New York.

Sheffield plate, the name given to the metal produced by fusing a thin layer of silver to a thicker copper base was invented in England in 1743 and regarded as peculiarly British. It does not appear to have found a foothold in France – where it was known as *plaqué* or *doublé* – until after 1768. In spite of opposition from the Goldsmiths' Guild, it received royal approval and in 1770 Jean-Vincent Huguet was authorized to specialize in the process. A fine *pot-à-oille* from his hand, now in the Louvre, is as satisfyingly neoclassical as equivalent works in silver. Huguet was joined by other goldsmiths; the most celebrated were Marie-Antoine-Joseph Tugot and Jacques Daumy. Tugot opened a specialist workshop in the Hôtel de Pomponne, rue de la Verrerie, and thereafter the fused plate became known in France as *pomponne*.

EWER AND BASIN, *silver-gilt. Paris, 1787. Maker: Henry Auguste. Fashioned in the French Empire style to the design of the French sculptor Jean Guillaume Moitte, this ewer and basin were bought in Paris in 1802 by the English connoisseur William Beckford of Fonthill Abbey. Height of ewer: 40 cm (15¾ in) Diameter of basin: 35 cm (13¾ in)*

CANDLESTICKS WITH MATCHING BRANCHES, *set of four, silver-gilt. London, 1775–6. Makers: Daniel Smith and Robert Sharp (candlesticks), Thomas Heming (branches). These candlesticks, in the purest neoclassical form, are decorated with water leaves and ribbon-bound reeding. The branches, incorporating swags, pateræ and flame finials, were fashioned by the royal goldsmith Thomas Heming. Height overall: 43 cm (17 in) (Brand Inglis Limited, London)*

· NEOCLASSICISM IN ENGLAND ·

The arrival in England of the new style was for once quite independent of developments in France. It coincided fortuitously with the accession in 1760 of the youthful George III. The untimely death of his father, Prince Frederick Louis, in 1751, had robbed Britain of a cultured and enlightened patron of artists: George was unfitted both by temperament and upbringing to follow in his father's footsteps. Throughout the country, however, there prevailed a spirit of national optimism and self confidence which was reflected in the Arts.

The new style set out not merely to please but also to instruct, and its principles, practised initially by the architects, were the well-tried tenets of classicism. Cabinet-makers and goldsmiths were swift to appreciate its importance. Their clients had been nurtured on Roman poetry, and no wealthy young Englishman's education was considered complete in the eighteenth century without several years spent in Italy on the Grand Tour. The more serious-minded, influenced by their opportunity for studying antiquity, arrived back in England brimming over with ideas and laden with antique vases, statues and engraved gems. They found on their return an informed body of architects whose interest in classicism was not confined to Palladio but founded on studies, made *in situ*, of Roman buildings. Few, it is true, had undertaken the difficult journey to Greece, but Paestum was accessible and Le Roy's engraved *Ruines des plus beaux monuments de la Grèce* became available in 1758 and Stuart and Revett's *Antiquities of Athens* in 1762.

The excavation of Herculaneum and Pompeii (the latter begun in 1755) made the ancient world very immediate and revealed a wealth of domestic rather than public architecture. Enormous interest was aroused by the uncovering of the decorations and works of art which embellished homes buried since 79 AD. The English competed for the objects that came on the market as a result of excavations, and many great collections were formed or enlarged at this time.

Robert Adam was in Italy during this period of discovery. He returned to London in 1758, his highly acclaimed survey of the Palace of the Emperor Diocletian at Spalato (Split) completed, and quickly established himself as an architect and interior designer of near genius, his name synonymous with the style in which he worked. To describe a piece of silver as 'Adam' conveys an instant idea of style and proportions, although he was not a prolific designer of silver. Only a few of the thousands of drawings by Robert Adam and his brother James, now in the Library of Sir John Soane's Museum in London, relate to silver; none of these appears to have been commissioned by a goldsmith – they seem instead to have emanated from aristocratic and wealthy patrons. Adam was meticulous in his attention to detail and it was essential to the success of his interiors that everything, including the silver, should be in harmony. It had to conform to the Attic shapes, and these were derived from Greco-Roman art rather than Greco-Roman plate, of which little was available at the time.

That well-worn symbol of antiquity, the tripod, captured the imagination of designers from the earliest years of the neoclassical period. It was particularly appropriate for the candelabrum, in itself an important decorative object. An Adam drawing inscribed 'Candlestick for Sir Watkin Wynn Bart. Adelphi 9 March 1773' in Sir John Soane's Museum in London shows an elegant two-branch tripod candelabrum. The London goldsmith John Carter translated it into silver in 1774, working closely to Adam's design. The pine-cone finial, rams' heads, scrolling friezes, festoons, palmettes, *pateræ* and guilloche borders which decorate this piece, now in the collection of Lloyd's of London, had become part of the standard repertoire and were *de rigueur* by the 1770s. John Carter had been fashioning candlesticks to Adam designs as early as 1767 (a pair of

TEAPOT *(left), silver. Boston, 1796. Maker: Paul Revere. Revere's client, Jonathan Hunnewell, was charged £14.11s. for this teapot. A matching stand and basket-shaped sugar bowl are in the same collection. The tassel motif of the bright-cut engraved decoration was a direct copy of one used by the London goldsmith Robert Hennell in the 1780s, losing much of its strength in the transition. Height: 15.5 cm (6⅛ in) (Metropolitan Museum of Art, New York)*

that date is at Temple Newsam House, Leeds); others, the work of Sebastian and James Crespel, bear the assay date-letter for 1769–70. Neither London goldsmiths nor the Adam brothers had the monopoly of elegant candlesticks: Sheffield produced a large number by such specialist makers as John Winter, John Parsons, George Ashforth and Matthew Fenton. They too were quick to realize that the classical column made an ideal shaft for a candlestick. The individual goldsmiths' variations on this theme, however, were not always strictly classical, and some of their twisted pillars owe more to bamboo than fluted stone.

Antique vase and urn shapes were found to be eminently suitable for hollow-ware. Sir William Chambers, the distinguished architect, defined 'the character of Urns' as 'simplicity, to have covers, but no handles, nor spouts, they are monumental'. Vases, on the other hand, 'might be used for libations, & other sacrificial, festive and culinary uses, such as Ewers, open vessels Ect.'[1] One of two drawings, inscribed by Adam 'Vase for Thomas Dundas Esqr. for a Prize', was realized in silver-gilt in 1770 by Daniel Smith and Robert Sharp for the Richmond race prize and is an example of the magnificence of the trophies of the period. Two designs for urn-shaped tureens were commissioned from Adam by the Duke of Northumberland in 1779. The urn form was also used for sauceboats, wine-coolers and jardinières. The vase shape came into its own with communion flagons, ewers, jugs for milk and hot water, coffee and chocolate pots. The London goldsmith Henry Greenway excelled himself in 1777: his chocolate pot in the Victoria and Albert Museum is based on a Greek amphora complete with (built-in) tripod support. Tea-caddies and sugar containers were made as vases, and smaller versions were used for condiments; the latter are so recorded in the ledgers of George Wickes as early as 1749 and continue to be described as such under his successors John Parker and Edward Wakelin throughout the neoclassical period.

CONDIMENTS AND WINE COASTER *(right), silver. London, 1774–1790. Makers: Hester Bateman (casters); Thos. Daniel (salts); Robert Hennell (mustard pot and wine coaster). Neoclassical preoccupation with urns and vases is apparent in the shapes, finials and decorative motifs. Bristol glass liners. Height of casters: 15.6 cm (6$\frac{1}{16}$ in)*

Certain everyday objects, such as teapots, waiters and bread baskets, were not susceptible to antique forms but were made very successfully in the classical idiom by the use of design motifs that were readily available from the growing number of archaeological publications which served as pattern books. The Greek key pattern, as well as many forms of *pateræ* and animal heads, could be found as early as 1753 in *The Ruins of Palmyra* and from 1757 in *The Ruins of Balbec*, both by Wood and Dawkins. A wealth of decorative borders and motifs was available from 1766 in d'Hancarville's *Collection of Etruscan, Greek and Roman Antiquities from the Cabinet of the Hon^{able} Wm Hamilton His Britannick Majesty's Envoy Extraordinary at the Court of Naples.* Some motifs were already in the goldsmiths' repertoire: the guilloche had been in use since the late sixteenth century, and the wave of the sea pattern or Vitruvian scroll was familiar, known perhaps from Raphael's decoration in the Vatican Loggia. Decoration of this kind was all the more effective because it was, for the most part,

PLATE *130 from* Antiquités Etrusques, Grecques et Romaines tirées du Cabinet de M. Hamilton. *Edited and published by d'Hancarville. Florence, 1801–8. The expressed purpose behind d'Hancarville's four illustrated volumes describing Sir William Hamilton's collection of Etruscan, Greek and Roman antiquities was 'to contribute to the advancement of the Arts' and to make 'an agreeable present to our manufacturers of earthenware and China, and to those who make vases in silver, copper, glass, marble etc.' The goldsmiths were quick to benefit from this wealth of material, and the inspiration behind many of their finest neoclassical pieces can be traced to this source. (Victoria and Albert Museum, London)*

used sparingly. The large areas of reflecting surfaces left unadorned served to emphasize the felicity of the shapes and the grace of the proportions. The plain surface could have been a perfect foil to fine engraving, at which the English excelled, but the art was, inexplicably, on the wane during the neoclassical period and even armorial work seems to lack vitality. The only kind of engraving to be widely used was a form known as 'bright cutting', popular in the 1780s. This was a new technique achieved by cutting small shallow facets of varying steepness which caught the light and gave a glittering effect (soon diminished when worn down by handling and polishing).

The most restrained and one of the most charming of the ornaments in limited use was the applied silver medallion, based directly on James Tassie's celebrated reproductions of classical and Renaissance gems and cameos. The proximity of the workshops of Tassie and Andrew Fogelberg in Soho, London, no doubt accounts for the number of these medallions adorning Fogelberg's early pieces and those he made later in partnership with Stephen Gilbert; there are several examples in the Victoria and Albert Museum. John Schofield and Burrage Davenport also decorated their pieces with medallions depicting classical themes, but few other goldsmiths followed suit.

No mention of Tassie's medallions has yet come to light in the working ledgers of John Parker and his partner Edward Wakelin, arguably in the first rank of goldsmiths of the neoclassical period. Their brief entries do, however, convey both shape and ornament, unlike those of the rococo period (where the objects may well have defied description). In March 1771 Lord Digby purchased from them 'A pair Goats head Candlesticks'; 'a sett of fluted festoon Vase Castors and Spoons' (for condiments) was sold a month later; an 'Antique Tea Vase wth Water leaves & Vetruvia [sic] foot' is entered in the account of William Fellowes Esq. in 1773; Sir Robert Burdett bought in May 1776 'a fine Antique Coffee Pot wth festoons and Water Leaves'.

Unfortunately none of the pattern books used by Parker and Wakelin appears to have survived. John Parker, scion of an old Worcestershire landed family, would have received a gentleman's education (he sent his own son to Eton and Oxford) and been conversant with the classics. The design possibilities of the published works stemming from the excavations at Herculaneum and Pompeii would not have been lost on him. He would have had easy access not only to the books already cited but also to J. F. de Neufforge's *Recueil élémentaire d'Architecture* (1757–72), the Comte de Caylus's *Recueil d'Antiquités* (1752–67) and Piranesi's *Parere su L'Architettura* (1765). Few goldsmiths were so purist that they were content slavishly to imitate the Ancients, and Parker and Wakelin found acceptable alternatives in the Florentine mannerist designs of Stefano della Bella's *Raccolta di Vasi diversi* – first published in Paris in 1646 – which were often mistaken in some quarters for the genuine antique forms. The shape used by Parker and Wakelin in 1770 for a condiment vase in the Victoria and Albert Museum is closely related to a della Bella design on Plate 6 of the *Raccolta di Vasi diversi*, and interpreted by way of a drawing by Robert Adam[2] who is known to have had in his collection designs by Stefano della Bella.

At the beginning of the neoclassical period the reputation of the London goldsmiths stood high, the new style being ideally suited to their skills and temperament. Their complacency was rudely shattered in the 1760s, however, by competition from the provincial cities of Sheffield and Birmingham. The cost of producing fine hand-made silver in London was high, and only the rich could afford to buy it in any quantity. The growth of a prosperous middle class with social aspirations created a market for cheaper goods, and this demand was met by Birmingham and Sheffield through the introduction of new labour-saving techniques. Sterling silver was still out of the reach of most purses, but fused plate was an acceptable substitute.

Old Sheffield, or fused plate, was the invention of Thomas Boulsover, a humble working cutler of Sheffield. He discovered in about 1743 that silver and copper stretched at almost identical rates: experiments showed, moreover, that copper when alloyed with small quantities of zinc and lead behaved like sterling silver. It only remained to find a method of fusing the two metals to produce an ingot of copper with a thin layer of silver. This accomplished, it was reduced to the required thickness by rolling (the first attempts were flatted by hand), and was then ready to be hammered and raised into the requisite shapes. It could not, however, be cast, and parts such as spouts and finials had to be made from die-stamped sections of sheet metal soldered together. Nor could it be pierced without revealing the copper until the introduction of double plating (c.1765) and the technique known as fly punching, which burred the silver over on both sides. The manufacturers of Old Sheffield Plate were thus able to produce, at a fraction of the cost, a wide range of objects which were at first glance indistinguishable from solid silver.

Birmingham very soon acquired the techniques for manufacturing fused plate and was quick to recognize the advantages of Sheffield's invention of die stamping, not only for fused plate but also sterling silver. Mass production of parts by this method meant considerable savings to the manufacturers which could be passed on to their customers. The progress made by the goldsmiths of Sheffield and Birmingham began to alarm their London counterparts, particularly in 1773 when the provincial makers decided to petitition Parliament for the right to set up their own assay offices. Hitherto most of their goods had been sent to London for hallmarking, occasioning much expense, delay and damage. The campaign was not without acrimony, and its eventual success owed much to the energy and brilliance of one man, the Birmingham manufacturer Matthew Boulton.

Boulton's name is inseparably linked with the silver of the neoclassical period, not only for the technical advances he pioneered, but also for his preoccupation with authentic antique forms. Many of his pattern books are now housed, appropriately, in the Birmingham Reference Library: a perusal of them establishes Boulton's awareness of the design sources of his day. It is known that Boulton sent his emissaries to Europe: in 1767 Wendler, his agent in Italy, added his employer's name to the list of subscribers to d'Hancarville's volumes on Sir William Hamilton's collection; Emsley, Boulton's London bookseller, was charged with acquiring for him 'such of the volumes of the Museum Florintina [published in Florence in the 1760s] as . . . will be useful to us' as well as five of the volumes published on the archaeological findings at Herculaneum. Boulton's indebtedness to Pergolesi's *Original Designs* (published 1777–1801) is evident in his work. He probably became acquainted with Pergolesi through Robert Adam, who seems at one time to have employed the Italian as an assistant. Adam and Boulton had much in common as their correspondence in the early 1770s testifies, and from time to time Boulton worked to Adam's designs on certain prestigious orders. The architect James Wyatt also designed for Boulton, as did Sir William Chambers.

Faced with this imposing array of talent and business acumen, the London goldsmiths had perforce to accept the status quo. They continued to meet a steady demand for pieces in the classical

SALVER, *one of a pair, silver. London, 1772–3. Maker: Ebenezer Coker. This gadroon-edged salver, or waiter, is remarkable for the exceptionally fine engraving. The ribbon bows and swags surmounting the central armorials are repeated in the wide decorative frieze. Here neoclassical urns of differing design are interspersed with four portrait profiles. Engraved profiles are rarely found on the silver of this period, and it is probable that they had a significant allegorical purpose and were not mere decorative motifs. Diameter: 39.4 cm (15½ in) (Brand Inglis Limited, London)*

TEA URN *(right), silver. London, 1772–3. Makers: John Parker and Edward Wakelin. It is based on a design published in Stefano della Bella's* Raccolta di Vasi diversi *(third vase from the right in the illustration on page 142). The dolphin spout on the tap does not appear on the original sketch. Height: 44.5 cm (17½ in)*

EPERGNE *(below), silver, parcel-gilt. Birmingham, 1775–6. Makers: Matthew Boulton and John Fothergill. The classical female terms which support the frame appear in several Pergolesi designs. Similar figures decorate a stand and burner of 1775 by these makers in the Metropolitan Museum, New York. Height: 42.8 cm (16¾ in)*

taste until the 1790s, when small but significant changes began to emerge. The tops of handles were flattened, straight lines replacing the elegant etiolated curves. A certain angularity is apparent in the shapes of tureens, while sauceboats, cruets, jugs and teapots become distinctly bellied, the latter acquiring a slight collar which deepens later into a veritable cowl. The neoclassical motifs of the Adam era, which had begun to lose their charm in the 1780s, finally gave way to plainer decoration as the century reached its close.

· SCOTLAND AND IRELAND ·

In Scotland, simplicity and functionalism have always characterized silver. Unlike their English counterparts, goldsmiths north of the border lacked the stimulus of large numbers of wealthy fashion-conscious patrons and based their skill on an innate respect for and appreciation of the unadorned metal. Lairds and merchants were often content to order their domestic plate from local burghs such as Banff and Elgin, but such comparatively simple wares would hardly have satisfied the small number of wealthy nobles and landowners educated abroad, particularly in France where the Auld Alliance still obtained. They would have placed their orders in Edinburgh, Glasgow or Aberdeen, where a cautious taste for the rococo had by the 1730s begun to manifest itself.

Although a certain amount of imitation of southern styles is apparent, few of the more outlandish features were adopted. Spouts were sometimes cast as grotesque birds, but for the most part the influence of the rococo is to be seen in a form of flat chasing, so delicate and restrained that at its best it resembles fine lace. This is found particularly on the bullet teapots so popular in Scotland. Table pieces such as salvers, coffee pots, tea-kettles and urns, tea-caddies, scalloped cream jugs and sugar basins lent themselves to rococo decoration. Naturalistic flowers were much favoured, together with shell motifs and trellis work. Handles and feet are gracefully scrolled, but there is little evidence of asymmetry.

The reluctance of the Scots to espouse the more extreme rococo fashions facilitated a smooth transition to neoclassicism. Silver designs began to reflect the interest aroused in the architectural activity of Edinburgh, not least that of Robert Adam, who was born in Scotland and whose name was to become synonymous with the style of silver produced in Britain in the last quarter of the eighteenth century.

It usually took some ten years for London fashions in silver to reach Ireland, but once they were there the Irish goldsmiths invested them with a poetic quality that is instantly recognizable. Their introduction to the rococo was due in part to the many wealthy Anglo-Irish families whose close links with Ireland led them to make their homes there. Fine houses were built in the latest English fashion or older mansions refurbished, and the interior decoration, furniture and silver had to be *à la mode*. Their owners travelled abroad, particularly in France, and followed French fashions very closely. For example, in 1745 the Earl of Kildare (created Duke of Leinster in 1766) commissioned from his London goldsmith George Wickes candelabra that were direct copies of a design by Thomas Germain. Continental influence is also apparent in the superb rococo dinner service (known as the Leinster Service and now in a private collection) which Wickes made for him between 1745 and 1747; it is one of the few that has survived virtually intact. No doubt the Earl's friends and neighbours lost little time in setting local goldsmiths to work, fashioning similar pieces to enable them to keep pace with the Kildares.

The rococo manifested itself tentatively at first, in ornament rather than form, but by the early 1750s undulating borders and exuberantly chased motifs had become predominant, with flowers, fruit, foliage, scrolls and asymmetrical cartouches jostling with dolphins, fishes, birds and farmyard animals. The charming rural vignettes have an insouciance which is peculiarly Irish: proportions and perspective have no place here – cows are dwarfed by milkmaids and shepherds by their sheep. Bucolic designs in rich variety were favourite motifs for dish rings (the so-called potato rings) – which are regarded almost as an Irish speciality – and for the exquisite pierced covers made between 1750 and 1755 which were probably placed over bowls of pot-pourri. These designs seldom appear on coffee pots, which frequently have spouts formed as bird-heads. Birds also feature as cast handles which curve over sauceboats, reminiscent of those made in London by Kandler, and cast eagles are applied to the bodies of sauceboats in such a way that they seem to emerge from them. Human masks are found above the feet of the ubiquitous cream jugs (especially those made in Cork), and lion masks were also popular.

In the last quarter of the eighteenth century the rococo gave way to neoclassicism, ending, as it had begun, some years after its demise in England.

· HOLLAND AND IBERIA ·

In Holland, Huguenot goldsmiths (such as the Mettayer brothers from Rouen) who had emigrated from France after the revocation of the Edict of Nantes in 1685 inevitably brought with them French stylistic influences. They found in Holland a flourishing bourgeois craft supported by a strong, stable economy based on maritime power. Many commodities, which had hitherto been scarcely known, had entered Europe through Dutch ports, and goldsmiths in Holland adapted their wares to meet the new demands. Certain pieces such as coffee urns and tobacco jars were peculiar to Holland. Divergences of form resulted from the division of the country into petty states: the existence of thirty-eight assay towns also contributed to regional variations.

TEA-KETTLE, LAMP AND STAND *(left), silver. Haarlem, 1762. Maker's mark: RB in oblong. The Dutch predilection for organic forms is apparent in this tea-kettle which resembles a pomegranate; the lid and finial complete the illusion. The scrolled stand with its pierced and chased apron is decorated with rococo foliage and trefoils. Height: 27 cm (10⅝ in)*

The native Dutch feeling for the brilliance of the metal and a preference for plain (ungilded) surfaces militated against the extravagances of the French rococo movement, and the fantastical soon gave way to swirling, fluid lines which afforded a wealth of reflections. Although the first sign of the rococo appeared in Holland between 1735 and 1740, it was restricted to trinkets; it did not become current in domestic wares until 1750 when it prevailed for some twenty years. True *rocaille* decoration is seldom found: the quasi-natural small flowers and foliage applied to coffee pots, candlesticks and tureens (notably an important one made in The Hague by Engelbart Jooster in 1766 and now in the Municipal Museum there) are a world away from Meissonnier and Germain. The Dutch favoured organic forms, decorating melon-shaped teapots and milk jugs on twig feet with leaf lids and finials.

By 1770 the Dutch predilection for plain reflecting surfaces had reasserted itself. Swirling rococo candlesticks were replaced by architectural fluted columns in the style advocated by Robert Adam. The Vitruvian scroll, or wave of the sea pattern, was widely adopted in Holland where it was known as the Running Dog Pattern. Beading, a

CANDLESTICK *(above), silver. Dublin, c.1745. Maker unknown. This airy fantasy illustrates the poetic quality of many Irish rococo pieces. Leaves decorate the asymmetric broken scrolls which form the open structure. The tulip-shaped candleholder is chased with stem spirals and bunches of grapes. The nozzle is detachable: its band is chased with shells and fish scales. Height: 26.7 cm (10½ in) (National Museum of Ireland, Dublin)*

fashion copied from England, was much used, particularly on the pairs of boxes for cakes and biscuits which were to be found in every self-respecting household. The decorative possibilities of pierced work were recognized and exploited to some effect. Perhaps the most graceful object of the period – and one peculiar to Holland – was the elegant vase designed to hold chestnut purée.

In Portugal, goldsmiths of the eighteenth century benefited little from their monarch's passion for wrought silver. King John V (1706–50) and his Court preferred to patronize the great French *maîtres orfèvres*, notably Thomas Germain and his son François-Thomas. The indigenous craftsmen, who included a number of French and Italian immigrants, worked mainly for the Church, and while French influence is apparent in their rococo pieces, their work in the neoclassical period owes much to England. In Spain, a country rent by internal and external strife, few outstandingly important pieces were made in the eighteenth century. Church plate was given priority, but some fine secular objects were also produced. French influence is seen in the use of shallow, spiral fluting. As might be expected, the styles of the Iberian motherlands were copied – often in a debased form that might include Indian motifs – in their South and Central American colonies.

CENTREPIECE *(above), silver. Augsburg, 1761–3. Maker: Bernhard H. Weyhe. Part of a service. Width: 72.5 cm (28½ in)*

JARDINIÈRE *(below), one of a pair, silver. Rome, c.1780. Maker: Luigi Valadier. Length: 32 cm (12½ in)*

· GERMANY AND ITALY ·

Many of the capital cities of the numerous small states that made up Germany – such as Dresden, Berlin, Frankfurt and Stuttgart – were renowned for their goldsmiths, as were several of the cities of the old Austro-Hungarian Empire. The most important, however, was undoubtedly Augsburg. The plate made there was much sought after by foreign visitors, including Lady Mary Coke who wrote in 1771: 'This town is famous for plate. They reckon they make it as well here as in any part of Europe, and I saw some that was really very fine.'[3] The large number of commissions placed with Augsburg's goldsmiths for huge dinner services amounted virtually to a monopoly. Not only did they supply the courts of Dresden, Stuttgart, Württemburg and Munich, but also the Russian Imperial Court and that of Gustav V of Sweden.

The silver, both secular and ecclesiastical, that was produced in the rococo period shows extraordinary artistic confidence and fluency. The Augsburg goldsmiths followed Paris, but they invested their work with a quality wholly and unmistakably German. A large number of German pattern books produced in the rococo period emanated from Augsburg. J.H. Haid (1710–76), of Augsburg and Vienna, was among those who published such designs. The chinoiserie centrepiece (left), made for a prince-bishop, derives from a series of drawings, one signed by F.J.Degle, in the Augsburg Staats und Stadtbibliothek, which Bernhard Heinrich Weyhe adapted. Another version, also with Court musicians, is in the Wadsworth Athenaeum, USA.

A certain reluctance to abandon the rococo was apparent at the beginning of the neoclassical period. Form gradually took precedence over decoration, but finials *à la Meissonnier* vanished only very slowly from the lids of tureens. Vase and urn shapes became popular and Vetruvian scroll borders appeared in the familiar company of swags, water-leaves, *paterae* and anthemions.

In Italy, the most important centres for the production of silver were Rome, Turin, Genoa, Venice and Naples. Turin and Genoa, being on the borders of France, were subject to its influence, but much of the secular plate produced in Italy was

inspired by Augsburg. Many Italian goldsmiths, however, invested their work with an exuberance which contrasts strangely with the restraint shown by their mentors. While bold curves – seen to advantage in the *trembleuses* of Genoa and *écuelles* of Turin – were acceptable in the rococo period, they appear less suited to neoclassical pieces.

The best goldsmiths, such as the Roman master Luigi Valadier, brought a sculpturesque quality to their work. Many of their finest pieces were made for churches throughout Catholic Europe. Rome, Naples and Catania were famous for ecclesiastical plate: so too was Messina, where members of the Juvarra family produced many important works.

· RUSSIA, THE BALTIC AND · · SCANDINAVIA ·

In Russia, enthusiasm for western European culture did not end with Peter the Great's death in 1725, and goldsmiths of the calibre of the Swiss-born Jérémie Pauzié and Jean-Pierre Ador continued to emigrate to Russia. Far from imposing European standards on the Slavs, the immigrant masters adapted to Russian taste and produced work that satisfied their clients' preference for the large and colourful. The exceptions to this were the fine gold boxes set with jewels made in St Petersburg for the Empress Catherine II, which owed much to French influence.

The goldsmiths had been content to follow seventeenth-century German fashions until the 1740s when they changed to a somewhat ponderous rococo style. The objects made for the Court did not, however, lack refinement, among them many finely embossed tall cups and covers in silver-gilt. Rococo slowly gave way to classicism, epitomized by the gold Orlov vase made by Ador.

A reaction against classical and western styles took place towards the end of the century, and brought a revival of the filigree, enamel and niello techniques for which the Russians were justly famed. Moscow was the chief centre of niello work in the eighteenth century and Alexey Ratkov one of its greatest exponents.

Baltic silver followed traditional Swedish forms prior to Peter the Great's conquests during the Great Northern War. Thereafter, while such centres as Riga and Estonia were politically dependent on Russia, in cultural matters they were closely associated with Germany. However, many Baltic goldsmiths emigrated to Russia, congregating especially in St Petersburg particularly in the last quarter of the eighteenth century.

In Denmark, the first stirrings of the rococo appeared in about 1740 and showed a marked French influence. Fluting, profusely curved, was the standard form of decoration, becoming twisted and swirling in the 1750s. Rococo shells, somewhat crudely chased, were popular, together with C-scrolls, cross-banded reeding and, occasionally, flowers. Asymmetry was not adopted until after 1750.

The tureen assumed great significance and was given pride of place in the centre of the table. The preferred form appears to have been the bellied outline of the *pot-à-oille*, bulbous shapes being much favoured for all hollow-ware. French influence is also visible in the scroll salts. A vogue for grotesque spouts prevailed: reminiscent of prow decoration on Viking ships, they may have been inspired by French designs published in the 1730s. They are found on many tea urns, teapots and coffee pots. Spoons are based on French patterns, while the pear-shaped tea canisters may well have been influenced by English fashions.

VASE, *two-coloured gold and enamel. St Petersburg, 1768. Maker: Jean-Pierre Ador. This early example of Louis XVI style in Russia is decorated with enamel* grisaille *plaques and the cypher of Prince Orlov, favourite of Catherine II. Height: 28.5 cm (11¼ in) (The Walters Art Gallery, Baltimore)*

DESIGN *(above), for a centrepiece. Christian Precht, c.1750. This is one of a series of delicate rococo designs for table centrepieces. In some of Precht's sketches the baskets are filled with fruit and flowers. He occasionally incorporates scrolling candlesticks, but here the basket, cradled in its frame, is set on a plateau and flanked by a silver caster and a glass ewer cruet mounted in silver. Dimensions: 49 × 69 cm ($19\frac{1}{4}$ × $27\frac{1}{8}$ in) (Nationalmuseum, Stockholm)*

PAIR OF CASTERS *(above right), silver. Pernau, Estonia, c.1785. Maker: Ernst Diedrich Rahm (probably). A certain naïveté in these casters does not detract from their charm. The Estonian goldsmith's regional interpretation of neoclassical form and ornament suggests the influence of Sweden rather than that of Russia. Height: 20.5 cm (8 in)*

Vases, urns and pillars – the stock-in-trade of neoclassicism – began to appear in Copenhagen in the 1770s, but a tendency to the bulbous was still apparent even in vase shapes. In the 1790s Sheffield Plate with blue glass liners was being imported from England.

In Norway, reluctance to give full rein to rococo exuberance is evident in the silver made in the 1750s. There was inevitably a time lag between the inception of the style in France and its cautious acceptance in most parts of Scandinavia and even then it had to co-exist with Bérainesque decoration which the Northerners were loth to abandon.

A fine maker in the rococo idiom was Tore Andreas Friis of Trondhjem. Also in Trondhjem was Johs Kelberlade, whose speciality was floral candelabra, which were also produced in Bergen. Cruet sets on salvers were common to both centres: their swirling fluted bodies are frequently surmounted by the birds with long necks and wide wingspan which were in constant use as finials on all kinds of domestic hollow-ware. Grotesque spouts are to be found on fluted pear-shaped coffee pots, and also on oil and vinegar containers.

Neoclassicism reached Norway from France, England and Germany in the 1770s and 1780s. Its decorative motifs, particularly the medallion and the swag, were transformed by the Norwegian goldsmiths into something approaching folk ornament.

In Sweden, the lure of Paris, although stronger than in the rest of Scandinavia, was tempered by the high prices charged by the French goldsmiths. The problem was partly overcome by aquiring drawings from France to serve as models for the Swedish goldsmiths. The archive thus formed, now in the National Museum at Stockholm, is a rich and valuable source of information on French designs.

The most brilliant of Sweden's rococo goldsmiths was Christian Precht. In 1727, the year he qualified as a journeyman, Precht set out for London where he worked for the Augsburg goldsmith Augustin Heckel. Paris was his next port of call and there, inevitably, he fell under the spell of Meissonnier and Thomas Germain. After visiting Augsburg and other German cities he returned to Stockholm in 1731 and began to work in the rococo style. In 1737 he was granted the privilege of conducting his trade as an independent artist free of Guild intervention. This however debarred him from the right to a maker's mark and without it silver could not be sold to the public although it could be supplied to the Court. Unfortunately the considerable quantity of royal plate made by Precht has been melted down and refashioned. Those pieces believed to be by him which have survived are marked with the makers' punches of fellow goldsmiths prepared to submit them for assay: their attribution to Precht is based on the fact that they far excel in design and quality other pieces made by the goldsmiths whose marks they bear. The high rococo baptismal ewer and basin of 1745 with the mark of Johan Colin (Eriksberg Castle) is a case in point: scholars are convinced that such a masterpiece can only have been made by Christian Precht. There is, however, no doubt about his authorship of the silver designs in the National Museum at Stockholm. His deftness and delicacy of touch were ideally suited to the airy flights of rococo inspiration – skill of the highest order would have been needed to translate them into silver. Porcelain beckoned to Precht in Stockholm as it did to Sprimont in London: designs made by him for the Marieberg faience factory are known, and it is possible that he may also have worked for the important firm of Rörstrand.

Enthusiasm for the rococo did not completely oust the old styles. Beakers continued to be made in the traditional trumpet shape and here the only acknowledgment of the existence of the new style is a band of engraved ornament beneath the rims in which *rocaille* mingles with Bérainesque strapwork.

In the last quarter of the eighteenth century Sweden turned once more to France for inspiration. Her ambassador in Paris, Count de Creutz, was able to avail himself of Robert-Joseph Auguste's incomparable work, but the Swedish goldsmiths of the day, lacking the exceptional gifts of a Precht, produced pieces in the neoclassical taste which were often massively handsome but seldom elegant.

· NORTH AMERICA ·

Silver produced in the American Colonies during the rococo and neoclassical periods, though often well made, was rarely more than a provincial version of that of one or other of the motherlands.

The rococo reached the American Colonies in the late 1740s, more than a decade after its adoption in England. It is evident from the newspaper advertisements of the time that large quantities of plate were imported from England. They not only served the American goldsmiths as models, but spurred them to compete on the highest level for their economic survival. Their interpretation of the rococo style was more restrained, and manifested itself mainly in elegant pear-shaped forms, double-scrolled handles and cast shell and C-scroll ornament, venturing only occasionally into asymmetry.

Little silver was made during the Revolutionary War, and by the time it ended rococo had given way to neoclassicism, whose extreme simplicity appealed to the new republic. Cultural ties with England were unimpaired, and the design source for the new forms was still to be found in English imported plate. The urn shape was very popular: it was even chosen as a symbol by the goldsmiths of Philadelphia who portrayed the Genius of America holding a silver urn on a banner carried by them on 4 July 1788. Bright-cut engraving was also extensively used.

Canada's dependence on France in the first half of the eighteenth century is reflected in the work of her goldsmiths, who followed the styles fashionable in the mother country, albeit in a far less sophisticated form. Although contact with France became more difficult after Canada passed into British hands following the Treaty of Paris in 1763, Canadian goldsmiths such as Laurent Amyot were still sent there to learn their craft even in the 1780s. Simplicity of form and sobriety of decoration are evident, even during the rococo period. Its influence, more apparent in church silver than secular pieces, continued well into the last quarter of the eighteenth century until it finally merged imperceptibly into neoclassicism.

CHALICE *(above), silver and silver-gilt. Quebec, 1784. Maker: François Ranvoyzé. Ranvoyzé's work was clearly based on earlier French styles. This chalice is more colonial rococo than metropolitan neoclassical. Height: 26 cm (10¼ in) (The National Gallery of Canada, Ottawa)*

TEAPOT, JUG AND SUGAR VASE *(left), silver. Philadelphia, c.1785. Maker: Abraham Dubois. The vase shape predominates, relieved by beading and by the pierced gallery – borrowed from England – which was peculiar to Philadelphia. Height (teapot): 28.8 cm (11¼ in) (Yale University Art Gallery, New Haven)*

· 7 · THE NINETEENTH AND EARLY · · TWENTIETH CENTURIES ·

More plate was made in the course of the nineteenth century than at any other time, before or since. One trigger for this unprecedented increase in production was the phenomenal growth in the population of the western hemisphere, which began in the mid-eighteenth century but accelerated after 1800 when the population of Europe was already 180 million. By 1900 that figure had more than doubled, despite mass emigration between 1815 and 1914, when about 40 million Europeans made a new life for themselves in the USA, Canada, Australia and other parts of the world. The emigrants carried their own national traditions to their new countries, creating a ready market for goods imported from their homelands, and manufacturers of silverwork in Europe were among the beneficiaries of this spread of European culture.

The population grew fastest in the countries transformed by the Industrial Revolution, of which Britain was a prime instance. The expanding manufacturing towns attracted agricultural labourers as well as craftsmen, who saw their livings disappear as mechanization advanced; long before the end of the century Britain had changed from an agricultural to a manufacturing nation. Steam, replacing water, wind and animal power, shortened and cheapened the production process; after 1830 it drove the locomotives and ships that took the finished goods all over the world.

One man who recognized the importance of modern technology was Prince Albert of Saxe-Coburg-Gotha (1819–1861), who came to England as the consort of Queen Victoria in 1840. He saw in it both a force for international free trade and an instrument for effecting unity between nations, and expressed these views at a banquet in 1850 given by the Lord Mayor of London for the purpose of raising funds for the proposed Great Exhibition the following year. The Prince spoke of living 'at a period of most wonderful transition'. 'Science', he said, 'discovers these laws of power, motion, and transformation; industry applies them to the raw matter, which the earth yields us in abundance, but which becomes valuable by knowledge.[1]

Prince Albert's unquestioning faith in the benefits of industrial development was characteristic of his time, and survived war, revolution in Europe and periodic trade depressions. Fifteen years after his death the biggest slump of the century drastically affected world trade and accelerated the rate of emigration from Europe. The apparent failure of industry in several countries precipitated a reaction which rejected machinery in favour of a return to craftsmanship. England, the forcing-house of the Industrial Revolution, became in the 1880s the cradle of the Arts and Crafts Movement, whose earnestly amateur and idiosyncratic silverwork was emulated the world over. The commercial silver trade in England, on the other hand, already battered by further technological innovations which put other countries in the lead, never fully recovered. Elsewhere in Europe and America, experimental work by artists and craftsmen had more effect on the great commercial silversmithing firms than it had in England, and France, Austria, Germany, America and Scandinavia all contributed more than England to the evolution of Art Deco silverwork.

· THE UNITED KINGDOM ·

As the eighteenth century gave way to the nineteenth, the Industrial Revolution in Britain was still in the process of transforming the old craft trades. The innovations introduced by Sheffield plate manufacturers, such as rolled sheet-metal components and decorative details stamped from steel dies by means of first horsepower and then water-power, were augmented in about 1820 by steam-powered lathes, which facilitated the mass-production of bodies on preformed chucks. The Sheffield manufacturer Samuel Roberts (1763–1843), a particularly fecund inventor, was responsible for several further improvements in the production and decoration of fused plate.

The new techniques spread from Sheffield and Birmingham, where machines were commonplace, to London. Leading manufacturers there realized their importance, particularly in the initial stages of silver-making, though the best work

FRUIT STAND *(facing page), silver. London, 1812. Maker: Paul Storr for Rundell, Bridge & Rundell, Royal Goldsmiths to George III. Storr, one of the most brilliant goldsmiths to work for Rundell's, also made silver-gilt versions of this piece, one of which is in the first Duke of Wellington's service at the Wellington Museum, Apsley House, London. Height: 35.2 cm (13⅞ in) (Victoria and Albert Museum, London)*

THREE-PIECE TEA SET *(above left), silver. Sheffield, 1868. Makers: Roberts & Belk. The circular bodies are each flat-chased with a cartouche and a frieze of classical figures on a matted ground between two engraved bands of laurel. The hinged cover of the teapot has a helmet finial. Height of jug: 28 cm (11 in)*

TEAPOT *(above right), silver. London, 1833. Maker: Edward Farrell. Farrell often used genre scenes inspired by seventeenth-century Dutch paintings in his naturalistic rococo pieces. Height: 19 cm (7½ in) (Victoria and Albert Museum, London)*

continued to be fashioned by hand. Provincial manufacturers of Sheffield plate used the same techniques for silverwork in the spare and elegant style of the early neoclassical period.

The Soho Manufactory, founded in the previous century by Matthew Boulton on the outskirts of Birmingham, employed able designers. From the 1760s onwards, silver and plated wares from Soho were exported in some quantity. Boulton had many contacts on the Continent and, like the Sheffield manufacturers, he issued catalogues to facilitate business. The influence of these catalogues on plate design in Scandinavia and America appears to have been considerable. Boulton died in 1809, and though Soho went on until 1848, its great days were over.

Edward Thomason, the first knight of the Birmingham trades and former apprentice to Matthew Boulton, set up on his own after his father's death in 1793. His factory in Church Street, Birmingham, turned out a diverse range of wares. One of his most prestigious works was a long table plateau of silver, mirror-glass and wood, made in 1818–19 in a mixed Gothic-classical manner for the Duke of Northumberland. According to Thomason's *Memoirs during Half a Century* (1845), the piece was designed by the Duchess; it was further extended – to nearly 216 cm (7 ft 1 in) – in 1841–2 by Robinson, Edkins & Aston for the Soho Manufactory. An exercise in eighteenth-century Georgian Gothic, the Northumberland table plateau was clearly made to consort with Robert Adam's Gothicization of the interior of Alnwick Castle in the 1760s.

Eighteenth-century antiquarianism continued into the nineteenth century, stimulating the archaeological revival of several historic styles, all of which flourished together. Experimental work in these, carried on in London during the first decade of the century, had a wide influence the world over. To the revived rococo, baroque, Renaissance and Gothic styles, and occasional forays into the Chinese manner, was added the exploration of naturalism.

Rundell, Bridge & Rundell of Ludgate Hill in the City of London, Royal Goldsmiths to George III and the royal family from 1804, had a stable of designers on whom they called from time to time. One of these was the French artist J. J. Boileau, who came to England in about 1787; three years later he was introducing in his silver a severe Greek style based on pre-Revolutionary French work. His designs are comparable with work of the late 1780s by the Royal Goldsmith to Louis XVI, Henry Auguste, whose sturdy forms and dignified ornament were later enshrined in English and Regency silver. Boileau was perhaps responsible, too, for bringing the Egyptian motifs which had characterized some French designs of the 1780s to English work just before 1800, predating the publication of Vivant-Denon's *Voyage dans la Basse et la Haute Egypte* (1802), which drew wider attention to Egyptian ornament.

Some of Boileau's work was executed by Paul Storr who, in sub-partnership with Rundell's, directed their workshops in Dean Street, Soho, from 1807 until 1819. Rundell's first workshop, started in 1802 in Lime Kiln Lane, Greenwich, was managed by Benjamin Smith, variously in partnership with Digby Scott, his brother James Smith and finally his own son, Benjamin junior. This workshop closed with the Smiths' departure in 1813. William Theed (1764–1817), the painter and sculptor who in 1804 joined Rundell's as their chief modeller (and later junior partner), lived in Greenwich for several years to be near the workshops, where orders for large table services in silver-gilt and silver, magnificently adorned with cast decoration, were executed. Rundell's continued, however, to use outworkers such as Storr, Philip Cornman & Son and the two William Pitts, father and son. Once the Dean Street manufactory was started, the work went to whichever workshop had spare capacity at the time. Scott and the elder Benjamin Smith produced, among other pieces, the earliest of the Trafalgar Vases designed by the sculptor John Flaxman (1755–1826), commissioned by Lloyd's Patriotic Fund for distribution to the admirals and captains who fought with Nelson at the Battle of Trafalgar in 1805. Subsequent versions were executed by Storr.

After Storr's departure, Rundell's retained the Dean Street workshops, and the plate produced there bears the marks of Philip Rundell (until 1823) and then of John Bridge (until his death in 1834). The remaining partners then relied solely on outworkers, all in London, most of whom had earlier associations with the firm. Among them were William Bateman II, (probably) Thomas Wimbush, John Angell, and Edward Barnard & Sons. Barnard's, which has continued as a manufacturer to this day, is more important than it seems. It anonymously supplied ten major items to firms participating in the 1851 Great Exhibition, including a combined centrepiece and candelabrum designed by Charles Grant, adorned with figures by E. G. Papworth (1809–66). The centrepiece was made for Lambert & Rawlings of Coventry Street, London, who were awarded a Prize Medal; the other exhibitors of Barnard's work included Widdowson & Veale of the Strand, Emanuel of Hanover Square, Payne's of Bath, Joseph Mayer of Liverpool and Martin, Baskett & Co. of Cheltenham.[2]

John Flaxman was Rundell's most distinguished artist, but most of his silver designs were modelled by others, such as his pupil Edward Hodges Baily (1788–1867). Both Flaxman and William Theed, who had earlier been employed by Wedgwood, the potters, were masters of the neoclassical repertory of shapes and motifs. This was derived in part from classical architectural detailing and carved stone artefacts, like the Medici krater in the Uffizi Gallery, Florence, and the Borghese krater in the Louvre, Paris. Both vases were engraved for publication by G. B. Piranesi (1720–78), the architect, artist and restorer of classical fragments in Italy. The Warwick Vase (now in the Burrell Collection, Glasgow) is probably the best-known example of Piranesi's restoration, and was much copied; reduced versions were made as wine-coolers and cups by Storr and others. Piranesi's *Vasi, Candelabri, Cippi, Sarcofagi* (1778) was widely used by designers and silversmiths. Storr had a copy in his workshop, and in 1808 Smith executed a set of silver-gilt wine-coolers for the Prince of Wales, based on the two antique kraters cited above. Greek pottery vases such as those in the Hamilton collection (published by d'Hancarville in the 1760s) were equally important. D'Hancarville's illustrations were accompanied by geometric analyses of the forms, and it is clear that much early nineteenth-century neoclassical design is based on mathematical proportions. C. H. Tatham's *Designs for Ornamental Plate* (1806) and Thomas Hope's *Household Designs for Ornamental Furniture and Decoration* (1807) were two publications which also encouraged this development. Flaxman was interested in other modes too; his National Cup in the Royal Collection, designed in about 1819 and executed by Rundell's in 1824–5, is an exercise in the Gothic manner.

Flaxman was among the designers who also looked to nature for inspiration. Another was the painter Thomas Stothard (1755–1834), who also worked for Rundell's on occasion. Flaxman's group of nymphs clustering around the serpent guarding the tree with golden apples in the garden of the Hesperides, which forms the upper stage of a silver-gilt candelabrum of 1809–11, is remarkable for its realistic depiction of the curving tree trunk which acts as the supporting column for the top range of candle branches. Over the next three decades the naturalism now associated with neoclassicism increasingly eroded its symmetry and formality. The revival of the rococo also fostered an interest in nature, and an extra ingredient was added by the incorporation of genre scenes after seventeenth-century Dutch paintings, a speciality of the London silversmith Edward Farrell, who supplied the retailer Kensington Lewis.

In time, natural forms ceased to be used only as decorative motifs and took over the whole structure of objects, particularly between about 1825 and 1850. Much of the stylistic experimentation at this time was carried out for George III's eldest son George (1762–1830), successively Prince of Wales, Prince Regent and George IV, and an amateur antiquary who when he was King commissioned

THREE NATURALISTIC ITEMS, *silver.*
Artichoke dish. London, 1850. Makers: Charles Thomas Fox and George Fox. Height: 9.5 cm ($3\frac{3}{4}$ in)
Salt cellar in the shape of a sea urchin. London 1826. Maker: John Bridge. Height: 6.3 cm ($2\frac{1}{2}$ in)
Taperstick. London, 1840. Makers: Edward Barnard & Sons. Height: 10 cm ($3\frac{7}{8}$ in)
(Victoria and Albert Museum, London)

GROUP OF PIECES *designed by A. W. N. Pugin. Pair of salt cellars and spoons, silver, parcel-gilt. Birmingham, 1844. Maker: Hardman & Iliffe. Height of salt cellars: 9.5 cm (3¾ in) Dish, silver, parcel-gilt and enamel. Birmingham, 1847–8. Maker: John Hardman. Designed for Henry Benson in gratitude for his attempts to mediate between Pugin and the family of Helen Lumsden, to whom Pugin was secretly betrothed. Diameter: 41 cm (16¼ in) Chalice, silver, parcel-gilt, with champlevé enamel and garnets. Birmingham, 1850. Maker: John Hardman. Height: 26 cm (10¼ in) (Victoria and Albert Museum, London)*

Wyatville to gothicize Windsor Castle in the 1820s. The young A. W. N. Pugin (1812–52) designed some of the furnishings, and is now thought to have been responsible for two items of plate made by Rundell's for the King in 1827, when the designer was only fifteen years old. One was the so-called 'Coronation Cup', a jewelled piece in the Gothic style, hallmarked for 1826–7. Other revived styles were developed under the aegis of the writer, antiquary and collector William Beckford (1759–1844), notably Renaissance, Veneto-Saracenic and Chinese; there is an example of each of the three styles in the Victoria and Albert Museum, London.[3] The figurative silverwork made by Rundell's set a fashion which, like the revived styles, was followed by other silversmiths.

Rundell's successors as Royal Goldsmiths in 1843 were R. & S. Garrard, descended from George Wickes (see page 133). Garrard's preferred to be known as the Crown Jewellers. In 1833 they had recruited a bronzist, Edmund Cotterill (c.1795–c.1860), trained at the Royal Academy Schools, as their chief artist. Storr, who had retreated to workshops in Harrison Street, off Gray's Inn Road, after leaving Rundell's in 1819, went into partnership with John Mortimer in 1822, thereby acquiring retail premises in New Bond Street, and eventually secured the services of several artists who had worked for the Royal Goldsmiths, including E. H. Baily and Frank Howard (1805–66). In 1839 Storr and Mortimer took on as a partner Storr's nephew by marriage, John Samuel Hunt, a silver chaser who had worked with Storr in both Dean Street and Harrison Street. After Storr's retirement in the same year the firm was known for a few years as Mortimer & Hunt and then as Hunt & Roskell until the end of the century; they were taken over by J. W. Benson.

One of the best known artist-craftsmen recruited by Hunt & Roskell was the Frenchman Antoine Vechte (1799–1868), who had been spotted by one of the partners in Paris and given a commission to make a vase in the Mannerist style. After the Revolution of 1848 had deprived him of work, Vechte left his native country and became an employee of Hunt & Roskell in London. He influenced the young artists employed by the firm, including Henry Hugh Armstead (1828–1905) and Frank Hunt, who designed the Goodwood Cup in 1857. Vechte was a virtuoso artist-craftsman, embossing pieces in the manner of the late sixteenth and early seventeenth centuries. Even though he worked the silver into a prepared die, embossing (known as repoussé in the nineteenth century) was difficult because of the risk of tearing the metal. Inevitably likened to Cellini, he was acclaimed at the Great Exhibition of 1851, although the jury, while awarding the high distinction of a Council Medal to his employers Hunt & Roskell, gave Vechte only an Honourable Mention. Nevertheless, Vechte attracted the patronage of Prince Albert and Queen Victoria. His work was the antithesis of industrial production, combining old techniques and an old style in flamboyant objects which were admired by virtually everyone.

G. R. Elkington & Co. of Birmingham, the patentees in 1840 of the electroplating process which caused the demise of the manufacture of Sheffield plate,[4] took pains to offset their commercial image by recruiting French artists and craftsmen for their silverwork. One of the first designers and modellers to join them from Paris, attracted by the prospect of good wages and a stable society, was P.-E. Jeannest, who died in 1857. Jeannest was succeeded by Vechte's former pupil Léonard Morel-Ladeuil (1820–88) and by A. A. Willms (1827–99) (the latter having first come to England in the wake of the French goldsmith J-V. Morel, who settled briefly in Burlington Street in 1849). Morel-Ladeuil and Willms, working in both the classical and Renaissance manners and supported by the firm's French craftsmen, dominated Elkington's display at the international exhibitions between 1862 and 1873. Quick to follow suit, other firms started luring French designers to England; the London retailer Harry Emanuel, for instance, showed works by Aimé Chesneau at the 1862 International Exhibition in London, and C. F. Hancock employed the Italian sculptor Raffaele Monti (1818–81).

The virtuoso pieces flooding these exhibitions and securing all the attention bore out the observations made by a trade commissioner, Dr (later Sir John) Bowring, in his evidence to the Select Committee of Arts and Manufacturers of 1835–6. Bowring believed that the French national exhibitions encouraged firms to make special pieces for show instead of improving ordinary productions. The Select Committee supported Free Trade, but nevertheless held that English design had gravely deteriorated since the great days of the Regency. English manufacturers were threatened by the French, who had the edge on design. Much of the Committee's deliberations, therefore, addressed the question of what actually constituted good design, which was particularly difficult with so many revived styles on offer. The preferred solution was to rate some styles more highly than others. Those styles (usually classically based) which were interpreted with archaeological exactitude were more meritorious than, say, the rococo, which could be assembled casually from a few scrolls and flowers. Naturalism was, on the whole, approved of; it was already becoming one of the most interesting (and certainly the most original) early Victorian styles. The Committee's final report noted with approbation the plans for the establishment of the first School of Design, in London; recommended that museums be set up in the principal manufacturing towns to improve taste and furnish examples to designers; declared it desirable that patent protection be extended to designs (a proposal which eventually led to the Design Acts of 1839 and 1842); and made sundry other suggestions.

The Committee failed, however, to distinguish between designing for crafts and for the machine, and most of the witnesses who had anything to do with silverwork were biased towards hand-made articles. At the international exhibitions from 1851 onwards, excellence was to be represented by works embodying the craft principle almost to excess. The problem confronted Henry Cole, who distinguished himself on the Executive Committee at the Great Exhibition of 1851 and was rewarded by being put in charge of all Schools of Design in England, Scotland and Ireland, together with the new Museum of Manufactures, the ancestor of the Victoria and Albert Museum. The museum opened with five thousand pounds' worth of modern objects purchased from the Exhibition; within a year, however, Cole began to transform the collection by adding antique articles. In spite of his brief to train designers for industry, Cole never lost his preference for traditional craft techniques.

Cole and his associates were regarded as the cultural establishment of England, partly because they ran a government concern, but also because they were the instruments through which the Prince Consort hoped to realize his dream of a

TITAN *or* JUPITER VASE, *silver, partly oxidized and embossed with figures in high relief. London, 1847. Maker: Antoine Vechte. Vechte's strength lay in the difficult task of embossing figurative compositions of great complexity. Height: 75 cm (29½ in) (The Worshipful Company of Goldsmiths, London)*

CANDELABRUM, *one of a pair, silver-gilt. London, 1809. Maker: Paul Storr for Rundell, Bridge & Rundell. It is decorated with a group of the nymphs of Nysa with the serpent in the garden of Hesperides. The candelabrum's upper stages were designed by John Flaxman, RA. Height: 50 cm (19⅝ in) (Royal Collection, London. Reproduced by gracious permission of HM the Queen)*

TWO DECANTERS *designed by William Burges. Decanter (right), Chinese* sang-de boeuf *porcelain body mounted in silver-gilt with semi-precious stones and enamel. London, 1870. Maker unknown. Burges designed this decanter for his own collection, and the beaded foot carries the inscription 'WILLIELMVS BURGES EX LIBRO SUO ANO DNI MDCCCLXX'. Height: 28 cm (11⅛ in) Decanter (far right), silver, glass, carved crystal, stones and antique coins. London, 1865. Maker: R. A. Green. Height: 27.9 cm (11 in) (Victoria and Albert Museum, London)*

complex devoted to the arts and sciences at South Kensington, where the Museum was sited in 1857. Cole met the Prince, the President of the Society of Arts, after joining its Council in 1846, and rapidly acquired a reputation as an authority on industrial design when he launched a scheme in 1847 for the manufacture of articles designed by fine artists under the title, 'Felix Summerly's Art Manufactures'.

The Great Exhibition made a large profit, but in terms of design it was generally agreed that the British were outshone by the French. Naturalism ran riot through the English section in particular; while the remnants of early nineteenth-century neoclassicism, swathed in undisciplined acanthus foliage, adorned many objects. Tudor, baroque and rococo articles abounded, with a small presence of work of Oriental inspiration; the Gothic was largely confined to the medieval Court mounted by A. W. N. Pugin. Some critical sense had to be made of this mixture, and the task befell Cole's friend Richard Redgrave (1808–88), a Summerly artist soon to become part of the South Kensington establishment. Redgrave's *Supplementary Report on Design*, which was completed in November 1851, attacked naturalistic statuary silver treated with 'imitation ... textures', and 'the flimsy and tinsel-like appearance' of silver plant forms, which were as 'much beneath the impressive effect in metal of even mere plain surface, as they are wide of any pretensions to fitness or propriety as works in metal at all'. Other manners such as the baroque in his view demonstrated 'gross contempt of constructive principles'. Like the Select Committee on Arts and Manufacturers, Redgrave opted for the safety of neoclassicism – in his case the latest version, appearing in about 1840, which, though Greek in inspiration, was often called Etruscan. C. F. Hancock of Bruton Street, who received a Council Medal (the highest award) from the jury, and Joseph Angell of the Strand (a prize medallist) were among the 1851 exhibitors to show work in the Etruscan genre. The decoration was sometimes cast or flat-chased, but later stamped or engraved on mass-produced wares. The recurrence of Greek forms encouraged Redgrave to insist on functionalism; ornament, he maintained, must decorate form, not disguise it. Vechte also received great praise; Redgrave thought highly of the French practice of oxidizing the surface of figurative silver, which eliminated reflections and allowed the modelling to show;[5] and much statuary silver produced in London was later oxidized.

The teaching at the Schools of Design (later renamed Schools of Art by Cole) concentrated on classical styles, including those of the Renaissance, allied to functional form. The South Kensington approach is manifested by Owen Jones's *The Grammar of Ornament* (1856), in which motifs from virtually every known style are interpreted in a disciplined, two-dimensional angularity. The most outstanding graduate from the London School was Christopher Dresser (1834–1904) who afterwards gained a doctorate for his botanical research from the University of Jena. Dresser, who went to Japan in 1876, used a Japanese Shinto arch form for the handles of his silver and electroplated wares, which were designed for machine production with little or no surface decoration, and made by a number of firms.

Cole continued to play an active part in international exhibitions, and it was his influence, above all, which brought about the transformation seen in the British silverwork at the London 1862 Exhibition. A strong emphasis on the new neoclassicism, together with prestigious work in the late Renaissance manner by Vechte and others, caused the French considerable anxiety lest they be overtaken by the English.

The Medievalists in England were motivated partly by religious conviction, partly by antiquarian enthusiasm; the latter eventually predominated. Two gem-set and enamelled chalices designed in the medieval manner by Pugin, and made by John Hardman & Co. of Birmingham, were among the pieces bought from the 1851 Exhibition for the foundation collection of the South Kensington Museum. Pugin, architect, designer and writer, was converted to Roman Catholicism in 1835 and henceforth argued that the Gothic style was the only one fit for a Christian country, appropriate to both ecclesiastical and secular work.

His view influenced the followers of the Oxford or Tractarian Movement which in the 1830s and early 1840s argued that the true origins of the Anglican Church lay in the pre-Reformation Catholic Church. These tenets offended the powerful evangelical wing of the Church of England, and made it difficult for Tractarians openly to patronize Pugin and his fellow Catholic Hardman, the only people to make church plate and other furnishings in the antiquarian Gothic manner. Supporters of Tractarianism in Cambridge founded the Cambridge Camden Society (later to be called the Ecclesiological Society) for the study of medieval buildings and furnishings. In 1842–3, the Society launched its own scheme for the manufacture of articles in the Gothic style from the designs of the architect William Butterfield (1814–1900), whose church plate (by J. Keith & Son of Westmoreland Terrace, City Road) was represented at the Great Exhibition. Butterfield was succeeded as official designer to the Society in 1856 by G. E. Street (1824–81), who in turn gave way in 1864 to William Burges (1827–81). Burges, one of the most eminent antiquarian architects of his day, soon persuaded the Ecclesiological Society to drop Keith in favour of Barkentin & Krall of Regent Street. A master of Gothic idiom, his sumptuous, eclectic designs for domestic silverwork were executed by several silversmiths including R. A. Green of the Strand and Hart & Son of nearby Wych Street. The writer John Ruskin (1819–1900), self-appointed secular prophet of the Medievalists, adopted Pugin's view that machine production lacked the honesty of craft work and degraded the operative.

After the British triumph at the 1862 Exhibition, the trade fostered further historic revivals, including late eighteenth-century neoclassicism, as well as work in the Queen Anne manner which, though exceptionally popular from the 1870s and 1890s, had been in Garrard's repertory since the 1830s. Borrowing from the French, manufacturers laid renewed emphasis on the rococo manner, which, with neoclassicism and other historic styles, persisted well into the twentieth century.

The trade, though, was falling on hard times, exacerbated by the great Depression which began in the mid-1870s. Under pressure from the current fashion for Japonoiserie, British silversmiths considered themselves unreasonably shackled by the hallmarking laws which forbade the combination of precious and base metals. While Tiffany's of New York achieved a resounding success at the Paris 1878 Exhibition with their coloured and encrusted wares in the Japanese taste, English manufacturers, prohibited from using copper and other base metals as decorative motifs, were compelled to employ expensive coloured gold for their ornaments, or simply to engrave suitable motifs such as cranes and bamboo to evoke the style. Moreover, as was pointed out to the Select Committee on Hallmarking in 1878, the Americans paid no tax on wrought silver, as the British did, which gave them export advantages.

The decline of the British trade was underlined by statistics quoted by one witness to the Select Committee which showed that duty was paid on 994,360 troy ounces of manufactured silver in 1855, while in 1877 the figure was 798,206 ounces. The reduction was partly due to the doubled cost of working plate, but also to the increase in the manufacture of electroplate. The Gorham Plate Company (cited but unnamed) of Rhode Island, said to employ 800 people, produced 'more silver in one year than the whole of the British silversmiths put together'.[6] Ironically, Gorham's (see page 190) employed many Europeans, including Englishmen. Despite the protests, it was not until 1890 that the duty on wrought plate was abolished.

The illustrated catalogues issued in the 1880s by a London firm of middlemen, Silber & Fleming (in the Library of the Victoria and Albert Museum), show that patterns current in the early Victorian period continued to be produced, but manufacturers had also turned to making novelties for the big London shops. Flower-holders often replaced centrepieces with candelabra as the principal items on the table, as gas and then electric lighting were adopted. Hunt & Roskell, Garrard and other leading firms still made traditional sculptural silver, but even they had withdrawn from international exhibitions by the 1880s.

The principal English exhibitor at the Paris 1900 Exhibition was the Goldsmiths and Silversmiths Company of Regent Street, whose Silver Medal was gained largely for replicas of historic pieces in the Victorian and Albert Museum and other items in the antiquarian taste, though the jury report cited with approval a group of articles of modern design.[7] These were executed for the firm by the silversmiths William Hutton & Sons of Sheffield, who set up an experimental workshop in London and made up the designs of artists such as Kate Harris, a graduate of the South Kensington School. Kate Harris's style was formed partly by Continental Art Nouveau, partly by the silverwork of the Arts and Crafts movement. Elkington's also made a gesture in the direction of modernity by employing an artist, Florence Steele, as a designer, but the greater part of the firm's output continued much as before. Other firms,

AESTHETIC PIECES. *Egg coddler, silver. London, 1884. Designer: Christopher Dresser. Maker: H. Stratford. Plate, silver inlaid with two-coloured gold. London, 1878. Maker: D. & C. Houle. Tea service, silver, parcel-gilt. London, 1876. Maker: J. & W. Barnard. Height of teapot: 14.5 cm (5¾ in) (Victoria and Albert Museum, London)*

COFFEE SERVICE *(facing page, below), silver with an ivory handle on the coffee pot. London, 1898–9. Designer: Kate Harris. Maker: William Hutton & Sons for the Goldsmiths and Silversmiths Co. Height of coffee pot: 17 cm (6¾ in) (Kunstindustrimuseum, Oslo)*

such as Mappin & Webb and Walker & Hall of Sheffield, occasionally added modern designs to their catalogues; but in general it was the lesser Birmingham manufacturers who pillaged French Art Nouveau motifs.

A commercial enterprise launched in about 1899 under the title of Cymric Silver by A. L. Liberty of Regent Street, London, also married the designs of artists to mass production. The work was made in the factory of W. H. Haseler in Birmingham, and the artists, who unfortunately went unacknowledged, included Archibald Knox (1864–1933), the most brilliant designer connected with the scheme, Bernard Cuzner (1877–1956) and Oliver Baker (1856–1939).

The Arts and Crafts Movement came into being with the founding of the Art Workers' Guild in 1884, followed by the Arts and Crafts Exhibition Society four years later. It was a social and aesthetic movement, reflecting not only the widespread dissatisfaction with the quality of manufactured goods which had grown after the Great Exhibition, but also an admiration for folk art and for the old guilds of medieval craftsmen. Its ideas were enunciated by John Ruskin and given practical expression by William Morris. Among the Guild members was the sculptor Alfred Gilbert (1854–1934), whose spectacular baroque manner was brilliantly employed in an epergne (Royal Collection, on loan to the Victoria and Albert Museum), commissioned by the officers of Queen Victoria's combined military forces to mark her Jubilee of 1887.

Also influenced by Ruskin and Morris was Charles Robert Ashbee (1863–1942), architect, designer and writer, who started the School and Guild of Handicraft in the East End of London in 1888, and claimed – with some justice – to have realized their ideals most thoroughly. Ashbee took the step as a political and philanthropic measure, a gesture of defiance in the face of mass unemployment and misery generated by the slump. He was proud of rejecting commercial practices and of bringing designers and craftsmen together in small workshops. The Guild embraced several of the decorative arts, and Ashbee, inspiring and directing his largely inexperienced men and boys, taught himself the rudiments of metalworking by translating Benvenuto Cellini's treatises on sculpture and goldsmithing. His deployment of elegant multiple wires for the handles of hand-raised cups and decanters created one of the nearest English equivalents of the whiplash curves of French Art Nouveau, and he was also capable of juxtaposing delicate and effective plant ornament against plain beaten surfaces. Many Guild pieces are set with stones and ornamented with enamels, testifying to the influence of the Medieval Movement on Arts and Crafts metalwork. Ashbee encouraged the establishment by A. S. Dixon (1856–1929) and others of a similar organization, the Birmingham Guild of Handicraft, in 1890. Ashbee's Guild exhibited widely and was much admired on the Continent. The London Guild moved to Chipping Campden, Gloucestershire, in 1902, but in 1907, as Alan Crawford describes in *C. R. Ashbee* (London, 1985), financial difficulties brought the Guild to a formal end. Several craftsmen, however, most notably George Hart, continued to work in Chipping Campden.

Other Arts and Crafts metalworkers included Alexander Fisher, primarily an enamellist, who taught the technique to many of his fellows; Nelson Dawson, whose silverwork and jewellery were frequently enhanced by delicate floral enamels by his wife, Edith, trained as a painter; the architect Henry Wilson, and one of his assistants H. G. Murphy, who was entrusted with the execution of his rich Byzantine designs. Among the other members of the Movement were Wilson's former pupils J. P. Cooper and Edward Spencer, both of whom were associated with the Artificers' Guild; Harold Stabler; Gilbert Marks; Omar Ramsden and Alwyn Carr, both from Sheffield; and Arthur Gaskin of Birmingham.

The Movement lost momentum in the first decade of the twentieth century, and there were few new ideas apparent in the work sent to the exhibitions at Ghent in 1913 and Paris in 1914. Although he recognized its approaching demise, Henry Wilson did his best to keep the Movement alive by staging a major exhibition of its work at the Royal Academy in 1916; he himself turned increasingly to architectural sculpture.

In Scotland, Perth, Greenock and other provincial centres still flourishing in the early years of the nineteenth century were affected by an Act of 1836 requiring all plate to be marked only at the Edinburgh and Glasgow assay offices. Some makers, like Andrew Black of Alloa, riposted by using pseudo-Edinburgh hallmarks. In Edinburgh and Glasgow, silversmiths pursued fashionable styles, while at the same time keeping alive traditional designs such as the quaich, or drinking cup. After 1850 the rage for Scottish wares, much encouraged by royal enthusiasm, resulted in the widespread manufacture of pieces incorporating thistles and stags' heads and set with agates or 'cairngorms', stones originally found in Scotland but largely replaced by imports from South America.

Neoclassical articles made between 1800 and 1830 by firms such as W. & P. Cunningham and Marshall & Sons of Edinburgh are more austere than their London counterparts, but by 1820 revived rococo was flourishing. Floral and scroll ornament on tea services by J. McKay of Edinburgh and others was frequently flat-chased. Traditional shapes lingered: bullet teapots, for instance, were still current in the 1860s. Other revived styles, such as the Gothic, enjoyed less popularity, but after 1860 full use was made of the Louis XVI and Adam manners. Marshall & Sons sent Scottish ornaments, quaiches and silver claret jugs 'of antique shape and figures' to the 1851 Exhibition, while F. H. Thompson showed a group of more modest electroplated items.[8]

English styles were carried north by manufacturers to the trade, who also executed works with Scottish themes, sometimes to special commission. Edward Barnard & Sons of London supplied goods on occasion to Mackay, Cunningham & Co. and Hamilton & Inches of Edinburgh, and to D. C. Rait of Glasgow. Mackay, Cunningham & Co. also patronized Henry Holland of London; while in the mid-1870s Edward Charles Brown, another London maker, sold articles in the Aesthetic manner to J. Aitchison of Edinburgh.[9]

There was a burst of creative activity initiated in Glasgow in the late 1890s by the architect and designer Charles Rennie Mackintosh (1868–1928), which had repercussions as far away as Vienna. Mackintosh designed elegant, mannered flatware and a handsome silver casket, now in the Victoria and Albert Museum, which was presented to Sir James Fleming in 1909 to commemorate the opening of the architect's extension to his Glasgow School of Art. Another architect who started in the Mackintosh group, George Walton (1867–1933), designed flatware while working in England in the early 1900s, and Jessie M. King (1876–1949), primarily a graphic artist, was responsible for a delicate enamelled toilet service for Liberty's Cymric scheme. The Glasgow school of designers had only a limited impact on the trade, however, as did the Arts and Crafts designer and enamellist Phoebe Traquair (1852–1936) in Edinburgh.

Irish silver in the nineteenth century was hard hit by the Act of Union merging Ireland with Britain in 1801, as the abolition of protective tariffs threw it into direct competition with mass-produced wares from Birmingham and Sheffield. By 1850 not one silversmith was left in Cork or Limerick. A few managed to survive in Dublin,

DESIGN FOR THE FORESTER TESTIMONIAL *(above), pencil, pen and wash, with studies of the members of the Belvoir Hunt, by H.H. Armstead, c.1856. The Testimonial was made to commemorate an incident at a meeting of the Hunt, when a fox took refuge in a tree.*

MUFFIN DISH, LINER AND COVER *(above left), silver set with cabochon chrysoprases. London, 1900. Designer: Charles Robert Ashbee. Maker: The Guild of Handicraft Ltd. Ashbee started the School and Guild of Handicraft in London in 1888 and was committed to the ideals of Ruskin and Morris.*
Diameter: 22 cm (8⅝ in) (Victoria and Albert Museum, London)

FOOTED BOWL *(above right), silver-gilt with shaped glass liner. London, 1849–50. Maker: Jean-Valentin Morel. Morel was born to the jewellery trade in Paris where he made his name as a master chaser, embosser, gem-cutter and engraver before going to London in 1848. The Queen and Prince Albert were among his English patrons. He returned to Paris in 1852.*
Height: 24.3 cm (9¼ in) (Victoria and Albert Museum, London)

among them Richard Sawyer, who made variations of neoclassical designs in the first decade of the century, still using engraved ornament. By about 1810 heavier neoclassical forms were beginning to be adopted. A hot-water or tea urn in the National Museum of Ireland, made by James Henzel and hallmarked for 1812, shows traces of both English and French influence, but the overall shape and a Gothic arcade round the base appear to be purely Irish contributions.[10]

The rococo revival in England again focused interest on the flamboyant Irish version of the style, and by the 1820s articles lavishly covered with scrolls and flowers were being made by Edward Power of Dublin and others, and were produced until the mid-century and beyond. Other revived styles came from England, partly in the form of imports. G. & S. Waterhouse of Dublin, who originated in Sheffield, naturally inclined towards the goods produced by other members of their family in their native town. But Irish traditions were reasserted in the 1840s. Sometimes the material was paramount, sometimes the style: while Thomas Bennett of Dublin sent plate made from Irish silver in a variety of styles to the Great Exhibition of 1851, James West & Son of Dublin and G. & S. Waterhouse showed shawl-pins and other items based on Celtic penannular brooches of about AD 800. The revived Celtic style was given great encouragement at the Dublin International Exhibitions of 1853 and 1865, and several Irish manufacturers contributed work in the Celtic style to exhibitions abroad. Like Waterhouse, the West firm sold silver in addition to jewellery, including a tea service of late eighteenth-century form embellished with panels of Celtic interlacing, executed for them by John Smith between 1870 and 1874. One of the most famous of all Irish antiquities, the Ardagh chalice, discovered in 1868, was a fruitful source of inspiration to designers and manufacturers. Celtic-revival wares attracted both tourists and others with antiquarian inclinations, from Queen Victoria downwards, but far more jewellery was made than silver.

Possibly some goods were exported to London; Topham & White of Dublin, for instance, seem to have been connected with E. White of Cockspur Street, London, because they showed together at the Dublin 1865 Exhibition.[11] There is little doubt, however, that trade largely ran the other way. Thomas Prime & Son of Birmingham and Dublin, as they described themselves, were among the other exhibitors. They showed silver and electroplate, and were chiefly known for the latter. The patentees of electroplating, Elkington's of Birmingham, were represented in Dublin, which indicates that they sent goods to Ireland in some quantity, and the manufacturing silversmiths Edward Barnard & Sons of London supplied goods to West from time to time. All these wares were in currently fashionable English styles.

· FRANCE ·

The French Revolution of 1789 was followed by the dissolution of the craft guilds, and though the goldsmiths' guild was briefly reprieved, trade was in disarray. It began to recover when Napoleon became First Consul in 1799, though France was in the middle of the wars of conquest which gained it a vast European empire. In 1806 Napoleon, now Emperor, decreed the exclusion of British ships from all the European ports under his control. Thus, while some French influence percolated into

English design through unofficial channels, it was far stronger in most of the lands under French control. The influence was naturally represented by the style flourishing in Paris, the very sophisticated French version of neoclassicism. While derived – like the English – from Greek and Roman sources, Parisian neoclassicism in the age of Napoleon was characterized by narrow forms somewhat analogous to late eighteenth-century English silver. English Regency design, altogether more robust, looked back to pre-Revolutionary French shapes.

The most sumptuous French Empire plate is distinguished by a marriage of graceful profiles, sculptural elements from the Greek and Roman pantheon of deities, and finely detailed ornament piled in tiers. In some official plate, laurel wreaths evoking the victorious French campaigns were accompanied by a selection from the standard repertory of corn husks, rosettes, palmettes, acanthus, serpents, human and lion masks, swags, guilloche, ovolo and gadrooned ornament. The classical discipline and order of the style perfectly suited Napoleon, ever ready to equate his regime with that of ancient Rome. Indeed, he actively encouraged only one other mode, in effect a sub-style of neoclassicism, by sending an expedition to Egypt to record its antiquities. Vivant-Denon's findings, published in his *Voyage dans la basse et la haute Egypte* (1802), added to the Egyptian motifs already in circulation in France.

Napoleon's predilection for silver-gilt was shared by many European royalties (not least in England), and imitated in aristocratic and moneyed circles. Few, however, could rival the most magnificent objects in Imperial possession, such as the silver-gilt cradle of Napoleon's son, the King of Rome. Table services were sometimes of staggering size: the coronation service supplied by Henry Auguste to Napoleon and Josephine in 1804 comprised hundreds of silver-gilt items, some of which the goldsmith had to take from old stock so as to fulfil the order. French-made services found their way to Germany, Italy, Russia and other countries. The serving dishes, still designed to be placed on the table in the old fashion, were often ambitiously ornamented. Only towards the mid-century, when dishes began to be handed round by servants, did they become less elaborate.

J.-B.-C. Odiot, Henry Auguste and Martin-Guillaume Biennais, the main Parisian silversmiths, were patronized by the Imperial Court. They often worked from the designs of the architects Charles Percier and Pierre Fontaine, whose collected designs, *Receuil de décoration intérieure* (1812), included items which had been published as early as 1801. Among other leading designers were the painter Pierre-Paul Prud'hon, who collaborated with the architect A.-L.-M. Cavalier on the King of Rome's cradle, and Louis Lafitte, a painter whose designs for the goldsmith Jean-Charles Cahier were illustrated in C. Normand's *Modèles d'Orfèvrerie* (1822). Most designers, and many outstanding chasers and other craftsmen, spread their services over several firms, a practice followed by subsequent generations. Auguste and Odiot had both received gold medals in 1802 at the French national exhibition in Paris; these exhibitions had been instituted by the government in 1798 to encourage trade. Auguste went bankrupt in 1809 and most of his models were acquired by Odiot. Biennais, formerly a maker of fancy goods and toilet cases who turned additionally to silverwork (he employed nearly 600 people), showed plate at the national exhibition of 1806. He retired after 1819, and was succeeded by Cahier, his former assistant, but in the interim Biennais showed himself to be an innovator. It was he who introduced enamel decoration into a service made for the Empress Josephine. Enamel was to become increasingly important as the century progressed, and research into the various types was largely initiated in France at the Sèvres Manufactory in 1845, when a department was specially set up for enamelling on metals. Biennais and his fellow silversmiths also made some use of die-stamped ornaments for borders and small decorative motifs.

The restoration of the Bourbon monarchy in 1814–15 failed to dislodge the supremacy of neoclassicism which continued well into the 1830s, only slightly ravaged by the fashion for naturalism which encouraged an informal treatment of acanthus and other plant motifs. The style survived the Revolution of 1830 which deposed Charles X (reigned 1824–30) and installed Louis-Philippe of Orléans as King of the French (reigned 1830-48). Naturalism was deplored by influential collectors and critics, who united to condemn the activities of Odiot's son, Charles-Nicholas. In 1820 or shortly afterwards the younger Odiot returned to Paris from a stint at Garrard's of London; he brought with him a collection of powered machinery hitherto unknown in France, together with a liking for an eclectic naturalistic rococo style marked by relaxed, rather bulbous shapes and profuse ornament. The shock-waves caused by the introduction of this English mode and the counter-measures taken against it were documented by Albert, duc de Luynes, chairman of the goldsmithing section of the Great Exhibition of 1851, in a subsequent report for the French Commission published in 1854.[12] In De Luynes's view, *le genre anglais* resulted from the exigencies of machine production, a view accepted by Henri Bouilhet in his *Orfèvrerie française aux dix-huitième et dix-neuvième siècles* (1908–12). Despite sustained attacks, however, the rococo style survived in France, as elsewhere. A version more faithful to French eighteenth-century originals was highly fashionable in the 1880s and, with a revived interest in naturalism, contributed to the evolution of the French Art Nouveau manner.

The younger Odiot, succeeding his father, won a Gold Medal at the national exhibition of 1827, despite showing a number of works in the English taste. In 1834 his most remarkable exhibits were naturalistic pieces lacking all formal structure: a double salt cellar, composed of a clump of silver convolvulus and other flowers growing out of simulated earth (illustrated in Stéphane Flachat's *L'Industrie à Exposition de 1834*), is as completely organic as many contemporary English articles. At the Great Exhibition of 1851 he showed naturalistic wares as well as a dish representing a damask napkin, but he was also capable of working in the neoclassical taste and in other acceptable styles. A service in the Renaissance style, executed in the mid-1830s from the designs of P.-E. Jeannest (see page 161) and another artist, Combettes, for Baron Salomon de Rothschild, was admired but did little to offset Odiot's reputation as the man who introduced the suspect English manner.

Critical approval was more easily gained by his father's former assistant Jacques-Henri Fauconnier, who was patronized by the duchesse de Berry, the daughter-in-law of Charles X. Fauconnier participated only in the 1823 national exhibition, when he won a Gold Medal for *animalier* groups by Barye, but connoisseurs held him in high regard, principally for his romantic interpretations of the Renaissance style on which he embarked in the 1820s, using the designs of Aimé Chenevard (1790–1838). He and his supporters were almost certainly unaware of the earlier experiments in the Renaissance taste made for William Beckford in London (see page 160). Fauconnier's was a *succès d'estime* only; he died indigent in 1839, leaving his two nephews, the brothers Fannière, to serve in the artistic vanguard from their small workshop.

Chenevard also explored the Gothic manner, again treating it romantically. Known as the '*Troubadour*' or '*Cathédrale*' style, the Gothic figured prominently at the 1834 Exhibition, the first to be held during the reign of the citizen-king Louis-Philippe. François Durand, another of the elder Odiot's former assistants, made his debut at this exhibition; he was among the silversmiths to use the services of the sculptor and modeller J.-B.-J. Klagmann (1810–67), one of the major designers to the trade, whose preferred style was the Renaissance. The Gothic and Renaissance manners ousted neoclassicism in terms of prestige, their ascendancy owing much to Charles Wagner, a German who settled in Paris in about 1830 and associated himself with a goldsmith named Mention. A Gold Medallist in 1834, Wagner showed an interest in techniques matched only by his expertise as a designer, modeller and chaser. His revival of niello in western Europe, coupled with his use of repoussé and enamel, encouraged other goldsmiths to embrace old techniques in the execution of historicist designs.

After Wagner's death a few years later, his associate F.-J. Rudolphi, who had joined him from Copenhagen, exhibited under his own name in 1844. Rudolphi became celebrated for his decorative use of a variety of materials, including ivory, stones and enamels, in works shown at the Great Exhibition of 1851 and subsequently. While most of his objects were inspired by medieval or Renaissance devices, Rudolphi's antiquarianism, in common with that of many of his Parisian contemporaries producing secular silver, was far from literal. Archaeological accuracy was, on the whole, left to the ecclesiastical specialists. Exotic styles were also current, most notably the Islamic manner, stimulated by the French conquest of Algiers in 1830. Examples of designs in the Islamic taste appear in Jules Peyre's book *Orfèvrerie, nielle etc.*, brought out in Paris before 1842.

Among the best-known antiquarian makers of the era, aside from Rudolphi, were the Marrel brothers and Jean-Valentin Morel, who was born into the jewellery trade. Morel, a master chaser and embosser, gem-cutter and engraver, was also noted for his use of enamel decoration. He started out on his own in 1827 and then worked for Fossin, a jeweller. Again in his own business, Morel won a Gold Medal at the Paris 1844 Exhibition for a display which included a rock-crystal cup mounted in embossed gold with figurative motifs, and an enamelled reliquary cross inspired by sixteenth-century work. In 1848-9, in consequence of litigation with his partner Duponchel, Morel decamped to London with a large team of artists and craftsmen. He was glad to leave Paris, where the luxury trades had been devastated by the Revolution of 1848; and a patron, Joly de Banneville (1787–1870), established him in New Burlington Street. His principal designer of elaborate confections in the late Renaissance or Mannerist taste was Louis-Constant Sévin (1821–88);

THE ORLEANS CUP *(right), silver-gilt. Paris, 1840. Maker: François Durand. This cup was designed and modelled by J.-B.-J. Klagmann, one of the major designers to the trade, and given by the Duke of Orléans as a prize at the Goodwood races in 1841.*
Height: 66 cm (26 in)

A. A. Willms, later head of Elkington's design studio, was a junior member of the group. Morel numbered among his English patrons Queen Victoria, Prince Albert and Thomas Henry Hope, magnate, scholar and collector.[13] Morel's contribution to the Great Exhibition, made under the British flag, was honoured by a Council Medal, the highest award. A year later he returned to France. Duponchel, still in Paris with most of the craftsmen employed by him and Morel, showed works in the Oriental and Louis XIV and XV tastes (baroque and rococo) at the exhibition of 1849, but did not actually participate in the Great Exhibition.

The most celebrated antiquarian maker of all was François-Désiré Froment-Meurice, designated 'Goldsmith to the City of Paris'. The son of a goldsmith, in 1829 he joined the family firm then run by his stepfather, taking it over three years later. He made his first appearance at a national exhibition in 1839 and gained a Silver Medal for modest works of a reasonable price. But his own talents as a designer, modeller and chaser, recognized by his friends and clients in artistic and literary circles, drove him to aim higher. His display at the national exhibition of 1844, for which he won a Gold Medal, included an elaborate monstrance and a chalice for Pope Pius IX, and a presentation vase modelled by Klagmann, all of which were reshown at the Great Exhibition. His contributions to subsequent exhibitions demonstrated the range and quality of his designers and craftsmen, from the sculptors Jean-Jacques Feuchères (who numbered Antoine Vechte among his pupils), Pierre-Jules Cavelier, Geoffroy-Dechaumes, and the Fannière brothers, to chasers such as Vechte himself, Honoré and Dalbergue, and enamellers like A.-T. Gobert, Lefournier, Sollier and Grisée. Queen Victoria rhapsodized in her journal over the Froment-Meurice display at the Great Exhibition, which gained a Council Medal. Laden with honours, Froment-Meurice died on the eve of the Paris 1855 Exhibition; his widow oversaw the completion of the items to be shown and the subsequent major commission for the Prince Imperial's cradle executed in 1856.[14] Three years later her son P.-H. Emile Froment-Meurice assumed the direction of the firm, exhibiting in 1867 and afterwards.

The styles of the showpieces at the French exhibitions, national and international, filtered down to mass-produced wares, though the elaborate artistry and Renaissance decoration had to be considerably stripped before it was suitable for manufacture by machine. Sheffield-plated wares were made in France until the 1840s, when they

ANTIQUARIAN PIECES. *Bottle, silver and silver-gilt. Paris, c.1844. Maker: F.-J. Rudolphi. Height: 24.5 cm (9½ in) Tankard, silver and ivory inlaid with hardstones. Paris, c.1855. Maker: F.-J. Rudolphi. Height: 23 cm (9 in) Cup and cover, silver-gilt with champlevé enamelling and garnets. Paris. c.1851. Makers: Marrel frères. Height: 26.8 cm (10½ in) Flask with stopper, silver-gilt openwork over blue glass. Paris, c.1851. Maker: F.-D. Froment-Meurice. Height: 41.5 cm (16¼ in) Bowl and cover, silver, Paris, c.1862. Maker: Ferdinand Barbedienne. Height: 11.5 cm (4½ in) (Victoria and Albert Museum, London)*

TWO-HANDLED VASE, *silver, parcel-gilt. Paris, c.1865. Makers: Christofle & Bouilhet. It depicts Chiron training Achilles in running, and bears the arms of Napoleon III. It was given by the Emperor to the Cercle des Patineurs in 1867. Height: 73 cm (29¾ in)*

were largely superseded by electroplated goods. Patents for electroplating, taken out by De Ruolz in France in 1841 and 1842, were acquired by the Parisian jeweller Charles Christofle, trained by his brother-in-law Calmette, whom he succeeded in 1831. Christofle accepted that the Ruolz patents were overset by those of Elkington's of Birmingham, from whom he obtained an exclusive licence to operate in France for ten years.

Ceding his jewellery interests to his nephew and associate Léon Rouvenat in 1849, Christofle concentrated on producing electroplated wares to which, in the early 1850s, he added silver articles. By 1855 his firm employed over 1200 workers; four years later, he added a second factory in Karlsruhe. Like Elkington's, the Christofle firm employed reputable designers and craftsmen, especially for their ambitious silver wares. Mathurin Moreau (1821–1912) was among the sculptors working for Christofle, frequently collaborating with Auguste Madroux (d.1870), the firm's head modeller and ornamentist. Madroux worked on services executed for the Emperor Napoleon III, for the Hôtel de Ville, Paris, and, presumably, for the Emperor Maximilian of Mexico (reigned 1864–67), whose silver and electroplate service comprised nearly 5000 items.[15] Another silversmith and jeweller, Gueyton of Paris, used the electrotyping process (not covered by the plating patents) to execute original designs in silver by precipitating the metal on to a prepared mould in the plating bath until sufficient thickness was built up to enable it to be detached as an independent object. Gueyton won a Council Medal at the 1851 Exhibition, but the jury was more impressed by the firm's cast and chased silver caskets.

The Louis XVI style, a favourite of the Empress Eugénie, flourished especially during the last decade of the Second Empire (1851–70), and even the Odiot firm, still working in the English manner, successfully attempted this late eighteenth-century style. The Rennaissance manner, though now somewhat outmoded, retained something of its prestige.

Critical approval was also given to the archaeological Greek and Roman styles; designers and manufacturers had recourse to the Campana Collection of Classical antiquities, acquired by the Louvre with the encouragement of Napoleon III. The discovery of other hoards, such as the Hildesheim Treasure in Germany in 1868, gave further impetus to archaeological classicism, which was exploited by the bronzist and silversmith Ferdinand Barbedienne and many others who had earlier been concerned with the French Renaissance style.

The Gothic Revival influenced church plate a few years later than it did in England, but sprang from the same antiquarian roots. Manufacture was largely in the hands of specialists who worked in both precious and base metals. One of the pioneers was J.-C. Cahier, who had made an outstanding service of vessels in the neoclassical taste for use at Charles X's coronation in 1825. Cahier turned to Medievalism in the late 1840s, influenced by his brother, R. P. Cahier, a priest and celebrated antiquary. He met with little financial success, so he took himself and his models to a similar workshop started in Paris by Placide Poussielgue-Rusand in about 1848. Poussielgue-Rusand's principal rival was Thomas-Joseph Armand-Calliat of Lyons, who succeeded in about 1853 to a firm founded by his father-in-law (a pupil of J.-B.-C. Odiot), whose name he adopted as the second part of his surname. L. Bachelet of Paris was another manufacturer of church wares; he was one of the favourite makers of the architect and antiquary Eugène Viollet-le-Duc (1814–79), whose *Dictionnaire raisonné de l'architecture française* (1854–68) helped buttress his international reputation as a scholar. Didron's *Annales Archéologiques* was likewise used by many designers both in and outside France.

The firm of Poussielgue-Rusand, Prize Medallists at the Great Exhibition, reappeared at the Paris 1855 Exhibition, showing work by Viollet-le-Duc and again being rewarded. They were joined at the 1855 Exhibition by Armand-Calliat. These two firms, and Bachelet, contributed to the 1862 Exhibition in London and to many subsequent exhibitions. By 1889 Poussielgue-Rusand had died and been succeeded by his son, Maurice, who won a Grand Prix at the Paris 1900 Exhibition, using designs by the architect Corroyer. The jury report commented on the firm's international importance; their work was represented in many European countries and in North and South America. Georges Bachelet, on the other hand, who succeeded his father, gave up his ecclesiastical interests and by 1889 had turned to making domestic plate. The Armand-Calliat firm was continued by Joseph Armand-Calliat on his father's death in 1901.[16]

The London 1862 Exhibition was almost as significant for the French as for the English trade. The formidable contingent of domestic plate makers included E. Froment-Meurice, the Fannière brothers, Christofle, Gueyton and Odiot. Antique Classical styles were much in evidence: Christofle showed a great table centre in the Pompeiian manner, made with the assistance of casts brought from Naples for Prince Napoleon; and Gueyton exhibited an enamelled tea service in the Etruscan taste, one of many instances of a style adapted to vessel types unknown in the Classical era. But the French report sounded an alarm over the astonishing improvement in English silverwork, now considered to rival the French, so much so that a pressure group for the establishment of a South Kensington in Paris was formed. It wanted a combined museum and school system such as was presided over by Henry Cole in London. Tactfully re-forming under the guidance of the trade as the Union Centrale des Arts Décoratifs in 1864, the group exercised a powerful influence on design and was instrumental in founding the Musée des Arts Décoratifs in Paris.

The Paris 1867 Exhibition saw the increased participation of manufacturers to the trade; Paul Christofle, the author of the official report, cited no fewer than ten such makers, including E. Hugo, a concern founded in 1851, which manufactured both for home and export. But the President of the Union Centrale noted that most exhibitors, well known and otherwise, were feeding on the past without attempting an original style. Some silversmiths showed imagination and judgment in making their pastiches; others did not. Nevertheless, striking technical innovations were on view, including Christofle's electrically powered engraving, and some outstanding exercises in traditional techniques. Charles Lepec's enamels received particular praise.[17] But the rage for Japonoiserie in the late 1860s and 1870s, coupled with a renewal of interest in other Oriental styles, precipitated a shift of direction. Christofle, for instance, used their own electroprocesses to imitate the complex encrustations of Japanese metalwork, showing the results at Vienna in 1873 and at Paris in 1878, when Tiffany's of New York still managed to attract the greatest attention.

The end of the Second Empire in 1870, in consequence of the Franco-Prussian War, disrupted the trade during the ensuing siege of Paris, but produced no major stylistic change. The Japanese mania died down after 1878, however, and as antiquarianism returned with renewed force there came pleas for originality, particularly from the goldsmith and jeweller Lucien Falize, who thought that nature would provide the necessary inspiration. Natural forms certainly figured prominently in the revived rococo style of the 1880s and later, but in ambitious works, such as a set of six candelabra shown by C.-Gustave–E. Odiot at the Paris 1889 Exhibition, historicism was carried to the lengths of copying a design of Meissonnier, the prime originator of the eighteenth-century style. A Grand Prix went to Christofle in 1889 for a service in the rococo style, while the firm of Boin-Taburet, founded in 1873, was awarded a Gold Medal for a centrepiece after another design by Meissonnier. Hugo's successor, Tétard, using designs by Mathurin Moreau and others, exhibited works in a variety of styles, including a rococo centrepiece with figure groups inspired by Watteau; in the view of Falize, who wrote the jury report, Tétard's display was equalled only by that of Christofle.[18]

The sense of movement generated by the rococo was also expressed in other styles; explored a little further, a sinuosity developed which presaged the compressed whiplash curves of Art Nouveau. For example, the female figure across the body of a coffee pot of 1880 by the sculptor Albert-Ernest Carrier-Belleuse (1824–87) generates a tension qualifying it as a precursor. It has been argued that the whiplash can be traced back to William Blake via the Pre-Raphaelites,[19] though it may equally have derived from the scrolling on late seventeenth-century Japanese porcelain which found its way to the West.

A characteristic concern for technical perfection insulated the major French goldsmiths, who adopted Art Nouveau from the conscious amateurism of the English Arts and Crafts Movement. Whereas English silversmiths drew mainly on techniques practised by the Medievalists, that is, hand-raising and decoration and the use of a limited number of stones and enamel types, the French repertory was wider. *Plique-à-jour* enamel (an unbacked variety of cloisonné enamel) was popular; ivory and rock-crystal were used more lavishly than in England. Embossers and chasers such as Vechte and the Fannière brothers (who won a Grand Prix in 1889), had a worthy successor in Jules Brateau, a pupil of Honoré, one of the most distinguished chasers and craftsmen of his day. Though he worked principally in pewter, Brateau showed a silver goblet in 1889, when he won a Gold Medal, and chased a silver service in the modern manner for the silversmith Robert Linzeler which was shown at the Paris 1900 Exhibition.[20] The greatest genius of French Art Nouveau, René Lalique (1860–1945), won a prize in a Union Centrale competition in 1893 for a naturalistic cup very close to the mature Art Nouveau manner. Lalique executed few examples of plate, however, preferring to make jewellery until about 1910, when he turned increasingly to glass wares.

Outside the jewellery section at the Paris 1900 Exhibition, Art Nouveau manifested itself only intermittently in French goldsmiths' work, which continued to represent the Renaissance, Louis XIV, XV and XVI, and French Empire styles. However, among the historicist works by Christofle was a centrepiece, named 'Fire and Water', designed and modelled by René Rozet (b.1859) and executed in silver, opaline crystal glass and ivory, which showed the transition from rococo to Art Nouveau, and a series of vases

COFFEE POT, *silver-gilt. Paris, late nineteenth century. Designer: the sculptor Edmond Becker. Maker: A. A. Hébrard. This coffee pot, exhibited at the Salon de la Société des Artistes français in 1907, shows the influence of the Art Nouveau style. Height: 12 cm (4¼ in) (Musée des Arts Décoratifs, Paris)*

COFFEE POT *(above), silver. Paris, c.1880. Designer and modeller: Albert-Ernest Carrier-Belleuse. Maker: Christofle. The sinuosity of the figure across the body of the pot presages the whiplash curves of Art Nouveau. Height: 25 cm (10⅞ in) (Musée Bouilhet-Christofle, Saint-Denis)*

CHESTNUT VASE AND COVER *(facing page), one of a pair, silver. The Hague, 1803–4. Maker: François M. Simons. Height: 24 cm (9½ in) (Rijksmuseum, Amsterdam)*

including at least one with female heads and flowers designed by the great Art Nouveau ornamentist Alphonse Mucha (1860–1939).[21] To judge by an award to one of Christofle's employees, '*Arnoux, sculpteur, chef d'atelier de l'art nouveau*', Christofle took the style seriously. But F. J. Joindy (1832–1906), who had worked for both Christofle and Lucien Falize, was also commissioned by Harleux, a concern dating back to 1815, to model a service in the modern style. This was exhibited in 1900, together with another in the same manner by Eugène Lelièvre; Harleux won a Gold Medal. Keller freres, another Parisian firm to gain a Gold Medal, mounted a massive display of historicist services (one in the Louis XIV style), but varied these with a goblet and stand in gold, the work of Brateau, and a faceted jug of advanced functional form which at the same time looked backwards to the more outlandish experiments of Christopher Dresser and forward to the 1920s.

The preoccupation with enamel, especially with the effects obtainable from translucent and *plique-à-jour* varieties, was reflected in several awards made by the Exhibition jury. A Grand Prix went to the sons of Lucien Falize, who had succeeded to the firm on his death. They loyally included their father's last works in their display, many of which they had themselves completed. Other pieces were their own work. The jury report cites mounted vases by Gallé and the Lucerne goblet, executed and enamelled by André Falize in tribute to his year's apprenticeship to Bossard, the Swiss silversmith. Emile Froment-Meurice, another Grand Prix winner, exhibited some works in enamel and ivory; Frédéric Boucheron's well-known firm gained a Gold Medal for works partly designed and executed by Lucien Hirtz, designer and enamellist, and modelled by Joindy. The latter, who had worked in the trade for forty years, received a Grand Prix, and Hirtz a Gold Medal. A Grand Prix also went to the enamellist Tourrette and gold medals to Alfred Meyer, once associated with the department for enamelling on metal at Sèvres, and to Eugène Feuillâtre (1870–1916), among others.[22]

Feuillâtre, celebrated for his remarkable *plique-à-jour* enamels on silver, showed a dish with a fish modelled in relief at the Turin 1902 Exhibition, when Art Nouveau was still at its zenith. The sharp reaction against the style which occurred towards the end of the first decade of the twentieth century resulted in a return to classicism. Some of the great nineteenth-century firms were already in decline: Odiot, for instance, had last shown under their distinguished name in 1889, passing afterwards to one of the firm's employees who exhibited in 1900 as Prevost et Cie, winning a Gold Medal for a largely historicist display which nevertheless failed to place him in the first rank. On the other hand, the name of Puiforcat, a minor concern manufacturing for such firms as Boin-Taburet in the late nineteenth century, was made illustrious by Jean Puiforcat after 1923.

· HOLLAND AND BELGIUM ·

From 1795 until 1813 Holland was subjected to French domination. In 1806 Napoleon raised his brother Louis Napoleon (1778–1813) to the kingship; Louis's Queen, Hortense, was the Empress Josephine's daughter by her first husband. After Napoleon's defeat, the Congress of Vienna created the Kingdom of the North and South Netherlands. The peoples of the South broke away to form the separate state of Belgium in 1830, and Holland, though still a colonial power, inevitably became less important.

Throughout the chequered years of French domination, Dutch silversmiths showed considerable independence of the more elaborate aspects of the French Empire style. Fashionable decorative motifs were often translated into engraved ornament, exemplified by a vase and cover (one of a pair) executed in 1803–4 by François M. Simons (1750–1828) of the Hague, as part of a table service for King Louis Napoleon's minister of finance, I. J. A. Gogel. Though disciplined, the amount of decoration in the vases shows that Simons was, in fact, probably more influenced by French fashions than many of his fellow countrymen. Amsterdam silversmiths generally displayed a pointed preference for strong plain forms and rarely allowed ornament to dominate. One of their number, Diederik L. Bennewitz, was born in Germany. In pieces by him and his fellow goldsmiths (and his successors, Bennewitz & Zonen) the decorative element is often confined to the wide reeded bands also noted in Danish silver and to bold gadroons which were popular. As late as 1850 the Bennewitz firm favoured the strong profiles of forty years earlier, adding minimal engraved decoration.[23]

A decade or so after the Kingdom of the Netherlands lost its southern territories, the stability of Dutch silver design was assailed by the antiquarian revived styles and mechanized techniques. At first the ornament was kept under control; even foliage was conventionalized and kept in low relief. The capitulation of leading goldsmiths was signified at the 1851 Exhibition by the display of J. M. van Kempen III of Utrecht, goldsmith to the King of the Netherlands. Van Kempen showed nineteen articles in the Greek, Gothic, Renaissance, Louis XIV and *rocaille* (rococo) styles, all of which he discussed at length in an illustrated pamphlet, 'On the Forms of Gold and Silver Works'. Deploring the absence of an original contemporary style, the goldsmith allied himself with archaeological purity, seeing the best hope in an intelligent imitation of genuine Greek forms,[24] a view shared by the Cole circle in England. Even so, van Kempen followed earlier antiquarian precedent to the extent of employing Gothic architectural motifs in a royal commission for a communion service in 1856. The firm used the services of designers such as Gerardus W. van Dokkum (1828–1903), Th. K. L. Sluyterman (1863–1931) and H. A. van den Eynde (1869–1940).[25]

At the Paris 1867 Exhibition the firm, now C. van Kempen & Zonen, were described as the most important in Holland; their current productions on show, mainly produced in second-quality silver with the aid of machinery at their factory in Voorschoten, still echoed English styles. They also showed electrotypes made by a process evolved by Louis van Kempen. They participated in the Vienna Exhibition in 1873, where their display included items in the Greek style.[26]

The award of Gold Medals at the Paris 1878 and 1900 Exhibitions justified their policy of employing artists and educating their workmen. Several well-known goldsmiths were trained in their workshops, including Yvo T. van Erp of Leeuwarden and W. Hoeker of Amsterdam. Hoeker & Zonen, who also exhibited in 1900, were credited by the jury with having aided the training of designers and craftsmen. Some of their exhibits, which gained them a Gold Medal, showed the influence of Art

TEAPOT, *silver with an ivory handle. Brussels, c.1867–8. Maker: Jean Dufour & Frères. Its design is in the neoclassical taste of the late eighteenth century. The hinged lid has a finial in the shape of a hound.*
Height: 24.7 cm (9¾ in)

Nouveau, though their style was allegedly Merovingian, marrying simple forms with coloured stones and enamel, niello and filigree decoration. Another leading firm, Begeer of Utrecht, also exhibiting in 1900, employed designers such as M. J. Lens, who in 1889 based a royal table service on Meissonnier engravings. One of the firm's exhibits in 1900 was a 'marvellously executed' tea service with seaweed reliefs. At that time Begeer's designers included Professor A. F. Gips, exponent of the mannered curves of Art Nouveau, whose kettle was exhibited at Turin in 1902.

Aside from Jan Eisenloeffel (1876–1957), who seems to have spread his services around van Kempen, Begeer and Hoeker, the Begeer firm's major artist in the years leading up to the 1920s was Carel J.A. Begeer (1893–1956). His work ranged from *Jugendstil* (Art Nouveau) through all the popular revived styles to plain shapes apparently influenced by early nineteenth-century design. Eventually, in 1919, the firms of van Kempen, Begeer and Vos & Co. of Rotterdam were united.

Goldsmiths specializing in church plate, such as Janssen & Co. who won a Bronze Medal in 1900, adhered to the Gothic style, unlike most makers of domestic silver. There was nevertheless a strong traditional element in Dutch life which meant, for instance, that local costume was worn with pride. De Haas of Sneek, a Bronze Medallist in 1900, was said to make traditional jewellery to match the costume, as well as plate and trinkets intended as souvenirs for tourists and modest collectors. The firm, however, also made extensive use of machinery.[27] Its pastiches can be paralleled by others in Leeuwarden, Groningen and elsewhere in Holland. Manufacturers of this kind met the indigenous demand for reproductions of traditional presentation spoons and the like but, as in Germany, they exploited tradition in the interest of profitable exports. Favourite wares were brandy-bowls, baskets in the late eighteenth-century Dutch manner, loving cups in the form of windmills or female figures, often engraved with dates appropriate to the originals and fake marks.[28]

During the period in which Belgium was successively under French and Dutch control, silversmiths like Joseph Germain Dutalis of Brussels worked largely in the French manner. Others inclined to the simplified Dutch version of neoclassicism, renewing their inspiration by referring to engravings of Roman antiquities from time to time. A silver prize cup executed by Josse Allard for the Namur races of 1843 took the form of a spreading gadrooned vase plainly inspired by a Roman marble original, on an elaborate pedestal adorned with ram's heads and other devices. After generalized historicism took effect, stylized Gothic devices surprisingly reminiscent of the pierced motifs in late eighteenth-century Sheffield plate appear in such items as an oil and vinegar cruet executed by E. Wolfers of Brussels after 1832; later, Louis Wolfers indulged in the pear-shaped forms and floral motifs of the rococo.[29]

Queen Victoria's uncle, Leopold of Saxe-Coburg (1790–1865) who accepted the throne of Belgium in 1831, extended his royal patronage to firms such as Jean Dufour & frères of Brussels. Among the royal commissions Dufour executed was a parcel-gilt silver trophy for presentation by the King to the Belgian Yacht Club in 1856. This was a classical vase with rim, knot and base dissolving into naturalism in the English manner of the 1830s; the handles were formed as prows. The Dufour firm also made fine articles inspired by Flemish work of the 1770s, as well as plate in the Louis XVI manner which they showed in London in 1862. Dufour also contributed several naturalistic pieces to the Paris 1867 Exhibition, a dangerous move, for the jury was far more disposed to admire the church plate of Bourdon de Bruynes of Ghent,[30] well-known on the international exhibitions circuit. Indeed, in 1878, the Ghent firm was the only Belgian silversmithing concern to exhibit.

A flurry of activity in the 1880s and 1890s led to the founding of societies and periodicals designed to promote art, architecture and the decorative arts. Ashbee's Guild of Handicraft and other members of the English Arts and Crafts Movement were among those invited to exhibit in Belgium, and their influence on the new Belgian style could be felt; but that style was not homogenous. Henry van de Velde, for instance, then based at Uccle, near Brussels, worked out a rational system of vigorous angular curves (by the turn of the century, though, van de Velde had settled in Berlin and his work is cited under Germany).

Another form was developed by Philippe Wolfers (1858–1929), sculptor and goldsmith, who trained under his father Louis in the family firm and subsequently travelled widely, seeking orders; Wolfers pursued the new art in the French fashion through an exploration of nature. In the 1890s he set up his own workshops, where unique pieces were made to his design with the aid of assistants, but he continued to act as chief designer for the family firm. Wolfers produced more jewellery than plate (though there are examples of the latter in the Musée des Arts Décoratifs, Ghent, and in the Musées Royaux d'Art et d'Histoire, Brussels). His exotic pieces, which frequently make use of the ivory then being imported in vast quantities from the Congo, are constructed round figurative and plant motifs. In 1908, having exhibited widely, Wolfers signified the end of Art Nouveau by turning to sculpture, finally embracing the machine production of silverwork in 1920.[31]

WINE COOLER, *silver. Berlin, c.1855. Maker: Hermann Julius Wilm. In the rococo style, it has a detachable liner, rim and dish. Its elaborate decoration includes applied Bacchanalian masks and vines, and a monogram which is probably that of Augusta, daughter of the Grand Duke of Saxe-Weimar-Essen, who married in 1829 Friedrich Wilhelm of Prussia, later King and first German Emperor (as Wilhelm I, reigned 1861–88). Height: 39.7 cm (15⅝ in)*

· GERMANY, AUSTRO-HUNGARY AND · · SWITZERLAND ·

During the years that Germany was under French occupation (1806–13), the levies demanded by Napoleon to finance his armies, together with a lack of interest in Germany's historic treasures, meant that much plate was sacrificed, and municipal collections of silver were decimated. By contrast, Napoleon's act of making his brother Jérôme King of Westphalia, coupled with the alliances confirmed by sacrificing his relatives to dynastic marriages, brought elaborate French table services to the courts concerned (most notably Bavaria), providing models for German silversmiths.

In 1813 Prussia mounted a costly war of liberation against Napoleon; and despite gaining additional territories in the form of the Rhineland at the Congress of Vienna in 1814, King Friedrich Wilhelm III (1770–1840) and his successor, Friedrich Wilhelm IV (1795–1861), could afford to make only modest acquisitions of silver. Under the peace treaty a loose German confederation comprising thirty-nine states, each under its monarch or princeling, was set up under the Presidency of Austria; and it was only after Prussia had achieved the unification of Germany by 1871 that Austria was formally expelled from Germany's affairs. The political exclusion of France after 1814 failed to eradicate an interest in French design, however. This was exemplified by a pair of large salt-cellars on winged griffin feet, made in about 1815 by Johann Martin Schott of Frankfurt.[32]

Other influences on German silver arose from the archaeological research that sent some German designers to Roman artefacts. Piranesi's engravings from the antique were also used, as in other countries. For example, the architect K. F. Schinkel (1781–1841) used Piranesi's engravings of the Borghese vase (which is now in the Louvre) as a basis for his work. In turn, Schinkel's dedication to the classical and Gothic styles, which he saw as complementary, is reflected by a frieze on a cup executed by the Berlin goldsmith J. G. Humbert.[33]

English influence was chiefly manifested in the widespread adoption in Germany of steam-powered machinery in the 1820s. This revolution in manufacture was to make Hanau the chief centre for wares of this kind, followed by Schwäbisch-Gmünd and Geislingen. Machine-made objects in high- and low-quality silver represented good value to the purchasing public at home and abroad, but French observers such as the duc de Luynes said that German silverware was on the thin side.[34] The use of sheet silver from the rolling mills to make articles which were spun or stamped and decorated with engine-turning, or stamped motifs filled with cement to prevent them collapsing (a technique borrowed from Sheffield plate) did not result initially in the bulbous shapes and rococo/naturalistic motifs of English work, so deplored by the French. The current German preference was for a simplicity later described as the Biedermeier style, from the adjective *bieder* (plain or unpretentious) and Meier, one of the most common German surnames. Biedermeier design, however, began to disappear by the late 1820s, when even royal goldsmiths like J. G. Hossauer of Berlin, who had worked in Paris between 1815 and 1819, succumbed occasionally to the swelling forms of English design.

Hossauer also experimented with the antiquarian Gothic manner and the use of enamel, as well as electrotyping. At the Great Exhibition his firm was awarded a Council Medal for a silver shield decorated with gold, enamel and engraved gems, conceived by King Friedrich Wilhelm IV of Prussia as a belated christening gift to his godson Albert Edward, Prince of Wales, later King Edward VII (1841–1910). Though one chaser (August Mertens) was cited as working on the shield,

TEA SERVICE, *comprising teapot, tea caddy, slop bowl, creamer, sugar bowl and matching tray, second-quality silver. German, late nineteenth or early twentieth century. The creamer, sugar bowl and slop bowl bear the mark of Storck & Sinsheimer, the rest are struck with pseudo-hallmarks. This service is in the rococo taste.*
Length of tray: 63.7 cm (25 in)

Hossauer employed five others in a staff which numbered well over sixty in 1844.[35]

The customary range of revived styles was represented in the work of the German contingent at the Great Exhibition. Most notably, M. F. Schneider of Berlin exhibited a striking enamelled silver and gold inkstand in an eclectic Gothic and cinquencento design, while a large classical centrepiece over 1.3 m (50 in) high with naturalistic details won a Council Medal for E. A. A. Wagner, nephew of Charles Wagner of Paris and son and successor of Johann Wagner, royal goldsmith and jeweller. The jury report cites the 'exalted character' of the work which was emblematic of the 'Progress of Mankind to Civilization, under the Guidance of Genius', a theme incorporating figures modelled by August Fischer. The repoussé work was executed by Wagner himself.[36]

In a centrepiece by M. H. Wilkens & Söhne of Bremen, shown at the London 1862 Exhibition, several styles, from the Gothic to the baroque, together form a base for a naturalistic sculptural group of a boar under attack from dogs beneath a stricken tree. It was admired by the *Art Journal*, as was another shield with which Fischer was also concerned. This was executed in 1858 by Hossauer's successors as royal silversmiths, Sy & Wagner of Berlin, in frosted silver with enamel decoration, as a marriage gift from the Rhineland to Prince Friedrich Wilhelm of Prussia and his bride, Victoria, Princess Royal of England. It gained the firm a medal and, exhibited again in Paris in 1867, a Gold Medal.[37]

More symptomatic of future German trends, which were closely bound up with the wars of unification, was a silver tea and coffee service shown in the 1862 Exhibition by Koch & Bergfeld of Bremen, described as in the 'German antique style'[38] and expressive of nationalistic aspirations. Koch & Bergfeld were later also known for claret jugs and other items set in stamped silver mounts in the Renaissance manner, which were exported to Sweden and elsewhere. Exhibiting at the Paris 1855 and 1867 Exhibitions were D. Vollgold & Söhne of Berlin, classed by the French with Sy & Wagner for the exceptional quality of their work (though like Hossauer they used electroprocesses in addition to conventional methods of manufacture). French tolerance was stretched to its limits, however, at the Vienna Exhibition in 1873 when several patriotic pieces were shown by the Vollgold firm. One item was a ceremonial helmet intended for the German Emperor, which was surmounted by a laurel wreath for the German victories of the Franco-Prussian War of 1870–71. J. Ludwig of Trier was among several goldsmiths showing Gothic church plate at this exhibition, while W. Wollenweber of Munich, equally skilled in the rococo style, won praise for a Renaissance vase.[39] Classical work in the archaeological mode (shown under the aegis of an agent, E. G. Zimmerman of Hanau) was sent to the Philadelphia Centennial Exhibition of 1876,[40] but the German contingent abstained from exhibiting in Paris two years later in what was clearly a political move, holding aloof until the great Paris 1900 Exhibition. In the interim the German export trade in silver wares, already a subject of French comment in 1867, expanded considerably.

The manufacture of electroplated goods which commenced towards the middle of the century was centred mainly upon Munich and Geislingen, where by 1900 about 177 establishments employed nearly 1000 hands. Britain, whose silver trade was then in decline, became one of the many markets for German manufacturers. P. Bruckmann & Söhne of Heilbronn, for instance, with a workforce amounting to some 800 in 1900, had offices in Holborn Viaduct by 1889, as well as in Madrid, St Petersburg, Vienna, Paris and Brussels.[41] Some German silver was executed at least partly by hand in a variety of styles from Gothic to rococo, and then struck with false marks. This makes it impossible to identify the manufacturer. It is known, however, that the firm of Simon Rosenau of Bad Kissengen, antique dealers and purveyors of jewellery to the German royal family, made pastiches of old plate in first- and second-quality silver. The use of pseudo-hallmarks was widespread. B. Neresheimer & Söhne of Hanau, who exhibited at the Paris 1900 Exhibition, are thought to have used the old Nuremberg hallmark, the Gothic letter 'n', to mark their objects, which included medieval cups, nefs and figures of knights and ladies. These were so popular in England that several merchants such as Berthold Müller and S. P. Landeck registered makers' marks (in fact sponsors' marks) at the assay offices in London, Chester and elsewhere, so that they could have their imported silver marked. This lucrative trade ended with the First World War.

The wealth and power of united Germany brought a series of important commissions to the leading goldsmiths. For example, a wedding present from the cities of Prussia to the Crown Prince of Germany, the future Emperor Wilhelm II, comprised a table service of more than 800 items on which Sy & Wagner and Vollgold & Söhne worked between 1881 and 1883. Encouraged by the existence of the Imperial Court, many German cities, having rebuilt or enlarged their municipal buildings, set about replacing the plate lost at the beginning of the century. The medieval style was much favoured, and one of the most striking of such municipal confections was commissioned by the city of Cologne. Made in the workshop of a local goldsmith, Gabriel Hermeling, and exhibited in Paris in 1900, it is an allegory of the Rhine made in textured gold and silver with the addition of enamel. The river, its tributaries, castles, churches and legendary Rhine maidens all support the symbolic figure of Father Rhine bearing on his head a crystal galleon laden with allusions to Prussia and the Rhineland. The piece was noticed kindly by the exhibition jury, as were several works by the Bavarian sculptor Fritz von Miller (1840–1921), who studied in the academies of Berlin and Munich. His pike of St Bernard, the patron saint of Munich, was made of horn and silver embellished with gold, and rests on a block of rock crystal, while a bust of the saint shelters in a corner of the wooden base.[42]

Fritz von Miller's pike was representative of the type of pieces designed by academic artists and teachers who had not yet caught up with the new art movement known as *Jugendstil*, the German version of the Art Nouveau style. More angular than the French version, it owed much to S. Bing, the art dealer from Hamburg who commissioned the Belgian artist and designer Henry Van de Velde (1863–1957) to design room settings for his shop in Paris, 'L'Art Nouveau', which opened in 1896. Sections of the shop were shown in Berlin the following year, and Van de Velde went to work in Berlin, moving in 1901 to Weimar, where his liking for severe contours sharpened by lively whiplash curves was expressed in such items as a silver tea kettle of 1903, now in the Kunstgewerbemuseum, Zurich.[43] The new style was adopted by the schools of applied art in numerous German cities, and practised in workshops. The most important were in Munich and Darmstadt, where the architect Peter Behrens (1868–1940) and the Austrian Josef Maria Olbrich (1868–1908) worked in an artists' colony set up under the patronage of the Grand Duke of Hesse.

In the early years of the twentieth century the linear rhythms of the style were reflected in the work of many influential designers. Richard Riemerschmidt (1868–1957), who in 1897 founded the Munich workshops, later turned to designing for machine production, and was a founder member of the Deutsche Werkbund in 1907. His tea service

COFFEE MACHINE, *silver. Vienna, 1825. Maker: Stefan Mayerhofer. This piece, ornamented only with a palmette above the tap and a suggestion of foliage on the handles and finial, reflects the Biedermeier taste for simplicity. Height: 43 cm (17 in) (Österreichisches Museum für Angewandte Kunst, Vienna)*

STANDING CUP AND COVER, *silver, parcel-gilt. Vienna, 1844. Maker: Mayerhofer & Klinkosch. It celebrates the first Austrian railway network and incorporates railway locomotives in its essentially Gothic design. Height: 73 cm (28¾ in)*

for the Deutsche Werkstätte, which subscribed to the new ethic, is sturdily undecorated.[44] Both Theodor Wende (1883–1968), a member of the Darmstadt colony, and Emil Lettré adhered to traditional methods of working but took the austerity of early nineteenth-century German classicism as their point of departure. Ernst Riegel (1871–1939), then serving an apprenticeship in Cologne, went back even further in time: his design for two silver-gilt baskets decorated in rock-crystal, enamel and amethyst, produced for the Deutsche Werkbund exhibition at Cologne in 1914, employed an abstraction of Romanesque filigree ornament sympathetically executed by Hermeling.[45] Riegel's work was a surprising exhibit for the Werkbund, which tended to stress standardization and the machine; but the founders were in fact divided, and Van de Velde, who thought its aim too restrictive for the creative designer, resigned his post in Weimar in the same year and in 1917 went to Switzerland. (He was succeeded by Gropius and the way was open for the Bauhaus.)

In the first years of the century, sharp-angled *Jugendstil* curves characterized the work of silversmithing firms such as M. H. Wilkens – associated with Peter Behrens in an Italian commentary on Turin in the 1902 Exhibition.[46] The style survived longest in the productions of the Württembergisches Metallwaren Fabrik of Geislingen, which turned out electroplated nickel alloy wares of a quality unusual at the cheaper end of the market.

After 1815, the territories of the Habsburg Empire were enormous, stretching from Venetia and Lombardy in Italy to Bohemia (now Czechoslovakia) in the north, Hungary and Transylvania in the west and Croatia in the south. In 1859 Lombardy, and in 1866 Venetia, were incorporated into the new Kingdom of Italy; and in 1867 there was nationalist unrest in Hungary and elsewhere, which was partly conciliated by the institution of the Dual Monarchy in 1867, when the Emperor Franz Josef became simultaneously Emperor of Austria and King of Hungary. The interest of minority groups – the Czechs, Poles, Slovaks, Serbs and Rumanians – were sacrificed to German and Magyar domination until 1918.

Austria's financial difficulties during the Napoleonic Wars were such that the Emperor Franz II issued a proclamation confiscating all articles of gold and silver, whether in public, church or private ownership. Only a small number of objects was saved from destruction, on payment of a high duty in gold and silver coinage. Following the Congress of Vienna of 1814, the silver trade staged a modest recovery, and in the 1820s French influence was paramount in Vienna and, to an extent, in Budapest, though the forms used were largely simplified versions of those current in France some ten or twenty years earlier. The Biedermeier taste for simplicity, however, ensured that decorative devices were used sparingly. For example, an urn by Josef Kern of Vienna is an austere version of a tea urn illustrated in Percier and Fontaine, *Receuil de Décoration Intérieure* (1812), while a coffee machine of 1825 by Stephan Mayerhofer is ornamented only with a palmette above the tap and a suggestion of foliage on the handles.[47]

In Hungary a form of neoclassicism was practised by such craftsmen as József Szentpétery, who settled in Pest after becoming a master silversmith in 1809, moving to Losonc (Lučenec) two years later, where he received commissions from the local nobility. Many Magyar aristocrats, however, refrained from patronizing silversmiths and platers in Budapest, preferring to bring even modest items from Vienna or Paris, though as the century progressed firms like Prandtner & Giergl took to machine production and recruited large numbers of apprentices, indicating that the firm flourished on middle-class custom. The same may be said of other parts of the Empire, where goldsmiths concentrated mainly on standard or traditional works which included fine filigree work and mainly modest items of domestic plate. Makers of ecclesiastical works were to be found everywhere. At Pressburg (now Bratislava), Gerhard Weidner was a respected name in the mid-century,[48] while royal jeweller H. Grohmann of Prague, the capital of Bohemia, showed assorted wares in the London 1862 Exhibition and church plate at the Vienna 1873 Exhibition.[49] The recognition of Hungary as a kingdom encouraged Franz Josef's patronage of silversmiths in Budapest. One showed an ambitious table service made for him at the Paris Universal Exhibition of 1900.[50]

Between about 1835 and the late 1850s, the revived styles popular elsewhere penetrated Austrian silverwork, together with a growing interest in mechanized production. The most popular manner has been recognized in the eponymous term for the period, the second rococo, though this term subsumes other styles. As a leading silversmith, Stefan Mayerhofer naturally ranged over several such styles: rococo scrolls and flowers decorate a service made by him in 1834, and reappear on a silver-gilt ewer and basin of 1835, set with cameos and bearing the arms of the Potocki family.

From 1838, Mayerhofer was in partnership with Josef Klinkosch, producing not only silver but also Sheffield (called English) plate. The firm's mastery of historic styles was again demonstrated in 1844 with a Gothic cup and cover which, celebrating the first Austrian railway network, managed to incorporate railway locomotives. By 1873, when Mayerhofer & Klinkosch showed at the Vienna Exhibition, they were said to be the largest silversmithing concern in Vienna; their 250-strong staff included a French sculptor and modeller, Deloye, and several chasers lured from France by high wages. (The head of their chasing workshop had worked for fifteen years in Paris before joining the firm.) The firm's exhibits ranged from a mounted crystal cup in the Renaissance style – in which the beady eye of a French workman descried a debt to a piece shown by Froment-Meurice at the Paris Exhibition of 1867 – to a reliquary in oxidized silver, gold and enamel.[51]

In the last forty years of the century, several goldsmiths in Vienna, perhaps inspired by the objects made for the Emperor Rudolf II in Prague in the sixteenth century, began to specialize in engraved crystal or glass articles set in enamelled mounts. The most costly examples were sometimes gem-set in the approved Renaissance manner. Hermann Ratzersdorfer, who had shown a toilet glass with a Baroque silver frame at the Great Exhibition of 1851, became a leading exponent of the genre. In common with other Austrian goldsmiths he abstained from exhibiting in Paris in 1867, but sent a selection of his mounted wares to the London International Exhibition of 1871. The 1873 Exhibition, held on their own ground, gave Ratzersdorfer and his fellow specialists the opportunity of showing a huge variety of these historicizing wares. Ratzersdorfer's display included mounted crystal drinking horns, cups and covers, and other vessels, which were generally admired and exported for decades afterwards to many countries, including France. Ludwig Politzer and Hermann Böhm of Vienna were among the best-known makers. Conventional figurative pieces in the archaeological classical, baroque and rococo styles, requiring the services of modellers and chasers, were shown in 1873 by such goldsmithing concerns as V. Mayer Söhne and Hermann of Vienna. The latter employed another French-trained chaser, Karl Waschmann, who later exhibited a centrepiece in the form of the Palace of Schönbrunn on his own account at the Paris 1900 Exhibition, triumphing over the former firm, whose Louis XIV table centre was ignored by the jury. Alfred Krupp, with a factory in the village of Berndorf employing over 3000 workmen, largely specializing in base-metal flatware and hollow-wares, represented Austria as vice-president of the international jury. His ambitious silverwork, probably made for the exhibition, was applauded.

The Hungarian exhibitors in 1900 included the Union of Mines and the artist Paul Horti, who was

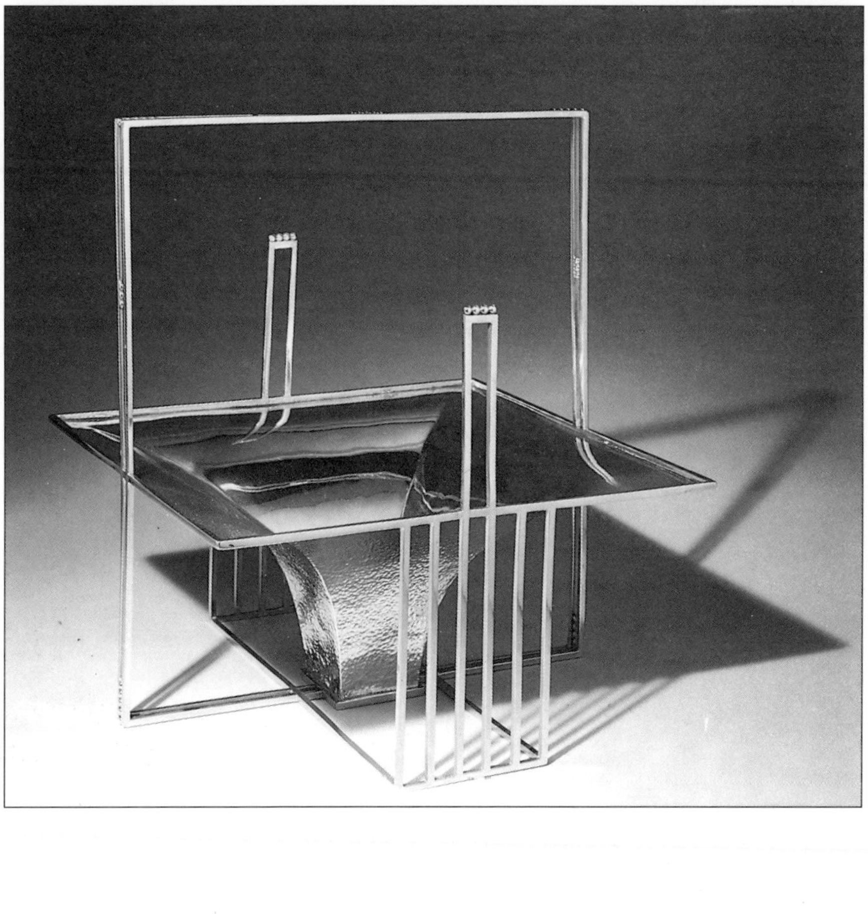

FRUIT BASKET, *silver. Vienna, c.1904. Designer: Josef Hoffmann (1870–1956). Makers: Wiener Werkstätte. The Wiener Werkstätte came into existence in 1903 with the aim of creating 'an intimate connection between public, designer and craftsman'. Hoffman's early designs for the school were invariably geometric and graceful. Height: 27 cm (10⅝ in) (Victoria and Albert Museum, London)*

EWER AND TWO CUPS, *silver-gilt, enamel and rock crystal. Vienna, last quarter of the nineteenth century. Makers: Hermann Ratzdorfer (cup and cover) and others. The wager cup, in the form of a maiden, her skirt and bowl enamelled with mythological scenes, is in the sixteenth-century taste. The cup and cover have borders painted with classical friezes. The ewer has* basse taille *enamelled bands. Height of ewer: 21 cm (8¼ in)*

given a Bronze Medal for an encrusted and enamelled casket. Bosnia and Herzegovina, administered by Austria after 1878, showed encrusted wares made from French and Viennese designs by students of the Sarajevo School of Arts and Crafts. The French looked kindly on these efforts, because Christofle and Lucien Gaillard of Paris had helped by providing patterns.

Maurice Wisinger of Budapest showed a repoussé shield designed by Horti in Paris in 1900, and sent examples of enamelled wares to the Turin Exhibition of 1902, when the Austrian contingent included J. C. Klinkosch who exhibited vessels embellished with swirling silver mounts designed by the Viennese architect and designer Otto Wagner (1841–1918).[52] Wagner's pupil, the architect Josef Hoffmann (1870–1956), was to give the *Jugendstil* a characteristic Austrian turn. He reinterpreted the Biedermëier tradition in the light of the soaring geometric elegance of Charles Rennie Mackintosh who, with C. R. Ashbee, had been invited to exhibit in 1900 with the avant-garde Viennese society of artists and craftsmen, the Secessionists.

Hoffmann and the designer and graphic artist Koloman Moser (1868–1918) taught at the school of arts and crafts attached to the Österreichisches Museum für Kunst and Industrie, both institutions founded in the 1860s on the lines of South Kensington. Hoffmann admired Ashbee's theories; in 1903, following a discussion between Hoffmann, Moser and a young businessman, Fritz Wärndorfer, who provided the financial backing, the Wiener Werkstätte came into existence, with the aim of creating 'an intimate connection between public, designer and craftsman . . .' Hoffmann's early silver designs were invariably geometric and graceful, while Moser's work and that of one of their associates, Carl Otto Czeschka (1878–1960), was spiced with fantasy.

The Wiener Werkstätte exhibited in Berlin and other German cities, and went on to show

their work in many countries, including England in 1906. But their most remarkable foreign monument is the house in Brussels, commissioned from Hoffmann by the Belgian millionaire Adolphe Stoclet and furnished by the workshops, complete with flatware and glasses. The first phase of the Wiener Werkstätte came to an end in 1906–7, with Moser's resignation and Czeschka's departure from Vienna. Among their successors was Dagobert Peche (1886–1923), who arrived in 1915 and managed a branch of Wiener Werkstätte in Zurich in 1917–18.[53]

In Switzerland, a satellite state of France between 1799 and the restoration of independence in 1814–15, the craftsmen's guilds were disbanded and many native traditions lost, as in France; but small village workshops scattered through the cantons went on making small items such as spoons, which were popular archery prizes. Goldsmiths in towns and cities tended to transform French models into strong and emphatic shapes. Among the leading goldsmiths active during the first half of the century were Georg Adam Rehfuss and Ludwig Friedrich Brugger of Berne, Hans Caspar I Wüest and Johann Jacob Rordorf of Zurich, and the brothers Marc and Charles Gély of Lausanne. In Berne, Rehfuss was considered the most important silversmith of his day. A man of artistic sensibility, according to the duc de Luynes, he had a large workshop and was much patronized by his fellow citizens.[54] But none of these was able to produce enough to satisfy local demand, and the deficiency was made up largely by imported goods from France and Germany.

The growing archaeological mood of the second half of the century was most notably exploited by a goldsmith in Lucerne, Johann Karl Bossard, who succeeded to a firm founded in 1775. Born in 1846, Bossard became a familiar contributor to major international exhibitions. At the Paris 1889 Exhibition, where he claimed already to have a diploma from Zurich in 1883 and a Silver Medal from Nuremberg in 1885, he was rewarded for a collection of items based on historic Swiss and German designs mainly of the late Gothic and Renaissance periods, derived, reportedly, from surviving documents and drawings. One dish was made after a design by Holbein in the museum at Basle. Bossard seems to have played an unusually active part in the preparation and execution of these pieces, which were all made in his workshops, even, presumably, to the carving of the coconuts mounted as cups of sixteenth-century design. His productions were widely admired for their authentic appearance, and his exports reversed to an extent the flow of foreign silver into Switzerland. He failed to contribute to the Paris 1900 Exhibition, although his name figures on the supplementary jury. Switzerland was then largely represented by G. Hantz of Geneva, awarded a Gold Medal principally for a buffalo horn mounted in silver and decorated with enamels of alpine subjects.[55]

SHIELD, *silver and damascened iron. Milan, c.1873. Maker: Giuseppe Francosi. Shown at the Vienna 1873 Exhibition, this elaborate shield is set with figurative silver plaques said to represent Noah's Ark and the Flood. Height: 56.5 cm (22⅛ in)*

· ITALY, IBERIA, GREECE AND MALTA ·

In 1797 Napoleon defeated the Austrians in Italy and created the short-lived Cisalpine Republic of northern Italy. In 1805 he formed the Kingdom of Italy (with himself as King); and, having installed his brother Joseph on the throne of the Two Sicilies, moved him to Spain in 1808 and replaced him with his brother-in-law Joachim Murat. At the Congress of Vienna Italy was again fragmented, until unification was finally achieved between 1861 and 1870, after decades of insurrection. It is this history of insurgency which probably accounts for the minor role played by most Italian silversmiths on the international scene during this period.

In the Papal State of Rome, dislike of the Napoleonic soldiery during the occupation did not preclude admiration for French neoclassical design. Giovacchino Belli, patronized by the sculptor Antonio Canova (1756–1822), was among the Roman silversmiths who turned the traditional oil lamps with reflectors (made all over Italy and in other Mediterranean countries) into a vehicle for mythological subjects. Belli made a Cupid lamp with a butterfly reflector in about 1805, matched by another with Psyche.[56] Another goldsmith, Roberti Tombesi, formerly (like Belli) an assistant to Luigi Valadier, one of the best-known silversmiths in Rome in the late eighteenth century, set up on his own in 1801, producing silver in the French Empire style with echoes of the forms he had used earlier. After Napoleon's defeat, British interests in Rome were not forgotten: the great goldsmithing concern founded by Fortunato Pio Castellani in about 1814 catered for both French and English taste, and though concentrating on jewellery, Castellani's interest in archaeological design influenced the plate produced by his compatriots.

Further south in Naples, where goldsmiths were slower to adapt to foreign styles and technology, baroque elements still often appeared in neoclassical designs, as in a large monstrance which was designed by the architect Domenico Barillari and the goldsmith Antonio Russo and executed in 1820 for a church in Serra San Bruno. Russo was a temporary resident, transferring his workshop to Naples for the sole purpose of carrying out the commission.[57] But naturalism crept in before 1840. Gabriele Sisino, who became a goldsmith in 1830, was among those who even essayed the rococo, making a lobed coffee pot and sugar bowl heavily encrusted with shells, foliage and flowers. Despite de Luynes's report in the early 1850s that Neopolitan silversmiths were still using the techniques of their forebears, they showed signs of capitulation to modern techniques by 1862, when one Neopolitan silversmith exhibited an electrotype in London.[58]

While most Italian goldsmiths plodded along the path of historicism, turning out domestic wares, ambitious works were also made. In Milan, a service of plate for the high altar of the Cathedral was commissioned from the two Scorzini brothers, Giovan Battista (d.1835) and his brother Luigi, a sculptor and modeller. Comprising twelve pieces in all and completed in 1838, the service is a monumental exercise in neoclassicism, using motifs from bas-reliefs to acanthus foliage.[59] The sculptural tradition, adapted to Mannerist forms, was maintained in works like an ambitious ewer and basin chased by Giovanni Bellezza (1807–76) of Milan, from the designs of Ferdinand Albertolli and Luigi Sabatelli. Commissioned by the Municipal Council in 1842 for presentation to the Archduchess Adelaide of Austria (1822–55) to commemorate her marriage to the future King of Italy Vittorio Emmanuele of Sardinia, the pieces were not finished until 1847. In the same year, the French artist and embosser Antoine Vechte completed the Jupiter, or Titan, Vase.

It was pointless to claim, as the French often did, that Vechte inspired Bellezza, when both were looking to early seventeenth-century Italian models. Antonio Cortelazzo of Vicenza was another virtuoso embosser and chaser, whose display of encrusted works at the Paris 1867 Exhibition possibly included a tea service with repoussé panels of damascened steel bearing the arms of Narishkine. Like Vechte, Cortelazzo was lauded as the modern Cellini. His English patrons included Sir A. H. Layard (1817–94), the excavator of Nineveh. Giuseppe Francosi of Milan sent to the Vienna 1873 Exhibition an elaborate damascened iron shield set with figurative silver plaques representing Noah's Ark and the Flood, and the iron ground the wrath of God, according to a French commentary.[60]

Traditional Genoese filigree, represented by the work of J. Bennati, J. Loleo, Emilio Forte and others, appeared regularly at exhibitions such as those in London in 1862 and Vienna in 1873. Italian silversmiths continued to participate in international exhibitions, though their work was only unofficially represented at the Melbourne Exhibition of 1888–9 (through A. Rizzo of Russell Street in that city).[61] In the eyes of the jury of the 1900 Exhibition they increasingly relied on reproducing artefacts from the past or copying slightly outdated German and French models. The latter complaint is probably a reference to an alleged debt on the part of Italian artist-craftsmen to Vechte and his pupil Morel-Ladeuil. The truth of the former is demonstrated by the copies of ancient artefacts in the Museum of Naples which were shown by Giacinto Melillo of the same city in 1900.

Melillo was given a Silver Medal, not because his work was in any way original, but because it was so skilfully executed in the traditional manner learned by him when he worked for Castellani. Mascetti of Rome was awarded a Bronze Medal for similar pieces, and so were makers of filigree work in Lucca and Milan. The Accarisi firm of Florence essayed more fashionable goods, showing a centrepiece modelled by Faraori. The modeller and his employers were each given Silver Medals.[62]

The Turin Exhibition of 1902 was intended, at least in part, to give Italian designers and makers a chance to show their paces. One of the most adventurous exponents of Art Nouveau was the painter, sculptor and designer Carlo Bugatti (1856–1940), who exhibited room settings and furniture produced in his Milan workshops. It was only after he left Milan for Paris in 1904 that he began to add silver to his repertory. Employing the standard Art Nouveau motifs of plant, insect and animal forms, Bugatti invested his designs with a bizarre individuality. They were executed by silversmiths working under the aegis of A. A. Hebrard, a founder of art bronzes who exhibited Bugatti's plate in 1907 at his showroom in the rue Royale, Paris. The artist also regularly sent his silver to the annual Salon des Artistes décorateurs, although in 1910, when progressive thinking had turned to austerity and functionalism, a writer in *Art et Décoration* challenged the logicality of Bugatti's work.[63]

A substratum of manufacturers in Italy capitalized on the late nineteenth-century vogue for pastiches and, as in Germany, Holland and elsewhere, produced goods which sometimes bore no maker's mark or were stamped with pseudo-hallmarks, a practice which has persisted in the present century.

Napoleon found Spain an uncomfortable and troublesome country, which he had forced into war against Portugal in order to deprive Britain of access to Iberian ports. In May 1808 he installed his brother Joseph as King, but the people rebelled and Britain came to their assistance, pinning down French troops in the Peninsular War, which lasted until 1814. The Royal School and Factory for Silversmiths, founded in Madrid in 1778 by Antonio Martínez Barrio, goldsmith and citizen of Saragossa, who died in 1798, managed to survive the war; it continued under the patronage of King Ferdinand VII (1784–1833) in difficult times for the luxury trades. The factory was helped by the quality of its productions, for Martínez had adopted steel dies from the first, recognizing their superiority over iron during a visit to England in 1775–6. Among pupils of the school were José Marti and Francisco Moliner, who settled respectively in Barcelona and Saragossa. A number of craftsmen had been sent to the Spanish colonies in South America, but this ceased after the loss of these countries in 1823.

The Royal Factory came under the management of Pablo Cabrero, a soldier not a silversmith, who married Martínez's daughter. Its work in the neoclassical manner, still being produced in the 1850s, is characterized by bold decorative detail. The factory looked to its past for inspiration, and in 1840 adapted the form of Hispano-Moresque pottery for a fine silver 'Alhambra' vase overlaid with gold detail. This vase was presented to the Earl of Clarendon following his term as British Ambassador to Spain, from 1833–9. Although Cabrero, who died in 1846, introduced the manufacture of plated wares to Spain, the factory declined and closed down in the mid-century.[64] The duc de Luynes referred to Martínez and his factory in his report on the Great Exhibition, citing also Pescador and Francisco Moratilla of Madrid. But of the three, Moratilla was the only one to exhibit in 1851, his sole contribution a huge jewelled Gothic tabernacle in silver for the Cathedral of Arequipa. The jury was duly impressed and recommended the award of a Council Medal, but this was overruled and the goldsmith received a Prize Medal instead.[65] Moratilla sent the same piece to the Paris 1867 Exhibition.

The Spanish silver trade clung to traditional designs and techniques, including the making of filigree. L. Gómez, M. Elena and F. Tello, all of Salamanca, comprising half the Spanish contingent in the goldsmithing section, exhibited filigree work in the London 1862 Exhibition. The only Spanish goldsmith at the Vienna 1873 Exhibition was a manufacturer of church plate, while at the Paris 1900 Exhibition the Spanish Pavilion was largely given over to a retrospective display of tapestries, arms and armour and goldsmiths' work, the only modern silversmith a maker of ecclesiastical wares, Martínez y Fraile, who was rewarded with an Honorable Mention for a silver-gilt ciborium set with stones, in customary homage to the Middle Ages. The piece was far removed from the original architectural work in Barcelona of Antonio Gaudí y Cornet (1852–1926), the outstanding Spanish exponent of Art Nouveau. Few goldsmiths followed his example, and of these the most notable was the jeweller Luis Masriera. In Barcelona, again, the classical mood which succeeded Art Nouveau found expression in the work of artist-craftsmen like Ramon Sunyer and Jaume Mercadé.[66]

In Portugal, the Duke of Wellington's victory in the Peninsular War in 1814 was commemorated by a handsome silver-gilt toilet service presented to him by the Prince Regent. Made in Lisbon between 1811 and 1816 by Vicente Pires de Gama

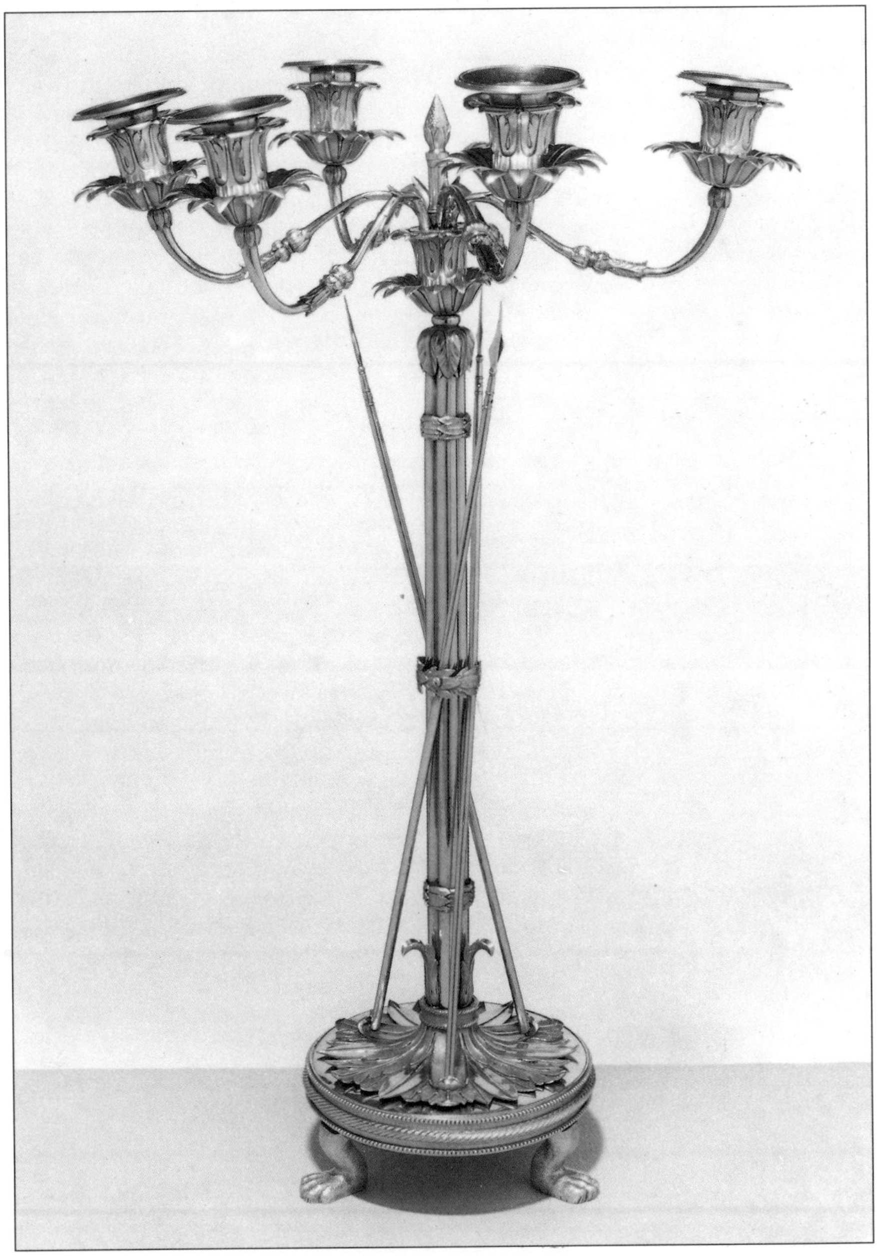

CANDELABRUM, *silver-gilt. Lisbon, 1811–16. Designer: Domingos Antonio de Sequeira. Makers: Vicente Pires de Gama and Joâo Teixero Pinto. This piece belonged to a large toilet service in the neoclassical manner presented by the Prince Regent of Portugal to the Duke of Wellington, to celebrate his victory in the Peninsular War. Height: 58.4 cm (23 in) (Wellington Museum, Apsley House, London)*

and João Teixeira Pinto, the service comprised some ninety pieces designed by the painter Domingos Antonio de Sequeira with appropriate emblems of war, executed in a sophisticated neoclassical manner. At Wellington's instigation, some Portuguese silversmiths went to work at Garrard's of London during the Peninsular War.

The final separation of Brazil from Portugal in 1825, and struggles over the constitution and the throne, however, were not conducive to artistic innovation: tea services made in Oporto in the late 1830s and early 1840s retain the sagging sides of early nineteenth-century English vessels. Before the mid-century, though, Portuguese goldsmiths took up the revived styles and naturalism. An apple and pear inkwell on a vine-leaf stand, bearing the name of Dias of Lisbon and probably made in the 1850s, may have derived from English work of the 1840s, but similar objects were produced all over Europe. A tea kettle in the rococo style, made in Lisbon between 1825 and 1850, is more closely related to French originals.[67]

In the early years of the twentieth century José Rosas junior, a member of a family firm of goldsmiths and jewellers founded in Oporto in 1851, went to London to pursue his studies at Goldsmiths' College and the Royal College of Art, before returning home to interest himself in traditional filigree work. He used the technique in a modern way, wrapping a frieze of filigree and enamel fish around a faience vase by Rafael Bordal Pinheiro in 1909 to create the effect of translucent (*plique-à-jour*) enamel. His firm's principal designer, Antonio Teixeira Lopes, who had studied and exhibited in Paris, conformed to orthodox French tastes of a decade or so earlier in designing and modelling a large centrepiece in the Louis XVI manner, shown by the firm at the Paris 1900 Exhibition. The jury was unenthusiastic, preferring the Louis XV style, but awarded a Bronze Medal to Rosas for an embossed tea service.[68]

Greece was the first of the countries under Turkish rule to be liberated, in 1830, and Ottoman Power in the Balkans was also undermined in the 1830s, when the Serbians and Rumanians of Moldavia and Wallachia asserted their independence (though substantial minorities of these peoples remained under Turkish rule for decades longer). The continuing unrest in the Balkans meant that the traditional Levantine baroque style persisted in the decorative arts; and goldsmiths in Greece and elsewhere were noted for their filigree work.

Malta, captured by Napoleon in 1798, was retaken by the British, whose right to the island was confirmed by the Treaty of Vienna in 1815. Maltese goldsmiths such as G. Lebrun, however, leaned more to Italian than English models for both domestic and church plate (see fn.56). Italian work was also commissioned for Maltese churches; the duc de Luynes cited a silver altar-frontal executed for St Paul, Valetta, by Vincenzo Belli of Rome. Late eighteenth-century Italian forms for coffee pots were brought up to date towards the middle of the century and later by the addition of chased scrolls and floral ornament.[69] As silversmithing declined, increased emphasis was placed on the making of the filigree wares, which were popular tourist souvenirs. Specimens appeared at several international exhibitions and at the Colonial and Indian Exhibition held in London in 1886.[70]

JARDINIERE WITH FLOWER VASE, *silver. Stockholm, 1827. Maker: Adolf Zethelius. Zethelius was an outstanding exponent of the French Empire style. This piece belonging to the Gothic service for the royal collections was inspired by the Medievalism reaching Sweden in the late 1820s. Height: 42 cm (16½ in) (The Royal Collections, Stockholm)*

· SCANDINAVIA ·

In 1810 a Frenchman, Prince Bernadotte, formerly one of Napoleon's Marshals, was elected the Swedish heir apparent. Bernadotte joined the allies against the French in 1812 and served as a military commander. Nevertheless Sweden lost Finland to Russia under the Treaty of Vienna, receiving instead Norway, taken from Denmark. Despite Bernadotte's espousal of the allied cause, Swedish goldsmiths were influenced by French design. Adolf Zethelius of Stockholm was an outstanding exponent of the French Empire style, adopting in 1813 the rounded lid and fluted forms of French sugar bowls for a version of his own, supported by dolphins (now in the Nordiska Museum, Stockholm).

Nevertheless, evidence of a far more complex flow of fashion is afforded by a lotus-bud finial on a coffee pot in the French manner, produced by the same maker in 1817; an identical finial had been used in 1813 by the London goldsmith Paul Storr, whose master was the Swedish goldsmith Andrew Fogelberg.[71] Medievalism reached Sweden by the late 1820s, inspiring a Gothic service for

COFFEE POT, *silver-gilt and enamel. Oslo, c.1880–90. Designer: Johan Lund. Maker: David Andersen. Gilded silver threads separate the different enamel colours. In 1888 Andersen established the first workshop in Oslo with steam-powered machinery. Height: 16.7 cm (6½ in) (Kunstindustrimuseum, Oslo)*

the royal collections, for which Zethelius produced an elaborate fruit stand in 1827, mixing neoclassical and medieval motifs with panache. At this stage Swedish silversmiths succumbed to the gamut of English revived styles, including the naturalistic manner, and to mechanical methods of production, and English influence largely replaced French for several decades. Björn Hedstrand has traced the development of the trade in his *Silvervaror i Sverige, 1830–1915* (Stockholm, 1975), illustrating it with parallel English and Swedish articles, and later German and Swedish pieces. These include a naturalistic rococo dessert stand with a figure column made by Benjamin Smith in 1845–6 and a similar work by Gustaf Möllenborg.

It is possible to add other parallels, and Hedstrand refers to a coffee pot of 1852 by Gustaf Theodor Folcker, describing it as Gothic, and another of 1856 by Frans Holm of Vadstena. Both are based on a design for a 'Tudor' tea and coffee service by Edward Barnard of London. One such service was presented to William Chadwick, the chairman of Richmond Railway, in 1849.[72] A sugar vase of 1861 in the English rococo style, by Möllenborg-Féron, is close to a rococo service exhibited by Joseph Angell in 1851.[73] The second round of revived styles, chiefly Greek, Louis XVI and Renaissance, flourished from the 1860s to the early years of the twentieth century, together with a species of baroque, exemplified by a covered tankard of 1882 by Erik Johansson of Gävle. Classical, Renaissance, baroque and Louis XVI pieces were among the wares imported by the Möllenborg concern from Koch & Bergfeld of Bremen and the Gebrüder Deyhle of Schwäbisch-Gmünd in the 1880s.

National traditions inspired mounted drinking horns, and pieces of this kind, together with virtually all the revived styles introduced during the nineteenth century, were still in production in the late nineteenth and early twentieth centuries. Many historicist pieces were reminiscent of English models, even to a version of a Dresser decanter.[74] The firm of G. C. Hallberg, said to employ 250 workers, showed royal plate designed by Lindegren, Kronberg, and Andrén in the eighteenth-century manner at the 1900 Exhibition, and nudged themselves into Art Nouveau by adding an inkstand delicately ornamented with motifs from nature by the sculptor Ferdinand Boberg, a leading artist-metalworker. The Möllen-

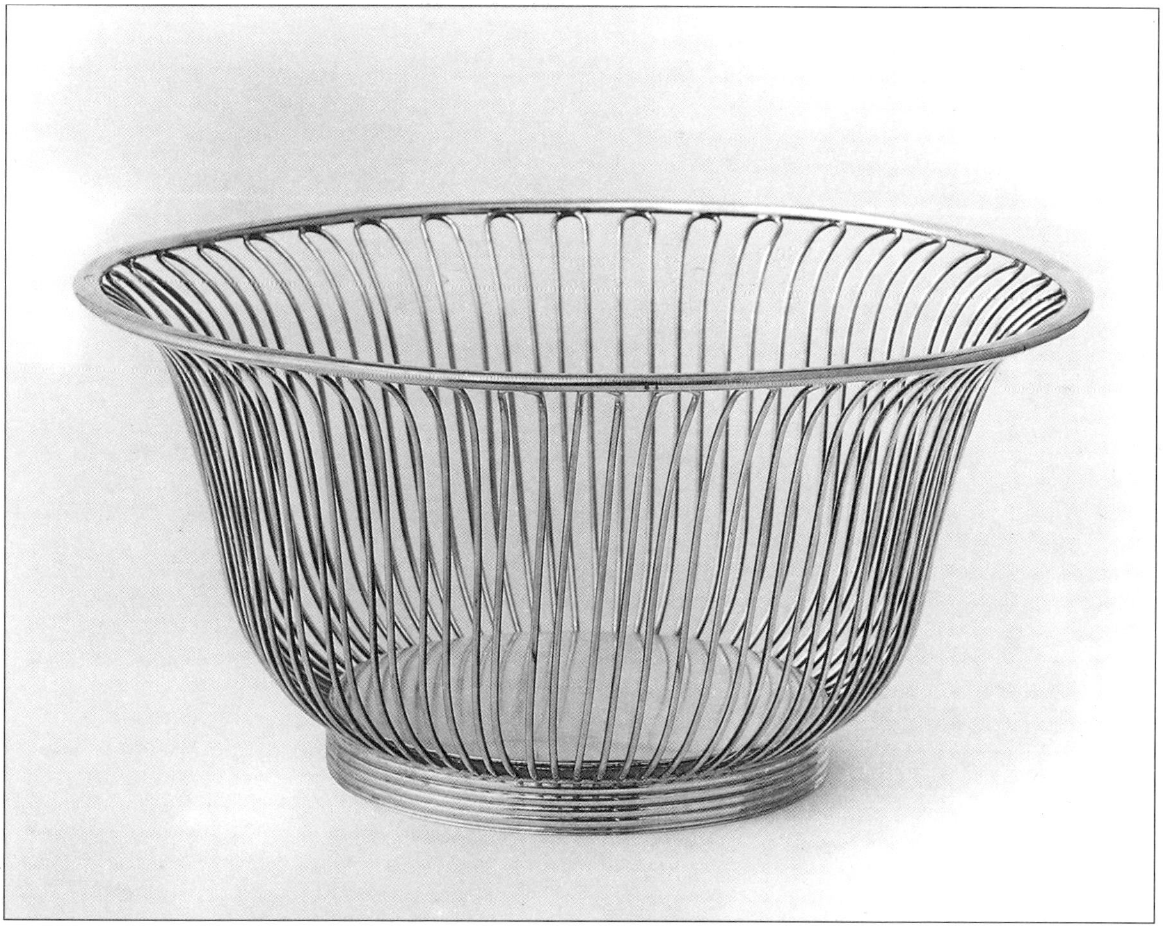

FRUIT BOWL, *silver wire. Copenhagen, 1813. Maker unknown. Made in the manner of late eighteenth-century Sheffield plate, it is a simplified version of a plated fruit dish made in Sheffield in 1803. Height: 12.4 cm (4⅞ in) Diameter: 25.5 cm (10 in) (Kunstindustrimuseum, Copenhagen)*

borg firm, on the other hand, confined itself to copies of Swedish work of the previous two centuries, the jury report remarking on the generally conservative nature of the trade.[75]

Norwegian and Danish goldsmiths shared a preference for English over French patterns. From the late eighteenth century this usually meant the elegant simplicity of Sheffield plate, the forms of which were as well known from catalogue illustrations as from imported pieces. A Norwegian combined sugar bowl and spoon rack by Ahasverus Kass, a goldsmith working in Christiania (Oslo) from 1809 until 1859, relates to one in fretted Sheffield plate which appears in a catalogue produced by an English plater especially for export in about 1784. Moreover, Jacob Tostrup of Christiania used a version of the Warwick Vase as a model for a silver copy (both this and the sugar bowl are in the Kunstindustrimuseum, Oslo.)[76]

Many silversmiths had been using die-struck filled borders in the manner of Sheffield plate since the late eighteenth century, but whether they made these ornaments with hand-operated presses or imported them is unresolved: machinery was not introduced into Norway until about 1830. Tostrup, who in his travels in Europe had seen mechanized methods in use in Copenhagen and St Petersburg workshops, installed power-driven die-stamping machines on his own premises in 1838. He also opened showrooms in Christiania and took to advertising his wares, actions necessitated by the slow decay of the old craft guilds and by the competition of mass-produced wares from abroad. Provincial goldsmiths were slower to adopt machinery, though Theodor Olsen and Marius Hammer of Bergen led the way in the 1870s.

David Andersen established a workshop in Christiania in 1888 with up-to-date steam-powered machinery. Ten years later steam was replaced by electricity, and Andersen had a staff of about a hundred workmen; other Christiania goldsmiths followed his example. Historicist styles were taken up in due time, absorbed and often simplified. The lobed and faceted forms fashionable in England between the 1820s and 1830s were used by both Tostrup and N. M. Thune of Oslo in the 1850s, while restrained naturalism was embodied in such pieces as 'The Bear Fight' – made in about 1860 by Björn Gudmundsen from Telemark for Tostrup – in which the figures are overshadowed by a tree rendered with delicately traced branches (Oslo Bymuseum). Tostrup frequently took part in international exhibitions and showed, for instance, a tankard, coffee pots and similar domestic wares at the exhibitions in London in 1862, Paris in 1867 and Philadelphia in 1876.[77]

Nationalism motivated Norwegian goldsmiths to look to their past, and they began to use the forms and techniques of peasant silver and the interlaced decoration of Viking art. The Tostrup firm exploited both, adding an interest in enamel, especially in *plique-à-jour*, probably at the instigation of Olaf Tostrup, who was impressed by the work he had seen at Vienna in 1873 and Budapest in 1884; the firm's example was followed by David Andersen. Their products became fashionable, and expanding tourism confirmed the demand.

In the second half of the century S. Hammer of Bergen (also an antique dealer) and Henrik Bertram Møller, who set up in business in Trondheim in 1884, were among those who catered for tourists on a large scale, turning out everything from jewellery to spoons, and large objects in the form of horns, ships and goblets, mainly in a fanciful Old Norse style. Both Tostrup and David Andersen sent work to the Paris Exhibition of 1900, together with Hammer and Olsen. Tostrup was awarded a Grand Prix, and the jury spoke admiringly of his enamels and silverwork with interlaced decoration. David Andersen, who received a Gold Medal, impressed the jury chiefly with his use of traditional motifs.[78]

The jury did not mention Gustav Gaudernack (1865–1914), a glass designer born in Bohemia and trained at the Vienna School of Applied Arts, who moved to Oslo in 1891. After a year at his old craft, Gaudernack began to design enamelled and plain silver for David Andersen before setting up on his own in 1910. A stylish silver vase with a bowl of lily-of-the-valley in *plique-à-jour* enamel, executed to Gaudernack's design for Andersen in 1905, recalls some of the movement of the new art.

One of his masterpieces of *plique-á-jour*, comparable with French work, is a bowl with dragonfly handles made by David Andersen in 1907 and now in the Kunstindustrimuseum, Oslo.[79] The influence of Art Nouveau waned towards the end of the first decade of the twentieth century, but traditional motifs continued to be used in silver design.

Examples of Danish plate made during the first decade and a half of the nineteenth century emphasize the debt to Sheffield plate: a sugar bowl and spoon rack of 1812 by Christen Dues; even more, a fruit bowl of 1813 in the Kunstindustrimuseum, Copenhagen, recall English prototypes. The bowl, bearing Copenhagen marks, is walled by inverted U-shaped wires held at the top by a ring and at the bottom by a reeded base: it is a simplified version of a plated wire dish of 1803 owned by the Cutlers' Company of Sheffield.

In the 1830s Jørgen Balthasar Dalhoff of Copenhagen produced neoclassical pieces with affinities to both French and English work of twenty years earlier, but with ornament more reticent than either.[80] The Dalhoff firm was among the manufacturers who took to plating and electroplating; though H. C. Drewson of Copenhagen was the first to do so, in 1846 gaining an Honourable Mention for his goods at the Paris 1855 Exhibition. Two of Drewson's catalogues, issued in 1861 and 1883, are reproduced in Christian Waagepeterson, *Dansk Sølvplet før 1900* (1975). The revived styles came together with the adoption of machinery, which must have occurred before 1838 as Tostrup saw a mechanized workshop in Copenhagen before he set up on his own.

By the early 1860s, however, historicism was chiefly expressed in two forms, both archaeological. The first was a reversion to styles of Denmark's past, medieval and earlier; the second was classical design. There were, inevitably, exceptions: E. F. Dahl of Copenhagen showed a centrepiece at the London 1862 Exhibition with a classical tripod base supporting a draped classical woman overshadowed by a bowl encased in rioting foliage, which would not have been out of place at the Great Exhibition. Vilhelm Christesen, goldsmith and jeweller of Copenhagen, submitted a more orthodox centrepiece in the Greek style. It is worth noting that S. Vigfusson of Reykjavik, Iceland, exhibited with the Danish contingent in 1862. Christesen's contribution to the Paris 1867 Exhibition included a remarkable horn in oxidized and gilt silver designed by the sculptor C. Peters and illustrating the story of a knight's rescue of a princess immured in a castle by a sorcerer. With medieval fantasy, the figure of the knight rides up to attack the dragons guarding the princess.

Later work by Christesen in the classical style, such as a candelabrum exhibited in Philadelphia in 1876, is marked by a more saturated ornament.[81] Royal patronage, rather than his own predilections, were said to have led Karl Michelsen of Copenhagen to work in the mid-eighteenth-century manner. His firm, the most important in Denmark at the turn of the century (he was the court jeweller), was founded by his father in 1841; he succeeded to the management in 1877. Searching for a new direction, Michelsen took to setting Copenhagen porcelain in Art Nouveau silver mounts, exhibiting examples in 1900.[82] The architect and designer Thorvald Bindesbøll (1846–1908) was among his designers.

The major Danish figure of the early twentieth century was Georg Jensen, a sculptor, ceramicist and goldsmith influenced by English theories of workshop practice. After a stay in Paris in 1900–01, he opened his own workshop in Copenhagen in April 1904, gathering around him such artists as Johan Rohde (1856–1935), whose designs were characterized by a refined simplicity; Harald Nielsen, who became Jensen's art director; and the sculptors Gundorph Albertus, who joined the firm in 1911, and Arno Malinowski.[83]

· RUSSIA ·

Russia's brilliant resistance to Napoleon in 1812 and its part in his final defeat was rewarded at the Congress of Vienna by the grant of Finland and part of Poland. This resulted in many goldsmiths migrating from Helsinki and elsewhere in the Russian Empire to St Petersburg, the capital, where, even in the eighteenth century, foreign

KOVSH *(above left), silver-gilt, enamel and garnets. St Petersburg, c.1890. Maker: Anders Johan Nevalainen for Fabergé. Kovshi (drinking scoops) were Russian vessels traditionally made (until 1821) for presentation by the Tsar to certain of his subjects for services rendered. Length: 11.4 cm (4½ in)*

EWER AND STAND *(above right), martelé silver. Rhode Island, 1903. Designer: William C. Codman (1839–1921). Maker: Gorham Manufacturing Co. The word 'martelé' means hammer-wrought and refers to the hammer marks left on the surface. Height of ewer: 49.2 cm (19¼ in) Diameter of stand: 32 cm (12⅝ in) (St Louis Art Museum, St Louis. Bequest of the Harry Edison Foundation)*

craftsmen had outnumbered the native guild. Among the Finns in St Petersburg was Carl Johann Tegelstein, who arrived as an apprentice in 1817 and became a master goldsmith in 1833. A silver-gilt tea kettle and stand, made just before his death in 1852 as part of the service for Grand Duke Nikolai Nikolayevich (1831–91), is in the Philadelphia Museum.[84] Gustav Fabergé, born in the Baltic region and of French Huguenot ancestry, was another hopeful lured to the capital where, in 1842, he founded one of its most celebrated firms.

Foreign influences, especially French, persisted in the early years of the nineteenth century. The firm of J. & A. Fraget of Warsaw, founded by two Frenchmen in 1824, introduced Sheffield plate and electroplate into Russia, establishing depots in St Petersburg, Moscow and other cities. Staffed by mainly Polish and Russian workers who had the benefit of schools set up by their employers, the firm flourished. Russia's principal contribution to the West was niello, which reached France by way of Wagner of Germany. The technique was practised in St Petersburg by masters mainly from Velikiy Ustyg.

In Moscow, reduced to a provincial centre after the Court moved to St Petersburg in the early eighteenth century, niello was used more widely, chiefly to decorate snuff or souvenir boxes. One of the few privileges retained by goldsmiths in Moscow was the honour of making the traditional kovshi (boat-like drinking scoops) for presentation by the Tsar to his subjects in acknowledgment of services rendered, but this custom ceased in about 1821.[85] Goldsmiths, however, continued to make kovshi and other vessels for general sale.

Power-driven machinery broke into this conservative haven in about 1830, accompanied (or followed) by the revived styles popular in the West. The styles were adopted and transformed, and the machinery was pressed into service in Moscow, St Petersburg and elsewhere. Well before the mid-century, determined efforts were made to make the Russian goldsmith trade independent of foreigners. The moving force was the Sazikov firm, founded in Moscow in 1793 by Pavel Fedorovich Sazikov and by 1810 large enough to be described as a factory. In 1842, the firm opened a branch in St Petersburg; four years later it was granted the Imperial Warrant. By the mid-century Sazikov employed over 300 designers and workmen, all Russian, with schools in design and modelling attached, for the craftsmen's children. The results were clearly demonstrated at the 1851 Exhibition, when Ignatiy Pavlovich Sazikov, then head of the firm, was awarded a Council Medal for a display of historicist articles and several works in the naturalistic style, exemplified by a centrepiece (engraved by the *Illustrated London News*) in which the Grand Duke Dmitri Donskoi was represented wounded and supported against a fir tree while learning from his soldiers of a battle won. The jury report regarded it as superior in design and execution to anything of its kind; even the duc de Luynes called it brilliant.[86] The firm survived several more decades, producing work adapted from Western fashions as well as in the Russian manner, using niello and enamelling techniques.

The Sazikov concern was rivalled by the firm founded in Moscow in 1853 by Pavel Akimovich Ovchinnikov and continued by his three sons.

This firm flourished until the Revolution. In 1873 Ovchinnikov established a branch in St Petersburg, receiving the Imperial Warrant two years later, and by 1881 he employed 300 workmen and had set up a training school in Moscow. It was reputedly the first concern to devote itself entirely to producing enamel and other wares in the Russian national style; but it also absorbed external influences, translating Japanese motifs, for instance, into lacquer-paintings on silver. A third important concern was founded in St Petersburg in 1867 by Ivan Petrovich Khlebnikov and transferred to Moscow in 1871, continuing until 1917 as warranted Court purveyors. In 1882 the firm had some 200 craftsmen.[87]

All three concerns were among the Russian firms contributing to international exhibitions, invariably attracting attention for their enamelled and niello work. When they formed part of the Russian contingent at the Vienna 1873 Exhibition, another Russian passion, *trompe-l'oeil* silverwork, was represented on Sazikov's stand in the form of a dish with a simulated damask napkin worked in silver.[88] (Odiot of Paris had shown a similar piece in 1851.) Articles in the same genre were made by many silversmiths in Russia in the second half of the century: basketwork and wood-grain textures were popular. Gustavovich Klingert of Moscow capitalized on Russian designs and techniques for export to Germany, England, France and America.

At Chicago the repetitious enamels of Russian work aroused criticism, but the adoption of Art Nouveau designs towards the end of the century enlarged the repertory. The saturated colours of traditional enamelwork were avoided by Fabergé and others in St Petersburg, who concentrated on the more delicate techniques of *guilloché* or transparent enamel laid over a textured gold ground in objects of *vertu*, a more important aspect of their production than their silverwork. The Fabergé concern was run from 1870 by Peter Carl Fabergé, who entrusted the execution of designs by the firm's artists to a number of workmasters. The workforce at times amounted to as many as 500 people. The firm received the Imperial Warrant in 1884–5, and afterwards opened branches in Moscow, Odessa, Kiev and London, building its reputation on impeccable workmanship until brought to a halt in 1918.[89] Fabergé himself served as a juror for the jewellery section of Paris 1900 Exhibition and was therefore precluded from receiving an award. Among his exhibits cited in the silversmithing report was a candelabrum in the Louis XVI manner in which nephrite, bronze and silver were combined. Other exhibitors who received awards were Ovchinnikov, Grachev Brothers of St Petersburg (famous for their enamels) and several goldsmiths using traditional techniques in the Caucusus.[90] The Poles, still struggling for independence, were unrepresented, although firms such as Malcz of Warsaw had earlier gained considerable mastery of western European revived styles.

· THE USA AND CANADA ·

The United States, at war with Britain in 1812, gaining territories such as the northern provinces of Mexico, and torn by the hostilities between the northern and southern states in the early 1860s, emerged after the mid-century as a major political and industrial power. The millions of European immigrants who poured in contributed in no small way to this new status.

The craft tradition of American silverwork, largely confined to the eastern states in the early nineteenth century, was revived there and elsewhere in its closing years. In the interim, firms of international renown such as Tiffany's of New York and the Gorham Plate Company of Providence, Rhode Island, using advanced methods of production, successfully began to challenge the European trade in the 1870s. Until the 1860s American silverwork reflected European styles at some distance, although neoclassicism lingered for most of the first half of the century. During the early Federal period (1795–1815) late eighteenth-century French taste mingled with English, while heavier forms were eventually introduced, and the late Federal period (1815–25) saw the increasing adoption of Empire and Regency designs.

The legacy of the Colonial period noticeably affected early Federal productions. In Boston Paul Revere, Jr., and others such as Ebenezer Moulton, used simple neoclassical shapes to great effect, as did the Richardsons, Abraham Dubois and Christian Wiltberger in Philadelphia. In the late Federal period, Jesse Churchill and his partner David Treadwell of Boston adapted the popular English barrel tankard form into a wine-cooler presented to Commodore O. H. Perry to commemorate his victory over the English in September 1813. It is possible that the design was inspired by what they saw in Sheffield platers' catalogues.[91] The demand for testimonials to the war heroes of 1812–14 gave a great fillip to the silversmithing trade.

Thomas Fletcher and Sidney Gardiner ran a prolific and much respected firm in Baltimore, and sometimes drew on the designs of Percier and Fontaine. Their tureen of 1817, part of a service presented to Commodore John Rodgers, recalls in form and decoration (especially the cast border of the cover) a monteith in the great service of plate by Henry Auguste presented by the City of Paris to Napoleon for his coronation in 1804.[92] Fletcher travelled to England, and so may have seen the silver versions of the Warwick Vase made by Storr for Rundell's in 1812, but his own variation, first produced in the form of a pair of covered urns in 1824–5 for presentation to De Witt Clinton, is thought to derive from an engraving by Henry Moses for *A Collection of Antique Vases*, a popular compendium published in London in 1814. Moses's book may also have been used by other American silversmiths. The De Witt Clinton vases made a lasting impression. An entry in Philip Hone's diary dated 14 February 1838 (in the

PITCHER *(right), silver. New York, c.1845. Maker: Zalmon Bostwick. This jug was copied from a stoneware jug of 1842 produced by the English firm of Charles Meigh. (Brooklyn Museum, New York)*

TUREEN *(below), one of a pair, silver. Philadelphia, 1817. Maker: Fletcher & Gardiner. This tureen was part of a large service of plate presented by the city of Baltimore to Commodore John Rodgers in gratitude for his part in the defence of the city against the British in 1814. Width: 38.8 cm (15¼ in) (Smithsonian Institution, Washington, D.C.)*

New York Historical Society) refers to the urns and then to the makers: 'Nobody in this "world" of ours hereabouts can compete with them in their kind of work.'[93]

Empire and Regency neoclassicism were still in full spate when the first of the revived styles crossed the Atlantic in the early 1820s. This was the revived rococo, which seems to have reached Baltimore at roughly the same time as it did Paris. The Baltimore version, characterized by compressed embossed motifs, recalls Irish rococo design. One of the principal exponents of the style, Andrew Ellicott Warner of Baltimore, is known to have had family ties with Ireland. Samuel Kirk of the same city executed his first rococo piece by 1822, but the later introduction of genre scenes and angular handles enabled the firm to carry the style into the 1860s.[94] The Philadelphia firm of Bailey & Co. exhibited breakfast and tea services and a coffee urn in the same style as one done by Samuel Kirk in 1835 at the New York 1853 Exhibition.

Gothic motifs crept into American silver here and there, but a full-blown rendering like the piece by Zalmon Bostwick of New York is rare. Made with a matching goblet in about 1845, the pitcher is based on a stoneware jug of 1842 by the English pottery firm of Charles Meigh of Hanley, Staffordshire.[95]

Naturalism was often combined with the rococo; a fine example, a kettle and stand of about 1850, executed by John Chandler Moore for Ball, Tompkins & Black of New York, is in the Metropolitan Museum of Art.[96] Renaissance and baroque forms also found their way into standard repertories, or sometimes in combination with the dominant style of the 1860s, the archaeological classicism flourishing all over Europe. The influence of Owen Jones's *Grammar of Ornament*, first published in London in 1856 and the epitome of South Kensington aesthetics, was strongly felt in America. Jones's geometric treatment of all historic styles, even of the naturalistic manner (plant forms, sternly disciplined into two-dimensional formality, were drawn for him by Christopher Dresser), influenced many American silversmiths.

European technological innovations were also adopted, and America contributed some of its own. Powered stamping, spinning and other techniques required large items of equipment and led to the establishment of substantial factories, where immigrants swelled the labour force. Leaders in the field were Gorham & Company, founded in about 1815–18 by Jabez Gorham in Providence, Rhode Island. In 1831, with a new partner, H. L. Webster, Gorham turned to the manufacture of silver spoons. His son John, who joined the firm in 1841, was quick to see the advantages of mechanical aids to production and, having observed what England was capable of, designed and made some machinery himself. In 1863, after several changes of title (listed in *Gorham Silver, 1831–1981* (1982) by Charles H.

Carpenter, Jr.), the firm became the Gorham Manufacturing Company, with retail premises in Broadway, New York. They had already extended their production into electroplated nickel wares a few years earlier, and in the 1870s their knowledge of electroprocesses was exploited further in colouring Japanese-style wares. Nevertheless, they were always capable of using traditional techniques to make presentation pieces. By 1889 they had over 1000 employees.

The company's principal designers were two Englishmen, both from Elkington & Co. of Birmingham, the patentees of electroplating in 1840. The first was George Wilkinson, who arrived at Gorham's in the 1850s and gained a Silver Medal at the Paris 1889 Exhibition; he may well have been responsible for Mrs Lincoln's tea service in the Smithsonian Institution. Wilkinson was succeeded by William Christmas Codman, who had apparently left Elkington's for Cox & Son of London before becoming Gorham's chief designer in 1891; he retired in 1914. C. R. Ashbee of the Guild of Handicraft, then in London, visited the Gorham works in 1896 and again in 1900–01, when he discovered how much the firm used the machine as against hand work. The 'application of machinery', he wrote in his journal, 'has been carried to a pitch of excellence and precise skill in its use for the making of silver ware, which no firm in England can come anywhere near . . . In England the great silversmiths' houses are dying, they have not the capital, nor the means, nor the wits to put in the newest American machinery . . .' Codman told Ashbee that English workmen from Elkington's, Mappin's and the like comprised seven tenths of the workforce (which totalled 2000 in Providence and New York), the rest being largely of Scandinavian origin.[97]

It is surprising that Codman is famous chiefly for hand-finished silver in the fluid naturalism of Art Nouveau, introduced in 1897; the hammer marks left on the surface inspired the name given to the range, Martelé, after the French word meaning hammer-wrought. Martelé silver, shown by Gorham at the Paris 1900 Exhibition, was admired by the jury for the technical dexterity used in its making. The jury was even more enthusiastic about the Rookwood pottery which was decorated by the firm with electro-deposited silver, and about the patterns of flatware, for which the French artist and die-sinker Antoine Heller was responsible (Heller was first recruited by Tiffany before 1878). Gorham was awarded a Grand Prix, being placed by the jury above Tiffany. Several members of the firm, including Edward Holbrook, its president, Codman and Heller (already a Gold Medallist at the 1889 Exhibition) gained medals. The firm went on to show a remarkable ivory and gold service at the Turin 1902 Exhibition,[98] and contributed to the St Louis Exhibition of 1904. In the first decade of the twentieth century they expanded further.

Tiffany, the most famous American manufacturer of silverware, was founded in New York in 1837 as Tiffany & Young, becoming Tiffany & Co. in 1853 after an intermediate change of title. Then importers and retailers, they brought over fancy goods from Europe and the East, and had showrooms first on Broadway and then in Union Square. Much of their silver was purchased from France and England, but they also acquired goods from John C. Moore of New York, a manufacturer to the trade. Moore's son, the silversmith and designer Edward Chandler Moore, took over the business on his father's retirement in 1851. An agreement by which Moore manufactured exclusively for Tiffany's was continued until 1868, when Tiffany & Co. became a corporation and bought the Moore concern. The Moore company, which employed about 500 craftsmen at one stage, had developed into a factory using some mechanized processes in combination with handwork; electroplating was added to silver manufacture shortly

HOT-WATER URN, *silver. Baltimore, c.1835. Maker: Samuel Kirk. Part of a tea and coffee service, it is decorated with Chinese scenes in the rococo style. Height: 39.5 cm (15½ in) (Minneapolis Institute of Arts, Minneapolis. Lent by the family of John Booth Cooley)*

COFFEE SET, *silver encrusted with silver, copper and gold. New York, c.1877. Maker: Tiffany & Co. This set, comprising coffee pot, sugar bowl and creamer, was almost certainly shown at the Paris 1878 Exhibition. Height of coffee pot: 21.5 cm (8½ in) (Victoria and Albert Museum, London)*

afterwards. It was Edward C. Moore, director of the newly acquired factory, who in fact created (with his designers) the characteristic bold and intricate decoration of Tiffany silver.

Tiffany's also sold articles by Grosjean & Woodward of New York and by Gorham. A Gorham cheese scoop in the Metropolitan Museum, New York, for example, has a handle in the Medallion pattern patented by Gorham in 1864, and bears the name of maker and retailer. The scoop, like many other pieces made for Tiffany's after about 1851, was executed in silver of the English sterling standard. Under Moore's direction, the variations on classical themes made for the firm in the 1860s took on an English quality of angularity, and Moore's importance as chief designer and supervisor of the silver manufacturing was recognized from 1868 to 1891 by the initial 'M' stamped on Tiffany articles.

At the Paris 1867 Exhibition, Tiffany's appeared as the sole representative of American silversmiths, and the official report spoke of pleasing tea services well and tastefully executed.[99] (Elkingtons of Birmingham are said to have bought half-a-dozen items purely for copying.) Moore's predilection for Eastern artefacts, reflected in his personal collections, spurred the firm's workforce to experiment with Islamic (his so-called 'Saracenic style') and Japanese metalworking techniques. The designer Christopher Dresser, visiting the Philadelphia Centennial Exhibition in 1876 *en route* for Japan, was commissioned by Tiffany, participating in the exhibition, to purchase examples of Japanese encrusted metalwork for the firm to study. Dresser did as required, and Tiffany's, who had already experimented with polychromatic effects obtained from the use of copper inlaid with silver, went on to gain a Grand Prix at the Paris

1878 Exhibition, largely for their encrusted goods, which included copper wares in the Japanese taste, embellished with electro-deposited silver, and other works in the same style in silver. Another of Tiffany's exhibits was an electrotype copy of the Bryant Vase, a work of classical form and floral decoration designed by James H. Whitehouse for presentation in 1875 to the poet William Cullen Bryant. The vase had been exhibited at the Philadelphia Exhibition before Bryant gave it to the Metropolitan Museum, New York in 1877.[100] Responding to the contemporary vogue for enamelling, niello, damascening, and hardstone decoration including rock-crystal, Tiffany also produced articles, often of an impressive size, incorporating horn, ivory and tortoiseshell.

The Americans loved colour, as the distinguished French goldsmith Lucien Falize observed of Tiffany's display at the 1889 Exhibition. (It was Falize who also declared that the firm had benefited from learning Japanese encrustation techniques first-hand, a claim which has since been denied.) The technical and stylistic experimentation was welded by the early 1890s into a distinctive form of American exoticism, exemplified by the Magnolia Vase in the Metropolitan Museum, New York, one of the oustanding works at the World's Columbian Exposition at Chicago in 1893.[101] Designed by John T. Curran and made in silver, with handles derived from the Toltec culture (representing early America) above an enamelled frieze of magnolias, the body is chased with the native flowers of America, some of them worked in gold.

American daring appealed to the French, but Tiffany's exercises in orthodox European revived styles such as English neoclassicism found less favour. Nevertheless, at the Paris 1900 Exhibition Tiffany was placed second only to Gorham in the foreign section, and the report enthusiastically cited the gold and stone-set Adams Vase (in the Metropolitan Museum, New York) designed by Paulding Farnham, chief designer and director of the firm's jewellery division; this was executed between 1893–5 for presentation by the stockholders and directors of the American Cotton Oil Company to their chairman, Edward Dean Adams.[102] Farnham himself received a Gold Medal for his work.

After decades of importing silverwork from England and France, Tiffany's was exporting silver to Europe well before the end of the century, using their premises in Paris and London (established respectively in 1850 and 1868) as clearing houses. Charles L. Tiffany, the founder of the firm, remained in charge until 1902; he was the father of the great artist-designer, Louis Comfort Tiffany (1848–1933), of Associated Artists and Tiffany Studios.

Another well-known firm was the Meriden Britannia Company, established in December 1852 at Meriden, Connecticut, by several manufacturers, some of whom already had experience in the production of Britannia metalware. By 1855 the Company had added silver-plated hollow-ware and flatware to their Britannia metal goods, and in 1862 acquired the tools and dies of Rogers, Smith & Co. of Hartford, Connecticut, flatware manufacturers. Concentrating on machine production, the company prospered, and in 1889, when they were awarded a somewhat contentious Gold Medal at Paris, the jury report remarked that about 2000 workmen were contributing to the firm's financial success, turning out some ten million items of flatware yearly (and hollow-ware in proportion) under the supervision of John Jephson, formerly of Elkington's. The engraved work was carried out under the direction of one Hirschfeld, a German who had been with the company since 1852. The firm traded all over America, and were also represented in Rio de Janeiro, Buenos Aires,

THE MAGNOLIA VASE, *silver, gold, enamel and opals. New York, 1893. Designer: John T. Curran. Maker: Tiffany & Co. Height: 79 cm (31 in) (The Metropolitan Museum of Art, New York. Gift of Mrs Winthrop Atwell, 1899)*

TEA AND COFFEE SERVICE, *silver. Providence, Rhode Island, c.1859. This eight-piece service is said to have been given to Mrs Abraham Lincoln by the citizens of New York, and is engraved with her initials – MTL for Mary Todd Lincoln. Height of hot-water kettle and stand: 49.4 cm (19⅜ in) (Smithsonian Institution, Washington, D.C.)*

Melbourne, London and, from 1889, Paris.[103] Six years later the company bought a small silversmith's workshop in New York and moved it to Meriden, incorporating it in 1898 into the International Silver Company of Meriden.

The Arts and Crafts Movement affected America early, the prime influence coming from England. L. C. Tiffany turned to the decorative arts in 1879, with the encouragement of Edward C. Moore and Samuel Bing, the dealer in Paris, who supplied both Moore and Tiffany with Oriental objects. Although the latter, when he came to found the Tiffany studios in 1902, preferred bronze to silver, his father's new workshops at Forest Hills, New Jersey, housed a young German-born silversmith, George Christian Gebelein (1878–1945), who was sent to Tiffany's in 1897 after his apprenticeship with the Boston silversmiths Goodrow & Jenks. After several moves, Gebelein rented a bench in 1903 at the Handicraft Shop in Boston, set up by A. A. Carey two years earlier to enable craftsmen to work and exhibit their productions under the aegis of the Arts and Crafts Society, itself founded by admirers of William Morris in 1897. Late in 1908 Gebelein left to work on his own at 79 Chestnut Street, Boston; he prospered, supplementing his own productions by dealing in (and collecting) antique English and American silver.

Chicago also had an Arts and Crafts Society, opened by Clara Barck Welles in 1900, which turned out simple silver hand-made to her designs. In 1905 she married Robert Jarvie, who had taken to metalwork as an amateur in the 1890s, and became a professional in 1904 when he started the shop bearing his name in the Fine Arts Building, Michigan Avenue. He developed into an outstanding silversmith and metalworker before going out of business between 1917 and 1920. Examples of his work, and of other Arts and Crafts metalworkers, are in the collections of the Chicago Historical Society and the Chicago Art Institute.

According to J. E. Langdon, *Canadian Silversmiths and their Marks* (1960), silversmiths in Canada, who were largely of French, English, Scottish and Irish origin, were augmented in the late eighteenth century by American Loyalist craftsmen. A five-fold increase in population during the first half of the nineteenth century attracted a corresponding increase in immigrant craftsmen, mainly from Europe. More people meant new churches, which had to be furnished with plate, which was imported or made locally.

Despite the new British regime, French influence remained strong in Quebec, though traditional articles such as the *écuelle* did not survive long. Several Montreal silversmiths, mainly of French and English descent, including Pierre

Hughet dit Latour and Robert Cruickshank, supplied the Government Department of Indian Affairs with articles for the Indian trade. A surviving order placed with Cruickshank in 1800 included gorgets, wristbands and other items of silver jewellery. Silversmiths in Nova Scotia, New Brunswick and Ontario favoured the use of imitation English hallmarks, partly to counter the competition from imported British work.

Robert Hendery of Montreal, who came to Canada some time before 1840, working briefly with Peter Bohle in the 1850s and with John Leslie from 1887 until 1895, was a leading manufacturer. He adopted the English lion passant and sovereign's head as marks, and his firm supplied silverwork, often also bearing the dealer's mark, to over 100 retailers in Nova Scotia, New Brunswick, Quebec, Ontario, and even as far afield as British Columbia. Hendery retired in 1895 and Leslie carried on until 1899, when the business was sold to Henry Birks & Sons, who continued using the imitation marks in a concern which still flourishes in Montreal. Birks was born in Montreal in 1840 to parents who had emigrated from Yorkshire in 1832, and started his own business in 1879, first as a retailer and then as a manufacturer. Branches were opened in Ottawa in 1901 and Winnipeg in 1903, while the firm afterwards acquired existing businesses in Ottawa, Toronto, Vancouver, Halifax, Calgary and elsewhere.

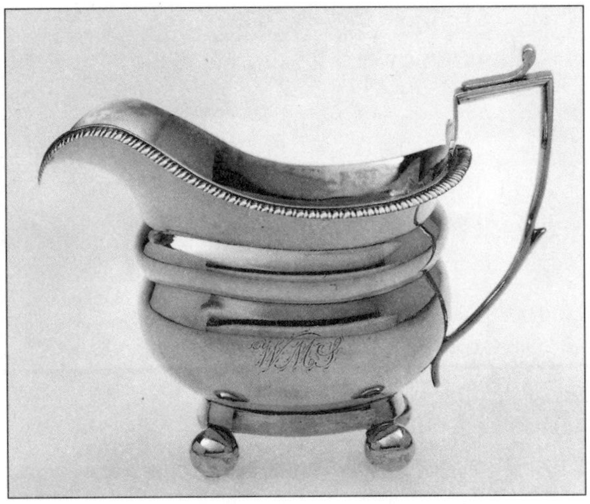

CREAM JUG, *silver. Quebec, c.1830. Maker: J. Smellie. Height: 11.5 cm (4½ in) (Royal Ontario Museum, Toronto)*

· CENTRAL AND SOUTH AMERICA ·

The silversmithing traditions established in Spanish and Portuguese colonial possessions led to the production of strong, florid church plate in the baroque and rococo manners, styles which also influenced domestic silver. The neoclassical style came to Mexico when the Royal Academy of San Carlos was established in 1785. Its greatest exponent was Manuel Tolsá, a silversmith born and trained in Valencia, who left Spain for Mexico in 1791. Tolsá died in 1816, but his simple forms and decoration continued to influence Mexican silverwork for several decades, especially the plate produced by Mexican Indians who were able to practise the craft after the country gained independence in the early 1820s. According to Lawrence Anderson in *The Art of the Silversmith in Mexico, 1519–1936* (New York, 1941) the trade then began a decline, exacerbated by the cessation of important commissions for church plate after ecclesiastical properties began to be nationalized in 1859. Some silversmiths, however, many of Spanish descent, were happy to return to the more florid forms of revived baroque and rococo art after independence, both in Mexico and in South America where late eighteenth-century neoclassicism had belatedly taken hold. For example, rococo floral trails and a scroll handle are married to an essentially classical profile in a jug made in Mexico in the 1860s (in the Field Collection of the Albuquerque Art Museum). Anderson thought French influence resulting from the invasion of Mexico in 1863 was of profound importance, outlasting the execution of the Austrian Emperor of Mexico, Maximilian, in 1867.[104] Maximilian certainly imported a huge French service, but inevitably owned Austrian pieces. A pair of mid-nineteenth-century rococo candlesticks by V. Fuster, bearing Maximilian's emblem and the name of his empress Carlotta, is in the Morley Collection, Museum of New Mexico, Santa Fe.[105]

Traditional types of object, such as maté cups for the infusion of Paraguayan tea and the accompanying *bombillas* or sipping tubes, continued to be made in the former colonies after independence; examples survive from virtually every country, including Peru, Bolivia and Chile. Equally important was the attempt in Peru, where the most productive silver mines were sited, to resuscitate pre-Columbian motifs during the early Republican period (c.1820–60). A mid-nineteenth-century Peruvian candelabrum with the central column formed as an Inca noble (Museum of New Mexico) characterizes the revived Mestizo style, combining European forms with decorative devices drawn from the past.

The Inca symbolized Peru, and was often shown standing on a lion emblematic of Spain. A simpler variant, the Andean manner, current in Peru between about 1825 and 1900, deployed the plain surfaces of ancient Inca work with figurative devices from the same source. Silver filigree introduced from Spain in the sixteenth century was still flourishing in Peru in the nineteenth. In Argentina, a land of vast ranches, silver was used for stirrups, spurs, riding whip handles and sheath knives, and for horse trappings, as in the past. Daniel Avila, a silversmith of San Miguel, San Salvador, received an Honourable Mention at the Paris 1889 Exhibition for a flower vase decorated with native flowers and a bird.[106] Spanish colonial designs are currently being reproduced throughout Latin America; it is not difficult to imagine that nineteenth-century models will suffer the same fate.

· 8 · ART DECO AND AFTER: 1920–60 ·

The silver manufacturing trade has, in the twentieth century, undergone fundamental changes as a result of largely external forces. The combined effects of increased mechanization and a significant widening of the consumer market, together with the increasingly competitive character of both the manufacturing and retail sectors, has changed the emphasis of the industry. Commercial exigencies, such factors as the cost of tooling up for new ranges which make only a long run a viable proposition, have made caution, and therefore conservatism, the depressing realities.

The trend during this century, already a feature of the trade in Britain by 1920 through the activities of the silversmiths of the Arts and Crafts Movement, has been towards a widening of the gulf between artist and industrialist. The self-styled artist-craftsman has tended increasingly to pursue his craft in isolation, willing to take commercial risks in the cause of creative freedom, while the major industrialized manufacturers have endeavoured to protect their businesses by catering to a safe market, manufacturing cautiously diluted and, therefore, inevitably debased versions of fashionable styles or, perhaps more usually, by mass-producing machine-made derivations of traditional styles. Such travesties appeal to the uninformed public, which prefers the reassurance of a style it recognizes to the shock of the new.

The craft of working silver in innovative styles has been kept alive by a few artisans and workshops of note. It owes its survival to individuals who have combined artistic creativity with sufficient business acumen to create a market for their wares and, most notably in Scandinavia and in Britain after 1945, to enlightened government sponsorship and support from the industry.

The polarizing of artist and industrialist has significantly undermined the silver manufacturing trade, and at the same time raises the question of the role of crafts, not only in silver but in all areas of applied art, in our society. The situation as it affected the silver trade was well expressed in 1967 by Graham Hughes in his study *Modern Silver*: 'the pattern ... repeated in most countries today,' he wrote, was one in which 'well-intentioned private societies try to keep alive techniques that are outdated and useless, to sell products that are unfashionable and therefore unsaleable, to perpetuate the myth that what is difficult to make must be intrinsically desirable.'[1]

Nevertheless, crafts play an important humanizing role in our society. Liberated from the restrictions and dictates of commerce, they might aspire to more lofty roles, broadening the range of media of artistic expression, allowing the creation of objects which would satisfy a genuine need for artefacts with individual emotional content. Hand-made objects were defined by Octavio Paz in a quotation cited by craft-furniture maker John Makepeace in 1975 as a mediation between the industrial object and its opposite, the work of art. The forms of craftwork, he explained, were governed 'not by the principle of efficiency but of pleasure ... Handcraftsmanship is a sort of fiesta of the object: it transforms the everyday utensil into a sign of participation.'

If there was a role for the individual artist-craftsman between 1920 and 1960, there was also urgent need for industrial designers able to define new aesthetics appropriate to machine production. In the twentieth century the silver industry has suffered a considerable international decline, largely because of its failure to accept the need for guidance from designers willing to reconcile the various demands of function, commercial expendiency and 'honest' form. In the first half of the century there was considerable debate about the notion of the industrial designer, though only in the post-war decades did this role acquire respectability. The big silver manufacturers that survived years of crisis often did so through turning to distinguished designers for guidance, and also through a realization that mass-production and a 'precious' material were incompatible and that the future lay in the series production of simple, functional designs in stainless steel. In fact, stainless steel has, since the Second World War, largely replaced electroplate for domestic and contract hollow-ware and flatware.

Since the First World War a small number of artists have shunned the safe and easy option of

THE SEA BEAKER *(facing page), silver. London, 1929. Designer: R. M. Y. Gleadowe. Engraver: George Friend. Maker: Murphy & Falcon. This finely shaped vase symbolizes the sea. Round the base are waves, chased in low relief; above them is an elaborate, finely engraved drawing of mermaids, dolphins and fishes with the winds blowing. Gleadowe was one of the ablest designers who worked with silversmiths, and this early experiment in freehand engraved designs shows the delicate line work that was typical of him. Height: 14 cm (5½ in) (The Worshipful Company of Goldsmiths, London)*

THREE APPLES ON A BRANCH *(right), silver. Vienna, 1925. Designer: Dagobert Peche. Made in the Wiener Werkstätte workshops. Presented to Josef Hoffman to mark his fiftieth birthday. The whimsical delicacy of this piece is typical of the highly wrought style of silver produced by Peche and other members of the Werkstätte from about 1915 until Peche's death in 1923. Height (without base): 38 cm (15 in) (Österreichisches Museum für angewandte Kunst, Vienna)*

CLOCK *(right), silver. Copenhagen, c.1925–30. Designer: Johan Rohde. Maker: Georg Jensen. Height: 33 cm (13 in) (Private collection)*

reworking old styles, and made their mark by working silver in forms which caught the mood of their era. The output of these talented designers was very small beside the vast, uninspired production of the big manufacturers, but it is through their diverse achievements that the medium has preserved its dignity and has a story to tell of creative evolution. Indeed, through the work of artists of this calibre, including Jean Puiforcat, Dagobert Peche, Johan Rohde, Henning Koppel, Sigurd Persson, Lino Sabattini and Gerald Benney, can be traced the history of the applied arts in general during this half-century.

· STYLISTIC DEVELOPMENTS ·

The 1920s and 1930s were years of great achievement and of marked contrasts within the decorative arts. This period saw the Modernist ideal of pure line and form and unadorned surface challenging the traditional equation of high style with conspicuous opulence of materials, form and decoration. The French enjoyed international pre-eminence in the 1920s with the Art Deco style, which achieved its fullest expression in the exhibits at the 1925 Paris Exposition Internationale des Arts Décoratifs et Industriels Modernes. French Art Deco brought together various elements: disciplined floral motifs; formalized, sometimes abstract geometric patterns; neoclassical proportions or softened curves (in contrast to the energetic curvilinear excesses of Art Nouveau); and a profusion of exotic materials. The style found expression in silver designs by Süe et Mare, Cardeilhac, Jean Serrière and a few others, but did not distinguish itself in silver to the extent that it did in other media. By contrast, the leading school of decorative design in Austria in the 1920s, the Wiener Werkstätte (founded in 1903), flourished with a charming, sometimes whimsical style graciously expressed in decorative silverware by Josef Hoffmann, Dagobert Peche and others.

In Scandinavia, where silver first attracted attention between the wars and in the post-war years has rightly won international acclaim, the industry owes much of its success to the Scandinavians' consistent refusal to see craft and industry as conflicting forces. Their respect for handwork does not blind them to the potentials of machine production; their ideal is a happy balance between mechanization and hand finish, between a love of natural materials and gentle silhouettes and the necessity for rationalized production lines. Scandinavian functionalism is concerned with making objects that are easy to use and pleasing to live with. Whilst enjoying the benefits of craft co-operatives and government promotion of art in industry, Scandinavian designers fully accept that the test of their abilities must be the market-place. The Danish firm founded by Georg Jensen has led the market in the promotion and sale of a truly modern style in silverware.

In the 1920s and 1930s, while Jensen was evolving the gracious, unadorned style with which this firm and other Scandinavian manufacturers were to lead the field after the war, designers and silversmiths in France, Germany, Britain and elsewhere took the pure lines and geometric forms of Modernist theory and used them as the basis of a style which was to become an end in itself. Form did not follow function: form was all. The results ranged from the high-quality, sculptural shapes conceived in Paris by Jean Puiforcat, a supreme stylist, to the proliferation of awkwardly proportioned, hard-edged, 'Modernist' electroplate tea-services, which seem to have been popular in the 1930s, the debased versions of a lofty ideal which had its noble precursor in Dr Christopher Dresser's revolutionary designs of around 1880.

British and American silver between the wars was rarely of great stylistic distinction, though such firms as Tiffany and Garrard produced wares that made up in sumptuousness for their lack of invention. In both countries conservatism was a seemingly universal characteristic of the industry and the large commissioning retailers. In the USA the most interesting silver on sale was arguably that imported from Scandinavia or Vienna. In Britain no other production matched the graphic elegance of Liberty & Co.'s 'Cymric' range and the handsome Arts and Crafts designs of C.R. Ashbee for the Guild of Handicraft, though a few designers produced pieces of some merit. It was not until the emergence from post-war austerity heralded by the Festival of Britain in 1951 that British silversmiths once again achieved distinction. This flowering of the craft of the silversmith in Britain in the 1950s and 1960s was largely due to the exemplary efforts of the Worshipful Company of Goldsmiths, a still vital craft guild which has encouraged a revival in the traditions of civic and corporate patronage and, in so doing, has allowed a great measure of artistic freedom to designers who, between them, have won international respect for this British renaissance. Only the Scandinavians overshadowed the British achievement during the 1950s and later, as their spare, gracious silver was marketed throughout the West as part of a major export drive, and contributed to the widespread acceptance of modern Scandinavian design as the absolute measure of good taste.

In the early post-war years a variety of new styles found favour. In Britain a richly decorative style incorporating heraldic and other allegorical motifs caught the patriotic mood of the Festival of Britain, soon to be succeeded by a preference for noble proportions in pieces usually bare of decoration and sometimes achieving a bold monumentality. In the 1960s Gerald Benney introduced new techniques of texturing and started an international vogue, still popular today.

In the 1950s in France and Italy, a few designers devised shapes for silver in the 'free-form' style then fashionable. The master of this style in silver, however, was a Dane, Henning Koppel, designing for Georg Jensen. His sculptural forms for hollow-ware and jewellery are among the most representative artefacts of their era and will, no doubt, come to characterize their period, as Jean Puiforcat's work characterizes the years around 1930.

The early 1960s witnessed the return of a new version of the Modernist style, marked by minimal, clean lines and the elimination of decoration. The stylistic exercises of the previous decade were toned down, and many leading silversmiths created simple, disciplined but exciting forms, different nonetheless from those associated with the first flowering of Modernism some thirty years previously. The Scandinavians and the British maintained their international pre-eminence in this period, and the simple, elegant forms created in silver by the most distinguished designers and silversmiths have, in turn, given a stylistic lead to industrial designers seeking appropriate shapes for mass production in stainless steel. It was characteristic of the open-minded attitude of the gifted designer David Mellor, based in Sheffield, that he applied his rationalist ideas to both silver and stainless steel with equal flair and success; similarly it was characteristic of the far-sightedness of the firm of Georg Jensen that it commissioned prominent designers to create ranges of stainless-steel tableware to be sold alongside their silver, obviously at lower prices but with no reduction in the quality of the design or the product.

The story of achievements in silver, as in any other aspect of craft or design, is the story of those designers who have captured the mood and defined the style of their era, and who have also succeeded in creating a genuine demand for their products.

TEAPOT, *electroplate and hardwood. Paris, c.1930. Designer: Gérard Sandoz. Like Puiforcat, Sandoz was a member of the Union des Artistes Modernes, many of whom produced silver of a dramatic, geometrically precise style. Like pieces by Puiforcat, the hollow-ware produced by Sandoz often used blocks of dark wood, as on the handle of this teapot, as a counterfoil to the silver.*
Height: 9.5 cm (3¾ in) (Victoria and Albert Museum, London)

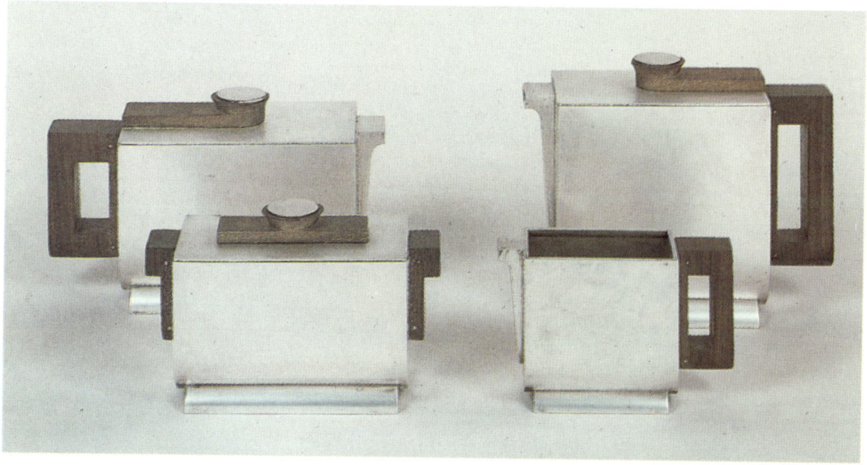

TEA SERVICE *(top), silver and hardwood. Paris, c. 1930. Designer: Jean Puiforcat. This is an example of Puiforcat's mature style, showing his belief in the magic and symbolism of pure geometry. (Sydney and Francis Lewis Collection, Richmond, Virginia)*

TEA SERVICE *(above), silver. Paris, c.1930. Maker: Tétard Frères. Tétard Frères were one of the leading Paris firms producing and retailing silver in the clean-lined Modernist style associated with Puiforcat. Height: 14.5 cm (5¾ in)*

· FRANCE ·

The French led the world in the 1920s in most areas of the decorative arts, both in the sophistication and the consummate refinement of their craftsmanship. France's foremost decorative designers found, in the Paris Exposition Internationale des Arts Décoratifs et Industriels Modernes of 1925, a sumptuous showcase for their achievements, and French Art Deco, as defined by the displays in the various pavilions, was a style which found able exponents in many media. In silver, however, with the notable exception of Jean Puiforcat, the undisputed master of French silver, the French did not achieve the distinction which they certainly attained in other areas, notably furniture, lacquer-work, ironwork, glass and ceramics.

In a special Summer 1925 issue of *L'Art Vivant*, art critic 'M.G.' (presumably the journal's editor, Maurice Martin du Gard), recounting his visit to the metalwork section of the exhibition, finds little to say concerning the *orfèvrerie* on display, simply listing contributors who included Aucoc, Cardeilhac, Christofle & Cie, Tétard Frères, Boulanger, Puiforcat and Sandoz. He illustrates a handsome *coupe* by Puiforcat and also, significantly, a teapot by the decorating firm of Süe et Mare. While most major commissioning or manufacturing retailers produced work too cautiously traditional to attract attention, a few distinguished Art Deco designs for silver were made, not by silversmiths but by leading Art Deco designers better known for their work in other fields. Foremost among them was Süe et Mare, which produced attractive Art Deco hollow-ware, services and dressing-table pieces in a style characterized by bulbous segmented forms. Emile-Jacques Ruhlmann, the leading Art Deco cabinetmaker, designed in various media, and his elegant mirror in silver-plated bronze, the circular frame supported on twin reeded horn-shaped legs, is a perfect example of his disciplined neoclassical style. An interesting exception to the prevailing timid Deco style was the work of silversmith Jean Serrière who created bold and simple shapes for hollow-ware which also had a distinctive hand-hammered surface.

By the late 1920s a new, strongly geometric style, inspired by the theorists of Modernism, gave a renewed vitality to French silver. The designers working in this style were to rally together as the Union des Artistes Modernes, a group founded in 1930 with common ideals formulated in the late 1920s. The UAM membership included several artists who were to produce outstanding work in silver, especially Jean Puiforcat, Raymond Templier, Gérard Sandoz and Jean Fouquet. This group of designers, together with a few others including Paul Brandt and Desny, between them created a body of work of considerable merit both in design and execution, unified by their liking for strict geometric forms and decoration, but each with a recognizable personal style. A representative selection of their work was published contemporaneously by Charles Moreau (c.1930–32) in the folio *Bijoux et Orfèvrerie*, volume sixteen within the

CIGARETTE CASE, *silver and lacquer incorporating crushed eggshell. Paris, c.1930. Designer: Paul Brandt. The strict geometric form and decoration of this piece typify Brandt's style. Dimensions (open): 14 × 16.5 cm (5½ × 6½ in) (Private collection)*

series *L'Art International d'Aujourd'hui*, selected and introduced by Jean Fouquet. The volume presents outstanding works from a brief but remarkable phase in French silver design. Here are dramatic, geometrically precise, almost architectural vases, services, samovars, *coupes*, table lamps, cigarette cases and jewels. The hollow-ware by Puiforcat and Sandoz used blocks of dark wood or clear glass as a counterfoil to the smooth silver. Desny used the device of building cubes from squares of glass to diffuse light from lamps of architectural proportions. Fouquet, Brandt, Sandoz and Templier used plain lacquers or lacquers incorporating crushed eggshell in dynamic decorations on cigarette cases or within the crisp angles and curves of bracelets and other items of silver jewellery.

The majority of the designers within this avant-garde group were second-generation jewellers or silversmiths with the facilities of family workshops available to them. They could, therefore, pursue their uncompromising design ideas without the need for major capital investment and without an initial concern for commercial acceptance. Fouquet and Templier were the sons of jewellers and carried on the family traditions in exciting new styles; Sandoz showed great flair as a designer of silverware and jewellery, much of which was made up in his father's workshops, but this career was short-lived and he turned his attentions in the 1930s to film-making, graphic design and painting. Puiforcat (1897–1945) learnt his craft in his father's workshops and established an independent reputation as one of the great silversmiths of all time.

Jean Puiforcat's early studies were broken off by the First World War and his enlistment, and it was not until his return to civilian life after the war that he turned his attention to practical training in the craft of silver work in his father's atelier. He also found time to practise sculpture under the tutelage of Louis Lejeune, and his sculptor's training provided an education in the emotive power of abstract forms which was to serve him well in his pioneering approach to silver design.

In 1923 Puiforcat participated for the first time in the annual Salon des Artistes Décorateurs, by which point his work had already acquired its individuality. His early works were distinguished by a lack of surface decoration, with the emphasis

JEAN PUIFORCAT, *photographic portrait. Undated.*

DISH AND COVER, *silver with jade handle. Paris, c.1925. Designer: Jean Puiforcat. Maker's mark: EP. An assured handling of form – the only decoration here is a sunray pattern on the lid and rings round the base, formed by incised lines – and an emphasis on harmonious proportions, soft curves and slightly bulbous, segmented shapes are what distinguished Puiforcat's early designs. Diameter: 25 cm (9⅞ in)*

on harmonious proportions. Their soft curves and slightly bulbous, segmented forms were in keeping with the fashions of the time, but distinctive for the nobility of their proportions and the assurance with which decoration was eliminated. The 1923 exhibit included a coffee service incorporating lapis lazuli and, while shunning decoration, Puiforcat appreciated the value of using such materials as lapis, jade, ivory, crystal or dark wood for handles and finials. Throughout his career he was to use these materials regularly, and always judiciously, as a counterpoint to the smooth polished surface of silver.

By 1925 Puiforcat's mastery of silver was undisputed, as was shown by his contributions to the Paris Exposition Internationale in that year. He was invited to display his work not only alongside that of his fellow silversmiths but also within the most prestigious pavilion of all, Ruhlmann's Pavillon d'un Collectionneur for which he created a 'surtout de table' and other pieces, displayed on the large sideboard of Ruhlmann's dining room.

By 1930 Puiforcat's mature style was fully developed, a style based on quasi-religious beliefs in the magic and symbolism of pure geometry. In a letter written to Comte Fleury in 1933 he explains the path of his evolution:

> My earliest designs were dictated by fashion until, after so much work inspired by traditional designs, I came to realize that something mysterious was eluding me. I had learned the principles of composition and proportion from the classic masters but felt that there was a more profound goal. And in pursuit of this I devised a scheme based on geometry. But this alone was not the answer; I felt that I had not truly progressed and had yet to find the key to the problem. Some links seemed self-evident, the majority remained obscure. I went back to the study of mathematics, delving ever more deeply beyond my earlier, superficial studies and discovered Plato. The way was now open. Through Plato I learnt about the relationships between arithmetical truth, geometry and ideals of harmony; I learnt about the five famous Platonic elements, later illustrated by Leonardo de Vinci: the dodecahedron, the tetrahedron (fire), the octahedron (air), the icosahedron (water), the cube (earth). I immediately appreciated the divine nature of art and I pursued the study of ancient religions in which numbers are universally regarded as endowed with a mysterious power and as the key to all things.[2]

Puiforcat was a profoundly religious man, and concentrated much of his energy in the 1930s on the creation of ecclesiastical plate, an aspect of his work much in evidence in his contribution to the Paris Exposition Internationale of 1937, for which he created an entire suite of chapel furnishings. The Second World War marked the effective end of Puiforcat's career, despite a brief spell of activity in Mexico in the 1940s.

Puiforcat had been a founder member of the Union des Artistes Modernes and when, in 1949, René Herbst, then president of the UAM, compiled a memorial volume (published in 1951), his fellow designers were invited to pay tribute to their colleague, and did so in terms of unqualified praise for the purity of his vision and the importance of his role in the history of French silver.

Puiforcat was a perfectionist. He raised his craft to the level of the abstract sculptor's art.

France produced no successor to Puiforcat. The major manufacturing firm of Christofle responded to changing fashions in the post-war period with the introduction of flatware designed by Tapio Wirkkala and with a stylish range of free-form hollow-ware by Lino Sabattini; and artist-craftsman René Robert created sculptural vessels in the fashionable curvilinear style which were eccentric rather than beautiful.

· AUSTRIA AND GERMANY ·

Two schools of design in the 1920s provide a fascinating contrast in the story of modern silver. While in Germany, the designers of the Bauhaus school were pursuing ideals of supposedly pure functionalism in silver and metalwork, in Vienna, more or less simultaneously, the Wiener Werkstätte was enjoying its last, decadent flowering and producing fanciful silverwork, charming yet lacking the vigour which had characterized the group's work in the years immediately after its inception in 1903. The contrast between the creations of the two schools reflects the conflict between the Modernist pursuit of 'pure' form and the popular demand for decoration.

The pure, angular lines and minimal grid designs which had made the early silver of Josef Hoffmann and Koloman Moser at the Werkstätte so revolutionary enjoyed only brief favour: within a decade a more highly wrought, decorative mode came to characterize the silver manufactured by the group. The shift in style during and after the war, while possibly dictated by commercial factors, was also to a great measure surely ascribable to the departure of Moser in 1906, disappointed at his colleagues' willingness to compromise their ideals, and to the increasingly important role subsequently played by Dagobert Peche after he joined the group in 1915. Peche was, first and foremost, a decorative artist, and his influence seems to have eclipsed even that of Hoffmann during this second phase of the Werkstätte's activity.

In eight years of intensive work, until his death in 1923, Peche made his mark in every area of the decorative arts, but perhaps his most successful achievement was his novel silverware. His hand-wrought silver usually bears the surface texturing of hammer marks, and he would tease the metal into delicate shapes, often with spiral fluting and seemingly featherlight scrolling handles and decorations. The surface of vases, jewellery, boxes and other pieces would often be repoussé with whimsical floral motifs. The style of Hoffmann's silver of this period was close to that of Peche, and they enjoyed commercial success, with Werkstätte retail outlets creating an international market for their work in silver and other media. The profusion of capricious ornament of the late Werkstätte style, however, was the symptom of a movement in decline, and Peche's death effectively marked the close of a fascinating Viennese experiment in design and decoration.

At Weimar in Germany, Walter Gropius had founded (in 1919) the Bauhaus, a school of architecture and applied arts which was to have a central and revolutionary role in the history of modern design. The Bauhaus sought a synthesis of all areas of the arts: functionalist theories, harnessed to a visionary ideal of a brave new world in which man and machine lived in harmony, were the basis of the school's approach. In the Bauhaus silver and metalwork department several talented designers were able to express themselves, creating pieces which reflected the Bauhaus dream. Most noteworthy among them were Marianne Brandt, Wilhelm Wagenfeld, Christian Dell, Josef Albers and Wolfgang Tumpel. Their dramatic style – starkly, even aggressively, geometrical – was fully developed by about 1924, from which period date some of their most outstanding pieces. These included Wagenfeld's cylindrical silver caddies, Dell's silver and ebony cylinder and cone carafe, Brandt's bronze, silver and ebony hemispherical teapot and a circular fruit bowl in silver, glass and wood by Josef Albers.

The Bauhaus's *oeuvre* in silver or electroplate, though neither numerically nor commercially significant, was important because it demonstrated the valid principle of form both following and expressing function, and reflected the search for an aesthetic relevant to the Machine Age. The Bauhaus concern for expressive form had the perhaps unavoidable effect of subjugating the needs of function to the dictates of style; and Bauhaus silver became the stylish expression of laudable intellectual theories.

At a more popular level, in Germany as elsewhere, the large manufacturers trod a more cautious path. The major German cutlers, Pott of Solingen, became an exception in the late 1930s when Carl Pott, son of the founder, determined to raise the aesthetic standards of the factory's range. An able artist trained in the ideals of the Deutscher Werkbund, Pott introduced his own elegant modern designs and commissioned further ranges from other designers including Josef Hoffmann. Germany's largest silversmiths, WMF, the Württembergische Metallwarenfabrik, produced little of creative merit in the 1920s and 1930s, despite a commercial success which allowed them to set up factories in Berlin, Cologne, Vienna and Warsaw as well as at Geislingen.

TEAPOT WITH STRAINER *(below), copper, silver plate inside, silver (strainer), with ebony handle. Weimar, 1924. Designer: Marianne Brandt. The dramatic, geometrical style of Bauhaus designers is fully exemplified in this hemispherical teapot. Height: 8 cm (3⅛ in) (Germanisches Nationalmuseum, Nuremberg)*

VASE *(right), silver. Vienna, c.1920. Designer: Josef Hoffmann. This piece is characteristic of the highly wrought silver of the Wiener Werkstätte. Height: 18.5 cm (7¼ in)*

MAZER BOWL *(below), maplewood mounted in silver and silver-gilt with enamel. London, 1932. Maker: Omar Ramsden. The central boss is engraved and enamelled with the arms of the Goldsmiths' Company. The chased decoration includes eight crowned leopards. Diameter: 33.6 cm (13¼ in) (The Worshipful Company of Goldsmiths, London)*

· BRITAIN ·

The 1920s and 1930s were an interesting period of transition for British craft silver. The spirit of the Arts and Crafts Movement was still evident in the output of several small workshops, while other artist-craftsmen and designers introduced new stylistic features, notably in the 1930s, anticipating the renaissance that the craft was to enjoy after the war. The popular market for tableware was catered for by the established large manufacturers, with the industry still centred around Sheffield and Birmingham. Such firms as Adie Brothers, Elkington's, Mappin & Webb Ltd., William Hutton & Sons, Walker & Hall Ltd., and Arthur Price & Co. Ltd. were more concerned with maximizing output than with educating public taste; and the commissioning of fresh ideas from talented industrial designers such as Keith Murray, who produced a new range for Mappin & Webb in the 1930s, was the exception rather than the rule.

Omar Ramsden (1873–1939), in partnership with Alwyn Carr, ran a small workshop till 1918, when Ramsden registered his own mark. His work was strongly historicist, reviving and reinterpreting decorative ideas from Tudor silver, but nonetheless imbued with a sense of vigour. The Ramsden workshops produced civic, corporate and ecclesiastical plate and many presentation pieces. Typical of the Ramsden style were his wood and silver mazer bowls. A charming detail on many of his pieces was the inscription 'Omar Ramsden me fecit', suggesting a degree of personal involvement in the manufacturing process that evidently won much custom, just as it has inspired a present generation of collectors.

Sybil Dunlop made silver jewellery and decorative tableware in a slightly fussy Arts and Crafts style enriched with enamels and semi-precious stones. The Modernist, functionalist style made little impact on British silver, though the 'Cube' teapot made by Napper & Davenport, Birmingham, was a prophetic exception, establishing a link between Christopher Dresser (d. 1904) and the pure lines of British silver in the late 1950s and 1960s. Changes in the inter-war years were cautious, but the seeds of a new style were sown and the encouragement given by the Goldsmiths' Company (especially after the appointment of Graham Hughes as Art Director) should not be under-estimated. At the forefront were H.G. Murphy, Leslie Durbin, Harold Stabler and R.M.Y. Gleadowe, and among the changes they introduced were preferences for engraved decoration and for smooth polished surfaces in reaction to the ubiquitous hammered texture of Arts and Crafts silver. Gleadowe, a designer rather than a craftsman, showed great sympathy for the medium and conceived charming engraved figural decorations on well-proportioned pieces.

The Second World War had a crippling effect on the silver industry in Britain, as in other countries where the metalworking industries were obliged to redirect their energies towards the war effort. Breakdowns in international trade dramatically limited the supply of the raw material and these combined circumstances caused a brief hiatus in the history of British silver. The speed with which creativity was revived after the war owed a great deal to the promotional activities of the Goldsmiths' Hall. At first, British silversmiths and designers worked in a style appropriate to the

mood of a country emerging from the hardships of war and anxious to express a sense of national pride. Their work was still essentially decorative, in contrast to the Scandinavian concern with form, and they continued applying the types of decoration, notably engraving, which had characterized the best British silver of the 1930s. There was an element of traditionalism, in keeping with the nation's need to reaffirm its sense of history and to assert the national character.

The Festival of Britain in 1951 and, two years later, the coronation of Queen Elizabeth II provided suitable occasions for the commissioning of commemorative silver, and many of the pieces made to celebrate these events made use of heraldic motifs such as the rampant lion or symbols of pageant and festivity. Foremost among the artists to distinguish themselves in this mode were Leslie Durbin (b.1913), designer and maker; Robert Goodden (b.1909), a designer who had trained as an architect and who played a leading role in the Festival of Britain, where he was responsible for the Lion and Unicorn building (he went on to become professor of silver and glass design at the Royal College of Art); Alex Styles (b.1922), who became in-house designer for Garrard in 1947, and brought an element of creativity to a range in which reproductions predominated; and R.G. Baxendale, who designed handsome commemorative pieces for Mappin & Webb. Typical of this phase was a magnificent tea service in parcel-gilt silver designed by Robert Goodden and made by Leslie Durbin in 1950 for the Royal Pavilion in the Festival of Britain. This service, now in the Victoria and Albert Museum, London, was conceived on the theme of the sea and might have been seen, within the pageant of the Festival, as an assertion of Britain's mastery of the seas, Britannia ruling the waves.

In 1939 the Worshipful Company of Goldsmiths had presented an exhibition, 'Modern British Silver', organized before the outbreak of war. In 1951, within the Festival of Britain pro-

The tea service (above) is inscribed: (the hot water jug) 'Waters bear vessels; yet where hot meets cold; One vessel has both waters in its hold'; (the teapot) 'When mountain buds unfold beneath the sea/ Thirsting and quenching shall each other be'; (the sugar bowl) 'Unnatural nature if by your design/The sweetest crystals should be found in brine'; (the cream jug) 'White from the green, pearls from the emerald turf/And the green ocean creaming into surf'

TEA SERVICE *(above), silver, parcel-gilt. London, 1950–51. Designer: Robert Goodden. Maker: Leslie Durbin. Made for the Lion and Unicorn Pavilion at the Festival of Britain. Height (hot-water jug): 25.7 cm (10⅛ in) (Victoria and Albert Museum, London)*

COFFEE POTS *(left), silver and heat-resistant nylon. London, 1959. Designer: Stuart Devlin. Maker: Wakely & Wheeler. By using heat-resistant nylon for the bases, Devlin was able to dispense with handles and create sleek silhouettes of great sophistication. Height: 32.5 cm (12¾ in) (Private collection)*

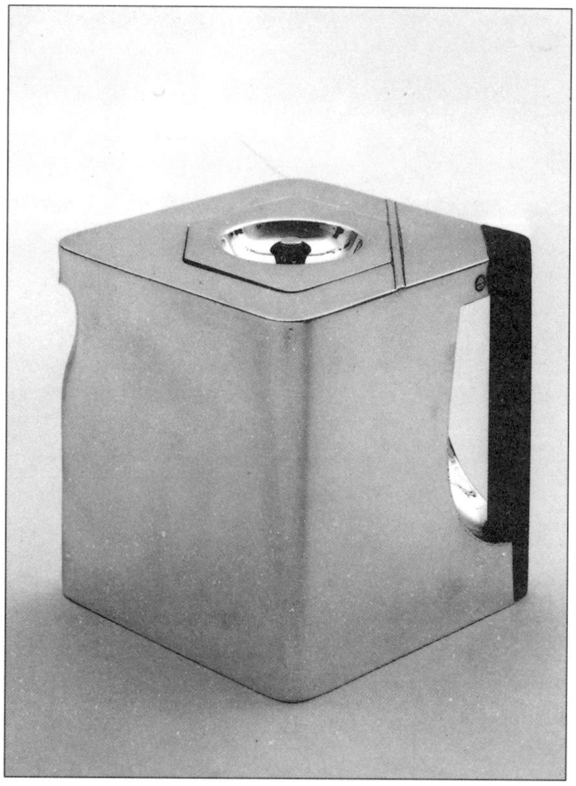

'CUBE' TEAPOT *(right), silver. Birmingham, 1922. Maker: Napper & Davenport. The Modernist, functionalist style of this teapot was unusual in its time, and forms a link between Christopher Dresser's liking for austere geometrical forms and the pure lines of British silver made in the late 1950s.*

BOWL WITH COVER *(below), silver. London, 1960. Designer: Alex Styles. Maker: Wakely & Wheeler. This commemorative piece was made for Garrard, the Crown Jewellers. (The Worshipful Company of Goldsmiths, London)*

SWEETMEAT DISH *(facing page, below), silver. London, 1925–6. Maker: Omar Ramsden. Ramsden revived and reinterpreted decorative ideas from Tudor silver, imbuing his pieces with a sense of vigour. Diameter: 16 cm (6¼ in) (Victoria and Albert Museum, London)*

gramme, the Goldsmiths' Hall organized another exhibition, 'Ceremonial Plate by Contemporary Craftsmen', to demonstrate the restored vitality of the craft. This was followed by further, regular promotional exhibitions at home and abroad which gave encouragement to British silversmiths and earned international respect for their work. The Hall established a policy of commissioning and collecting fine examples by leading silversmiths and, indeed, by new, otherwise unrecognized talents. For example, the Hall acquired for its collection an elegant coffee service in silver and nylon, designed by Stuart Devlin while he was still a student at the Royal College of Art, and made by Wakely & Wheeler in 1959. By using heat-resistant nylon for the bases, Devlin was able to dispense with handles and create sleek silhouettes of the greatest sophistication.

While its collection provides education, publicity and inspiration, the Hall has also been instrumental in reviving and encouraging the tradition of commemorative plate and, on its advice, many cathedrals, churches, companies, corporations and universities have commissioned fine work from leading British designers. In addition the Hall has commissioned a piece of modern silver for each of the new universities as an incentive to them to start collections of contemporary work in the tradition of college plate. Examples of such commissions include the mace designed by Peter Inchbald for the University of Hull in 1955, the ciborium made by Gerald Benney for the new Coventry Cathedral in 1958 and the centrepiece bowl also made by Benney in the same year for Leicester University.

Benney, born in 1930, was perhaps the most influential of the new generation of silversmiths who superseded the Festival of Britain style and gave a strong new character to British silver in the late 1950s and 1960s. He studied at Brighton College of Art and the Royal College of Art, and set up his own workshop in 1955 and very soon made his mark with his combination of strong design sense, concern for quality, and commercial flair. The stylistic evolution of the 1950s involved a reaction against figurative decoration, a renewed interest in form with the emphasis on sleek modern shapes, rather in the manner associated with Scandinavian silverwork, for hollow-ware and bold, sculptural forms for major display pieces. Perhaps Benney's most influential innovation was the revival of surface texturing. His earliest textured piece dates from 1956, and within a decade the use of richly textured surfaces, often gilt, had become a widespread feature of contemporary silver. Stuart Devlin was to become enamoured of such effects, which became a dominant and commercially successful feature of his work.

Benney's generation included several designers of note, not least David Mellor, also born in 1930, and a student at Sheffield College of Art and the Royal College of Art. Mellor has proved his ability to design on every scale, from handsome presentation pieces to practical yet elegant flatware. Robert Welch, born in 1929, is another versatile designer-craftsman, who set up his Chipping Campden workshops in 1955 after studying at Malvern and the Royal College of Art. While Benney, Mellor and Welch have each produced outstanding works in silver, their achievements as creators of finely made precious objects should perhaps be regarded as secondary to their influential roles as industrial designers. Each has designed ranges of flatware or hollow-ware in stainless steel which combine practical concerns with elegant modern styles appropriate for mass production.

The great achievement of the post-war British renaissance in silver has been in creating a genuine role for the artist-craftsman, able to preserve the vitality of his craft while also able at the same time to apply himself to the needs of the mass market.

· SCANDINAVIA AND GEORG JENSEN ·

The early decades of the century were years of considerable social and political change in the Scandinavian countries, where a trend towards a new democratic socialism was paralleled by a widespread concern with the formulation of a new aesthetic which acknowledged craft traditions while creating a happy alliance between artist and manufacturer. The Scandinavians were among the first to find a role for the industrial designer and to set high standards which would apply equally to machine-made and hand-made goods. Each country had its influential supervising body: the Swedish Svenska Slöjdforeningen (Society for Industrial Design), founded in 1845, had one of the longest histories of any such society; the Danes had followed suit in 1907 with the Lands Foreningen Dansk Brugskunst Og Design (Society of Applied Art and Industrial Design); the Finnish designers' association Ornamo was founded in 1910; and Norway set up its Foreningen Brukskunst (Society of Applied Arts) in 1918.

Functionalist ideas had their first significant impact at the Stockholm Exhibition of 1930, and from that time until after the war the Scandinavians were to promote their functionalist style increasingly through individual national exhibits or participation in joint exhibitions and international exhibitions. The obvious feature of this functionalism, as applied to silver, was an emphasis on simple, generally unadorned forms. The lasting success of the functionalist movement in Scandinavian silver, however, was in the restraint with which the new principles were applied as worthy design ideals rather than as justification for extremes of style. While designers of the Bauhaus or the UAM created eye-catching pieces which, half a century later, are seen as dramatic statements of stylistic theory, the best Scandinavian silver of the 1920s and 1930s has a truly timeless beauty.

The Swedes embraced the superficial stylistic characteristics of Modernism, but silversmiths such as Jacob Ängman (1876–1942) and Wiwen Nilsson (b.1897) nonetheless softened the angles of their designs with the judicious counterpoint of discreet decorative details or gentle curves, shunning too austere or rigid a geometry. Ängman worked for Sweden's largest silver manufacturer, Guldsmeds Aktiebolaget, from 1907 till his death, and won many prizes internationally for his understated functionalist designs. Nilsson, who had been apprenticed in his father's workshop in Lund and subsequently studied in Copenhagen and in the Paris workshops of Jensen, set up his own workshop in 1927.

The Norwegian firms of Tostrup and David Andersen sought a compromise between tradition and modernity, and were for the most part restricted creatively by their caution. Oskar Sørensen, designing for Tostrup, produced some interesting work, notably sculptural vessels in the shape of birds, highly stylized into geometric forms.

The field of Scandinavian silver was dominated by the Danes, and names of note included A. Michelsen, an old-established firm with designer Kay Fisker producing outstanding work in the functionalist mode, and Hans Hansen, who had set up his workshops in 1906 at Kolding. However, all these were overshadowed by the firm of Georg Jensen.

Georg Jensen (1866–1935) was already an experienced silversmith and trained sculptor when he set up his own silver studio in 1904 in Copenhagen. He was a perfectionist in love with his craft, and his aesthetic was dominated by the pursuit of harmony between elegant forms and ornamentation which could on occasion veer towards an opulence which was becoming unfashionable. Nonetheless, Jensen's fine craftsmanship and sure taste raised his work above the whims of fashion and were the basis of one of the great successes in the history of the Danish decorative arts.

Jensen's success, however, also owed a great deal to certain equally talented members of the Jensen team, particularly Johan Rohde (1856–1935), a painter and designer who entered into partnership with Jensen in 1906. Rohde was a purist who rejected ornament in favour of classically perfect forms, and the grace of his creations is deceptively simple. Edgar Kauffman Snr., of the New York Museum of Modern Art, reminds us, in an essay on Jensen written in 1966, that '. . . the purity of his expression came from unremitting study and revision'.[3] The same sentiment was expressed by Swedish design critic Äke Stavenow, who said of Rohde that 'He was a functionalist before functionalism was a conscious program. His larger pieces are so natural in form that they seem inevitable. Yet study of his numerous sketches reveals the effort required to achieve such extraordinary simplicity.'

Harald Nielsen joined the firm in 1909 and his work, like that of Rohde, was characterized by a

CHALICE *(below), silver, parcel-gilt. London, 1958. Maker: Gerald Benney. This is one of the first pieces on which Benney used surface texturing as a form of decoration, an idea invented by him and widely practised since. Height: 30.3 cm (12 in) (The Worshipful Company of Goldsmiths, London)*

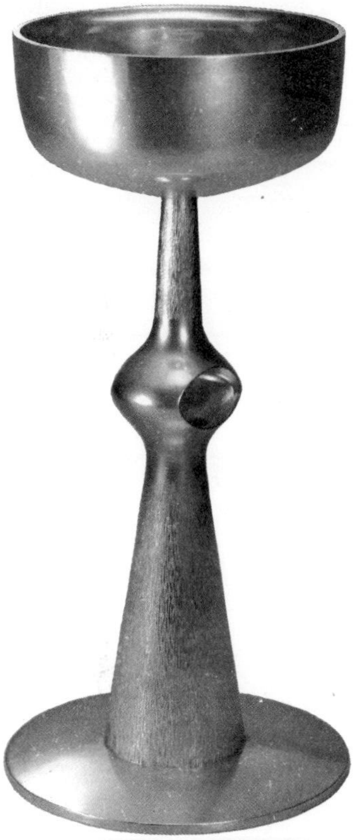

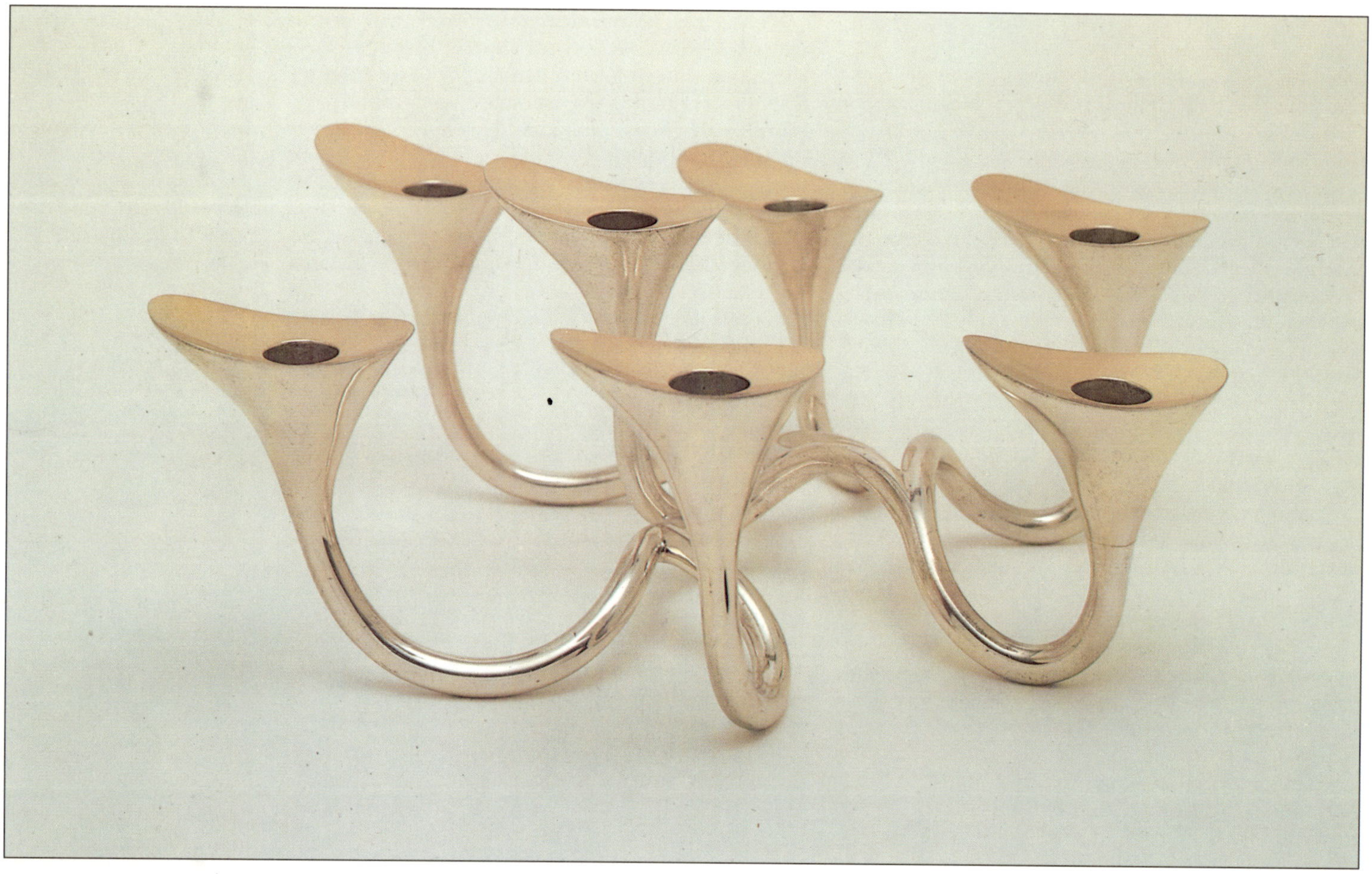

CANDELABRUM, *silver. London, 1956. Designer: Jeus Andreason. Maker: E. H. Skilton for Asprey's. Width: 33.5 cm (13¼ in) (Private collection)*

gracious functionalism. He was Art Director for a number of years and outlived both Jensen and Rohde. Their deaths in 1935 marked the close of an era for the firm; their successor in influence was Count Sigvard Bernadotte (b.1907), a gifted designer who had joined the firm in 1930. Bernadotte was of a generation more willing to accept the extreme, hard and coldly elegant aspects of functionalism. Although there was some conflict between his crisp, mathematical style and the work of his peers at Jensen, his was to be the guiding influence that led Jensen with renewed success into the post-war era. Another important figure at Jensen was Frederick Lunning, responsible for the New York outlet opened in 1922. He proved himself an accomplished salesman and, indeed, did much to promote every aspect of Scandinavian design in the United States.

After the Second World War the Scandinavian Modern style, a mellow refinement of the functionalist ideals which had dominated design before the war, developed and was to become perhaps the most influential style of the 1950s. Finnish designers, led by Tapio Wirkkala, had triumphed at the Milan Triennale of 1951; Norway, Finland, Denmark and Sweden, the four Scandinavian countries which took part in the 1954 Triennale, enjoyed a considerable, combined impact. The success of the Scandinavian Modern style was encouraged by the co-operative efforts of the Scandinavian countries, as evidenced in their joint venture 'Design in Scandinavia', a major travelling exhibition which toured museums in the United States and Canada between 1954 and 1957. By the close of the decade the Scandinavian style, with its gracious forms, a simplicity which avoided austerity and a preference for understatement in the sensitive crafting of natural materials, was the strongest international influence on domestic design.

Scandinavian firms and individual craftsmen and designers achieved international success in the field of silver design, as in other areas. The Danes were at the forefront, with Jensen maintaining its supremacy as the firm most successful in finding a wide market for modern silver designs. Other firms and small workshops shared in the glory with their own versions of the Scandinavian Modern style, while several highly acclaimed designers applied their talents to the creation of models for manufacturing in either silver or stainless steel.

Although overshadowed by Jensen, there were several other Danish firms worthy of note, including Just Andersen, A. Michelsen and Hans Hansen. Hans Hansen produced high-quality wares in a pure, simple style which belied the meticulous crafting of the metal. Bent Gabrielsen Pedersen, who had worked briefly for Jensen, joined the firm in 1953 and worked with Karl Gustav Hansen in a

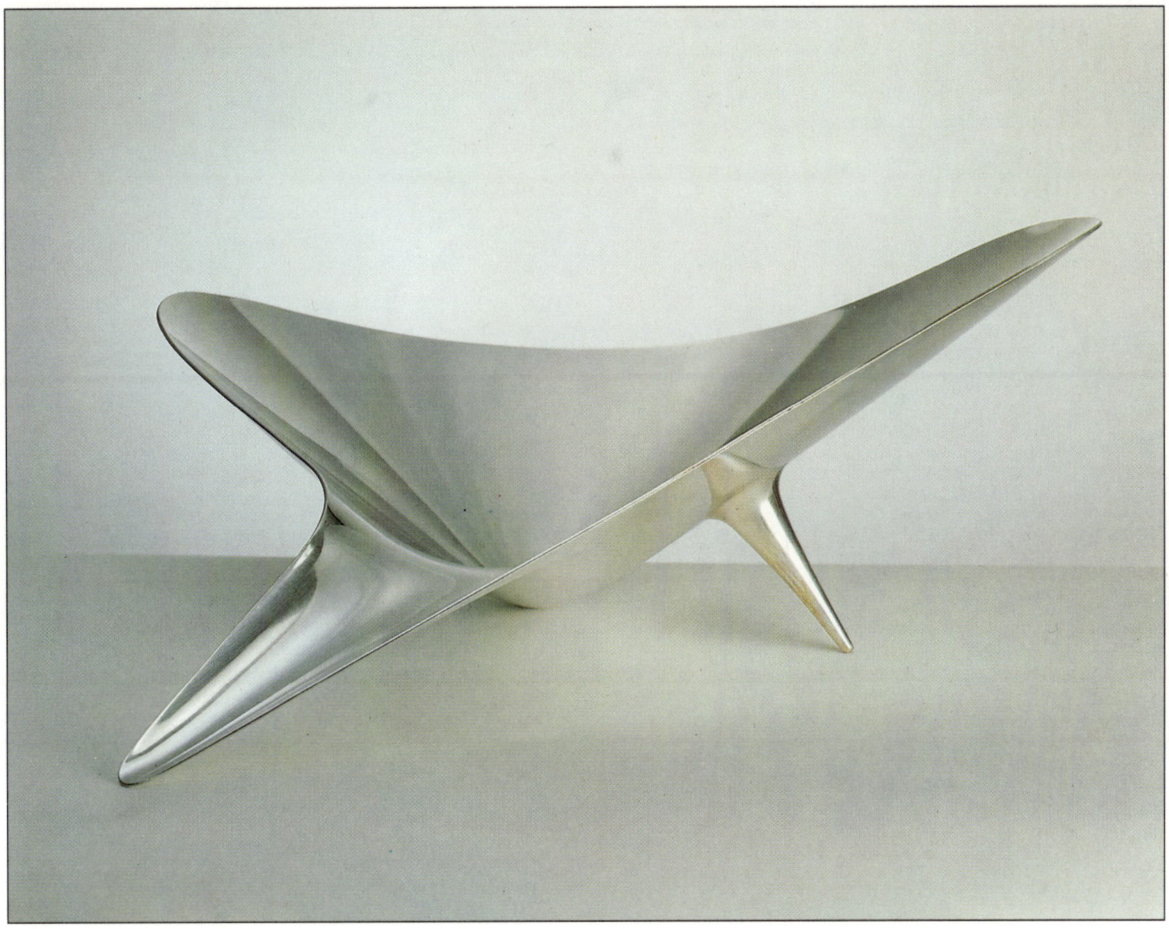

timeless, understated modern style which won the firm international acclaim and numerous prizes; and Kay Bojesen continued working in the elegant, pared-down style which she had first explored before the war, winning a Grand Prize at the Milan Triennale of 1951.

The Norwegian manufacturing retailers David Andersen were responsible for elegant silverware, including pieces in a sculptural, free-form style. Perhaps the most highly lauded Scandinavian silversmith of the post-war era, however, was the Swede Sigurd Persson whose strength lay in preserving the values of the small-scale artist-craftsman's workshop in the face of an increasing trend towards less personalized manufacture, even from the most distinguished craft studios. Persson, born in 1914, trained under his father and completed his studies in Munich and Stockholm, graduating in 1943 from the Stockholm Konstfackskolan. His work as an industrial designer provided him with the financial stability to pursue his interests in silver. He has kept a very small workshop with a limited output, but with no compromise in the application of his ideas. He has forged a strong, simple aesthetic based on practical design sense and the sure eye of a sculptor, winning many prizes, including awards at the Milan Triennales of 1951 and 1954. While Persson has preserved the craft ideal, individuality in Scandinavian silver has to some extent been sacrificed in the unified commercial promotion of an international Scandinavian style.

The 1950s were exciting years in the evolution of new sculptural forms for flatware. Distinguished designers such as the Finn Tapio Wirkkala, Tias Eckhoff (a Norwegian) and Arne Jacobsen (a Dane) applied the science of ergonomics and an aesthetic of curvilinear modernism to the creation of beautiful and innovative ranges.

Several talented designers joined Jensen after the war and contributed to the continuing prosperity of the firm and its reputation as a stylistic innovator. First came Henning Koppel (b.1918), followed by Søren Georg Jensen (b.1917), a son of the founder. Both had trained as sculptors and brought fresh and quite distinctive visions to the medium of silver. Jensen's style was rigid and strongly geometric, whereas Koppel was a supreme exponent of the asymmetrical free-form Modernism which was such an exhilarating aspect of design in the post-war years. His jewellery and hollow-ware of the late 1940s and 1950s exploited the dynamic interplay of curves and the amoeboid forms which became part of the popular vernacular of design. He won the highest award, the gold medal, at three successive Triennales, in 1951, 1954 and 1957.

Architect Magnus Stephensen (b.1903) brought to Jensen a rational design sense, which was applied to silver but more profitably to the

DISH *(above left), silver. Copenhagen, c.1950–55. Designer: Henning Koppel. Maker: Georg Jensen. This piece shows Koppel's mastery of the sculptural free-form style. Height: 22.2 cm (8¾ in)*

BRACELET *(above), silver. Copenhagen, 1947. Designer: Henning Koppel. Maker: Georg Jensen. Koppel was a supreme exponent of free-form Modernism in both his jewellery and his hollow-ware. Length: 20.8 cm (8$\frac{3}{16}$ in) (Private collection)*

creation of stainless steel hollow-ware and flatware, an increasingly important part of Jensen's production. Stephensen shared many of the qualities of his predecessor Gilbert Rohde; both of them were rigorous perfectionists. Stephensen's functionalist spirit was well adapted to the creation of ideal forms for practical vessels and utensils which were destined for high-quality series production.

Nanna Ditzel brought a fresh approach to jewellery design, with her creations for Jensen during the 1950s and 1960s. She worked in both silver and gold, and would use large cabochons of semi-precious stone as a contrast to the plain surfaces of the polished metal. The simple, boldly sculptured forms that characterized her work gave a lead to the contemporary fashion for unfussy and strongly sculptural jewellery. Her style was much copied, but rarely equalled.

In 1954 Jensen celebrated its half-centenary with an open competition for flatware. This was won by Tias Eckhoff, one of several distinguished designers to contribute to the Jensen range on a freelance basis. By 1966, the centenary of the founder's birth, the firm had showrooms in nineteen countries and had clearly demonstrated by its remarkable example that the pursuit of quality and commercial success need not be incompatible ambitions.

· OTHER COUNTRIES ·

In the USA, the 1920s and 1930s were somewhat unproductive years for silver. The American Arts and Crafts Movement had failed to make the impact on silver manufacture that had certainly been evident in the production of furniture and ceramics. The big manufacturers such as Gorham, the International Silver Company, Oneida and Reed & Barton were primarily concerned with turnover and profit, and were happy to cater to the lowest common denominator of taste. The prestigious firm of Tiffany's was in a period of decline from which it did not recover until the 1950s. The Crash of 1929 and the difficult years of the Depression stifled any possibilities of innovation in the silver industy, though a home-grown streamlined version of Modernism made some impact in the 1930s, influencing designs for silverware in a limited way.

In the post-war years the United States silver industry produced little of merit, failing to compete with the high standards of design and quality of work imported from Scandinavia. Tiffany & Co.'s declining fortunes were to be revived, however, after 1956 by the appointment as Vice-President of the creative and dynamic French designer Jean Schlumberger. His arrival turned the tide, and Tiffany was to regain something of its former glory. Tiffany's production was aimed at the top of the luxury market, but in the area of domestic or contract silver and metalware design the philosophies of disposability and built-in stylistic obsolescence which were a feature of American industrial design were hardly conducive to the creation of pieces to rival the Scandinavian ideal of timeless beauty. Some industrial designers, such as Russel Wright, designing for John Hull Cutlers Corporation, evolved elegant modern forms and, as in Europe, the trend was towards the use of stainless steel for the mass-production of flatware and hollow-ware in modern styles.

Switzerland produced one isolated but outstanding talent, in the person of Meinrad Burch-Korrodi. Trained in London, New York and Paris, he returned to Switzerland to set up his own workshop in 1925, moving from Lucerne to Zurich seven years later. He specialized in church plate and enriched his creations with enamelling, bringing a sense of style and a shrewd commercial mind to this area of silver.

In Italy, a highly wrought archaeological style enjoyed considerable popularity in the 1950s, while the designer Lino Sabattini proved himself Italy's most interesting exponent of the undecorated sculptural style. Milanese architect Cesare Lacca adapted traditional shapes, eliminated detail and created elegant hollow-ware.

'COMO' TEA SERVICE *(facing page, above), electroplate. Bregnano, 1957. Designer: Lino Sabattini. Sabattini was Italy's most interesting exponent of the sculptural style. Height (coffee pot): 17.75 cm (9⅝ in)*

COFFEE POT *(facing page, below), silver with black rosewood handle. Stockholm, 1958. Maker: Sigurd Persson. Persson has a strong, simple aesthetic based on practical design sense and a sculptor's eye. Height: 23 cm (9 in)*

'SPHERE' TEA SERVICE *(above), electroplate. USA, c.1930–35. Maker: Wilcox S. P. Co. Marked 'made exclusively for Carole Stupell'.*

· 9 · CONTEMPORARY SILVER ·

Silver is once again being put to its most appropriate use, as a metal for items of luxury and decoration. Modern silver reflects a revival of vitality in craftsmanship; attempts in this century to mass-produce silver have failed, and throughout the Western world the number of silver factories has steadily declined. There remains only a small band of dedicated hammermen, whose declared aim is not to furnish hotels and railways with objects of utility, but rather to create beauty for special clients.

Craftsmen in precious metals have often worked in gold or platinum as well as silver. Since the 1970s in the West, their metallurgical vocabularly has widened still further, perhaps because of growing knowledge and awareness of the East, particularly Japan. There is hardly any gold there, and the arts of making arms and armour, based on steel, have always been prominent. The cleverest Japanese craftsmen have now inspired the West with a new fertility of invention. With today's wider horizons and better communications, craftsmen now enjoy experiments, mixing materials and even using the products of new technology like titanium, tantalum or niobium, which have become easily available only in the last decade.

The word goldsmith derives from very early times. For instance in Anglo-Saxon poems, gold was identified with perfection: then, since solid gold was beyond the reach of most, silver was gilded to resemble gold because the gold colour was the grandest. Today's goldsmiths may be at home in any one of half-a-dozen materials; they make jewellery as well as tableware, and they may be industrial designers too, designing anything from cars to condiment sets, because that is where the money lies. It is ideas which are important, not just the metal used, as was once the case.

Silver has never been suited to the design vocabulary of the machine. Smooth surfaces with no incident are what the machine can produce easily, but there seems little point in going to the expense of buying an object made of such a precious metal, if that metal looks as smooth as stainless steel, or if the job it does could equally well be done by lowly pewter. Silver is best suited not to the monotony of a machine-induced finish, but to the caressing touch of the hand.

As recently as a generation ago nearly all the bigger factories producing silverware were not actually factories in the modern sense of the word but 'villages' of craftsmen, grouped according to the skill each had mastered, whether it be chasing, hand-raising or planishing. In a traditional British factory, such as James Dixon of Sheffield or Elkington's of Birmingham, there might be four hundred men or more, twenty or so working in each big room, using no more machinery than stamps and lathes and finishing every stage of the manufacture by hand. It was the same almost everywhere: at Tiffany's near New York, at Carl Pott in Solingen (the German steel and cutlery centre), and at Jensen of Copenhagen, Gorham at Providence, Rhode Island, Krupp in Milan, Christofle of Paris, Wiskemann of Brussels and WMF of Geislingen. Even at Jensen, which until the 1960s made more silver than any other firm, the dream of mass production had had only a very limited impact on the old hand techniques. In the new Jensen kitchenware factory in Jutland, set up to produce saucepans designed by the sculptor Henning Koppel, high technology, with its spot welding, precision dies and elimination of human error, thrived only on steel and copper, not silver. Highly mechanized production was concentrated on stainless steel, as at the Gense factory in the Swedish steel town of Eskilstuna, where fine, clean designs were produced for knives and forks which had been made without ever being touched by a human hand. Factory-made silver, now almost dead, has actually never really been alive.

· THE ECONOMICS OF THE SILVER · INDUSTRY ·

The demise of so many old firms since the 1960s is partly due to the fact that the public likes its silver rich and decorative. That requires labour-intensive hand work which is done best and most cheaply by small artist-craftsmen in back sheds with low overheads, rather than in big workshops

PAIR OF CANDELABRA *(facing page), silver with acrylic stems. Youlgreave, Derbyshire, 1984. Designer: Brian Asquith. One of Britain's finest industrial designers whose industrial experience has influenced his work in silver, Asquith creates very strong forms and has evolved a personal use of acrylics for vivid colour effects. Height: 40.3 cm ($15\frac{3}{4}$ in) (The Worshipful Company of Goldsmiths, London)*

FAN BROOCH, *silver and titanium. San Diego, 1982. Designer: Arline Fisch. President of the Society of North American Goldsmiths and Professor of Art at the University of San Diego, California, Fisch is a jeweller specializing in woven metal and featherwork; her decorative effects are influenced by Mexico and Peru. This fan has a blue and gold woven construction which is reversible. Dimensions: 13 × 10.3 cm (5 × 4 in)*

whose high distribution and administration costs have become a decisive factor in business. It is partly, too, because of the increase in production in the Far East: Japan, with its cutlery city of Tsubame, north of Tokyo, and with its history of sword-making, has always made good knives; and now that Western furniture and flatware are displacing the traditional floor and chopsticks in smart Japanese homes, so Japanese products are made in a Western style and often adorn Western tables. Nevertheless, Japan is quite a small producer compared with Taiwan, Korea, the Malaysian Peninsula and Hong Kong. It was Hong Kong which first entered these lists, perhaps when Viners started making some of their Benney designs there in the 1960s; from all the Far East, stainless steel and electroplate have now caught the attention of the West. No longer does a major airline such as British Airways commission a craftsman such as Brian Asquith of Sheffield to design and supervise the production of tableware for a new aircraft, as it did for the VC10 airliner; American Airlines, one of the proudest in the USA, show the name of several countries on their cutlery, and America is only one of them. Contract buyers now go to the lowest bidder, which usually means the Orient. The centre of large-scale production has moved from Europe to the Far East.

Another equally important evolution that has changed the organization of the silversmith's craft is the rise in power of the retailer. Mappin and Webb closed their Sheffield factories a generation ago, yet the name lives on in their highly profitable retail chain of shops selling a wide range of china, leather and 'fancy goods' as well as silver. Selling is apparently easier, less dirty, more lucrative, and less personally demanding than manufacturing. The team spirit which used to inspire the factories has yielded to a wish for gain which is now possible for the first time because of high general wages. Chain stores such as Zales of the USA, Stern of Brazil and South America, and James Walker, H. Samuel and Ratners of Britain have captured the bulk markets. The older names retain a special power, however. Garrard, for instance, is one of the ancient manufacturing firms. After merging with the Goldsmiths' and Silversmiths' Company, they changed their emphasis from producing to retailing, greatly to their financial advantage. They still make some specialized pieces in their own workshops, but buy most of their stock from elsewhere, sometimes designed by their own good modern silver staff designers, Alex Styles and Richard Anderson. Some of the Garrard success is due to them, some to the romance of their history of over two and a half centuries, some because they are the British crown jewellers. Their connection with the British royal family is such that they made huge profits in a few months, for instance, selling royal souvenirs of the wedding of the Prince and Princess of Wales in 1981.

Asprey of London, Cartier and Boucheron of Paris, and Tiffany of New York, likewise handle silver as well as jewellery, and they, likewise, find their ancient prestigious names help them to make sales to new oil-rich clients in the Middle East and Africa. While their names are old, their activities are mostly new: they make only a fraction of what they sell and no longer support a big, stable manufacturing activity, but instead buy from many different suppliers to whom they offer little continuity or security.

A further cause of the decline in silverware production is the rise in the status of jewellery; jewellers now enjoy the glamour which once belonged to silversmiths. Les Must de Cartier – the old jewellery firm's new chain of smaller stores – has expanded rapidly in the 1980s, while silver firms have been contracting. Tiffany, too, started a worldwide jewellery expansion, opening in London in 1986. Until 1939 the wealth of the courts and noble houses of Europe was reflected in the quantity of tableware considered necessary in rich households. In a large mansion there would have been a great quantity of splendid silverware. Today there are no more servants to clean the

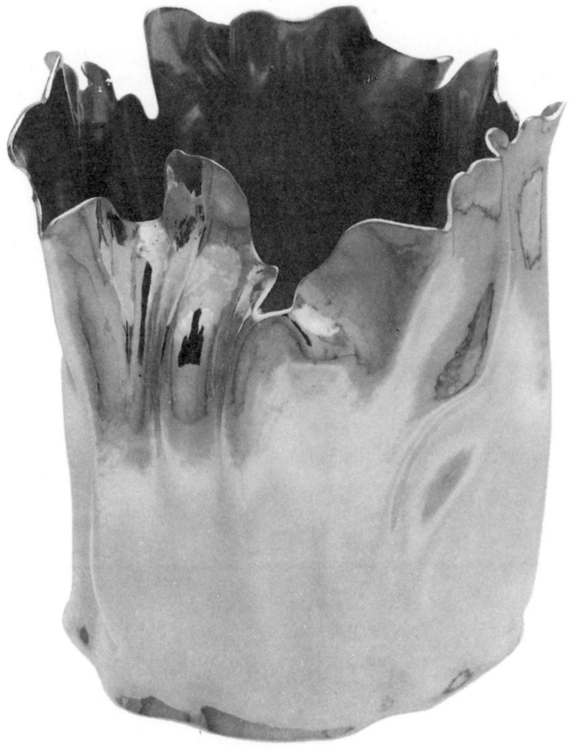

VASE, *silver. Copenhagen, 1979. Designed by Ole Kortzau for Georg Jensen. Until the 1970s Jensen made more silver than any other firm. Their mass production was concentrated on stainless steel; most pieces of silver continued to be made there by old hand techniques. Height: 15.5 cm (6 in)*

plate, and the increase in travel that leaves houses empty and vulnerable to burglars has meant that only a few people want, or can afford, to use the family silver. It used to be normal practice to add to the family plate, generation by generation, in the great houses such as Burghley and Althorp in England, or in one of the Newport mansions furnished by Tiffany in the USA. But now, instead of silver, it is jewellery with its endless capacity for variety which has become fashionable among collectors. Much of the old silver production was related to areas dominated by the male: ambassadorial plate, boardroom ornaments, government gifts, even the perpetuation of dynastic glory by engraving coats-of-arms on family and official plate, all these can be considered traditionally masculine activities, and silver made for them is steadily decreasing in quantity. Jewellery, fashion shops and fashion magazines are, by contrast, female in character, are expanding quickly, and absorb an ever-increasing proportion of the wealth of most families, as they do the skill of available craftsmen. The liberation of women may thus be said to have brought with it the downfall of conventional silverware.

In the 1970s artists and patrons moved together to create a new language of ornament by which jewellery was upgraded to the level of art, and began to enjoy the support of art institutions in a way that would have been unthinkable only ten years earlier. In the USA, for instance, the exhibitions of the new Society of North American Goldsmiths are mostly of the type of jewellery known as 'wearable art'; the current President, Arline S. Fisch, Professor of Art at the University of San Diego, California, is herself a jeweller specializing in woven metal and featherwork, a far cry equally from the diamonds of the Vanderbilts and the Astors and from the loving cups and salvers of the old university colleges at Harvard and Yale. The American Craft Council in New York, for more than a decade supported by Mrs Vanderbilt Webb but now a fully fledged independent body no longer financed partly by its President (for three years Barbara Rockefeller), has ten times more jewellers as members than silversmiths. The 1978 exhibition of American silver at Goldsmiths' Hall, London, was dominated by Finnish-born Heikki Seppa (Professor of Fine Arts at Washington University), and his pieces were portable decoration, not functional. The best US silversmith at the exhibition was Mary Ann Scherr of New York's Parsons School of Design; and her silver is perforated and angular, a startling and flighty departure from the old silver disciplines. Mary Lee Hu of Michigan State University, another distinguished artist, likewise directs her energies away from the beaten sheet, instead using silver wire to weave beautiful vessels and other forms. Aesthetically pleasing but almost impossible to use, they are table jewels rather than tableware.

Recent changes in educational theory have also hastened the flight of metalsmiths from solid silver, and its traditional techniques, into jewellery, with accompanying research into exciting new metals and materials. Formerly the aim of art schools was to teach the rudiments of technique; now, far from helping students to master difficulties, the emphasis is on short cuts and freedom of expression rather than on the capacity to emulate the skill of Benvenuto Cellini. People who want to learn crafts are turning away from the old disciplines towards the idea of self-expression. And the artist's personality is more evident in small items of jewellery made perhaps with fabric or wood, than in hard silver. Accompanying silver's beauty of texture and colour and line are the formidable problems of making the metal change its shape. Britain has far more art schools than any other country, but of the forty or so which teach silversmithing, only four or five make more silverware than jewellery: Camberwell, Sir John Cass (The City of London Polytechnic), Medway, Chesterfield and High Wycombe. The annual exhibition at Goldsmiths' Hall, London, called 'Passing Out', is a selection from all these metalwork schools, and nine-tenths of the pieces are jewellery. In 1983 a huge exhibition, 'Young Blood', in London's Barbican Art Gallery, told the same story: silversmithing, once deemed a vital craft discipline, a good stage in the training of any artist, has yielded its pre-eminence to jewellery.

Five centuries ago goldsmiths such as Cennino Cennini, Donatello, Ghiberti, and Cellini were famous in their time, whereas jewellers of the same period worked anonymously, their names unknown both then and now. Today, the roles may be changing: jewellers like Andrew Grima, who won the Duke of Edinburgh Award at London's Design Centre, and Gerda Flockinger and Wendy Ramshaw, who exhibited at London's Victoria and Albert Museum, are better known in the art world and in fashion magazines than their fellow silversmiths working with sheet silver.

The amount of silverware made in Britain may

have diminished as much as fifty per cent in the past ten years; certainly, the annual figures issued by the British Hallmarking Council indicate falling public demand. But to some extent quality has replaced quantity, the artist has stimulated the artisan, and the silverware made today seems to show a style born of confidence, as it did in the great periods of silversmithing of the past.

· THE PRE-EMINENCE OF BRITAIN ·

Famous goldsmiths have always had their own personal vision, so that their work can even now be recognized as distinct from that of their contemporaries: Dinglinger of Dresden, de Lamerie of London, the Auguste family of Paris in the eighteenth century, each wrought the precious metals in their own way, so that they not only became symbols of their age but also stood out from it. It was because the genius of these craftsmen rose up above a good common mean that the rococo period was so distinguished; and the same could be claimed for the 1970s. In Britain, a group of silversmiths has become established, working on commissions from clients who choose to mark their celebrations with a piece of silver. These are the banks and big commercial companies, the city livery companies of London, trade associations and professional bodies such as the Chartered Accountants and the Stock Exchange, the royal family (especially for such occasions as the Queen's Jubilee and the Prince of Wales's wedding), other great families up and down the land, and the Church.

The interest of these patrons in silver, though due in part to a national, centuries-old tradition of love of the metal, which is unique to Britain, has since 1970 been excited by the personality and enterprise of the younger British silversmiths, who have broken out of the theoretical mould of clean function and sensible shape into a sort of riotous abandon. The New York skyline expresses the enterprise of America, just as a London Queen Anne house shows the stability of Britain. In the same way it can be said that British silversmiths' present-day fantasy results from the quirkiness of the British character, in contrast with the fine lines and simple forms of modern Scandinavian silver, inspired by the quest for a pure, unpretentious life in the North.

Louis Osman has emerged as an outstanding creator of modern times. At Canons Ashby in Northamptonshire from 1970 till 1980, he and his craftsmen made a series of amazing creations in silver and gold which had much the same impact on established standards as Roger Fry's exhibitions of Post-Impressionist paintings at the Grafton Gallery before the First World War. An architect by training, Osman has said, 'People used not to mind if they made jewels or cathedrals. Now, an architect would feel put upon if he had to make so much as a button for his wife.' He urged

EPITHALAMIUM CUP *(above), silver set with moonstones. London, 1981. Designer: Jocelyn Burton. Made to commemorate the Royal Wedding of 1981. Height: 17.9 cm (7½ in)*

BOX *(right), gold, red enamel and fire opal. Beenham, near Reading 1972. Designer: Gerald Benney. Benney is one of Europe's great enamellers, often colouring whole pieces as well as details. Width: 10 cm (4 in)*

his craftsmen, such as Malcolm Green and Wally Gilbert, to put more passion into their surfaces, more weight into their hinges, more curves into their edges.

Quite unlike Fabergé, with his prim eighteenth-century idiom, and the Arts and Crafts practitioners from Ashbee to Bernard Cuzner to Leslie Durbin, whose roots were in technique, Osman starts with an idea, then finds out how to interpret it in metal. The results are always interesting, usually strong and dignified, and often very beautiful. His more important commissions, in which he was helped by his wife Dilys, a self-trained enameller, have been the crown for the Prince of Wales, used at his investiture at Carnaervon Castle and now in the National Museum of Wales in Cardiff; the box containing Magna Carta, given by Britain to the USA to celebrate the Bicentennial; a cross made for Ely Cathedral and (sadly) rejected, and many pieces in the ever-growing collection at Goldsmiths' Hall.

Osman now lives in another great historic mansion, at Byford Court near Hereford, where the unique richness of his imagination requires equally rich clients. He really needs a patron like Augustus the Strong of Dresden, who in the early eighteenth century diverted some of the wealth of Saxony into the goldsmith's workshops (we can now marvel at the results in the Grüne Gewölbe Treasury there). The wealth available to Osman from his principal clients, like the Worshipful Company of Goldsmiths, has never been on such a legendary scale.

Another country-house practitioner in Britain is Gerald Benney. Based near Reading at Beenham House, he is the product of two types of education: the art schools, in which Britain excels (Brighton and the post-graduate Royal College of Art, where from 1975 until 1984 he was Professor, albeit only part-time because he was always determined to concentrate on his own work); and the apprenticeship system, with Dunstan Pruden in the workshop complex at Ditchling near Brighton, founded by Eric Gill. Since the 1950s, Benney has been noted as much for his professionalism as for his superb designs. He is master alike of pricing, publicity, craftsmanship and design. He feared that his taut new shapes, sometimes likened to rockets at Cape Canaveral, sometimes to racing cars at Le Mans, might be copied, especially when Viners earned him fame through worldwide mass production. At the time, in the late 1960s, they were the biggest British firm with more than 1000 workers.

Benney used sophisticated technology: the 'no-scrap blank' – a spoon or fork shaped so that no metal had to be cut away and wasted – represented an obvious but unique technical advance. Benney made a fortune from his designer's royalties – his best pattern (in steel) made him a total of £65,000 in a dozen years. The automatic machine polishing of knife blades, the vacuum forming of coffee-pot bowls, doing away with the

DRAWING *(left) by Louis Osman for a* COVERED CUP *(below), gold and enamel. London, 1978. Designer and maker: Louis Osman. Enamellist: Dilys Osman. The bowl echoes an African stringed drum. The cover is engraved as the sea with foaming enamelled waves. The two sporting dolphins and the recumbent Thomson's gazelle carrying the drum are solid gold, carved and enamelled. The base bears the words: 'but always as friends'. Height: 12 cm (4¾ in) (Victoria and Albert Museum, London)*

DETAIL OF A HALLMARK SYMBOL *(above). Engraver: Malcolm Appleby. Aberdeen, 1982. This fascinating piece of heraldic symbolism appears on a cup commissioned by the Worshipful Company of Goldsmiths to celebrate the 500th birthday of the date mark at Goldsmiths' Hall. (The Worshipful Company of Goldsmiths, London)*

CUP *(above right), gold. London, 1969. Designer and maker: Louis Osman. Engraver: Malcolm Appleby. The four-sided base (England, Scotland, Wales and Ireland) gradually changing to circular form (unity) is engraved with the Royal Lion of England, the Unicorn of Scotland, the Dragon of Wales and the Harp of Ireland, as well as the Prince of Wales's feathers.*
Height: 10 cm (4 in)

tiresome moulds with their undercuts and their dusty, unsmooth surfaces, the vacuum evaporation and centrifugal casting which made possible the rapid production of handles or hinges, all these miracles of modern mechanical ingenuity could and did work with steel. But Benney's silver designs for Viners were always found to be too austere to impress the Viners sales force. Viners' customers wanted their silver ornate, but the firm found it uneconomical to produce Benney's magnificently ornate ideas. Viners are now, like Walker and Hall, defunct, but Benney thrives as always, designing and making silver by hand.

Seeing only a limited future in factory work, Benney learnt to make flawless enamels, and has evolved inimitable methods of striping and spotting his surfaces. Expertly using ideas passed on to him by Berger Beigersen, the master enameller from the extinct firm of Burch Korrodi of Zurich, Benney can apply enamel to his textured surfaces more perfectly than anyone else. His personal style is more fluent, less spiky than Osman's, and his production is larger. If Osman has sometimes been uncouth in expression, Benney can be flashy, though each admires the other, and both deserve the accolades they receive. Like Osman, Benney employs only two or three craftsmen at his own workshop, and much of his substantial production is made by outworkers in small workshops dispersed throughout the country, such as Brian Fuller in Amersham, who was general manager of Benney's London workshops from 1969 to 1975. They execute some of Benney's designs, then Benney puts his own sponsor's hallmark on the finished products, usually with the word Benney printed beneath; and if there is enamel, he always punches the name of the enameller beneath it. In this way, he feels he can encourage his enamellers, his most skilful experts, without confusing the public about who is the true originator and creator, namely himself: an elegant compromise.

Benney now limits himself to silversmithing, without any work in industry or teaching. Indeed, as if to underline his determination to be an artist rather than a technician, in 1983 he began to spend time painting large landscapes, seascapes and nudes. These particularly please his voracious American admirers: American collectors can be more positive than Europeans.

Unlike Benney, Robert Welch, Benney's friend and contemporary (established in part of what was the workshop of architect C. R. Ashbee in Chipping Campden, with a retail shop and gallery), continues his practice as industrial designer for clients such as Kitchen Devils (who make ultra-sharp knives) and the Japanese firm Yamazaki, who in 1983 chose him from an international submission to provide a new set of stainless-steel tableware. Another recent client is Shetland Croft on the Scottish island. But his heart is in his hands, and he enjoys making big, smooth, geometrically precise items of silver, which may sometimes be harsh but which are always sensible and often full of character because of their extreme restraint. Since industrial design is well paid, to some extent Welch's drawings for industrial products subsidise the silver made by him and his assistant John Limbrey.

Welch's establishment of small workshop, small and picturesque retail shop and art gallery, combined with his thriving industrial design activity, is the dream of many craftsmen, but few realize it. More often, it is teaching, not industrial design, which provides a steady income, not because teaching is easier, but because teaching jobs are easier to obtain than jobs in industry. In Britain the art schools need the ideas of an artist who runs a commercial workshop. Welch has produced two books to record his satisfying career so far.

A third distinguished contemporary of Benney and Welch is David Mellor. Always obsessed by the shape and grace of cutlery, he created his first big opening in the late 1950s. Supported by Peter Inchbald and the management of their big Sheffield company Walker and Hall, Mellor tried hard to develop a market for new, simple, clean silver designs, but they failed and the firm foundered. Mellor has now started his own factory in Sheffield at Broome Hall. With twenty men instead of 500, and producing his ideal designs in steel, not silver, he is achieving a triumphant success. He is now expanding into a new factory-home on a five-acre site at Hathersage, with Michael Hopkins his architect, and in London into Docklands.

In the field of handwork, David Mellor made his silver so plain that it had little decorative appeal to the layman. Consequently it was very difficult to sell and he eventually abandoned handwork at his modern and well-organized Sheffield studio, designed in 1960 by his architect friend Patrick

Guest. Not for Mellor any adaptation to market demands: he was determined to produce what he himself believed in. What interested him most was cutlery, the traditional trade of his home city. Having succeeded as an industrial designer of lamp-posts, street furniture, stoves and many other useful artefacts, and having been disappointed by the performance of his cutlery factory clients in Sheffield, he decided to go his own way and build his own factory, rather than a workshop, in his sixteenth-century home at Broome Hall, the bigger presses going into his fine Adam-style eighteenth-century dining hall. But to produce was not enough: he also had to establish his own retail outlets, two in London and one in Manchester, and very successful they have been.

Until 1984 Mellor was Chairman of the British government's Crafts Council, to which the government gives an annual subsidy of around £1.8 million, but he resigned because he could not achieve, through the committee system there, the perfection he had managed to impose on his cutlery. Despite his abandonment of hand-made silver, Mellor remains a true craftsman because he demands absolute control over all he does.

Australian-born Stuart Devlin, the most flamboyant designer of his generation to emerge in Britain, has evolved an almost frenzied degree of complication in his silverware, with pierced and filigree surfaces, echoed in his recent initiatives in jewellery and furniture. He keeps prices down by batch soldering and batch production of component sections. He exports all over the world, basing himself mostly in London with frequent rest trips to the West Indian island of Mustique, to Malaysia with its rapidly increasing wealth and consequent need for new homes, and to his cousins in his homeland. Until 1984 he had as partner one of the world's richer men, the Duke of Westminster. His Grace withdrew, and Devlin consequently had to close down his smart shop in Conduit Street, in London's West End, and reduce his force of craftsmen to a modest half dozen.

The long-term achievement of Devlin, however, is not so much the prosperity he brings to skilled craftsmen (and to himself); it is his discovery of a hidden streak of avarice in certain buyers who prize the limited edition. Devlin was the first to exploit this in silver: by presenting friends and clients with a last-chance unique opportunity to buy a piece, he might persuade some of them to buy simply in order not to be left out of what may prove to be a gainful and delightful annual sequence, even if they do not really need it. Devlin's chosen medium was the Easter egg, sometimes expensive and amusing like those by Fabergé, sometimes cheaper and perhaps of questionable taste and quality. Whatever the intrinsic worth of the object, however, the almost hysterical reaction of the client was and is what counts. A temporary, special chance causes a quick reaction. (The same instinct causes the public to queue for hours to see a special loan exhibition, when the same exhibits may be seen in more comfort and at less expense in a permanent showplace round the corner, at any other time.) Devlin has both the craftsman's talent to be able to make the eggs, with contents that are often surprising, and the salesman's ability to create a new market for them.

The trend in Britain is clear: it is towards more elaborate, more decorative, and less useful pieces in silver. Michael Rowe, for example, is one younger artist who has refined this movement of silver into the realms of pure art. His speciality is boxes, but not for keeping things in on a dressing table: they are purely decorative, because they do not open, they cannot hold anything, and they have unexpected gaps and cracks and angles down their sides. Just as many young painters prefer to work on huge canvases whose only possible buyer is a museum, so some young craftsmen prefer the useless to the functional, since the imagination can thus be given free rein – perhaps as a form of social protest. This 'art-craft' receives welcome publicity in the art press which usually shuns the practical crafts, but whether there is a future in it is less certain.

Another way to self-expression is to use unfamiliar techniques and materials, now easily available for the first time. Alastair McCallum has mastered the Japanese invention of laminating different coloured metals into luscious striations. This *mokume-gane* work in the form of small, useful bowls or dishes is wonderfully rich in colour and texture. Another master of unusual materials is Kevin Coates, renaissance theorist, maker of baroque musical instruments, and user of refractory metals such as titanium with silver. His miniature sculptured groups like his Magic Flute pendant, suggesting the complexities of the

WAFER BOX, *silver lined with yew. Chipping Campden, 1968. Designer: Robert Welch. Maker: Raymond Marsh. Carvers and engravers: T. and A. Wise. It has an applied Madonna lily, carved and engraved, on the lid. The box was privately commissioned as a memorial for the church at Elmley Castle. Dimensions: 11.4 × 7 × 3.8 cm ($4\frac{1}{2} \times 2\frac{3}{4} \times 1\frac{1}{2}$ in) (St Mary's Church, Elmley Castle, Worcestershire)*

CUTLERY *(above), silver. Sheffield, 1963–4. Designer and maker: David Mellor. Mellor produces cutlery of simple, clean and graceful shape. Length of longest knife: 23.5 cm (9¼ in) (The Worshipful Company of Goldsmiths, London)*

Mozart opera, are memorable, exquisite and entirely original. His 1983 cup in the Goldsmiths' Hall collection, associated with the London medieval Guilds of Goldsmiths and Fishmongers, is another miniature piece of great artistic integrity. Such 'table toys' were made in Frankfurt or Dresden in the seventeenth century, and it is a pleasure to see that they can still be made by a craftsman today.

The best engraver in Europe, trained to engrave the locks of guns, is Malcolm Appleby, whose studio is near Aberdeen at Crathes. His pictorial fantasy, deeply cut into precious metal with rare confidence and joy, often outlines Celtic legends with daring figures of wind and wave. Let's not be too critical, his fantastic creatures seem to say; like Rubens or Bosch, let's fill the surface with what we like.

Silversmithing in Britain has diminished in the past decade, both in the size of pieces and the scale of production, but the art may nevertheless be more creative, its spirit more fun, and the future more specialized and artistically more bright.

BOWL, *silver with copper inlay. London, 1980. Maker: Michael Rowe. Rowe specializes in elaborate and decorative silver objects, particularly boxes, that are not for functional use. Dimensions: 27.5 × 22 × 80 cm (10⅞ × 8⅝ × 31½ in)*

· SILVER IN OTHER COUNTRIES ·

Overseas, silversmithing is struggling to keep its vitality. Most people want their homes to be manageable rather than glorious, and that means fewer treasures lying around, less silver on the table. Britain led the Industrial Revolution in the 1760s, and it is Britain that has led the craft revival or, as some see it, the anti-machine reaction of the 1970s and 1980s. The machine is now seen as the arch-polluter of the environment, the cause of unemployment everywhere, as robot assembly replaces the human brain. In this context, William Morris's words, and the inherited craft skill of British silversmiths, have given an almost mystical impulse to present British artist-craftsmen. Each country is of course distinct, but none has had such a long love-affair with silver as Britain, and none has had such notable new achievements.

The future probably lies with individuals, not with groups. Sigurd Persson of Stockholm, born in 1914, is master of the angled bulge, and has published five epic books on his jewellery, his silver, his sculpture, design and glass. He is as sure of touch with industrial design as with silver, though the airy spirit of jewellery sometimes eludes his northern logic. He sells in craft co-operatives (Stockholm is particularly strong in this area), in galleries, and in Nordiska Company (NK), the big store. But there is a limit to the vocabulary of his plain surfaces.

Olle Ohlsson, also of Stockholm, born in 1928, is almost a contemporary of Britain's Benney, and, like him, has evolved his own scheme of surface textures, this time with a dentist's drill which makes the silver quite deeply pitted (and the flying particles have pitted the skin of his face, too). Whether his hot personal approach has taken root in the rather cold critical air of Sweden is questionable.

Still further north, in Finland, the financial recession has bitten deep; whereas silver in other countries has survived the anxieties of the past decade, Finland shows the signs of strain. Tapio Wirkkala, the most famous northern designer of them all and the most positive, worked in glass bottles and china and paper, as well as in his main field of product and building design in his last years, less in silver. Norway is famous for enamels, often from the old firm of Tostrup.

Denmark has always, since the pioneering work of Georg Jensen himself at the turn of the century, been in the forefront of silver design. Candles and silver go well together, and long Danish winter evenings encourage plenty of both. Copenhagen's Kunstindustriemuseet has regular modern silver shows, and the various craft societies keep silver well in the public mind, as an aristocrat among materials. But since the Royal Copenhagen Porcelain Company bought Jensen's, and other firms like Michelsen and Dragsted merged, some of the old vigour has gone: Danish art schools are not strong enough to keep the

creative spark alive, business leaders like Hans Hansen are too small for an international context, and rich individual patrons do not exist as they do in the South. It is in the South that the lustrous metal seems to have its future.

In Germany, the austere pre-war style of Andreas Moritz in Nuremberg has inspired Friedrich Becker (born in 1922) of Düsseldorf. He designs silver and cutlery for his friends in the Carl Pott works in nearby Solingen, but his real pleasure is to contrive ever more ingenious kinetic structures. Everything, from rings to table-centres to city-centre fountains, has to move, the spinning or rotating parts being mounted with engineering precision so that they move freely with no risk of jamming. He presented a big, cascading pendent feature to Düsseldorf Art School where he is Professor. It hangs down the middle of the well of

LEAF DISH *(above), oxidized silver and gilt. London, 1973. Maker: Stuart Devlin. Diameter: 41 cm (16 in) (The Worshipful Company of Goldsmiths, London)*

DUCK SPOON AND SALTS *(left), silver. London, 1983. Maker: Sarah Jones. Length of spoon: 11.2 cm (4⅜ in) (The Worshipful Company of Goldsmiths, London)*

TEAPOT *(right), silver with macassar ebony. Düsseldorf, 1977. Maker: Friedrich Becker. Becker designs silver, cutlery and jewellery as well as industrial products and ingenious kinetic sculptures. Height: 17 cm ($6\frac{5}{8}$ in) (Private collection)*

'ESTRO' SAUCE JUG *(facing page, above), silver. Como, 1977. Maker: Lino Sabattini. Sabattini, with a small band of craftsmen, makes silver of daring, unadorned design, often with a very bright polish more popular in Italy than in northern Europe. Dimensions: 9 × 24 × 20 cm ($3\frac{1}{2}$ × $9\frac{3}{8}$ × $7\frac{7}{8}$ in) (Private collection)*

DISH *(facing page, below), silver. Stockholm, 1979. Maker: Olle Ohlsson. Ohlsson has evolved his own scheme of surface textures, often drilling the silver to make it deeply pitted. Diameter: 40 cm ($15\frac{3}{4}$ in)*

the school's central spiral staircase, gently turning with the passing airs so that its transverse bars and balls catch the light and then turn dull again. Students love it and often try to emulate it; but such artistic insight is not often allied to adequate engineering ability.

In the old silver centre of Schwäbisch Gmünd, one of the few German towns entirely to escape the war, Pierre Schlevogt heads the silver academy. But, like Becker and like the Munich sculptor, jeweller and silversmith Hermann Jünger, he finds the school authorities are not very interested in silver. Even though handwork is thought by some education experts to be a vital therapy in times of high unemployment, in Germany the emphasis is still on economics and on possible earning power; so the craft industries and schools find themselves unfashionable and under pressure to conform.

Italy, like France, still has its big houses with servants and the consequent lifestyle. Unlike the French, however, Italians find new design as vital as air, and in most towns there are groups of artisans capable of making almost anything. The artist-craftsman Lino Sabattini of Bregnano, near Como, is typical: with some thirty craftsmen he makes daring unadorned silver for sale mostly to private clients in the region, or to progressive international retailers like Rosenthal. Salvatore Gregorietti of Milan, designer of the new show-cases in the Poldi-Pezzoli Museum, is one of the many Italian architects who turn their hand to everything, including silver. He designs silver as part of the wholeness of living, and thinks it no different from the furniture or china through which he also enlarges his life. But Italian silver tends to be too bright and shiny for British eyes: it seems to have too much dash, and too little feeling for the subtleties of the metal.

Most Italian designers are individualists who prefer to work on their own. They often organize the production of one or two fantastic objects which achieve publicity in the world's design media, but regular sales are another matter, and without sales the social relevance of this sort of silver is questionable. Gem Montebello in Milan, an establishment managed by the sister of the sculptors Arnaldo and Gio Pomodoro, concentrates on jewellery, commissioned from all over the world, but the pieces are sometimes so big that they can fairly be called tableware. Memphis, founded by Ettore Sottsass the architect as an expression of informal, light-hearted protest against the heavy, expensive sobriety of much modern design, concentrates on furniture.

The most spectacular Italian newcomer is the Cleto Munari collection of architect- and artist-designed silver. The style has an affinity with the Post-Modern, angular buildings of the American architect Michael Graves and the Briton Terry Farrell. Fashionable and famous names design for Munari: Hans Hollein of Vienna, Paolo Portoghesi, Sam Wirkkala (son of the Finnish pioneer, Tapio), and the late Carlo Scarpa. A parallel group was commissioned by the Italian firm of Alessi, including, in 1979/80, tea and coffee services by eleven top architects and designers, including Robert Venturi, Alessandro Mendini and Richard Sapper. Like Munari, it included Graves (with a spectacular kettle) and other prestigious names in modern design. The Max Protetch

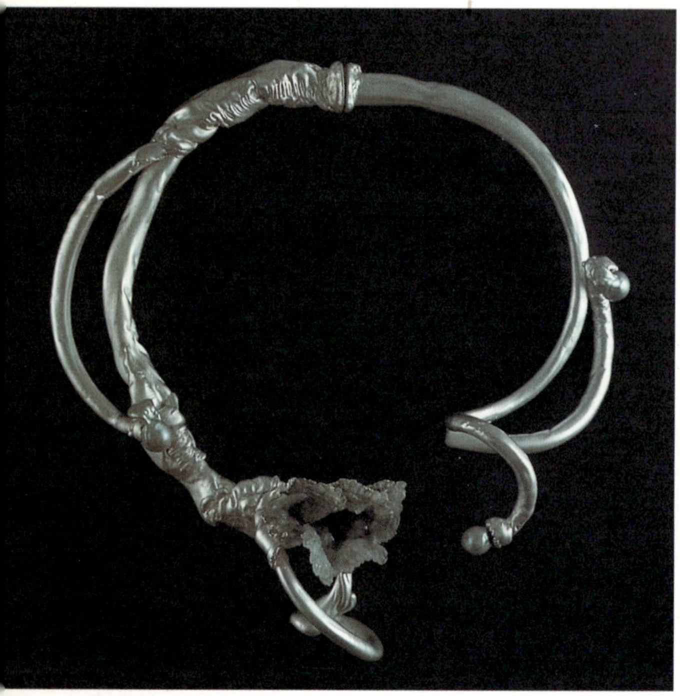

Gallery of New York has agency rights on the collection, and showed some of it in 1984. The Limn Company of San Francisco is also active in this field of highly contrived forms.

The New World is famous for its machines, not its hands, and for its stamped chromium, not for its wrought silver. Fine silversmiths like John Lewis of Boston, or Henry Shawah in Cambridge, Mass., are very rare even on the East Coast, and almost unknown elsewhere. Albert Paley of Syracuse has adapted his silversmithing skills to create a fascinating new idiom: his blacksmith's work, like the railings for the Smithsonian Institution in Washington, has generated extraordinary interest. He is now one of the leaders of a new school of architectural metalworkers, which includes David Watkins in London. Stanley Lechtzin of Tyler College in Philadelphia has conquered a new, large-scale method of fabrication by electroforming, but, like most of his US friends, he concentrates on jewellery rather than silverware. Half-a-dozen big American craft fairs like Rhinebeck of New York, now at West Springfield, Massachusetts, or Haystack Mountain tell the same story: craft silver has not yet gripped this vast economy. When it does, it will probably be not an offshoot of the European tradition of hand-raised good manners, but some exciting new statement based on a new technique, revitalizing an old craft.

Buyers of silver used to be private clients equipping themselves with objects to make their homes beautiful. Patrons today are companies and public bodies who use silver to enhance their boardrooms and their public image. In the 1920s and 1930s, silver was for everyone. Now, it is unashamedly for the luxury market, but designers have more creative freedom than they have had for centuries.

TORQUE *(above left), silver, quartz and pearls. Philadelphia, 1984. Maker: Stanley Lechtzin. Lechtzin has pioneered electroforming. Dimensions: 20.5 × 19.3 × 5 cm (8 × 7½ × 2 in)*

DAGGER AND SHEATH *(above right), gold, gulf pearls, rubies and diamonds. London, 1984. Maker: Grant Macdonald. Made for a customer in Oman, this is typical of many export orders. Length: 27 cm (10⅝ in)*

APPENDIX I

· THE CRAFT OF THE SILVERSMITH ·

The purpose of this chapter is not to be a do-it-yourself guide to the making of objects from precious metal (nor is it concerned with basic general workshop techniques such as turning, sawing, soldering, polishing and so forth), but to provide information about the technical background to the history of silver.

· THE MATERIALS ·

All the metals and alloys from which artefacts are traditionally made share certain basic physical characteristics (though in widely differing proportions). They have strength without unacceptable brittleness; they are ductile, that is to say they will stretch under pressure without immediately breaking, though certain treatments, including hammering when cold, will make some of them harder and therefore more brittle; they become softer when heated, and will eventually liquefy if the heat is raised enough (that is, to their melting point); they can be fused (welded) directly to themselves and to some other metals, or joined by means of another, more fusible, metal (solder); they can be drilled, cut and carved like wood; they can be filed and polished; and, finally, all of them except for gold and platinum are affected to some extent by corrosives, including those in the atmosphere and soil.

This fundamental uniformity has meant that the same fairly limited range of techniques has been used to shape and decorate metals, though with variations of emphasis according to the predominant characteristics of the one concerned and the technical resources available. For example, lead, which has a low melting point (621.3°F) and can be liquefied easily over an ordinary fire or gas-jet, has normally been formed by casting, that is by melting it and pouring it, like a jelly, into a shaped mould. Iron, on the other hand, has a high melting point (2802°F), and a special furnace is required to liquefy it in quantities sufficient to make the production of cast-iron objects a practical proposition. Only when the necessary comparatively advanced technology is available is it possible to produce such objects, and the most widely used method of forming iron has been the blacksmith's, that is, beating it into shape with hammers on an anvil (forging), usually under heat. Cast iron that has not been specially treated to make it malleable – a comparatively modern technique – differs from forged iron in being extremely hard and brittle, and so not workable with the hammer.

Silver has middle-range characteristics which, combined with the beauty of its surface appearance, make it an ideal material for producing the kind of decorative objects that form the subject of this book. It has considerable strength (though not, of course, comparable to the ferrous metals), and a low enough melting point for it to be cast without difficulty in a small workshop using simple skills and equipment – small quantities can even be liquefied under the jet of a mouth-operated blow-lamp. It is so ductile that it can easily be worked cold by hand-forging.

In its pure form silver is too soft for most purposes, and it has at all periods, except the very earliest, commonly been alloyed with another metal, usually copper, to harden it and increase its durability. The officially accepted variations in silver alloys are discussed in Appendix II, and it is only necessary to mention here that the commonest is the British sterling standard. This comprises 925 parts fine (pure) silver to seventy-five parts copper, and its melting point is 1640°F, as opposed to 1760.9°F for the pure metal.

Gold has similar properties but in its pure state it is much softer than silver and much heavier, with a slightly higher melting point (1945.4°F). It is likewise alloyed with other metals to increase its strength and durability, and also, more often than silver, to change its colour for decorative effect.

There are two imitation forms of silver plate, of which the earlier is Sheffield plate, sometimes called 'Old' Sheffield plate. This is, in effect, a sheet of copper sandwiched between two thinner sheets of silver, which are fused to it, and is produced under heat by rollers. The composite sheet can be worked more or less like a sheet of silver – though objects made of Sheffield plate have normally been produced by mechanical

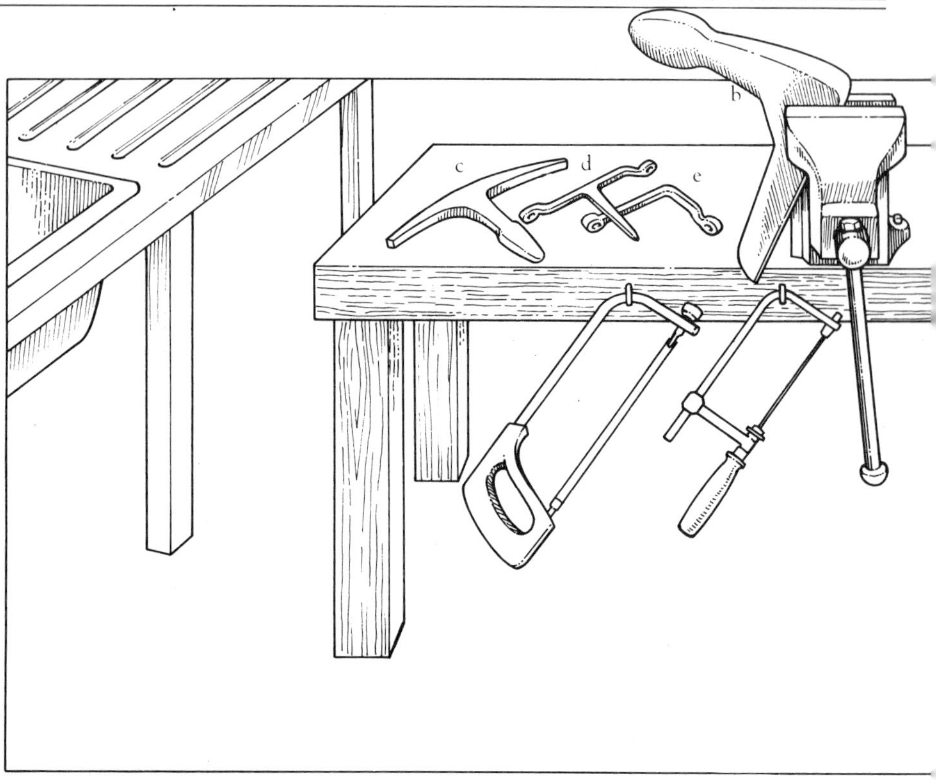

means, especially die-stamping – and the finished product is only distinguishable from one made entirely of silver after close examination. The technique was invented in 1742 by a Sheffield cutler, Thomas Boulsover, and produced the same effect as silver at much lower cost, since a much smaller amount of the metal was used.

The second method of imitating true silver plate is by electroplating, a process that rapidly supplanted Sheffield plate in the 1840s and still remains in very wide use. It was made commercially viable by a patent granted to Elkington's of Birmingham in 1840, and involves coating an object, which must be an electrical conductor, with a metal such as silver by the process of electrodeposition. A piece of the metal to be deposited and the object to be plated with it are attached respectively to the positive and negative terminals (cathode and anode) of a source of direct electrical current and suspended in a suitable solution. The current passes from the cathode to the anode taking with it charged metal particles (ions) from the former and depositing them on the latter. Thus electroplate, unlike Sheffield plate, does not exist as a separate composite metal from which items can be made. Any electroconductor can be electroplated, but the base materials normally found on plated versions of true silver plate are nickel alloys, and also, in the Victorian period, a form of pewter called Britannia metal.

A version of the electroplating process, known as electrotyping or electroforming, can be used for making metal reproductions. It involves coating a mould made from the object to be reproduced with a conducting agent, and then plating it with an appropriate thickness of the required metal. This will produce an exact replica of the original object which, if made of the same metal and carefully cleaned-up, can be very difficult to distinguish from the original. Most electrotypes, however, have been produced either as original works or, more commonly, as reproductions of antique pieces for educational purposes or as souvenirs for sale in museums and similar institutions. The base material for these last is almost invariably copper, coloured to match the original, where this is gold or silver, by plating it with whichever of these is appropriate. Unless they have been cleaned-up, reproductions of antique pieces can normally be distinguished from the originals by the distinctive granular appearance, like solidified sediment, of their undersurfaces.

Electrotyping was introduced at the same time as the electroplating process, and enormous numbers of examples of it exist. For example, Elkington's concluded an agreement with the British Department of Education and Science on 6 October 1853, in which they were granted the right to make reproductions of pieces owned by or lent to the South Kensington Museum (now the Victoria and Albert Museum), which were sold to the public. Many museums in other countries had similar arrangements.

The very first silversmiths no doubt smelted their own metal from the ore, but central production near the mines had already begun by the third millennium BC. The monk Theophilus – who was probably the same person as the goldsmith Roger of Helmarshausen – gives instructions in his famous craft-treatise, *De diversis artibus* (c.1100), for casting silver into appropriate flat plates for working with the hammer. It was probably the normal practice for silversmiths to do this themselves until at least as late as the second half of the eighteenth century, when the development of mechanized techniques – notably in connection with the manufacture of Sheffield plate – led to the commercial production of sheet silver. Even after this, however, craftsmen must still have continued to prepare some of the working metal themselves, since one of the most important sources of their business, until the decline in the use of table-silver after World War I, was derived from the melting-down and refashioning of old plate. Few, if any, modern silversmiths would do this: their normal practice is to buy their working metal in sheets and bars from a specialist supplier, and to send any old plate that has no antique value to a bullion-dealer for melting and refining.

· TOOLS AND EQUIPMENT ·

The modern mind tends to assume that elaborate results can only be achieved with complex, sophisticated equipment operated by a large number of workers. In fact, though many early workshops were no doubt large, the basic equipment needed to enable a skilled silversmith to produce work of the highest quality and sophistication need occupy an area no greater than about 3 × 2m (10 × 6ft). It

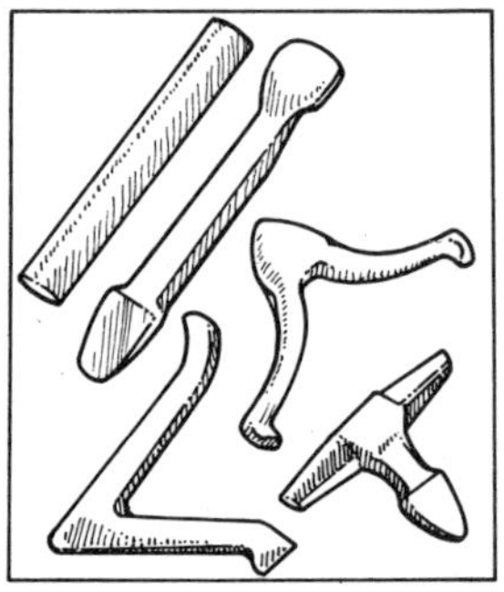

Various forms of stake.

PART OF A SILVERSMITH'S WORKSHOP *(top) with an anvil on a steady-block (a) and a bench bearing various tools, including stakes (b,c), a horse (d), a crank (e), pliers (f), files (g), a leather jeweller's skin for catching silver-filings (h), dies (i) and a cleaning vat (j). The horse and the crank are pierced to take shaped 'heads' to convert them into stakes. Both can be held in a vice, but the former, like the stake, is shaped at the bottom to fit into a hole in a steady or anvil.*

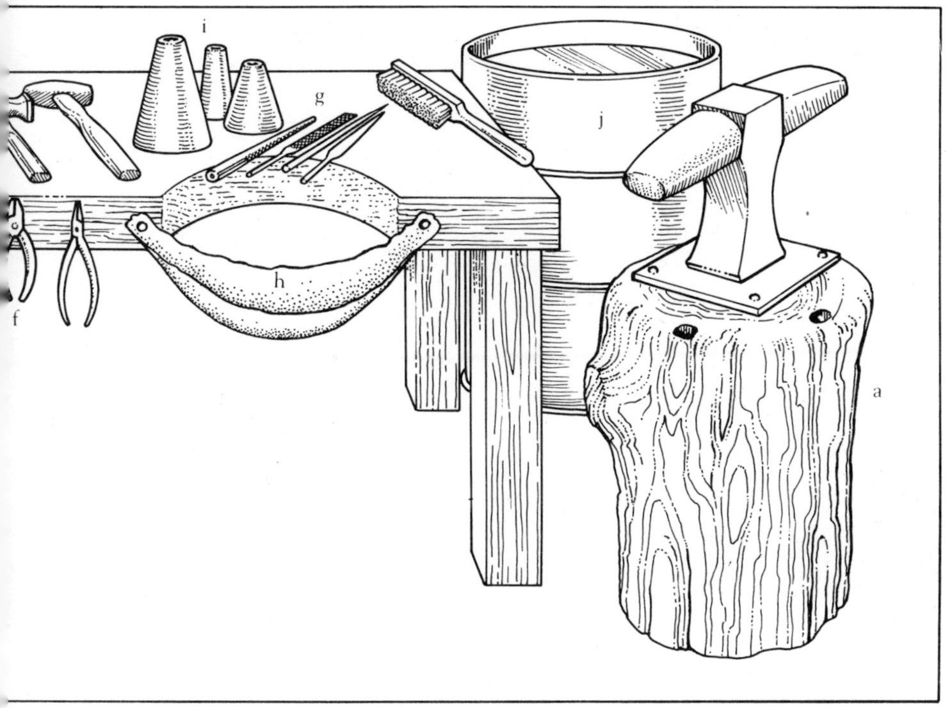

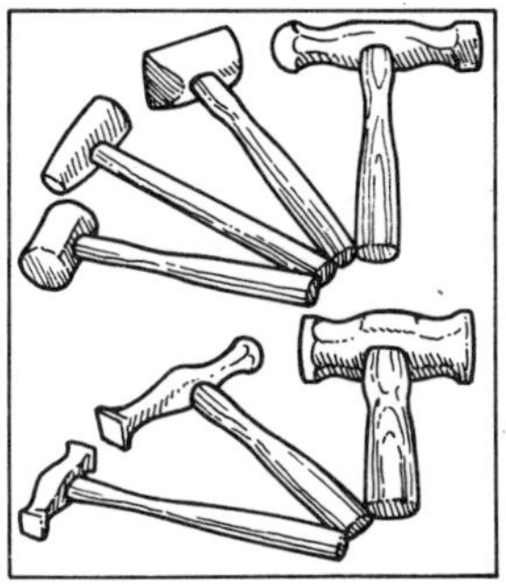

Various forms of hammer used by silversmiths.

comprises the following items:
1 A wooden work-bench with normal fittings, including a leg-vice. It must also have provision for the attachment of a jeweller's skin, a sheet suspended horizontally between the craftsman and the bench, especially during sawing and filing operations, to catch droppings of precious metal for remelting.
2 A hearth for annealing the metal (see below), which, in its simplest form, is a shallow tray of fireproof material, now usually iron, some 38–50 cm (15–20 in) square or round, filled with burning charcoal or pulverized coke, and mounted in or on a heat-resistant insulator of some kind. The heat is controlled by an air-jet, provided on very primitive hearths by a simple mouth-operated blowpipe, and on more sophisticated ones by bellows operated by hand, foot, water or electricity. The amount of heat that can be produced depends, of course, on the amount of blowing power available, but sufficient can be generated by hand operation to melt gold or silver in a crucible. A modern silversmith, however, would have one or more gas torches for applying localized heat, and might also have a special crucible melting-furnace and, if such techniques as enamelling are used, a muffle-furnace. This last is designed so that anything placed in it is protected from direct contact with the heat source or the products of combustion. The primitive craftsman, with only an open hearth, used a muffle-iron for the same purpose: this was a flat pan with a collander-like iron lid which could be covered completely with glowing charcoal.
3 A steady-block, a tree-trunk section with holes and depressions in it, in which the small anvils known as stakes (see below) may be fixed and metal may be shaped.
4 A vat containing pickle – in a modern shop normally a dilute solution of sulphuric acid – for making work chemically clean, an essential requirement for such processes as soldering.
5 A sink and board for washing and scouring work.
6 A selection of stakes on which metal – normally in sheet form – is worked with the hammer. These stakes have stems which are held in a hole in the steady-block when in use, or else in a vice. The simplest ones look rather like tall, polished, iron mushrooms, but a wide variety of forms is available, designed to provide anvil-heads to suit any shape of product: for instance, on a narrow arm to reach inside a cylinder.
7 A selection of hammers with different heads for different types of work.
8 A selection of mandrels, engraving- and chasing-tools, punches, drills, files, saws, shears, tongs, and the other minor tools of metalworking.
9 Cleaning and polishing materials.

In addition to the above, most established craftsmen in advanced societies have a lathe, which can be used for polishing as well as for turning. Many also have a draw-bench for making wire, despite the fact that it has long been mass-produced. This is a bench supporting a hand-operated windlass attached to a cable ending in a pair of tongs. Wire is produced by drawing gold or silver rods through holes of gradually decreasing size in iron plates (draw-plates) by means of the windlass. An extension of this is a frame in which two dies (swages) with identical but reversed recessed patterns can be clamped down with screws onto a wire, which is then pulled backwards and forwards, the swages being screwed down gradually the while, so producing wire of special section. Simple swages struck with the hammer have also been used for producing grooves, or even repeated patterns, in sheet metal. The date when drawn wire was introduced is still in dispute. The earliest written evidence for its manufacture is in Theophilus's treatise of c.1100, but it was probably introduced in late Roman times. The earliest methods of making wire were by rolling or spirally coiling thin strips of metal and working them by hand.

· FORMING TECHNIQUES ·

With the exception of electroforming, die-stamping and spinning, the techniques used by the modern silversmith go back at least as far as the first clearly defined development of the craft in the middle of the third millennium BC. Modern technology has done little more than provide a few powered mechanical aids to enable some of these techniques to be carried out with less physical effort and less dependence on personal skill and judgment, as well as being able to mass-produce supplies of working metal. The basic forming processes are still carried out by hand, as they have been for thousands of years, and if a western silversmith's workshop is bigger than those of his predecessors or some of his eastern contemporaries, it is mainly because modern powered equipment needs more room.

All the techniques described here are often used in conjunction with each other, while objects are commonly made in parts joined together, most frequently by soldering, but also by screwing and riveting.

CASTING

The very earliest metal artefacts, no doubt made from casual finds of natural metal, were probably worked by hammering. The true age of metals started with the discovery – probably in Anatolia in the fourth millennium BC – that they could be extracted from their ores under heat: it is likely, therefore, that the first true metalworking skill was casting. Casting involves pouring the liquid form of a material that will solidify into a suitably shaped mould and leaving it until it has solidified. The mould is then removed, leaving the material concerned with its outer configuration corresponding to that of the interior of the mould. A simple illustration of the basic process is provided by the ice-tray of a refrigerator, which is actually a mould for casting a material – water – with a very low melting-point.

The simplest form of mould is cut into a block of material – in the very beginning, stone – and the molten metal is simply poured into it from the top, like water into an ice-tray. This has the disadvantage of producing objects that are flat on one side. The next stage, therefore, was to produce a mould in two symmetrical, but reversed, halves that locked together, usually by means of studs and holes. Such a mould, like all closed moulds, must have an aperture through which the molten metal can be poured and, very important, ventilation-holes through which the air replaced by the metal, and any other gases, can escape. All these apertures fill with metal to form sprues which have to be removed when the casting is cleaned.

A simple one- or two-part mould can only be used to produce a casting that has no undercutting in its design – for example, a spoon or fork – since, otherwise, the two could only be separated by breaking the mould. The next stage, therefore, was to produce a multi-part mould, constructed and held together in a similar manner to the two-piece one, but so designed that the joins between the parts are arranged to enable all undercutting to be cleared. The much-used modern method of industrial casting in sand-moulds, first recorded in the sixteenth century, does not normally seem to have been used for precious metals. It involves forming a mould by making an impression in compacted sand with a model of the object to be cast.

Hollow objects – made to save both weight and metal – can be produced in a piece-mould, normally by including a core in its construction, but also by the method known as slush-casting.

INVESTMENT (WASTE WAX OR *CIRE PERDU*) CASTING

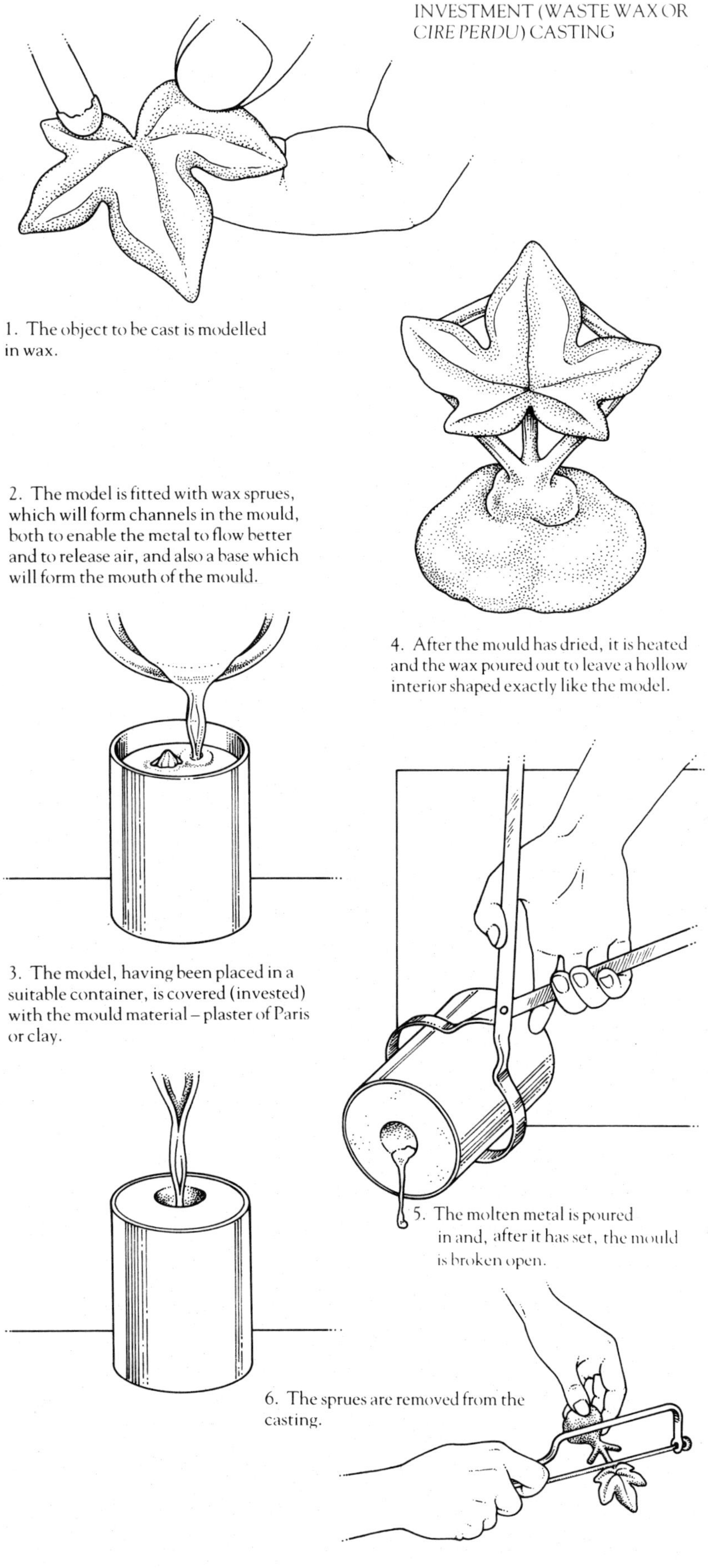

1. The object to be cast is modelled in wax.

2. The model is fitted with wax sprues, which will form channels in the mould, both to enable the metal to flow better and to release air, and also a base which will form the mouth of the mould.

3. The model, having been placed in a suitable container, is covered (invested) with the mould material – plaster of Paris or clay.

4. After the mould has dried, it is heated and the wax poured out to leave a hollow interior shaped exactly like the model.

5. The molten metal is poured in and, after it has set, the mould is broken open.

6. The sprues are removed from the casting.

This is only suitable for certain metals and is made possible by the fact that the parts that come into contact with the cold walls of the mould harden first. When this has happened, and formed a skin of the required thickness, the still-molten metal in the middle is poured out.

The most refined method of casting, and the one most used since the fourth millennium BC, is the investment or lost-wax (*cire-perdue*) process. It involves making a full-sized wax model of the object to be cast, on a suitable core if the finished object is to be hollow, and solid if it is to be solid. The model is fitted with wax 'sprues' to form pouring- and ventilation-vents, and is then invested – that is, completely covered – with clay or plaster, or some other suitable material for the mould. This is allowed to harden and is then gently heated or, in the case of clay, baked. The heat in both cases melts the wax which drains from the mould, and is then replaced with molten metal. It is essential that the metal fill the mould fully and firmly, and the modern caster uses centrifugal force for this purpose, on a special machine.

When the metal has cooled, the mould has to be broken away, so it can only be used once. Where a design needs to be repeated, a master model is kept from which piece-moulds for further waxes can be produced. In a modern workshop this would be a silicone-rubber impression, but formerly lead or plaster was used.

Casting is followed by a cleaning-up process which involves not only removing dirt and scale, the sprues, and visible traces of core-supports, but also the sharpening up of any details that may not have reproduced properly, and any polishing.

RAISING

This is the technique most used by the silversmith, and involves forming dishes and vessels (hollow wares), and other objects, out of sheet metal by working it cold with the hammer on a stake, one of the shaped anvils already mentioned. The technique was in use in the Near East by the beginning of the third millennium BC, and has remained basically unchanged ever since. With regular and carefully controlled blows of the hammer, a disc of silver can be converted into a bowl or jug without joins or seams. The hammer is used to fold the metal, and only minimally to stretch it, so that the craftsman can mould the vessel without making the metal thinner. What happens is similar to making a bowl shape out of a single disc of brown paper, which can only be achieved by folding, or by cutting gores and overlapping the edges, since the paper cannot be stretched. A silver bowl is formed in the same way, except that the metal, that in a less malleable material would be folded or overlapped, is worked away to the edges.

The compression of the cold metal under constant hammer blows causes it to harden and become unworkable after a time. It then has to be 'annealed', to restore its malleability, a process that merely involves heating it and allowing it to cool before further working.

RAISING A BOWL

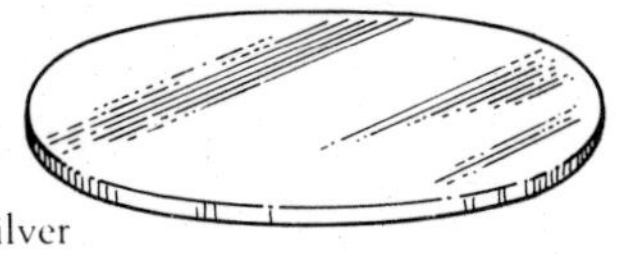

1. Disc of silver

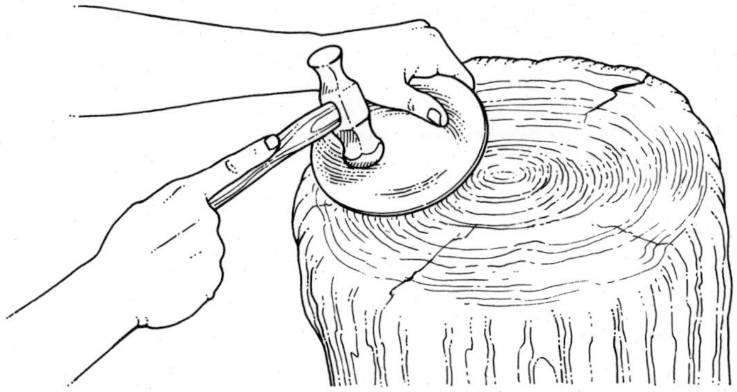

2. The bowl started by making the disc slightly concave with a hammer on a wooden surface.

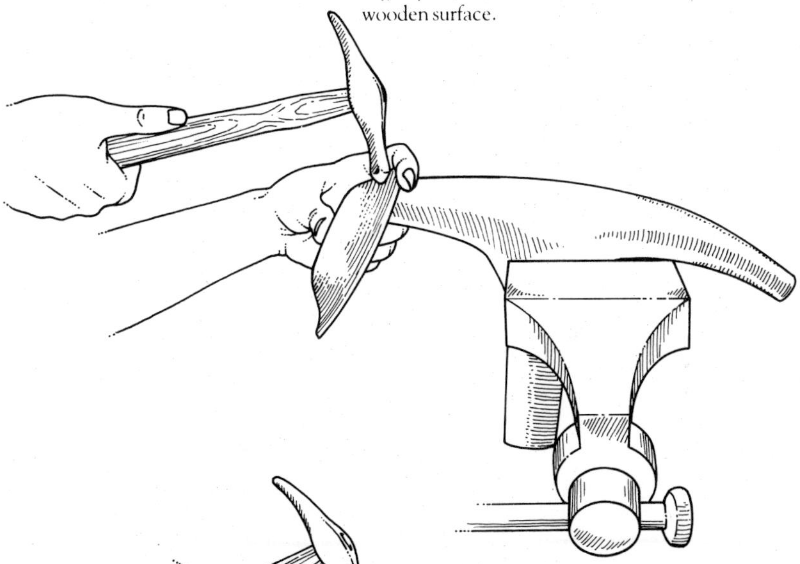

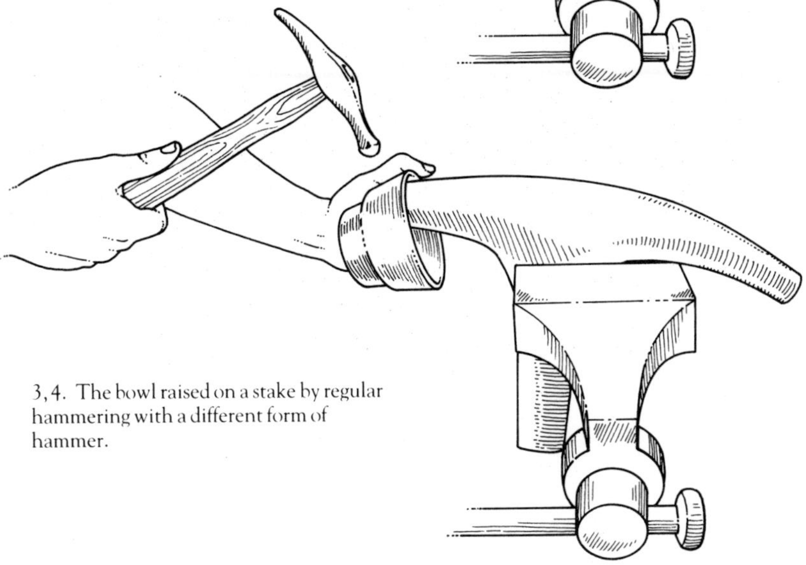

3,4. The bowl raised on a stake by regular hammering with a different form of hammer.

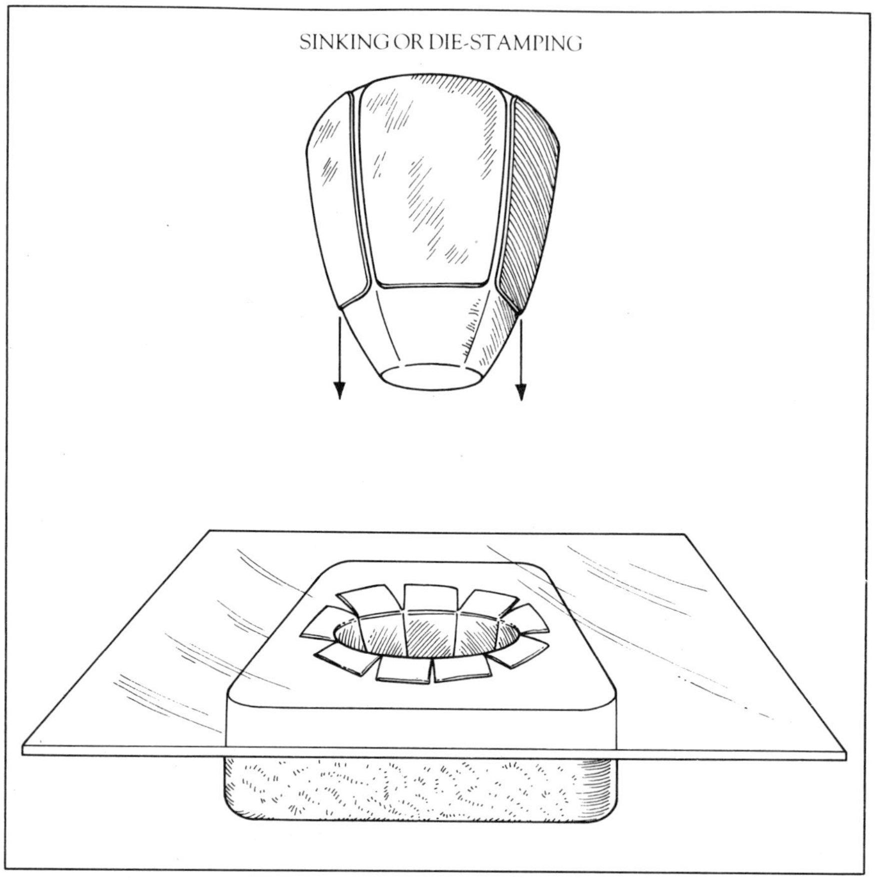

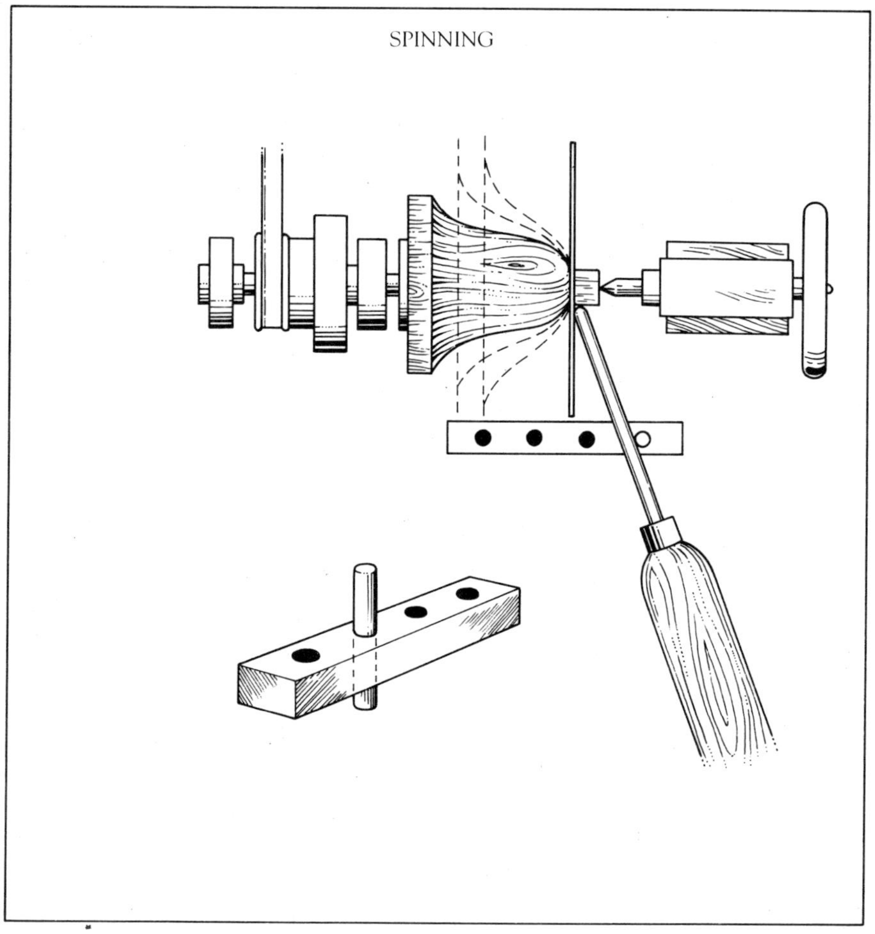

SINKING OR DIE-STAMPING

This involves forming something like, say, the body of a pepper-pot by forcing sheet silver into a hole conforming to the final external configuration of the finished body by means of a punch conforming to its internal one. A simple form of punch can be made of wood and struck with a hand hammer. In its most elaborate form – introduced in the second half of the eighteenth century – the punch and the hole are specially cut steel dies, mechanically operated and capable of stamping several sheets at a time: each bottom sheet as it fills the bottom die is replaced by an unstamped sheet on top. The metal in this process is, of course, stretched.

SPINNING

This process is used for the mass production of hollow wares by means of a lathe. An object is formed from a metal disc which is gradually pressed against a wooden former (the chuck) corresponding to its final internal configuration, until it finally takes its shape. The effect is as if the disc was slowly hammered over a former, but pressure in spinning is applied, not by the hammer, but by a lubricated metal-ended lever, resting against a vertical fulcrum and pressed sideways by the operator against the metal disc as both it and the chuck rotate on a lathe. Composite, disintegrable chucks are used for producing deep and complex shapes, from which a one-piece chuck could not be removed. The spinning process is still used for mass production and is surprisingly quick, the metal seeming to flow on to the chuck. The date of its introduction is a matter of controversy, but there does not seem to be any evidence for its use before the late Middle Ages, and it was probably only adopted generally in the late eighteenth century.

· FINISHING ·

The usual finish for gold and silver plate is a high polish produced with mild abrasives. Silver, however, has also commonly been coated with gold from an early date, partly to make it look like the more precious metal, but also to protect it from tarnish and acid: for instance, the interiors of silver wine-vessels were, and still are, commonly gilded. There is evidence for silver being gilded by burnishing gold leaf on to it as early as the middle of the second millenium BC in Egypt, and the technique remained in general use for this purpose until late Roman times. In about AD 300, however, it was being supplanted by the mercury- or fire-gilding technique, which had been in use in China at least 600 years earlier, and which was to be used universally for good-quality gilding on metal until supplanted after 1840 by electrogilding. Fire-gilding involves making an amalgam of mercury and gold – the two combine readily – and then brushing it on to the prepared surface to be gilded under heat. The heat dissolves the mercury in the highly dangerous form of free mercury vapour (gilders had short lives!) leaving the gold deposited on the surface.

Apart from gilding, it has been the practice for craftsmen sometimes – especially since the mid-nineteenth century – to colour the surface of their silver by oxidizing it chemically. This is usually done to provide a foil for bright areas, or applied or inlaid decoration in other materials.

· DECORATION ·

The decoration of gold and silver plate can be broadly classified into two types, integral and applied.

INTEGRAL DECORATION

All decoration forming part of the main material or design of an object is termed integral, including such details as mouldings and finials which have been cast separately and soldered into place. The techniques for producing ornament of this kind include casting, turning on a lathe, and using shaped punches, patterned stamps, saw and file, and also engraving and chasing.

Engraving involves producing designs made up of lines produced by gouging out strips of metal from the surface being decorated by means of a burin, a sharply-pointed engraving-tool.

Chasing, according to Bernard Cuzner in his *Silversmith's Manual* (2nd edition, London, 1949, p.153), '. . . is to be taken as including chasing, embossing, repousse [*sic*] work, and the modelling of solid metal with hammer and punch.' A number of different steel or iron tools, of about the same size as a pencil, are used for chasing, the most important probably being the tracer, which resembles a blunt screwdriver. Unlike engraving-tools, chasers are used for moving, but not *re*moving metal.

When sheet metal is chased it has to be supported on something that is both hard enough to give rigidity and plastic enough to yield to the work. A sandbag can be used for this purpose, but the material most frequently employed is a pitch-based compound with which the surface opposite the one being chased is coated. When the other surface has to be worked it is necessary to transfer the pitch to the opposing face.

The two main kinds of chasing are flat chasing and embossing, or repoussé. Flat chasing produces an effect that superficially resembles engraving, but the lines are the result of compressing, and not removing, metal along their length. It can often be identified by the presence of a ghostly reversed impression of the design on the back of the metal.

Embossing or repoussé involves modelling designs in relief by means of the hammer and chasing-tools. The basic principle is first to raise the parts of the design that are to be in relief from the rear, and then to work back their concavities from the front.

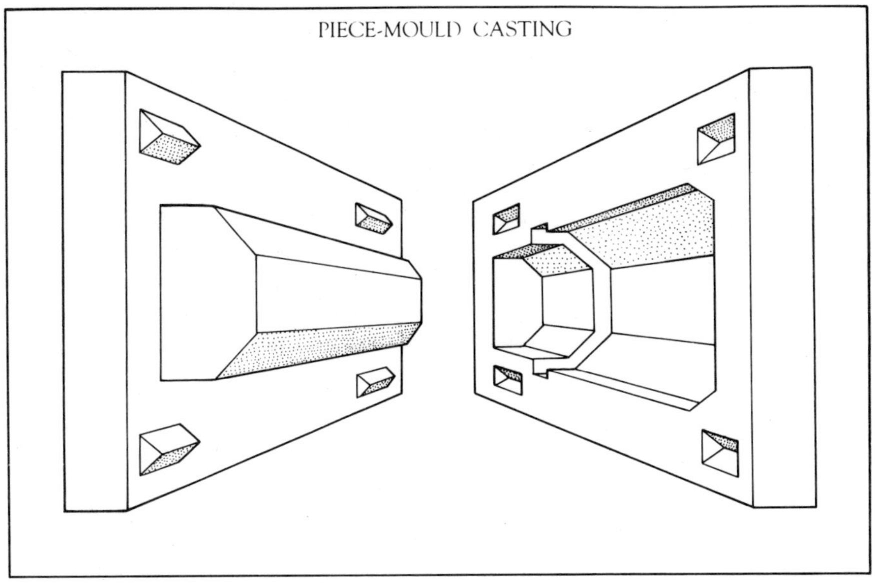

A TWO-PIECE MOULD FOR HALF A SPOUT *(above) with male (a) and female (b) halves held in the correct position by lugs and recesses at the corners. The parts are bound together with wire before use.*

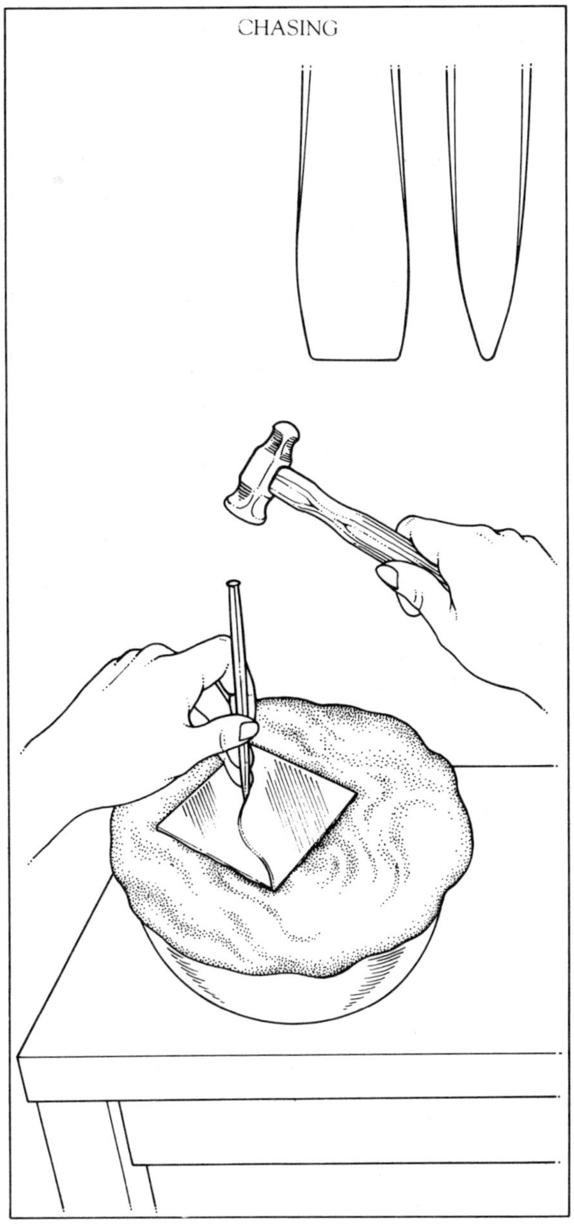

CHASERS *(left), and the method of using them on a pitch-block.*

APPLIED DECORATION

All decoration that does not form part of the basic design, construction, or material of the object, including such things as precious and other stones or crystals, either set in mounts or inlaid directly into the surface, and plaques cast in the same metal and soldered or riveted in place, comes into the category of applied decoration. Similarly, one metal can be inlaid into another – gold into silver, for example – and either polished flat, or left proud and sculptured with ornament in the form known as encrustation.

An other type of metal-applied-to-metal decoration is filigree. This is a very ancient and widespread technique involving the use of wire, usually formed into scrolls and similar motifs, soldered together to form panels and strips of decoration. Filigree can be used independently for jewellery and ornamental vessels such as caskets and vases, but has also frequently been soldered as applied decoration to gold and silver objects.

Granulation, another form of applied decoration, is a method of building up raised designs in minute grains of gold, normally grouped *en masse*, on a gold base. It is first recorded on a bead of the first half of the third millennium BC from the Hittite city of Ur, and was much used by the Ancient Greeks and Etruscans. The art of producing it was subsequently lost until the nineteenth century, when it was rediscovered by the jeweller Castellani. It is not certain that his methods were precisely those used by the Ancients (whose techniques are still a matter for some discussion), though they produced very similar results. The general principle was to attach with an adhesive the grains of gold in the required pattern to the surface to be decorated, and then to apply sufficient heat to 'solder' them together. Two gold surfaces will, in fact, fuse together at a temperature just below that of their melting point without the assistance of solder. It is very probable, however, that a form of solder in solution was included in the adhesive by means of which the granules were initially fixed to the base: for example, a finely divided copper mineral such as malachite (copper carbonate) or a copper salt in solution. The granules would have been produced by heating snippets of gold wire, or gold filings, in charcoal. (For the latest information on the technique, see J. Ogden, *Jewellery of the Ancient World*, 1982, pp.64–5).

One of the most frequently used methods of decorating gold and silver since the early Middle Ages is enamelling. Enamel is coloured ground glass made into a paste, applied to a suitable metal base and fired in a muffle-furnace until it revitrifies. In simple terms, it produces an effect like the glaze on a pot.

The earliest enamellers were unable to merge their colours, and so their designs were built up, like stained-glass windows, in compartments of different colours. Enamel of this kind falls into two main categories: cloisonné, in which the compartments (cells or cloisons) are produced by soldering filigree to the base, and champlevé, in which they are gouged out of it. From the fourteenth century, artists began to understand how to apply the colours like paint, without the need for divisions between them, and also how to produce completely translucent enamel which could be used with a design engraved underneath it. One remarkably delicate technique, apparently introduced in about 1400 but not widely used, is known by its French name of *plique-à-jour*. It comprises, what are, in effect, windows, the enamel being open on both sides and merely supported by its frame. It was probably produced by firing it with some kind of solid support on one face which was then removed.

Another frequently used type of applied decoration is niello, a mixture of silver, lead, copper and sulphur, melted to form a decorative black filling for designs cut into the surface of metal. It is analogous to enamel, but has a much lower melting point and so can be applied without the need for a special furnace. Niello was known in ancient times and is still widely used.

GRANULATION

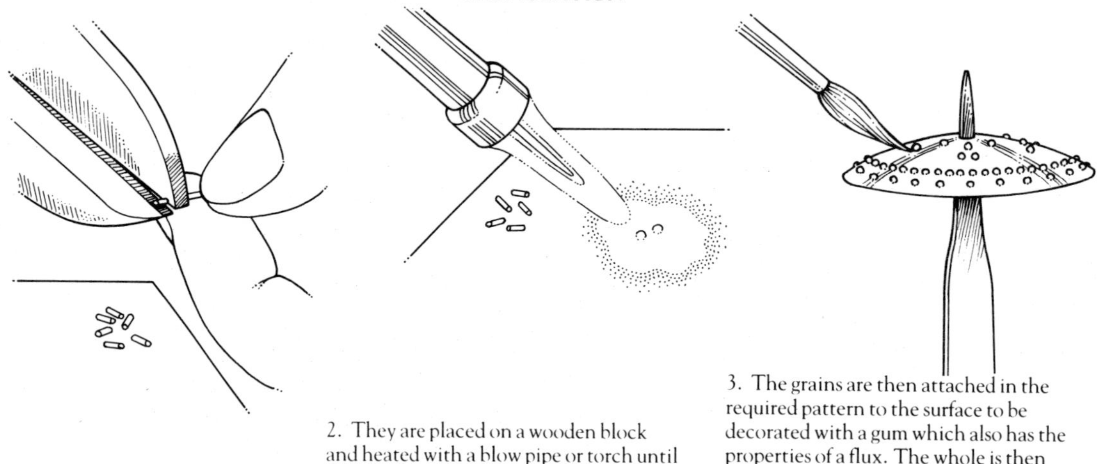

1. Gold wire is cut into fragments.

2. They are placed on a wooden block and heated with a blow pipe or torch until they form tiny grains.

3. The grains are then attached in the required pattern to the surface to be decorated with a gum which also has the properties of a flux. The whole is then heated until the grains fuse to the base.

APPENDIX II

· THE METALS: · HALLMARKING AND METHODS OF ASSAY ·

Silver is widely distributed in the earth's crust, and so it is not surprising that its unique properties were recognized in ancient times and that methods were devised for its extraction and for fashioning it into articles of beauty and utility. Because of its malleability and high intrinsic value it was also used in many countries to make coins.

· THE METALS ·

One of the forms in which silver occurs in nature is as silver chloride (horn silver), from which it is easily recovered. Occasionally it is found in its metallic state (native silver). These two forms were probably the main, if not the only, sources of silver for many centuries after it was first discovered, possibly in the fourth millennium BC. It was not until the third millennium BC, following its discovery in ores such as galena, where lead is the predominant metal, that it became widely used for making jewellery and larger articles. Other ores rich in silver were eventually discovered, but although some extensive mining operations are based on such deposits, most of the world's output is from ores consisting mainly of lead or other base metals.

Silver was first known and used to make vessels in Asia Minor and the Near East c.2500 BC. Eventually, mining spread to the West, and by 800 BC it had been established in the Iberian peninsula, which continued to be the main source of the metal until the Moorish invasion of Spain in the eighth century AD. There was also some production in other parts of Europe; for example, large quantities of silver were recovered from lead ores at Laureion near Athens, from about 600 BC to the first century AD. After a lull in mining activities between the eighth and thirteenth centuries, an area of great importance as a source of silver was developed in Silesia in central Europe, which supplied most of the demand. The position changed radically, however, with the Spanish conquest of the Americas; rich deposits of silver ores were discovered in Mexico, Peru and what is now Bolivia, and vast quantities of the metal shipped to Europe. Today, the principal producing countries in order of importance are Mexico, Peru, the Soviet Union, the USA and Canada, but many other countries including Australia and Japan also contribute to the world's supply.

Silver in its pure state is unsuitable for the manufacture of articles because it is relatively soft. However, by alloying with another metal it can be substantially hardened, a property known in early times. Copper has always been the metal most frequently employed for hardening, although others can be used. The proportion of silver in the alloy has varied from country to country and from one period to another – from as low as 50 per cent to 97 per cent. Below 80 per cent the alloy becomes yellow, so this is usually considered the lowest practical standard for silver articles.

A number of different methods have been used for the extraction of silver from ore deposits, the earliest depending on a process known as cupellation. The ore containing both lead and silver was first smelted and the resultant lead/silver alloy heated on a bed of bone ash, in such a way that a draught of air passed over the molten metals. Under these conditions the lead and any other base metals combine with oxygen in the air to form oxides, which in their molten states run off or pass into the bone ash, leaving a residue of almost pure silver. This does not, however, remove any of the other noble metals, such as gold, which may be present in the silver. A more modern method for extracting silver from lead ores is Parkes process, which relies on the greater affinity of zinc for silver than for lead. After preliminary smelting of the ore, zinc is added to the molten metal and the resulting crust of silver-zinc compounds is skimmed off from the lead, and the zinc is then removed by distillation.

In South America the amalgamation or so-called 'patio process' was employed from the sixteenth century for extracting silver from silver-rich ores; mercury was added to the crushed ore to form an amalgam with the silver and was subsequently removed by distillation. Another method, used in Mexico since the beginning of this century, is based on the use of sodium cyanide

UNITED KINGDOM
Makers' Marks

Early

c. 1700

Modern

UNITED KINGDOM
Date Letters

London
1478

London
1705

Birmingham
1952

All Offices
1984

solution which slowly reacts with silver, thus effecting a separation from the other constituents of the ore. The crushed ore is leached with cyanide solution and the silver precipitated by the addition of zinc. Silver recovered by these last two methods is still not pure, and a further refining is required, usually by cupellation with lead as already described. Nowadays an electrolytic method is normally used for a final refining operation.

Copper was known even before silver, and methods had been devised for extracting it from its ores. The silver-copper alloy used by silversmiths was, and still is, made by simply melting together the two metals in the correct proportions. The resulting ingot can be hammered or rolled into a flat sheet, drawn into wire, or used for casting. Apart from surface tarnishing by sulphur-containing gases in the atmosphere, it is fairly resistant to corrosion, and articles made from it even thousands of years ago have not deteriorated.

· SILVERWARE AND COINAGE ·

In early times there was often a close relationship between silverware and silver coinage, one being easily converted into the other. It was not uncommon during times of financial hardship for an owner to sell his plate for melting and conversion into coinage, just as he might purchase silverware as a form of saving in more prosperous times, knowing that its intrinsic value could always be realized if necessary. Thus, quite apart from any aesthetic considerations, there were two further important criteria for a potential purchaser of an article to bear in mind – its weight and its silver content. The first was easily assessed: articles would always be weighed when purchased. The second was not so simple to establish, as skilled tests were required. It was in the early fourteenth century that compulsory systems of assaying and marking of silver articles were introduced in several European countries, with the object of protecting the public and safeguarding the standard of silver. In some countries the coinage itself was subject to testing independently of those responsible for minting it. In Britain this independent test was called The Trial of the Pyx; dating from the thirteenth century, it was, and still is, carried out by the goldsmiths' guild, now known as the Goldsmiths' Company.

· HALLMARKING ·

Since it is impossible to tell by purely visual means what proportion of silver an article contains, there has always been a temptation for a dishonest craftsman to defraud a purchaser by selling silver of inferior quality. It was as a result of many such frauds that hallmarking was introduced in a number of European countries between the thirteenth and fifteenth centuries. In Britain for example, a statute enacted in 1300 decreed that no silver article was to leave the hands of the worker until it had been tested by the wardens of the goldsmiths' guild and marked with a leopard's head. In France, hallmarking had been started even earlier by the guilds in certain towns; other European countries followed suit. These systems had much in common, and a description of the British procedure will serve to illustrate the general principles which also applied to a number of other countries.

HALLMARKING IN BRITAIN

In 1238 King Henry III ordained that all silver wares should be of the sterling standard, that is, they should contain (using the modern notation) not less than 925 parts per thousand or 92.5 per cent of silver in the alloy. He also commanded the Mayor of London to appoint six discreet goldsmiths to superintend the craft. This proved to be an inadequate measure, and it was followed by the Statute of 1300 in the reign of Edward I, already mentioned. Thus was initiated the system of compulsory assaying and marking that has continued in principle to the present day. The Goldsmiths' Company, which received its first Royal Charter in 1327, is still responsible for hallmarking at the London Assay Office, one of four offices now operating in the United Kingdom; the others are at Birmingham, Sheffield and Edinburgh. The present law is contained in the Hallmarking Act 1973, which became effective in 1975.

In 1363 silversmiths were ordered to strike their own distinctive maker's mark alongside the official, or king's mark. The makers' marks were in the form of a device or emblem such as a bird or a cross; later, makers had to register their marks at the assay office in the form of the initials of their Christian and surnames, except during the period of the compulsory higher standard from 1697 to 1720 (see below), when they were required to use the first two letters of their surnames. For some years both a device and initials were often used together in a single shield, but today only the initials are permitted. The mark is now generally referred to as the 'sponsor's' mark; this is because it is not necessarily the mark of the maker, but more accurately the person or firm responsible for sending it to the assay office for assaying and marking. The maker's mark is extremely useful, especially so in the case of antiques, as it enables an article to be attributed to a particular person or firm, usually the actual maker.

It appears that in the years following the Statute of 1300 the wardens of the goldsmiths' guild, or Goldsmiths' Company as it was later called, maintained their control by regular visits to silversmiths' workshops, either carrying out tests on the spot or taking samples from the articles and assaying them later. Under its Charters the Company had been granted wide powers of search and seizure, and the wardens periodically inspected the premises of silversmiths in both London and other parts of England.

A further Statute in 1478 made the Goldsmiths' Company liable to a fine if any substandard article were found to bear its mark, and it was probably as a result of this enactment that the wardens made a change in their system. They appointed a permanent assayer, and required workers to bring all their newly manufactured wares to the assay office at Goldsmiths' Hall to be assayed and struck with the mark of the Hall – hence the origin of the word 'hallmark'.

At the same time a further mark, now known as the date letter, was struck by the side of the leopard's head. This was a letter of the alphabet which was changed each year, the object being to identify the assayer or warden responsible for assaying or marking the article. Twenty letters were used, and when one alphabet was completed the design of letter or shape of the surrounding shield was changed. The date letter has been continued to the present day and has proved of great value, giving as it does the year in which an article was assayed, normally the same as that of manufacture. The 'year' was not in fact the calendar year, but ran for twelve months (from the middle of May at the London Assay Office). Since 1975 the date letter has been changed on 1 January each year at all four assay offices, and the same letter is used at each of them.

A fourth mark was added in 1544 – a lion passant (a heraldic term for a lion that is walking). This mark is still used at the three English assay offices to denote silver of the sterling standard. At the Edinburgh office the standard mark is now a lion rampant (rearing up on its hind legs).

Between 1697 and 1720 the minimum standard was raised compulsorily from 925 to 958.4 parts per thousand, in order to deter silversmiths from melting coins of the realm for their raw material, a practice which had become prevalent due to the shortage and high price of silver. To denote the new standard the lion passant mark was replaced by the figure of Britannia. The sterling standard was restored in 1720, together with the lion passant mark, but the higher standard with the Britannia mark continued as an alternative and is still occasionally used.

Originally the only assay office was in London, but an Act of 1423 mentions seven other towns that were to have 'divers touches' or marks. Authorized assay offices were eventually established by the local goldsmiths' guilds in Chester, Exeter, Newcastle, York, Norwich and probably also in Bristol, although the evidence for the last named is scanty. During their active period large quantities of silver were marked at the first four of these offices, and articles bearing their marks are frequently encountered. Each office had its own distinctive assay office mark – for example a castle for Exeter and the city arms for Chester – and its own distinctive date letter cycle. Their marks sometimes also included the leopard's head.

London retained the leopard's head as its own assay office mark. It was surmounted by a crown between 1478 and 1820, after which date it has remained uncrowned. It has been used consistently on sterling silver assayed in London since 1300, but between 1697 and 1975 it was replaced by a lion's head erased (a heraldic term for a lion's head, in profile, with ragged lower edge) on silver of the higher (Britannia) standard. Since 1975 the leopard's head has been used at the London Assay Office on silver of both the sterling and Britannia standards.

The assay office mark thus usually makes it possible to identify the particular assay office where the article was tested and marked. This is an important point to note when using the hallmark for dating an article, because until 1975 each assay office used a different cycle of date letters.

Birmingham and Sheffield were important centres of the silversmithing trade by the latter part of the eighteenth century, but their products had to be sent elsewhere for hallmarking. It was the result of much energetic petitioning, particularly by Matthew Boulton, a manufacturing silversmith as well as a pioneer of the Industrial Revolution, that an Act of Parliament was passed in 1773 establishing the two assay offices which are still operating today. The Assay Office mark for Birmingham is an anchor and for Sheffield a rose (prior to 1975 a crown for silver and a rose for gold).

The standard for silver wares in Scotland was established by Statute in 1457 at eleven ounces in twelve ounces troy (916.6 parts per 1000). The statute authorized the appointment of a deacon in each town where goldsmiths worked, who was to set his mark alongside a maker's mark on articles brought to him, if they were up to standard. A further statute provided for a town mark, and it would appear that the law was followed, at least to some extent, as later pieces bear marks attributed to such places as Aberdeen, Arbroath, Inverness and Perth.

In 1586 the Edinburgh guild was granted special powers of search and seizure throughout Scotland, in addition to its hallmarking duties. The Edinburgh Assay Office was already in operation at that time and has continued ever since. Between 1552 and 1681 its hallmark comprised a maker's mark, the assay office or town mark – a castle – and a deacon's mark consisting of his initials, sometimes in monogram form. An assay master's mark, also in the form of his initials or a single initial, was substituted for the deacon's mark in 1681, and at the same time a date letter was introduced. In 1759 the assay master's mark was discontinued and a mark of a thistle was used instead. This mark continued until 1975 when a new standard mark – a lion rampant – replaced it.

The Glasgow Assay Office was opened in 1819 and closed in 1964. It is odd that, although the sterling standard applied at the Glasgow office from the date of its opening, the lower standard still applied to the rest of Scotland; it was not until

UNITED KINGDOM
Modern Standard Marks

Sterling silver

English Offices

Edinburgh

Britannia silver

All Offices

UNITED KINGDOM
Modern Assay Office Marks

London

Birmingham

Sheffield

Edinburgh

UNITED KINGDOM
Duty Mark

c. 1790

1836 that the standard for the whole of Scotland was brought into line with that of England.

There have been other marks, in addition to those already described, which have been used at different times for special reasons, the best known being the duty mark, struck by the assay offices between 1784 and 1890. This mark, which took the form of the head of the reigning monarch in profile was to signify that the excise duty had been paid. The amount of duty or tax depended on the weight of the article and was collected at the time of hallmarking by the assay offices on behalf of the excise authorities. A mark depicting the head of George I, George II, George III, William IV or Victoria will therefore be found on most silver articles bearing a hallmark within the above years.

A rare hallmark, used only between 1784 and 1785, is the duty drawback mark – a standing figure of Britannia in intaglio (that is recessed – not to be confused with Britannia standard mark). This mark signified that the article was to be exported and that the duty already paid had been refunded.

Since 1904 the assay office marks and standard marks struck on imported silver have been different from those used on British-made articles, although the same date letters have been used. The sponsor's mark on imported wares is usually that registered at the assay office by the importer rather than the mark of the maker.

Three further marks, not strictly hallmarks, were struck on silver articles by the assay offices at a manufacturer's request, to commemorate three royal occasions, the first being the Silver Jubilee of the reign of George V and Queen Mary in 1935, the mark for which was a representation of the two crowned heads. The other occasions were the Coronation of Queen Elizabeth II in 1953 and her Silver Jubilee in 1978, the mark portraying the crowned head of the Queen in both cases.

British silver wares normally bear the full set of hallmarks, but genuine pieces with only a maker's mark are not infrequently encountered, and small articles made in the eighteenth and early nineteenth centuries often have one or more of the marks missing. Articles weighing less than 7.78 grams may not be hallmarked at all, since such articles are exempt from compulsory hallmarking.

Marks sometimes found on antique silver articles have been ascribed to towns with no assay office, such as Taunton or Leeds. They were probably struck by the maker and are therefore not strictly hallmarks, although they are often of considerable interest.

HALLMARKING IN IRELAND

The Dublin Assay Office has origins dating from the early seventeenth century. When Eire became independent in 1921 the Assay Office continued as before, under the control of the Goldsmiths' Company of Dublin which had been incorporated by Royal Charter in 1637; the present system is in fact virtually identical to that in the United Kingdom. The assay office mark is the figure of Hibernia (not to be confused with the figure of Britannia, which is similar in appearance); it was originally struck in 1730 as a duty mark but continued in use after the duty had been abolished. The Irish standard mark for sterling silver is a crowned harp – there is no higher standard of silver in Eire corresponding to the Britannia standard in the United Kingdom. The date letter, first used in 1638, is sometimes missing on old Irish silver articles, making it difficult to ascertain their age, but recent research on the variations of the harp and Hibernia marks has enabled some uncertainties to be resolved.

HALLMARKING IN FRANCE

The French hallmarking system is straightforward in principle – it has always been based on compulsory assay and marking – but the diversity of the symbols used at various times can be confusing. For this reason only the more important marks are mentioned in this short account of its history.

From the late thirteenth century to the Revolution, control of the standard of silver wares was undertaken by the gold and silversmiths' guilds, in towns where they existed. The wardens, elected annually by the guild members, were responsible for the assay and marking, but from an early date they, in turn, were subject to the supervision of the local department of the Mint.

At first there was a single guild mark, then

UNITED KINGDOM
Earlier Assay Office Marks

London
fifteenth century

London
eighteenth century

London
(on Britannia silver only)
before 1975

Sheffield
before 1975

UNITED KINGDOM
Marks of former Assay Offices

Exeter

Chester

Glasgow

Newcastle

IRELAND
(Dublin)

Assay Office Mark

Standard Mark

FRANCE *Eighteenth-century Marks*

Maker's Mark
Paris

Guild Mark
Paris 1724/5

additionally in 1378 each maker was required to have a mark. Later, another mark was introduced, identifying the warden responsible for the assay. Changed annually, it took the form of a letter of the alphabet surmounted by a crown, and is thought to have been first used by the Montpellier guild in 1427 and adopted by the Paris guild in 1461. In the seventeenth and eighteenth centuries it was this mark alone that guaranteed the standard, although a separate town mark was sometimes used as well. The exact details of the warden's mark varied from one town to another, and it sometimes included an additional letter or letters or a device to identify the town concerned.

It is not therefore possible to consider early town marks, standard marks and date letters separately, since two or more of these functions were usually combined in the one warden's mark. For example, between 1784 and 1789 the combined town and standard mark for the Paris guild consisted of the letter P and the last two figures of the year surmounted by a crown. All wardens' marks had to be struck on a copper plate at the office of the local department of the Mint.

Makers' marks originally consisted of a symbol for the town – a fleur-de-lis for Paris, for example – with a device, such as a star or a cross, and a crown. From about 1500 the mark had to include the maker's initials in addition to his device. The marks of Paris silversmiths also included two pellets representing the minus tolerance (2 grains) which was allowed on the standard. The maker's mark was the responsibility of the silversmith himself, but after 1506 it had to be struck on a copper plate at the local department of the Mint, as in the case of wardens' marks. Although some plates have survived, it is mainly from other documentary records that extensive lists of makers' marks have been published.

In 1672 two new marks were introduced in connection with the tax which had first been levied on silver some years previously. The prerogative of tax collection was leased out under contract to '*fermiers*'. A maker had to bring to the *fermier* or his agent every article in an unfinished condition after it had been assayed by the guild, and at this stage the *fermier* applied the '*poinçon de charge*'. The maker then had to bring the article again after it had been finished, and when the tax had been paid the '*poinçon de décharge*' was struck in it. The *fermiers* had their own distinctive marks, and each new holder of the position could either use the punches of his predecessor or have new punches made. In the latter case he would apply a special mark known as a '*poinçon de recense*' to all existing articles bearing his predecessor's mark and still in the hands of their makers. Many of the *fermiers*' marks and *recense* marks are recorded, and they can be very helpful in deciding the date of a piece when the evidence from the other marks is inconclusive.

The standard for Paris was fixed at an early date, at eleven deniers twelve grains. Since twelve deniers were equivalent to pure silver and there were twelve grains to one denier, this was equivalent to 958.33 parts per thousand. The standard was confirmed in 1554, and although in principle it then applied to the whole country, territories which were attached to the French crown after that date maintained their own standards, which were generally lower. The Paris standard continued until 1797.

At the time of the Revolution the guilds lost their powers of control and the *fermiers* were disbanded; in consequence the standard of the silver rapidly deteriorated. It was eventually appreciated that this was having a deleterious effect on the trade, and in 1797 a new hallmarking law was passed which formed the basis of the modern system. Assaying, marking and tax collecting were henceforth to be undertaken by the State, and existing wares were required to be marked with a *recense* mark.

Two standards were authorized: 950 and 800 parts per thousand. The latter is still in force, but the former was replaced by the 925 standard in 1973. There were originally two marks, one for the standard and the other a guarantee mark. The standard mark depicted a cock with a small '1' or '2' in the same shield to denote the higher or lower standard respectively. The guarantee mark for large or medium-sized wares assayed by cupellation portrayed the head of an old man. A different symbol was used on small wares assayed by the touchstone method.

The marks were changed in 1809 and again in 1819. In both cases *recense* marks were struck on existing articles. There was a further change in 1838; from that date only one mark was to be used in place of separate standard and guarantee marks. For articles assayed by cupellation the mark was the head of Minerva with a small '1' or '2' to denote the higher or lower standard respectively; for wares of the 800 standard assayed by touch the mark was a boar's head for Paris and a crab for the provinces. In 1962 the boar's-head mark was replaced by the crab, but otherwise these marks are still in use.

The guarantee mark is struck by means of a steel punch bearing the appropriate symbol, the article being supported on an anvil also made of steel. Since 1838, in order to combat forgery, the

anvils themselves have been engraved with designs in the form of various insects. There is in consequence a further impression on the reverse side of the article.

Since 1797 the maker's mark has always been in the form of initials with a device in a lozenge- (diamond-) shaped shield. In addition to those described, a number of other marks have also been used, such as those specifically authorized for imported articles and antiques.

HALLMARKING IN THE NETHERLANDS

Little is known of the early activities of the gold- and silversmiths' guilds in the Netherlands, which were abolished at the end of the eighteenth century, their records being subsequently destroyed. They were, however, responsible for hallmarking, as were the guilds in Britain and France. The earliest regulation was in 1382, in a decree of the town of Utrecht; two marks were mentioned, a maker's mark and a town mark, the latter struck by the assay master of the guild. There were similar decrees for Middleburg in 1455 and Amsterdam in 1469. An assay master's mark which changed annually, probably in the form of a date letter, is also mentioned in the Amsterdam decree. A more general edict in 1489 in respect of the provinces of Holland and Zeeland stipulated that a town mark had in future to be struck on all silver wares wherever made, and the standard was fixed at 945 parts per thousand. In 1503 a further decree stated that all wares were to be marked with the town's coat of arms and a separate date letter; the same requirement applied to the province of Utrecht after 1507. In these provinces which were the most prolific centres of manufacture, similar regulations continued for three centuries. In other provinces the regulations varied, but they were eventually brought into line.

According to an edict of 1663 in the province of Holland, supervision of local assay masters was subject to the jurisdiction of the Mint. A fourth mark, the lion of Holland, was introduced in the same year and was gradually adopted in other provinces. The standard was fixed at 935 parts per thousand, but a lower quality was allowed for smaller articles. There was much confusion and variation concerning the lower standard until 1733, when it was fixed at 833. The Mint masters continued to supervise the guilds in the province of Holland, and their records provide a useful source of information about the system in the eighteenth century.

In 1798, the old system, whereby control was carried out by the guilds, was officially abolished, and when the country came under the jurisdiction of the French Empire in 1807, new regulations were introduced. Forty-two assay offices centrally controlled by the State were set up. There were two standards – 934 and 833 – and four marks: a maker's mark, a standard mark, an assay office mark and a date letter. A crown was the standard mark for large wares of the higher standard, and for the 833 standard the figure '10'. Small wares were simply marked '1' for the higher standard, '2' for the lower. There was also a different assay office mark for each of the forty-two offices, taken from the town's arms.

In 1811 the country was incorporated into the French Empire, and the French standards of 950 and 800 with the corresponding standard marks (q.v.) were introduced; at the same time the

HOLLAND

Marks used since 1953

925 835

Large Wares

835

Small Wares

Standard Marks

Assay Office Mark

Date Letter

GERMANY

Augsburg
seventeenth century

Augsburg
eighteenth century

Nuremberg
seventeenth century

number of assay offices was reduced to twelve. But after the downfall of Napoleon, the Kingdom of the Netherlands was established, and in 1814 a new hallmarking law came into effect. This preserved much of the French system, but the old standards of 934 and 833 were restored. For large wares there were four marks: a maker's mark; a lion rampant 'to sinister' (that is, facing the observer's right) with the figure '1' in the shield to denote the higher standard or a lion passant 'to sinister' with a figure '2' for the lower standard; an assay office mark – a helmeted head which included a letter to identify the particular office; and an annual date letter. Small articles carried a single symbol different from these marks.

In 1953 the law changed, and the standards were altered to 925 and 835, but the marks remained similar to those already in use. Between 1814 and 1953 additional marks were struck to signify payment of duty, and other marks have been used from time to time for special purposes, for example on antiques and imported wares.

MARKING IN OTHER COUNTRIES

In a number of other European countries, such as Austria-Hungary, Germany, Portugal, Spain and Sweden, control of the standard of silver wares was formerly exercised by the guilds. The marks on early pieces made in these countries can usually be ascribed to a particular town, and many of the makers' marks have also been recorded. For example, between the sixteenth and eighteenth centuries Augsburg and Nuremberg were famous as centres of silversmithing and fortunately, owing to the powerful guilds in these towns, surviving examples of their craft can usually be identified by the guild marks. The same applies to silver from many other centres with a thriving silverware industry – Antwerp, Bruges, Copenhagen, Lisbon, Stockholm, to name but a few. The standards varied considerably; it is strange, for instance, that the standard for Nuremberg silver in the sixteenth century (875 parts per thousand) was relatively low compared with, say, those for Paris and London.

Hallmarking, that is testing and marking independently of the manufacturer, continues to this day in many countries, usually administered by the State. The following have compulsory hallmarking requirements – Austria, Finland, Czechoslovakia, France, Hungary, Ireland, Netherlands, Malta, Poland, Portugal, Spain, Sweden, Switzerland (for watchcases only), the United Kingdom, USSR and Yugoslavia. Voluntary hallmarking systems are operated in Belgium, Denmark and Norway. In Italy the registration of makers' marks is mandatory and standards are laid down by law, but hallmarking is not required.

Outside Europe hallmarking is not widely practised, although several countries have recently introduced it, including Kuwait and Bahrain. Egypt has had a hallmarking system since 1916; South Africa and Japan have voluntary schemes.

There is no hallmarking system in the USA or Canada, but early pieces usually have makers' marks and some also have marks bearing a resemblance to British hallmarks but struck by the maker. The current laws in both countries specify standards for silver articles, namely sterling (925), with an alternative in the United States of 900, known as coin silver, which (apart from its former use in coinage) has never been popular.

Marks resembling British hallmarks but struck by the maker are sometimes found on nineteenth-century articles from South Africa (Cape of Good Hope) and Australia, and also on silver wares made in China for the British and American markets.

INTERNATIONAL HALLMARKS

In 1972 seven European countries were signatories to an International Convention on Hallmarking. Under its terms, an article bearing an assay office mark and a common control mark struck at an authorized assay office in one of the participating countries, and bearing in addition a sponsor's mark and fineness mark, is recognized by any of the other participants as being in full conformity with its own hallmarking requirements. This obviates the necessity for further assaying in an importing country and helps to promote trade in precious metal articles. The marks show that an article has been assayed by a method approved under the provisions of the Convention. There are now eight participating countries – Austria, Finland, Ireland, Norway, Portugal, Sweden, Switzerland and the United Kingdom.

The common control mark depicts a balance with the figure for the standard in parts per thousand. Three standards of silver are recognized

INTERNATIONAL CONVENTION

Common Control Mark

under the Convention – 925, 830 and 800. No country, however, is obliged to accept articles marked lower than its own minimum legal standard. In Britain, for instance, only the 925 standard is acceptable for silver articles.

IDENTIFYING HALLMARKS

It is naturally easier to identify a hallmark if the country of origin is known, but in the absence of such knowledge there are several general reference books which can be consulted. Some of these contain lists of symbols from which it may be possible to deduce the country concerned; recourse can then be made to a more specialized reference work, of which there are many.

In the case of a British hallmark, first to be identified should be the standard mark; next, the assay office responsible for marking; then the year of marking, which can be found from an appropriate list of date letters for that particular office; and finally any additional mark or marks, such as a duty mark, should be elucidated. The maker's or sponsor's mark can also be identified in many cases, again from a specialized reference work. It is seldom possible, however, to establish the identity of London makers working before 1697, as the records of the registrations before then have not survived.

The modern hallmarks of many countries consist of one or two symbols only; a date letter is not generally used nowadays, except in a few countries such as Finland and Holland as well as in Britain. Most official hallmarks show the standard of the silver, and there is usually also a maker's mark. The standard is normally denoted by a distinctive symbol, either alone or in combination with a number, or by figures showing the actual millesimal standard, for example '925', signifying the sterling standard. The symbol used will generally give a clue as to the country of origin of a piece as well as the standard of the silver used.

· METHODS OF ASSAY ·

The earliest procedure for determining the fineness of silver articles was the touchstone method, mentioned in the sixth century BC. While more often referred to in ancient literature in connection with the testing of gold, it was also used for silver. The touchstone method is still used in many parts of the world, although it cannot equal the accuracy of the cupellation or other later chemical methods. In its simplest form the test is carried out by rubbing the article on a touchstone – a hard black natural stone – until a streak of metal is produced, and comparing the colour of this with the colour of a streak made from a touchneedle – a piece of silver of known composition. The more copper present in the alloy the yellower will be the streak.

Another early procedure was the simple heat test. It relies on the fact that copper darkens when heated in air due to the formation of copper oxide, whereas silver in its pure state is unaffected; the more copper there is in a silver/copper alloy the darker will be the colour after heating. If the standard is below 850 parts per thousand it will turn almost black. The method was recognized in Roman times, and in the thirteenth century it was used by the silversmiths' guilds in France, where it was known as 'l'essai á l'échoppe' or 'essai à râclure', being applied to samples that were removed from the articles by means of a graver or scraper.

In the cupellation method, a sample of the material under test is weighed on an accurate balance, then wrapped in lead foil and transferred to a refractory cup, called a cupel, in a high-temperature muffle furnace. Cupels were originally made of bone ash, but in more recent times magnesia has been used. The base metals and the lead are oxidized and absorbed into the cupel, leaving a residue of pure silver which is weighed on an accurate balance, the weight being compared with the weight of the original sample. The principle is identical to that of the old refining technique which has already been described. It is not known exactly when the cupellation method was first used for assaying, but it was certainly known in the fourteenth century and possibly even earlier.

All three methods have been used for hallmarking purposes. In Britain in the fourteenth century the touchstone would probably have been the method adopted for routine testing and the cupellation method used less frequently, but by the fifteenth century the latter method was in daily use at the assay office. At that date either the touchstone method or cupellation, or both, were used in all countries operating a hallmarking system. The cupellation method, although much more accurate than the touchstone procedure, does nevertheless have certain disadvantages, more especially because it is to some extent dependent on the skill of the assayer. By the eighteenth century its shortcomings were realized. In the mid-nineteenth century it was superseded in France and later in other countries by a volumetric (titration) method, in which the sample is dissolved in nitric acid. A standard solution of sodium chloride is added until the equivalence point is reached – the point at which all the silver has been precipitated as silver chloride. The volume added is proportional to the silver content of the sample. This method was devised in 1830 by the celebrated chemist Gay-Lussac on behalf of the French Government. His and another volumetric procedure, known as the Volhard method, are extensively employed in modern assay offices. Although they are far more accurate than the touchstone test, the latter is superior in one respect, namely that it is non-destructive, whereas the former require samples to be removed from the articles under test, usually in the form of scrapings.

· NOTES ·

1 · THE ANCIENT WORLD

1 H. G. G. Payne, *Perachora* I, Oxford, 1940, p. 150.

2 B. Filow, *Die archäische Nekropole von Trebenischte*, Berlin, 1927, pp. 30–31.

3 Artiaco Tomb: *Monumenti Antichi* XIII, 1903, p. 245.

4 Vetulonia: I. Falchi, *Vetulonia e la sua necropoli antichissima*, Florence, 1891, pl. x, 8. Cumae: Artiaco Tomb, *Monumenti Antichi* XIII, 1903, p. 242.

5 L. P. de Cesnola, *Atlas of the Cesnola Collection* III, Boston and New York, 1901, pl. xxxix, 12.

6 Chiusi: Boston, Museum of Fine Arts, *AJA* 22, 1918, pp. 278–9. S. Paolo di Civitate: Taranto, Strong, 1966, p. 103.

7 *Sovetskaya Archeologiya* XIII, 1950, pp. 217–38.

8 E. Gjerstad *et al.*, *Finds and Results of the Excavation in Cyprus, 1927–1931* [Swedish-Cyprus Expedition III]. Stockholm, 1937, pls. XC: 5 and XCII d, p. 238.

9 M. I. Rostovtzeff, *Iranians and Greeks in South Russia*, Oxford, 1922, pl. XII.

10 *Archäologischer Anzeiger* 1913, pp. 184 ff.

11 *Antiquités du Bosphore Cimmérien*, Imperial Archaeological Commission, St Petersburg, 1845, xxxviii.5.

12 Persia: Mazanderan – (a) Kansas City, William Rockhill Nelson Gallery and Atkins Museum of Fine Arts, Nelson Fund, inv. no. 35–37/2, and (b) The Guennol Collection, formerly in the collections of Ernest Herzfeld and Joseph Brummer, New York. S. Russia: Aktanizovskaya Stanitza in the Taman peninsula – *Comptes Rendus de la Commission Impériale Archéologique*, 1900, pp. 105 ff. Euboea: G. Papabasileios, *Περὶ Τῶν ἐν Εὐβοία Ἀρχαίων Τάφων*, Athens, 1910, pl. Ie. Greece or Asia Minor: Washington, D.C., Dumbarton Oaks Collection, inv. no. 40.3. Balkans: Bohot, Bulgaria – *Bull Inst. Bulg.*, XII XIII, 1938–9, p. 445, fig. 238. Syria: Washington, D.C., Dumbarton Oaks Collection – Richter, *Dumbarton Oaks*, nos. 29–30. Italy: Ancona – Museo Nazionale di Ancona; Ornavasso, Cemetery of S. Bernardo – Willers, *Neue Untersuchungen*, p. 16, fig. 11. Spain: Cordova Treasure – British Museum, inv. no. PRB. 1937. 7–6 (2–24); Torre de Juan Abad (Ciudad Real) – Madrid, Museo Arqueológico Nacional, inv. no. 35. 644; Santisteban del Puerto (Jaén) – I: Madrid, Museo Arqueológico Nacional, inv. no. 35. 644; Santisteban del Puerto (Jaén) – I: Madrid, Museo Arqueológico Nacional, inv. nos. 28. 455, 28. 456, 28. 467, 28. 466; II: Jaén, Museo Arqueólogico

13 *Le Musée* III, 1906, pp. 75 ff.

14 68 *Berlin Winckelmannsprogramm*, 1908

15 *Bulletin de Correspondance Hellénique* 55, 1931, p. 490.

16 Hildesheim: Berlin, Staatliche Museen, Antikenabteilung, inv. no. (of one of the pair) 3779.13. Hockwold: British Museum, inv. no. PRB. 1962. 7–7 (1–9).

17 Hoby: Copenhagen, National Museum. Vize: Istanbul, Archaeological Museum inv. nos. 5709–5712. Boscoreale: Paris, Musée du Louvre. Italy: New York, The Pierpont Morgan Library, inv. nos. 1917. 527, 1917. 528.

18 Ingolstadt: Munich, Museum für antike Kleinkunst, inv. no. 3391. Turin Museo de Antichitã. Belgrade: National Museum.

19 Notre-Dame-d'Allençon: Paris, Musée du Louvre, no. 26 and inv. no. Bj 1992. Marwedel: Hannover, Landesmuseum, Abteilung für Urgeschichte, inv. nos. 104.47 and 6.64.

20 Strong, p. 169.

21 Chattuzange: British Museum, *BMCP*, no. 135. Syria: British Museum, *BMCP* no. 73.

22 Worcester Art Museum and Baltimore Museum of Art.

23 Graincourt: Paris, Musée du Louvre. Niederbieber: Bonn, Rheinisches Landesmuseum; nos. 18124, 18125, E 1708. Nicolaevo: *Bulletin de l'Institut Archéologique Bulgare* 4, 1914, pp. 1 ff.

24 Berthouville: Paris, Bibliothèque Nationale, Cabinet des Médailles Notre-Dame-d'Allençon: Paris, Musée du Louvre.

25 Chaourse: British Museum, *BMCP* nos. 170, 171, 172. Graincourt: Paris, Musée du Louvre, inv. no. Bj. 210. Mérouville (Eure et Loir): Lyon, Musée des Beaux-Arts, inv. no. T/M/3.

26 K. Majewski, *Importy Rzymskie w Polsce*, Warsaw, 1960, pl. XIX a.

27 *Rivista di Archeologia Cristiana* XII, 1935, pp. 313 ff.

28 Duke of Northumberland; on loan to the British Museum.

29 Diana Dish: Berlin, Staatliche Museen.

30 Belgrade, National Museum; Vienna, Kunsthistorisches Museum; Geneva, Musée de la Ville.

31 Madrid, Real Academia de la Historia.

32 Water Newton: British Museum, inv. nos. PRB. 10–2. 1–27. Kumluca: Washington, Dumbarton Oaks Collection; Antalya Museum, inv. nos. 1019, 1020, 1021, 1051, 1052, 1053, 1054.

33 Riha: Washington, Dumbarton Oaks Collection, inv. no. 24. 5. Stuma: Istanbul, Archaeological Museum, inv. no. 3759.

34 Phela: Washington, Dumbarton Oaks Collection, inv. no. 55. 17. Hama: Baltimore, The Walters Art Gallery, inv. no. 57. 632.

35 David and Michal: Nicosia, Museum of Antiquities. David trying on Saul's armour: New York Metropolitan Museum of Art, inv. no. 17. 190. 399. Anointing of David: New York, Metropolitan Museum of Art, inv. no. 17. 190. 398. Introduction of David to Saul: New York, Metropolitan Museum of Art, inv. no. 17. 190. 397.

4 · THE BAROQUE

1 J. von Sandrart, *L'academia todesca della architectura, scultura e pittura, oder Deutsche Academie der edlen Bau-Bild-und Mahlerey – Künste II* (Nürnberg, 1675) pp. 341–2.

2 Ibid.

3 Inv. nos. 1877–1898.

4 J. Guiffrey, *Inventaire Générale du mobilier de la Couronne sous Louis XIV* I. (Paris, 1885) p. 43 (1673).

5 *Parentalia: or Memoirs of the Family of Wrens* (London, 1750) p. 262.

6 Quoted by F. Kimball, 'J A Meissonier and the beginning of the *Genre Pittoresque*', *Gazette des Beaux Arts*, 6th series, XXII (Oct. 1942) p. 58.

7 Prints and Drawings Department, Victoria and Albert Museum, London.

8 C. Perrault, *Les Hommes Illustres*, Vol. I (Paris, 1696–1700) p. 99.

9 Quoted by A. Heal, *The London Goldsmiths* (Cambridge, 1935) p. 17.

10 Quoted by A. Franklin, *La Vie Privée d'Autrefois: les Repas* (Paris, 1889) p. 42.

11 Bibliothèque Nationale, Paris, Mel. Colbert, ff. 311r–312r.

12 E.g. Victoria and Albert Museum, London, inv. no. M104–1984.

13 'Kahwa', *Encyclopaedia of Islam*, IV (Leiden, 1978) pp. 453–4.

14 Victoria and Albert Museum, London, inv. no. M398–1921.

15 Maker's mark TL. Victoria and Albert Museum, London, inv. no. M7399–1921.

16 Inv. no. 92–1870.

17 Inv. no. 240–1879.

18 Inv. no. M21–1968.

19 M. Lavin, *Seventeenth Century Barberini Documents and Inventories of Art* (New York, 1975) p. 6.

20 K. Aschengreen Piacenti, 'I Piatti in Argento di San Giovanni', *Die Kunst des Barock in der Toskana* (Munich, 1976) pp. 188–207.

21 *The Twilight of the Medici: Late Baroque Art in Florence 1670–1743* exhibition catalogue (Florence, 1974).

22 *Oro di Venezia* exhibition catalogue, Ca'Vendramin – Calergi (Venice, 1983) pp. 87–94.

23 R. Bossaglia and M. Cinotti, *Tesoro e Museo del Duomo* (Milan, 1978) cat. no. 65.

24 *Barocco Piemontese* exhibition catalogue (Turin, 1963), 'Argenti', cat. no. 176.

25 H. Nocq, *Le Poinçon de Paris* IV (Paris, 1931) p. 111.

26 I. ter Molen, *Van Vianen, een Utrechtse familie van zilversmeden met een internationale faam* (Rotterdam, 1984) p. 38 and pp. 41–2.

27 Inv. no. M261–1984.

28 J. Hayward, *Huguenot Silver in England 1688–1727* (London, 1959) p. 18.

29 Illustrated in C. Hernmark, *The Art of the European Silversmith 1430–1830* (London, 1977), p. 290.

30 Inv. nos. M248–1956 and M470–1956 respectively.

31 M. Rosenberg, *Der Goldschmiede Merkzeichen* II (3rd ed., Frankfurt, 1925).

32 Inv. no. M65–1959.

5 · THE ROCOCO

1 Illustrated in Plate 4 of *Rococo Silver* by Arthur Grimwade.

2 George Vertue, *Notebooks*, The Walpole Society, Vol. XXII, III, p. 105.

3 Public Record Office C.104/58.

4 George Vertue, *Notebooks*, The Walpole Society, Vol. XXII, III, p. 152.

5 Victoria and Albert Museum, 66.Z., Vol. XIX, Account 83.

6 Vol. XIX, Account 246; Vol. XXIV, Account 63.

6 · NEOCLASSICISM

1 Letters of Josiah Wedgwood, ed. Lady Katherine Farrer, Vol. 1, p. 235.

2 As pointed out by Mr. Charles Truman of the Victoria and Albert Museum.

3 *The Letters and Journals of Lady Mary Coke*, Vol. III, p. 452.

7 · THE NINETEENTH AND EARLY TWENTIETH CENTURIES

1 Martin, II, pp. 247–8.

2 Barnard Ledger, Nov. 1850–March 1853, pp. 95–137; London 1851 exh., *Illustrated London News*, 7 June 1851, p. 531; *AJIC*, p. 137.

3 Bury, Wedgwood and Snodin, 'The antiquarian plate of George IV', *Burlington* magazine, CXX1, 1979, pp. 343–53; Snodin and Baker, 'William Beckford's Silver, 1 and 2', id., CXX11, 1980, pp. 735–748, 820–834. *Illustrated London News*, 31, 1857, p. 128 (*ill.*).

4 Bury, *Victorian Electroplate*, 1971.

5 London 1851 exh., reports, single-vol. edition, Cl. XXX, R. Redgrave, 'Supplementary Report on Design', pp. 708–49; id., Class 23, pp. 513, 516.

6 *Report from the Select Committee on Gold and Silver*, London, 31 July 1878, paras 40, 42, 213–16, 281–90.

7 Paris 1900 exh., rapport, Cl. 94, p. 316.

8 London 1851 exh., cat., II, Cl. 23, Marshall & Sons, no. 23; F. H. Thompson, no. 25.

9 See Sotheby's Belgravia, English and Foreign Silver (etc.), 13 Dec. 1979, lot 507; id., 19 Feb. 1981, lot 515.

10 Irish Silver from the seventeenth to the nineteenth century, Smithsonian Institution Traveling Exhibition Service, 1982, cat. nos. 58, 66.

11 Dublin 1865 exh., cat., Section 23, no. 654.

12 London 1851 exh.; D'Albert, duc de Luynes, *Travaux de la Commission Française*, VI, pp. 58–9; 63.

13 The Second Empire, 1852–1870, Philadelphia Museum of Art, 1978, cat. no. III–33; London 1851 exh., *Reports*, Cl. 23, p. 512.
14 H. Bouilhet, II, pp. 232–6, 251–60, 274.
15 H. Bouilhet, II, pp. 241–2; T. Bouilhet, pp. 8, 9; passim.
16 Collection Connaissance des Arts, *Les grands Orfèvres*, p. 310; Paris 1900 exh., *Rapports*, Cl. 94, pp. 222–6, 241–5; cited in Paris 1889 exh., *Rapports*, Cl. 24, 1891, p. 449; see also Sotheby's Belgravia, *19th and 20th century Silver* [etc.], 29 Sep. 1977, lot 229.
17 H. Bouilhet, II, p. 286, III, pp. xxi; 54–5; Paris 1867 exh., *Rapports*, 1868, Cl. 21, p. 278; 1867 *AJIC*, pp. 154, 169, 238 and (a dissentient view) 255.
18 Paris 1889 exh., *Rapports*, Cl. 24, pp. 464, 472, 478, 481.
19 Schmutzler, pp. 8–11. Paris 1889 exh., *Rapports*, Cl. 24, pp. 477, 513.
20 Paris 1900 exh., *Rapports*, Cl. 94, pp. 228, 271.
21 Barten, no. 1694; T. Bouilhet, pp. 196, 206–7.
22 Paris 1900 exh., *Rapports*, Cl. 94, pp. 221, 255–8, 246–54, 259–61, 268; *AJIC*, p. 234; Turin 1902 exh., Pica, p. 125. The dish is in the collections of the Victoria and Albert Museum.
23 Sotheby's Belgravia, English and Foreign Silver, 19 June 1975, 98; J. G. Meyer tea service for Bennewitz.
24 Information kindly communicated by Mr Karel Citroen.
25 Mensen en Zilver (exh.), Boymans Museum, Rotterdam; De Zonnehof, Ammersfoort, 1975–6.
26 Paris 1867 exh., *Rapports*, Cl. 21, p. 267; Vienna 1873, Lyons workmen's reports, p. 46.
27 Paris 1900 exh., *Rapports*, Cl. 94, pp. 327, 8. Turin 1902 exh., Pica, p. 267; Mensen en Zilver, 1975–6, cat. pl. 128.
28 Citroen, *Valse Zilvermerken in Nederland*; Vanwittenbergh, no. 273 and vase in the Musée Communal, Brussels; no. 277.
29 Sotheby's Belgravia, English, Russian and Foreign Silver, 22 Ap. 1976, lot 129.
30 London 1862 exh., cat. III, Belgium, Cl. 23, p. 33, no. 837; Paris 1867 exh., *Rapports*, III, Cl. 21, p. 267. Paris 1878 exh., Belgian reports, 1879, III, Cl.24, p. 211.
31 Wolfers, pp. 8–18.
32 Christie's New York. Important English, Continental and American Silver, 4, 5 Feb. 1981, 196.
33 Scheffler, *Berliner Goldschmiede*, pl. 108.
34 London 1851 exh., De Luynes, p. 79.
35 Scheffler, p. 435.
36 London 1851 exh., *AJIC*, p. 327; *Reports*, Cl. 23, p. 514; *Illustrated London News*, 9 August 1851, p. 188 (*ill.*).
37 London 1862 exh., *AJIC*, pp. 154, 220; Vogel, 1867, p. 682.
38 London 1862 exh., cat. III, Koch & Bergfeld.
39 Paris 1867 exh., *Rapports*, III, Cl. 21, pp.267–8; Vienna 1873 exh., Lyons workmen's reports, p. 17, Parisian workmen's reports, p. 47; Grandjean, pl. XXIX(1).
40 Philadelphia Centennial Exh., 1876, *Industrial Art*, pp. 99, 400.
41 Hughes, pp. 22–3; Paris 1900 exh., *Rapports*, Cl. 91, p. 352.
42 Orfèvrerie fantastique (exh.), 1977, Berlin; Aachen, no. 1, Cologne no. 49, Munich no. 89 (ill); Paris 1900 exh., *Rapports*, cl. 94, pp. 298–302.
43 Henry Van de Velde (exh.), 1964, cat. no. 93.
44 Pevsner, *Sources of Modern Architecture and Design*, pl. 171.
45 See f.n. 42, Cologne, no. 55.
46 Turin 1902 exh., Pica, p. 321.
47 Vienna in the Age of Schubert (exh.), 1979; cat. pl. 27, 28.
48 Toranová, nos. 179, 167.
49 London 1862 exh. cat., III, Cl. 33, p. 105; Vienna 1873 exh., Lyons workmen's reports, p. 12.
50 Paris 1900 exh., *Rapports*, Cl. 94, Orfèvrerie, p. 318.
51 Adjectives of History (exh.), 1979, no. 38; Vienna 1873 exh., Parisian workmen's reports, p. 20.
52 Paris 1900 exh., *AJIC*, 1900, p. 152; *Rapports*, Cl. 94, pp. 303, 306–7, 318–19; Turin 1902 exh., Pica, pp. 170, 171.
53 Vergo, pp. 132, 33.
54 London 1851 exh., de Luynes, *Rapports*, Cl. 23, p. 101.
55 Paris 1889 exh., cat., Sections Suisse, p. 24, Cl. 24, no. 49; *Rapports*, Cl. 24, pp. 560, 1; Paris 1900 exh., *Rapports*, Cl. 94, p. 334.
56 The Cupid lamp is in the Victoria and Albert Museum (436–1865) Designs for similar lamps are to be found in the V and A Print Room; for a Maltese example by G. Lebrun, see Sotheby's London, Silver from Europe (etc.), 11 Feb. 1985, lot 53.
57 Catello, pl. LXXI.
58 London 1862 exh., Kingdom of Italy cat., Cl. 23, p. 353; an electrotyped crucifix was shown by Giuseppe Masini, Naples.
59 Catello, p. 370; Bossaglia/Cinotti, pl. 428–40.
60 Sotheby's Geneva, European Silver, 14 Nov. 1984, lot 71; Bouilhet, III, p. 93; Paris 1867 exh., *Rapports*, III, Cl. 21, p. 270; Culme, p. 178; Sotheby's New York, Victorian International, 17 June 1983, lot 257; Vienna 1873 exh., Parisian workmen's reports, p. 49.
61 London 1862 exh., Kingdom of Italy, cat., Cl. 33, p. 353; Vienna 1873 exh., Parisian workmen's reports, p. 49; Melbourne 1888–9 exh., *Official Record*, p. 473, Cl. 21, no. 24.
62 Paris 1900 exh., *Rapports*, Cl. 94, pp. 319–21. Garner, *Carlo Bugatti*, pp. 13–30.
63 Garner, op.cit., pp. 26–28.
64 A. M. Johnson, 'The Royal Factory for Silversmiths, Madrid', *Notes Hispanic*, 1942, pp. 15–24; Christie's London, Important Silver (etc), 27 March 1985, lot 70.
65 London 1851 exh., De Luynes, p. 99; cat., III, p. 1345, pl. 203; *Reports*, Cl. 23, p. 515.
66 London 1862 exh., cat., III, Spain, Cl. 33, p. 65; Vienna 1873 exh., Lyons workmen's reports, p. 9; Paris 1900 exh., *Rapports*, Cl. 94, p. 309; *Poment*, 1920, pl. 98, 101.
67 Sotheby's Belgravia, Foreign Silver (etc), 13 July 1978, lot 209; Sotheby's London, Silhouettes . . . and European Silver, 4 July 1983, lot 288.
68 J. Rosas & C^{a}., fig 6; Paris 1900 exh., *Rapports*, Cl. 94, p. 329.
69 London 1851 exh., de Luynes, p. 84; Denaro, p. 95; Sotheby's Belgravia, English and Foreign Silver (etc.), 7 July 1977, 115.
70 For instance, at Melbourne in 1888–9; *Official Record*, p. 483; London Colonial and Indian exh., 1886, cat., p. 462, Malta.
71 Andrén, pl. 69 and 64; Penzer, pl. XLII.
72 Hedstrand, pl. 27 and 28; 29, 33 and drawings from Christian Hammer's studio, pl. 56, and *Connoisseur Period Guides, Early Victorian Silver*, pl. 52.
73 Hedstrand, pl. 59; London 1851 exh., *AJIC*, pl. 163.
74 Hedstrand, pl. 72; pp. 98, 99; pl. 118; pl. 66; p. 157.
75 Paris 1900 exh., *Rapports*, Cl. 94, pp. 332–3.
76 Polak, *Norwegian Silver*, p. 76; Bradbury, p. 57; Polak, op. cit., p. 96.
77 London 1862 exh., cat., III, cl. 33, p. 126. Paris 1867 exh., *Rapports*, III, cl. 21, p. 269; Philadelphia 1876 exh., Industrial Art, p. 317.
78 Polak, *Gullsmedkunsten i Norge*, pp. 90–91; Paris 1900 exh., *Rapports*, Cl. 94, pp. 326–7.
79 Riisøen and Bøe, fig. 25; Polak, *Gullsmedkunsten i Norge*, frontispiece.
80 Lassen, pl. 212, 216; Bradbury, p. 210; Lassen, pl. 219, 220.
81 London 1862 exh., *AJIC*, p. 152; cat., IV, Cl. 33, Denmark, p. 58; Paris 1867 exh., *AJIC*, p. 27; Philadelphia 1876 exh., *Industrial Art*, pp. 87, 435.
82 Paris 1900 exh., *Rapports*, Cl. 94, p. 307; see also Sotheby's Belgravia, English and Foreign Silver (etc.), 1 May 1975, lot 42.
83 *Mobilia*, Copenhagen, no. 131/132, June/July 1966.
84 Hiesinger, no. 63–186–2a, b, c.
85 von Solodkoff, p. 86.
86 London 1851 exh., *Illustrated London News*, 19, 23 August 1851, frontispiece and p. 252; *Reports*, p. 515; de Luynes, pp. 97–8; *AJIC*, pp. 266–7.
87 von Solodkoff, pp. 194, 201.
88 Vienna 1873 exh., Parisian workmen's reports, p. 42; de Luynes, p. 63.
89 Snowman, p. 154.
90 Paris 1900 exh., *Rapports*, Cl. 94, pp. 330–31.
91 Metropolitan Museum of Art, New York, 1970 centenary exh. cat., *19th century America*, no. 31; cf. a cylindrical wine cooler in Sheffield plate, c. 1810, Bradbury, p. 384.
92 A tureen (one of a pair) in the St Louis Art Museum; Fennimore, *Antiques Magazine*, 102, 1972, pp. 642–9. A collection of Fletcher's designs and working drawings is in the Metropolitan Museum, New York.
93 Moses, pl. 37; Gandy Fales, pp. 116–7.
94 Louisa Bartlett, 'American Silver', *St Louis Art Museum 1984 Winter Bulletin*, pp. 37–8.
95 *Connoisseur Period Guides: Early Victorian Silver*, pl. 57A.
96 Metropolitan Museum centenary exh., no. 141.
97 Ashbee, typescript Memoirs, III, p. 282.
98 Paris 1900 exh., *Rapports*, Cl. 94, pp. 311–2; Turin 1902 exh., Pica p. 69.
99 Paris 1967 exh., *Rapports*, III, Cl. 21, p. 271.
100 Bury, 'The Silver Designs of Dr Christopher Dresser', *Apollo*, December 1962; Carpenter, *Tiffany Silver*, pl. 1; Paris 1878 exh., E. Bergerat (ed.), *Chefs-d'Oeuvre d'Art*, I, 1878, pp. 122, 123 (ill.).
101 Paris 1889 exh., *Rapports*, Cl. 24, p. 538; Metropolitan Museum centenary exh. 1970, no. 258.
102 Metropolitan Museum Centenary exh., no. 281; Paris 1900 exh., *AJIC*, pp. 93–4.
103 Paris 1889 exh., *Rapports*, Cl. 24, pp. 542–3.
104 Anderson, p. 237; Boyland, figs. 15, 19A.
105 Ribera and Schenone, *Plateria Sudamericana* (exh.), 1981, no. 320, etc.; Boylan, figs. 17, 33B.
106 Paris 1889 exh., *Rapports*, Cl. 24, p. 530.

8 · ART DECO AND AFTER: 1920–60

1 Hughes, G., *Modern Silver* (London, 1967) p. 73.
2 Letter published in *Jean Puiforcat, Orfèvre Sculpteur* (Flammarion, Paris, 1951).
3 Cited in Jensen special issue catalogue, *Mobilia*.

· BIBLIOGRAPHY ·

1 · THE ANCIENT WORLD

For publications before 1966 see Strong, 1966. The following bibliography lists books, but not articles, published since that date.

Bank, A., *Byzantine Art in the Collections of Soviet Museums*, Leningrad, 1977.
Baratte, F., *Le Trésor d'Argenterie Gallo-Romaine de Notre Dame d'Alençon*, Paris, 1981.
Baratte, F., *Römisches Silbergeschirr in den gallischen und germanischen Provinzen*, Aalen, 1984.
Baratte, F., *Le Trésor d'Orfèvrerie romaine de Boscoreale*, Paris 1986.
Bruce-Mitford, R.L.S., *The Sutton Hoo Ship-Burial III*, London, 1983.
Cahn, H. A. and Kaufmann-Heinimann, A. (eds.), *Der spätrömische Silberschatz von Kaiseraugst*, Basel, 1984.
Cristofani, M. and Martelli, M. (eds.), *L'Oro degli Etruschi*, Novara, 1983.
Dodd, E. C., *Byzantine Silver Treasures*, Bern, 1973.
Effenberger, A. (ed.), *Spätantike Silbergefässe aus der Staatlichen Ermitage, Leningrad*, Berlin, 1978.
Gehrig, U., *Hildesheimer Silberfund*, Berlin, 1967.
Hill, D.K., *Greek and Roman Metalware*, Baltimore, 1976.
Kent, J. P. C. and Painter, K. S. (eds.), *Wealth of the Roman World, AD 300–700*, London, 1977.
Musso, L., *Manifattura Suntuaria e Committenza Pagana nella Roma del IV Secolo: Indagine sulla Lanx di Parabiago*, Rome, 1983.
Ninou, K. (ed.), *Treasures of Ancient Macedonia*, Athens, 1978.
Oliver, A. Jr., *Silver for the Gods: 800 Years of Greek and Roman Silver*, Toledo (Ohio), 1977.
Overbeck, B., *Argentum Romanum: ein Schatzfund von spätrömischen Prunkgeschirr*, Munich, 1973.
Painter, K.S., *The Mildenhall Treasure*, London, 1977.
Painter, K. S., *The Water Newton Early Christian Silver*, London, 1977.
Shelton, K. J., *The Esquiline Treasure*, London, 1981.
Strong, D. E., *Greek and Roman Gold and Silver Plate*, London, 1966.
Venedikov, I., *Thracian Treasures from Bulgaria*, London, 1976.
Weitzmann, K. (ed.), *Age of Spirituality: Late Antique and Early Christian Art, Third to Seventh Century*, New York, 1979.

2 · THE MIGRATION PERIOD AND THE MIDDLE AGES

Braun, Joseph, *Die reliquiare des christlichen Kultes und ihre Entwicklung*, Freiburg im Breisgau, 1940 (reprinted 1971).
Collon-Gevaert, Suzanne, *Histoire des arts du métal en Belgique*, Brussels, 1951.
Fritz, Johann Michael, *Goldschmiedekunst der Gotik in Mitteleuropa*, Munich, 1982.
Gauthier, Marie-Madeleine, *Emaux du moyen-âge occidental*, Fribourg, 1972.
Lasko, Peter, *Ars Sacra 800–1200*, Penguin Books (Pelican History of Art), 1972.
Lightbown, R. W., *Secular goldsmith's work in mediaeval France: a history* (Society of Antiquaries Research Report), London, 1978.

3 · THE RENAISSANCE AND MANNERISM

Clayton, Michael, *Christie's Pictorial History of English and American Silver*, London, 1985.
Clayton, Michael, *The Collector's Dictionary of the Silver and Gold of Great Britain and North America*, 2nd ed., London, 1985.
Collins, A. J., *Jewels and Plate of Queen Elizabeth I, The Inventory of 1574*, London, 1955.
Oman, Charles, *English Engraved Silver 1150–1900*, London, 1978.
Hackenbroch, Yvonne, *Renaissance Jewellery*, London, 1979.
Hayward, J. F., *Virtuoso Goldsmiths and the Triumph of Mannerism 1540–1620*, London, 1976.
Hernmarck, C., *The Art of the European Silversmith 1430–1830*, 2 vols., London and New York, 1977.
Leithe-Jasper, Manfred and Distelberger, Rudolf, *The Kunsthistorisches Museum Vienna, The Treasury and the Collection of Sculpture and Decorative Arts*, London, 1982.
Lightbown, R. W., *Tudor Domestic Silver*, London, 1970.
Mabille, Gérard, *Orfèvrerie Française des XVIe, XVIIe, XVIIIe Siècles*, Paris, 1984.
Oman, Charles *The English Silver in the Kremlin 1557–1663*, London, 1961.
Pechstein, Klaus, *Goldschmiedewerke der Renaissance*, Berlin, 1971.
Seling, Helmut, *Die Kunst der Augsburger Goldschmiede 1529–1868*, 3 vols., Munich, 1980.
Wenzel Jamnitzer und die Nurnberger Goldschmiedekunst 1500–1700 (exhibition catalogue), Nuremberg, 1985.

4 · BAROQUE SILVER, 1610–1725

Baudouin, P., 'Antwerp Silver in the early seventeenth century', *The Connoisseur*, April 1977, pp. 248–260.
Bulgari, C. G., *Argentieri, gemmari e orafi d'Italia*, Rome, 1958–74.
Catello, E. and C., *Argenti Napoletani*, Naples, 1973.
Dutch Silver 1580–1830 (exhibition catalogue), Rijksmuseum, Amsterdam, 1979.
Fales, M. C., *Early American Silver*, New York, 1973.
Fernandez, A., Munoa, R. and Rabasco, J., *Enciclopedia de la Plata Española y Virreinal Americana*, Madrid, 1984.
Frederiks, J. W., *Dutch Silver*, The Hague, 1952–61.
Gruber, A., *Silverware*, Fribourg, 1982.
Hayward, J. F., *Huguenot Silver in England 1688–1727*, London, 1959.
Hernmarck, C., *The Art of the European Silversmith 1430–1830*, 2 vols., London and New York, 1977.
Hood, G., *American Silver, a History of Style 1650–1900*, New York, Washington, London, 1971.
Nocq, H., *Le poinçon de Paris: répertoire des maîtres – orfèvres de la juridiction de Paris depuis le Moyen Age jusqu'à la fin du XVIIIe siècle*, Paris, 1926–31.
Oman, C., *Caroline Silver 1625–1688*, London, 1970.
Schliemann, E., *et al*, *Die Goldschmiede Hamburgs*, Hamburg, 1985.
Seling, H., *Die Kunst der Augsburger Goldschmiede 1529–1868*, Munich, 1980.
Solodkoff, A. von, *Russian Gold and Silver*, London, 1981.

5 & 6 · THE ROCOCO AND NEOCLASSICISM

Arts Council of Great Britain, *The Age of Neo-Classicism* (exhibition catalogue), London, 1972.
Bapst, Germain, *Etudes sur l'Orfèvrerie Française au XVIIIe siècle – Les Germains*, Paris, 1887.
Barr, Elaine, *George Wickes: Royal Goldsmith 1698–1761*, London, 1980.
Bennet, Douglas, *Irish Georgian Silver*, London, 1972.
Bouilhet, Henri, *L'Orfèvrerie Française aux XVIIIe et XIXe siècles*, Paris, 1908 and 1912.
Bulgari, Constantino G., *Argentieri, Gemmari e Orafi d'Italia*, Rome, 1958–69.
Clayton, Michael, *The Collector's Dictionary of the Silver and Gold of Great Britain and North America*, London, 1971.
Clifford, Timothy, *Some English Ceramic Vases and their Sources* (paper read at the Geological Museum, London, 18 December 1976).
Connaisance des Arts, *Les Grands Orfèvres de Louis XIII à Charles X*, Paris, 1965.
Dennis, Faith, *Three Centuries of French Domestic Silver*, New York, 1960.
Eriksen, S., *Early Neo-Classicism in France*, London, 1974.
Finlay, Ian, *Scottish Gold and Silver Work*, London, 1956.
Gans, M. H. and Duyvené de Wit-Klinkhamer, Th. M., *Dutch Silver*, London, 1961.
Grimwade, A. G., *The London Goldsmiths 1697–1837*, London, 1976 (rev. ed. 1982).
Grimwade, A. G., *Rococo Silver*, London, 1974.
Hayward, Helena, *English Rococo Designs for Silver* (proceedings of the Society of Silver Collectors, London, 1969–70).
Heal, Sir Ambrose, *The London Goldsmiths 1200–1800*, Cambridge, 1935.
Hernmarck, C., *The Art of the European Silversmith 1430–1830*, 2 vols., London and New York, 1977.
Lassen, Erik, *Dansk Sølv*, Copenhagen, 1964.
Munthe, Gustaf, *Christian Precht*, Stockholm, 1957.
Murdoch, Tessa, *Roubiliac and his Huguenot Connections* (proceedings of the Huguenot Society, 24, 1983).
Phillips, John Marshall, *American Silver*, London, 1949.
Roland Michel, Marianne, *L'Ornement rocaille: quelques questions* (Revue de l'Art 55, Paris, 1982).
Rowe, Robert, *Adam Silver*, London, 1965.
Snodin, Michael, *English Silver Spoons*, London, 1974.
Solodkoff, Alexander von, *Russian Gold and Silver*, London, 1981.
Taylor, Gerald, *Silver*, London, 1956.
Trudel, Jean, *Silver in New France*, Ottawa, 1974.
Victoria and Albert Museum, London, *Rococo: Art and Design in Hogarth's England*, London, 1984.
Ward-Jackson, Peter, *Some Main Streams and Tributaries in European Ornament from 1500 to 1750* (Victoria and Albert Museum Bulletin Reprints, 3, 1969).

Auction catalogues:
Christie, Manson and Woods
Sotheby's
Phillips, Son and Neale

7 · THE NINETEENTH AND EARLY TWENTIETH CENTURIES

Accascina, Maria, *I Marchi della Argenterie e Oreficerie Siciliane*, Trapani, 1976.
Alcolea, Santiago, *Orfebrería civil Hispánica, IV (Siglos XIX y XX)*, 1970.
Anderson, Lawrence, *The Art of the Silversmith in Mexico 1519–1936*, 2 vols., New York, 1941.
Andrén, Erik, *Swedish Silver*, New York, 1950.
Bardi, P. M., *Arte da Prata no Brasil*, Banco Sudaméris Brasil S.A., 1979.
Barten, Sigrid, *René Lalique, Schmuck und Objets d'Art, 1890–1910*, Munich, 1975.
Bartlett, Louisa, 'American Silver', *The Saint Louis Art Museum Winter Bulletin*, 1984.
Bennett, Douglas, *Collecting Irish Silver 1637–1900*, London, 1984.
Bennett, Douglas, *Irish Georgian Silver*, London, 1972.
Bøe, Alf, 'Gustav Gaudernack – tegninger og utførte arbeider', *Årbok 1959–62*, Kunstindustrimuseum, Oslo, 1962.
Bossaglia, Rossana, and Cinotti, Mia, *Tesoro e Museo de Duomo*, I, Milan, 1978.
Bott, Gerhard, *Kunsthandwerk um 1900. Kataloge des Hessischen Landesmuseums* No. 1, Darmstadt, 1965.

Bouilhet, Henri, *L'Orfèvrerie française aux XVIIIe et XIXe siècles*, 3 vols., Paris, 1908–12.
Bouilhet, T., *150 Ans d'Orfèvrerie*, Paris, 1981.
Boylan, Leona Davis, *Spanish Colonial Silver*, Museum of New Mexico Press, 1974.
Bradbury, Frederick, *History of Old Sheffield Plate*, London, 1912 (reprinted Sheffield, 1968).
Budapest, Museum Nationale Hungaricum, Kolba, Judit H. and Németh, Annamária T., *Goldsmith's Work*, Hungarian National Commission for Unesco, Corvina, 1973.
Bulgari, Constantino G., *Argentieri, Gemmari e Orafi d'Italia, Parte Terza, Marche – Romagna*, Rome, 1969.
Bury, S., 'The Silver Designs of Dr Christopher Dresser', *Apollo*, LXXVI, 1962, pp. 766–770.
Bury, S., *Victorian Electroplate*, London, 1971.
Carpenter, Charles H., Jr. with Carpenter, Mary Grace, *Tiffany Silver*, London, 1979 (1st ed. USA, 1978).
Carpenter, Charles, Jr., *Gorham Silver 1831–1981*, New York, 1982.
Catello, Elio e Corrado, *Argenti Napoletani dal XVI al XIX Secolo*, Naples, 1973.
Citroen, Karel, *Valse Zilvermerken in Nederland*, Amsterdam, 1977.
Collection Connaissance des Arts – 'Grands Artisans d'Autrefois', *Les Grands Orfèvres de Louis XIII à Charles X*, préface de Jacques Helft, Paris, 1965 (conçu et realisé par Claude Fregnac).
Connoisseur Period Guides, *Early Victorian Silver*. London, 1958.
Crawford, Alan, *C. R. Ashbee*, New Haven and London, 1985.
Crook, J. Mordaunt, *William Burges and the High Victorian Dream*, London, 1981.
Culme, John, *Nineteenth-century Silver*, London, 1977.
Darling, Sharon S. in association with Casterline, Gail Farr, *Chicago Metalsmiths*, Chicago, 1977.
Denaro, Victor F., *The Goldsmiths of Malta and their Marks*, 1972.
Fales, Martha Gandy, *Early American Silver* (paperback edition), New York, 1973.
Fornari, Salvatore, *Gli Argenti Romani*, Rome, 1968.
Gans, M.H. and Duyvene de Wit-Klinkhamer, Th.M., *Dutch Silver*, translated by Oliver van Oss, London, 1961.
Garner, Philippe, 'Carlo Bugatti 1856–1940', in *The Amazing Bugattis*, The Design Council, 1979 (published to coincide with the RCA exhibition, The Amazing Bugattis).
Grandjean, Serge, *L'Orfèvrerie du XIXe siècle en Europe*, Paris, 1962.
Gruber, Alain, *Silverware*, New York, 1982.
Hammacher, A. M., *Le Monde de Henry van de Velde*, Antwerp/Paris, 1967.
Hawkins, J. B. [and others], *Australian Silver 1800–1900*, National Trust of Australia (NSW), Sydney, 1973.
Hedstrand, Björn, *Silvervaror i Sverige 1830–1915*, Stockholm, 1975.
Hessling, Egon, *Dessins d'orfèvrerie de Percier, conservés à la Bibliothèque de l'Union Centrale des Arts décoratifs*, Paris, 1911.
Hiesinger, Kathryn B., *Styles 1850–1900*, Philadelphia Museum of Art, Philadelphia, 1983. One of: Guides to European decorative arts, no. 2.
Hope, Thomas, *Household Furniture and Interior Decoration*, London, 1807.
Howarth, Thomas, *Charles Rennie Mackintosh and the Modern Movement*, London, 1952, 2nd ed., 1977.
Hughes, Graham, *Modern Silver throughout the World, 1880–1967*, London, 1967.
Johnson, Ada Marshall, 'The Royal Factory for Silversmiths, Madrid', *Hispanic Society of America, Notes Hispanic*, New York, 1942, pp. 15–23.
Klapthor, Margaret Brown, *Presentation Pieces in the Museum of History and Technology, Contributions from the Museum of History and Technology: Paper 47*, Smithsonian Institute, Washington, D.C., 1965.
Kommer, Björn R. and Kommer, Marina, *Lübecker Silber, 1781–1871*, Lübeck, 1978 (Veröffentlichungen zur Geschichte der Hansestadt Lübeck).
Krohn-Hansen, Thv., *Trondhjems Gullsmedkunst 1550–1850*, Oslo/Bergen, 1963.
Langdon, John Emerson, *Canadian Silversmiths and their Marks 1667–1867*, Lunenburg, Vermont, 1960.
Lassen, Erik, *Dansk Sølv*, Copenhagen, 1964.
Leeuwarden, Fries Museum, *Fries Zilver*, Leeuwarden, 1968.
Leighton, Margaretha Gebelein with Swain, Esther Gebelein and Gebelein, J. Herbert, *George Christian Gebelein, Boston Silversmith, 1878–1945*, Boston, 1978.
Lie, Inger-Marie Kvaal and Opstad, Lauritz, (eds.), *Kunstindustrimeet i Oslo/En Kavalkade av aktuell kunstindustri gjennom hundri år i 1876*, Oslo, 1976.
Lightbown, R. W., *Scandinavian and Baltic Silver* (Victoria and Albert Museum Catalogue), London, 1975.
Madsen, Stephen Tschudi, *Sources of Art Nouveau*, 1st ed., Oslo, 1956. Reprinted (A Da Capo paperback), 1976.
Martin, Theodore, *The Life of His Royal Highness The Prince Consort*, 5 vols. 2nd ed., London, 1875–80.
Moses, Henry, *A Collection of Antique Vases, Altars, Paterae, Tripods, Candelabra, Sarcophagi, etc.*, London, 1814.
Neuwirth, Waltraud, *Josef Hoffman, Bestecke für die Wiener Werkstätte* (catalogue of exhibition at Osterreichischen Museum für angewandte Kunst), Vienna, 1982.
Neuwirth, Waltraud, *Lexikon Wiener Gold- und Silberschmiede und Ihre Punzen, 1867–1922*, 2 vols., Vienna, 1976.
Oman, Charles, *English Silversmiths' Work Civil and Domestic*, London, 1965.
Paris, Musée du Louvre, P. Verlet, ed. *Catalogue de l'orfèvrerie du XVIIe, du XVIIIe et du XIXe siècle*, Paris, 1958.
Penzer, N. M., *Paul Storr, 1771–1844, Silversmith and Goldsmith*, London, 1954. New ed., 1971.
Percier et Fontaine, *Receuil de décorations intérieures*, Paris, 1812.
Pevsner, Nikolaus, *The Sources of Modern Architecture and Design*, London, 1968.
Piranesi, Giovanni Batista, *Vasi, Candelabri, Cippi, Sarcofagi*, Rome, 1778.
Polak, Ada, *Gullsmedkunsten i Norge før og nå*, Oslo, 1970.
Polak, Ada, *Norwegian Silver*, Oslo, 1972.
Polak, Ada, *Henrik Bertram Møller 1858–1937, Gullsmedkunst og treskurd*, Oslo, 1979.
Poussielgue-Rusand, P., *Album de modèles dessinés par le P. Arthur Martin*, Paris, 1853.
Powell, Nicholas, *The Sacred Spring, the Arts in Vienna 1898–1918*, London, 1974.
Pugin, A. W. N., *Designs for Gold and Silversmiths*, London, 1836.
Pugin, A. W. N., *The Present State of Ecclesiastical Architecture*, London, 1843.
Rainwater, Dorothy T., *Encyclopedia of American Silver Manufacturers*, New York, 1975.
Riisøen, Thale and Bøe, Alf, *Om Filigran, Teknikk, Historikk, Filigran/Filigree, its Technique and History; Filigree in Norwegian ownership* (Kunstindustrimuseum, exhibition catalogue), Oslo, 1969.
Rosas, José & Cª., *Ourives Joalheiros, Porto, 1851–1951*, Porto, 1951.
Santos, Reynaldo dos and Quilhó, Irene, *Ouriverea Portuguesa nas Colecções Particulares*, 2 vols., Lisbon, 1959.
Scheffler, Wolfgang, *Goldschmiede Niedersachsens*, 2 vols., Berlin, 1965.
Scheffler, Wolfgang, *Berliner Goldschmiede, Daten, Werke, Zeichen*, Berlin, 1968.
Schmutzler, Robert, *Art Nouveau*, London, 1964.
Schümann, Carl-Wolfgang, *Clipeus virtutis, oder der Glaubensschild*, Sonderdruck aus der Festschrift Kauffmann/Munuscula Discipulorum, Berlin, 1968.
Schweiger, Werner J., *Wiener Werkstätte: Design in Vienna 1903–1932*, London, 1984.
Select Committee on Arts and Manufactures, *Report* and proceedings, London, 1836.
Select Committee on Gold and Silver (Hallmarking), *Report* (and proceedings), London, 1878.
Snodin, M. 'J. J. Boileau, a forgotten designer of silver', *Connoisseur*, 18, pp. 125–133.
Snodin, M. and Baker, M., 'William Beckford's Silver', 1 and 2, *Burlington* magazine, Nov., Dec. 1980.
Snowman, A. Kenneth, *Carl Fabergé, Goldsmith to the Imperial Court of Russia*, London, 1980.
Solodkoff, Alexander von, *Russian Gold and Silver*, London, 1981.
Stavenow-Hidemark, Elisabet, *Svensk Jugend* (Nordiska Museum exhibition catalogue), Stockholm, 1964.
Sutton, Arthur, *A. Edward Jones, Master Silversmith of Birmingham*, Birmingham, 1980.
Tatham, Charles Heathcote, *Designs for Ornamental Plate*, London, 1806.
Ticher, Kurt, *Irish Silver in the Rococo Period*, Shannon, 1972.
Toranová, Eva, *Zlatníctvo Na Slovensku*, Bratislava, 1975.
Udy, David, 'Piranesi's' 'Vasi', the English Silversmith and his Patrons', *Burlington* magazine, CXX, 1978, pp. 820–838.
Vanwittenbergh, Jacques, *Orfèvrerie au Poinçon de Bruxelles* (exposition présentée par la Ville de Bruxelles et la Société General de Banque), Brussels, 1979.
Vende, E., *Väärismetalltööd Eestis, 15–19 sajandini*, Tallinn, 1967.
Vergo, Peter, *Art in Vienna 1898–1918*, 1975, 2nd ed., Oxford, 1981.
Viollet-le-duc, E., *Orfèvrerie à l'Usage des Cultes. Dessins . . . gravés par P. A. Varin*, Paris, 1850.
Vivant-Denon, D., *Voyage dans la Basse et la Haute Egypte*, Paris, 1802.
Waagepeterson, Christian, *Dansk Sølvplet før 1900*, Copenhagen, 1975.
Wardle, Patricia, *Victorian Silver and Silver-Plate*, London, 1963.
Wolfers, Marcel, *Philippe Wolfers, Précurseur de l'Art Nouveau*, Brussels, 1965.

SOME RETROSPECTIVE EXHIBITIONS *in chronological order*

Victoria and Albert Museum, Exhibition of Victorian and Edwardian Decorative Arts. Catalogue, London, 1952.
Kunstindustrimuseet i Oslo. Kristiania – Sølv fra 1604–1854, Oslo, 1954.
Musée National d'Art Modern. The sources of the XXth Century. The Arts in Europe from 1884 to 1914, Paris, 1960.
Nederlands Zilver, 1815–1960, Gementemuseum, The Hague, 1960.
Treasures of Trinity College, Dublin, Burlington House, London, 1961.
Christofle, Orfèvre. Cent Ans d'Orfèvrerie d'avant-garde, de Napoleon III à nos jours. Musée des Arts Décoratifs, Paris, 1962.
Henry Van de Velde 1863–1957. Rijkmuseum Rijkmuseum Kröller-Müller, Otterlo, 1964.
19th Century America. Furniture and other Decorative Arts. An exhibition in celebration of the hundredth anniversary of the Metropolitan Museum of Art, New York, 1970.
Irish Silver, An exhibition of Irish Silver from 1630–1820, Trinity College, Dublin, 1971.
Victoria and Albert Museum, Victorian Church Art, London, 1971.
Nederlandse Silwer/Dutch Silver, 1600–1850, Kultuurhistoriese Museum, Kaapstad/Cape Town, 1971.
The Arts and Crafts Movement in America, 1876–1916. Princeton, 1972. Also shown at the Art Institute of Chicago and the Renwick Gallery, Smithsonian Institution, 1973.
The Age of Neo-Classicism, The Royal Academy and the Victoria and Albert Museum, London, 1972. The Fourteenth Exhibition of the Council

of Europe.
Birmingham Gold and Silver, 1773–1973. An exhibition celebrating the Bicentenary of the Assay Office, City Museum and Art Gallery, Birmingham, 1973.
Groninger Zilver, Groningen Museum, Holland, 1975.
Victoria and Albert Museum, Liberty 1875–1975 (catalogue of an exhibition to mark the firm's centenary), London, 1975.
Mensen en Zilver, Bijna Twee Eeuwen Werken voor Van Kempen en Begeer. Tentonstelling van Zilverwerk, Sieraden, Penningen, Tekeningen, Portreeten en Curiosa, Museum Boymans-Van Beuningen, Rotterdam, 1975–6.
Emil Lettré-Andreas Moritz. Zwei Deutsche Silberschmiede im 20. Jahrundert, Museen der Stadt Koln: Kunstgewerbemuseum, Cologne, 1976.
Orfèvrerie Fantastique/Fabelachtig Zilver. Trésors des villes allemandes (fin 19ᵉ siècle)/schatten der Duitse steden (eind 19ᵉ eeuw), Europalia 1977 Exhibition, Maison du Roi, Brussels, 1977.
The Second Empire, 1852–1870/Art in France under Napoleon III. Philadelphia Museum of Art, 1978 (also shown at the Detroit Institute of Arts 1979, and the Grand Palais, Paris, 1979).
Vienna in the Age of Schubert. The Biedermeier Interior, 1815–1848. Victoria and Albert Museum, London, 1979.
Blaauwen, A. L. den, (ed.), *Nederlands Zilver/ Dutch Silver, 1580–1830*, Rijkmuseum, Amsterdam, 1979 (also shown at the Toledo Museum of Art, Toledo, Ohio and the Museum of Fine Arts, Boston, Mass., 1980).
Crook, J. Mordaunt (ed.), *National Museum of Wales, Cardiff. The strange Genius of William Burges, 'Art-Architect', 1827–1881, A catalogue of a Centenary Exhibition organized jointly by the National Museum of Wales, Cardiff, and the Victoria and Albert Museum, London*, catalogue entries by Mary Axon and Virginia Glenn, Cardiff, 1981.
750 Jahre Zürcher Gold- und Silberschmiedehandwerk, Helmhaus, Zurich, 1981.
Ribera, A. L. and Schenone, H.H., *Platería Sudamerica de los Siglos XVII-XX*, Bayerische Nationalmuseum/Staatliche Museum für Völkerkunde, Munich, 1981.
Irish Silver from the Seventeenth to the Nineteenth Century (organized by the Smithsonian Institution Traveling Exhibition Service from the collections of the National Museum of Ireland), Washington, 1982.
The Adjectives of History, Furniture and Works of Art, 1550–1870. Selected and edited by Alvar González-Palacios assisted by Donald Garstang, P. & D. Colnaghi & Co. Ltd., London, 1983.

PERIODICALS

Foment de les Arts Décoratives, II, Barcelona, 1920.
The Decoratives Arts Society Newsletter, Vol. IX, no. 2, New York, June 1983.

8 · ART DECO AND AFTER: 1920–60

Eisler, Max, *Dagobert Peche*, Vienna and Leipzig, 1925.
Fouquet, Jean, *Bijoux et Orfèvrerie*, Paris, c.1930.
Hughes, Graham, *Modern Silver*, London, 1967.
Revere-McFadden, David (ed.), *Scandinavian Modern Design 1880–1980*, New York, 1982.
— *Georg Jensen 1866–1966*, Snekkersten, Denmark. (Mobilia, special issue, June-July 1966).
— *Jean Puiforcat: Orfèvre Sculpteur*, Paris, 1951.

9 · CONTEMPORARY SILVER

Camberwell Beauty, Oxford, 1981. Catalogue of exhibition at Oxford Gallery, of graduate students of Camberwell School of Arts and Crafts, perhaps the best school of its type in Europe; good photo survey of current interest in texture and in uncouth shape.
Email, Vienna, 1980. Catalogue of far-ranging and distinguished exhibition at Galerie am Graben, Graben 7, Vienna.
Hughes, G., *Modern Silver throughout the World, 1880–1967*, London, 1967.
Edward Jones, A., *Metalcraftsman*, Birmingham Museum and Art Gallery, 1980. A good account of the Midlands industry, its growth and decay.
Emil Lettre and Andreas Moritz, Cologne 1977. Catalogue of exhibition of two German silversmiths of outstanding austerity, held in Cologne, Kunstgewerbe Museum.
Olle Ohlsson, Hanau, 1980. Catalogue published by the Deutsche Goldschmiedehaus, Hanau, for his 1979/80 exhibition there.
Persson, S., *Silver; Jewels; Sculpture; Glass; Industrial Design*, Stockholm, 1980–86. Five handsome volumes produced by the artist from Hogbergsgatan, Stockholm.
Louis Comfort Tiffany, 1848–1933, Lausanne, 1974. Catalogue of exhibition at Galerie des arts décoratifs; good table decoration and lamp photos.
Philippe Wolfers, 1858–1929, Ghent, 1979. Catalogue of exhibition held at Ghent Museum, 1979; good silver and glass photos.

APPENDIX I

Bradbury, F., *A History of Old Sheffield Plate*, London, 1912. A valuable source of information about industrialized manufacturing methods.
Bury, Shirley, *Victorian Electroplate*, London, 1971.
Cuzner, Bernard, *Silversmith's Manual*, 2nd ed., London, 1949.
Knauth, Percy, *The Emergence of Man: the Metalsmiths*, New York, 1974. An excellent popular account of the early history of metalworking.
Ogden, Jack, *Jewellery of the Ancient World*, London, 1982. The best general account in English of the present state of knowledge of early goldsmithing techniques.
Theophilus, *On Divers Arts*, translated with Introduction and Notes by John G. Hawthorne and Cyril Stanley Smith, 2nd ed., New York, 1979. The best translation of this important work for those with a practical interest in the craft techniques it describes.
Tylecote, R.F., *A History of Metallurgy*, London, 1976.
Untracht, Oppi, *Metal Techniques for Craftsmen*, 2nd ed., New York, 1975. Probably the most comprehensive practical handbook of metalworking crafts available.
Untracht, Oppi, *Enamelling on Metal*, London and New York, n.d. [1957].

APPENDIX II

All countries
Beuque, E., *Platine, Or et Argent: Dictionnaire des Poinçons*, Vols. I and II, Paris, 1929.
Rosenberg, M., *Der Goldschmiede Merkzeichen*, Vol. IV, Berlin, 1928.
Tardy, *Les Poinçons de Garantie Internationaux pour l'Argent*, Paris, 1977 (English language edition, 1981).
Canada
Langdon, J. E., *Canadian Silversmiths 1700–1900*, Toronto, 1966.
Channel Islands
Mayne, R. H., *Old Channel Islands Silver: its Makers and Marks*, Jersey, n.d.
Denmark
Bøje, C. A., *Danske Sølvmaerker*, Copenhagen, 1962.
France
Carré, L., *Les Poinçons de l'Orfèvrerie Française*, Paris, 1928.
Helft, J., *Les Poinçons des Provinces Françaises*, Paris, 1968.
Nocq, H., *Les Poinçons de Paris*, Vols. I-IV, Paris, 1926.
Thuile, H., *L'Orfèvrererie du Languedoc: Catalogue des Orfèvres*, Montpellier, 1966.
Germany
Rosenberg, M., *Der Goldschmiede Merkzeichen*, Vols. I-III, Berlin, 1928.
Scheffler, W., *Goldschmiede Niedersachsens* (and other works), Berlin and New York, 1965, etc.
Seling, H., *Die Kunst der Augsburger Goldschmede 1529–1860*, Munich, 1980.
Holland
Citroen, K.A., *Amsterdam Silversmiths and their Marks*, Amsterdam, Oxford and New York, 1975.
Koonings, W., *Meestertekens van Nederlandse Goud en Zilversmeden 1850* – (several volumes), The Hague, 1963.
Voet, E., *Haarlemsche Goud en Zilversmeden en kunne Merken*, Haarlem, 1928.
Voet, E., *Merken van Amsterdamsche Goud en Zilversmeden*, The Hague, 1912.
Voet, E., *Merken van Friesche*, The Hague, 1932.
Voet, E., *Merken van Haagsche Goud en Zilversmeden*, The Hague, 1941.
Voet, E., *Nederlandse Goud en Zilvermerken 1445–1951*, The Hague, 1951.
Italy
Bulgari, C. G., *Argentieri, Gemmari e Orafi d'Italia*, Rome, 1958 (in progress).
Malta
Denaro, V. F., *The Goldsmiths of Malta and their Marks*, Florence, 1972.
Russia
Goldberg, T. and others, *L'Orfèvrerie et la Bijouterie Russes aux XV-XX Siècles* (Russian text, with French summary), Moscow, 1967.
South Africa
Welz, S., *Cape Silver and Silversmiths*, Cape Town and Rotterdam, 1976.
Sweden
Andren, E., and others, *Svenskt Silversmide 1520–1850*, Stockholm, 1963.
United Kingdom
Bradbury, F., *Guide to Marks of Origin on British and Irish Silver Plate*, Sheffield, 1985.
Culme, John, *Directory of English Goldsmiths and Silversmiths 1838–1914 in the Press*, Woodbridge, Suffolk.
Grimwade, A.G., *London Goldsmiths 1697–1837: their Marks and Lives*, London, 1976.
Jackson, Sir Charles, *English Goldsmiths and their Marks*, London, 1966.
Touching Gold and Silver, 500 Years of Hallmarks, Goldsmiths' Company, 7–30 November 1978.
United States
Belden, L. C., *Marks of American Silversmiths in the Ineson-Bissel Collection*, Charlottesville (Va.), 1980.
Ensko, S., *American Silversmiths and their Marks*, 3 vols., New York, 1927 (privately printed).

· GLOSSARY ·

(*'A' in brackets after the word indicates that it is Ancient Greek or Roman*)

ACANTHUS (A) Classical stylized leaf ornament based on the Mediterranean acanthus plant, notable for its thick, deeply scalloped leaves.

ALABASTRON (A) Elongated, narrow-necked vase for perfume.

ALLOY A mixture of two or more metals. Also used sometimes to denote the base-metal part of a precious-/base-metal alloy.

ALTAR-CRUET *See* cruet.

AMPHORA (A) A jar with two handles used for storing liquids.

AMPULLA A small flask for the consecrated oil (*chrism*) used for anointing in sacred rites.

ANDIRONS Iron supports for burning logs in an open fireplace, sometimes decorated with silver.

ANNEALING A technique for softening metal by heating it to a temperature below its melting point and allowing it to cool.

ANTHEMION (A) Stylized decorative motif based on the honeysuckle flower. Widely used in classical architecture.

APOSTLE SPOON A spoon with the *finial* of its stem formed as the figure of Christ or one of the Apostles. Theoretically made in sets of thirteen, but often produced singly as christening gifts.

APPLIQUÉ Motifs executed separately and then applied to the surface of an article.

AQUAMANILE A medieval ewer for ablutions at table, usually of latten (a brass-like *alloy*), often in the shape of a lion, dragon, or other fantastic beast.

ARABESQUE A form of ornament of Islamic origin, making use of scrollwork, tendrils and, sometimes, foliage.

ARCADING Type of ornament representing a series of arches forming an arcade.

ARGYLL A container, normally with a spout, for gravy or sauce incorporating a device for keeping it warm, usually some kind of jacket or subsidiary container for hot water, but sometimes a receptacle for a hot iron.

ASSAY Test for quality, especially to ascertain that an *alloy* contains the legally-required proportion of precious metal. *See* Appendix II, page 233.

ASSAY-MARK *See* hallmark.

ASSAY-OFFICE The establishment where gold and silver are assayed and marked. Also, in popular usage, the organization responsible.

AURICULAR An ornamental style, first developed in Holland by the van Vianen family in the first part of the seventeenth century, characterized by strange lobed shapes, often resembling the interior of a shell or else the human ear (hence its name), and interflowing ornamental curves.

BAROQUE An art style that developed in Italy in the second half of the sixteenth century and spread to the rest of Europe, remaining popular until the early eighteenth century. It is characterized by expansive curved forms, and often, a general air of formal pompous grandeur.

BEADING Small globular ornament, usually applied in a row like a string of beads.

BEAKER A handleless drinking-vessel, generally of tapering cylindrical form, common since the Middle Ages.

BLEEDING BOWL *See* porringer.

BOSS A raised ornament, usually circular.

BOTTLE-TICKET A silver label for wine, spirit or sauce, suspended round the neck of the bottle containing it. Now often called a *wine-label*.

BOUGIE-BOX *See* taper-stand.

BRATINA A type of Russian *loving-* or *welcome-cup* with swelling sides, narrow neck, short foot and, sometimes, a domed cover.

BRIGHT-CUT ENGRAVING A technique whereby the lines of engraving are cut with sides of varying steepness, so producing a bright and sparkling effect. Done by holding the graving-tool's cutting-point crooked, so that the groove is almost vertical on one side and almost parallel to the surrounding surface on the other.

CABOCHON An uncut, but polished, gemstone, usually convex on the upper side.

CADDINET (French: *nef-à-cadenas*) The successor of the medieval *nef*. An individual rectangular *salver* for use at table, with a narrow rectangular covered box across the front containing compartments for spices, napkins and cutlery. An attribute of rank in the French court in the seventeenth century, its use – always limited – later spread to the British and German courts.

CALYX Whorl of leaves forming the outer case of a bud or the envelope of a flower. Also applied to the ornament supporting and partly enclosing the bowl of a *chalice* or secular cup.

CAMAIEU, EN French term for painting in white or monochrome on a plain background in imitation of a *cameo*.

CAMEO A relief design, especially on gemstones, hardstones, and glass. The opposite of *intaglio*.

CAN *See* mug.

CARTOUCHE Scroll ornament, derived from the Ionic volute, arranged as a panel to frame armorials, inscriptions and vignettes.

CASSOULETTE A vessel in which perfumes are burned. Often supported on a tripod.

CASTER A container, usually more-or-less bottle shaped, with its cover pierced with many small holes for sprinkling (casting) its contents, used mostly for sugar, salt or spices.

CASTING The technique of producing an object by liquefying its material, usually metal, and pouring it into a mould. Also synonymous with 'sprinkling', as in *casting-bottle* (cf. *caster*). *See* Appendix I, p. 228.

CAUDLE-CUP A cup for caudle, a nutritious spiced drink made from oatmeal mixed with wine, beer or spirits, traditionally given to women after childbirth. The term appears to refer specifically to a baluster-shaped cup with two handles, with or without a cover, of a kind that was particularly popular during the period c.1650–90. It is now often – though erroneously – called a *porringer*.

CAVETTO A hollow moulding, its profile a quarter circle.

CENSER (THURIBLE) A vessel in which incense is burnt, especially one that is swung during a religious ceremony.

CHAFING-DISH A dish fitting on to a small charcoal brazier used for cooking food, or keeping it warm, at table.

CHALICE The cup for the wine in the service of the *Eucharist*. Also called *communion cup* in Protestant churches and chapels.

CHARKA A shallow Russian bowl for vodka, usually on ball feet.

CHAMPLEVÉ ENAMELLING *See* Appendix I, page 232.

CHASING *See* Appendix I, page 231.

CHEESE-SCOOP A spoon-like device with a scoop-shaped bowl of semi-circular section used for taking portions out of a cheese.

CHEESE-TOASTER *See* toasted-cheese dish.

CHINOISERIE A decorative style, invented in Europe, involving Chinese landscape scenes with figures, birds and animals. Copied from imported Chinese and Japanese objects.

CHRISMATORY A container, usually a small casket, for the ampullae for consecrated oil. cf. ampulla.

CIBORIUM A container for the *Host* for the *Eucharist*.

CLASSICAL To do with the civilizations of Ancient Greece and Rome. *Neoclassical* refers to the deliberate revival of classical art that began in the mid-eighteenth century.

CLOISONNÉ ENAMELLING *See* Appendix I, page 232.

COASTER *See* wine-coaster.

COFFEE-BIGGIN A form of cylindrical coffee-pot with strainer and spirit-lamp on a stand, which can be easily packed for travelling. Invented by George Biggin and used in the late eighteenth and early nineteenth centuries.

CRUET A small stoppered vessel, usually more-or-less bottle shaped, either for (a) condiments at table or (b) wine and water used in the celebration of the *Eucharist (altar-cruet)*. Table cruets are normally accompanied by a *cruet-stand* (*cruet-frame*) and the term *cruet* is often applied loosely to the whole.

CUT-CARD-WORK A form of decoration popular in the late seventeenth and early eighteenth centuries involving the soldering of sheet silver over the body of an object. This was sometimes pierced with scrollwork and foliage, but was otherwise plain.

DAMASCENING The inlaying of gold or silver into an object. *See* Appendix I, page 232.

DIAPER A trellised pattern.

DIE-STAMPING OR SINKING *See* Appendix I, page 230.

DISH-CROSS A support for a hot dish at table, often incorporating a central spirit-lamp. It is normally x-shaped, with the arms of the x made so that they can be adjusted to fit dishes of different sizes.

DISH-RING A deep ring-shaped support for a hot dish at table. Particularly popular in Ireland, where it is often erroneously called a *potato-ring*.

DOG-NOSE SPOON *See* wavy-end spoon.

ÉCUELLE In the Middle Ages, a plain shallow bowl with a flat rim used for eating all types of food. Later it acquired two handles, and later still, a cover, and was used for soup or gruel. The same as the English *porringer*.

ELECTRUM A naturally-occurring *alloy* of gold and silver.

ELECTROFORMING Another name for *electrotyping*.

ELECTROPLATING (ELECTRODEPOSITION), ELECTROTYPING (ELECTROFORMING) *See* Appendix I, page 226.

ÉMAIL EN RONDE BOSSE Enamel applied to contoured surfaces like ceramic glaze.

EMBOSSING *See* Appendix I, page 231.

ENAMELLING *See* Appendix I, page 232.

ENGRAVING *See* Appendix I, page 231.

EPERGNE Possibly a corruption of the French *épargne* ('saving'). A term used in Britain, but not in France, for a form of elaborate table dumb-waiter, variously fitted with holders for sweetmeats, fruit and condiments, and often incorporating candle-holders. cf. surtout-à-table.

EUCHARIST The sacrament of Christ's supper (Mass or Communion).

FESTOON A garland of leaves and flowers, sometimes with fruit, suspended at each side and occasionally in the middle.

FILIGREE *See* Appendix I, page 232.

FINIAL A knob, sometimes pointed, applied to the top of an object.

FLAGON A large covered vessel with a single handle for pouring.

FLANGE A rim or projecting surface.

FLAT CHASING *See* Appendix I, page 231.

FLATWARE Spoons and forks.

FLUTING Shallow concave grooves, vertical, oblique or curved, normally closely set in series. The opposite of *gadrooning*.

FONT-CUP A short-stemmed drinking-cup with a shallow bowl with vertical sides, popular in early-sixteenth-century England.

FUSED PLATE The same as *Sheffield Plate*.

GADROONING A series of rounded ribs, like inside-out *fluting*.

GILT With a thin wash of gold over all surfaces. *See* Appendix I, page 230. cf. *also* parcel-gilt.

GOTHIC The major art style of the later Middle Ages, especially in northern Europe, characterized by pointed, angular forms and intricate detail. It sank in the social scale during the early sixteenth century, but in the eighteenth century started to become the subject of a deliberate antiquarian revival (Gothic Revival) which eventually led to it becoming, in an academic form, the major style of the second half of the nineteenth century.

GRACE-CUP A cup, not of any specific form, used to drink a grace (thanksgiving) at meals and commonly circulated amongst those present. cf. loving-cup *and* welcome-cup.

GRANULATION *See* Appendix I, page 232.

GROTESQUE Decoration involving human and animal forms fantastically interwoven with scrolls, shells and foliage, often bizarre and distorted.

GUILLOCHE A continuous plaited scroll pattern, the interstices often filled with rosettes.

HALLMARK A mark stamped on a precious metal article by an official *assay-office* guaranteeing its standard of purity. Strictly, the term should be confined to the mark of an assay-office operating from a company hall, like that of the London Goldsmiths' Company, and *assay-mark* used for others.

HANAP A general medieval term for a bowl-shaped drinking-vessel, with or without a foot.

HIGH RELIEF Sculptured or embossed decoration which projects strongly from its background.

HOLLOW-WARE Plates, vases, cups, jugs, etc.

HOLY WATER STOUP A container for consecrated water.

HOST The consecrated bread of the *Eucharist*.

HUGUENOTS French Protestants. They were granted religious toleration by the Edict of Nantes of 1598, but as the result of persecutions, culminating in the revocation of the Edict in 1685, large numbers emigrated. Some of them were silversmiths who had an important influence on the development of their craft in their countries of adoption.

ICE-BUCKET (ICE-PAIL) A wine-cooler for individual bottles introduced in the second half of the seventeenth century. cf. wine-cistern.

INCENSE-BOAT A boat-shaped container on a foot for storing incense for use in a *censer*.

INTAGLIO A recessed design, especially on gems, hardstones and glass. The opposite of *cameo*.

INTERLACE A design of interlacing lines or *strapwork*.

KANTHAROS (A) A deep drinking-cup, often on a tall stem, with two handles that sometimes curve high above the rim.

KNOP (KNOT) The swelling or protuberance on the stem of a *chalice* or other cup. Its purpose is both practical – to provide a better grip – and decorative.

KOTYLE (A) A deep cup with horizontal loop handle, popular in Etruria in about the seventh century BC.

KOVSH A Russian boat-shaped drinking-vessel with a single handle, also used as a ladle.

KRATER (A) A bowl in which wine was mixed with water.

KYATHOS (A) A ladle.

KYLIX (A) A shallow drinking-cup with two handles, often on a tall stem.

LEKYTHOS (A) A bottle for perfumed oil.

LOTUS The Egyptian water-lily, used in stylized form for ornament.

LOVING-CUP A cup, not of any specific form but often large and two-handled, passed round the dining-table for those present to drink from in turn. It appears to have been a Romantic revival of the *grace-cup*.

LOW RELIEF Sculptured or embossed decoration which projects only slightly from its background.

MANNERISM A highly intellectual and idiosyncratic offshoot of the Renaissance style which appeared in Italy in the early sixteenth century and spread thence to northern Europe, surviving until the early seventeenth century. It was characterized, among other things, by the use of sinuous, attenuated and bizarre forms, along with precious stones and exotic materials.

MARTELÉ A French term – meaning literally 'hammered' – for a form of decoration in which the hammer marks are left on the surface of a wrought-metal object. Also used as a trade name by the Gorham Manufacturing Company of Providence, Rhode Island.

MAZARINE A flat, pierced plate that fits, slightly raised, into the bottom of a serving-dish and allows juices to drain away. Often used for fish.

MAZER A drinking-bowl made of close-grained wood, almost invariably maple (Old High German *masar*). It was very popular in northern Europe during the Middle Ages and the sixteenth century and was commonly fitted with a silver, sometimes even gold, rim and base. A *standing mazer* is a mazer on a tall, stemmed foot.

MEDALLION A circular or oval ornamental motif.

MOKUME The process of laminating different coloured metals and *alloys* together to produce a decorative striated effect. The term is Japanese.

MOLINET A form of whisk for hot chocolate, usually comprising four flanges, often of pierced silver, at the end of a wooden rod which was rotated between the palms of the hands through a hole in the lid of the chocolate-pot.

MONSTRANCE A receptacle for displaying the *Host*, either on the altar or in processions.

MONTEITH Variant of the *punch-bowl*, distinguished by a deeply notched rim (usually detachable) from which wine-glasses may be suspended by their stems. The purpose was allegedly to cool the glasses in cold water with which the monteith could be filled when not in use as a *punch-bowl*.

MUG (OR CAN) A drinking-vessel with a simple body, usually more-or-less cylindrical or baluster-shaped, a side handle and no cover. Now often popularly, but erroneously, called a *tankard*.

NAUTILUS CUP A cup with its bowl formed by the shell of the chambered nautilus, a cephalopod native to the Pacific and Indian Oceans.

NEF A boat-shaped (hence its name) container used at table by monarchs, great lords and high-ranking ecclesiastics in the Middle Ages and Renaissance. It usually held their personal table-utensils and also, sometimes, salt and spices. It was continued as the *caddinet*.

NEF-À-CADENAS *See* caddinet.

NEOCLASSICAL *See* classical.

NIELLO *See* Appendix I, page 232.

OINOCHOE (A) A one-handled jug for serving wine, the lip often pinched to form a spout.

OMPHALOS (A) A central boss in the base of a dish.

OPUS INCLUSORUM *See* verroterie cloisonnée.

OVOLO Half round or curved convex moulding.

PALMETTE Decorative motif in the shape of a fan formed of stylized palm-leaves.

PARCEL-GILT Partial gilding. *See* gilt.

PATEN A shallow dish on which the *Host* is laid at the celebration of the *Eucharist*, usually made to match a *chalice*. A *standing-paten* is on a low foot.

PATERA (A) A bowl with a single handle set at right angles to the rim, as on the later *porringer*. The term is often applied loosely to a circular classical ornament based on the bowl.

PAX (PAX-BREDE) A small tablet – not necessarily of metal – used to exchange the kiss of peace at Mass, it being first kissed by the priest and then successively by the congregation. Examples normally bear a religious scene and have a small handle at the rear.

PEG-TANKARD A large *tankard* with a vertical row of pegs inside forming a scale against which the amount of liquid consumed can be measured. The type appears to be Scandinavian in origin, but was made elsewhere.

PHIALE (A) A shallow bowl used for pouring drink-offerings. A *phiale mesomphalos* has a central boss.

PILGRIM BOTTLE A flask-shaped bottle, originally of similar design to the water-bottle traditionally carried by medieval pilgrims. It was designed for the bulk service of wine to the table before the general introduction of the glass bottle, though examples continued to be made thereafter.

PLANISHING The process of smoothing the surface of a metal object with a planishing-hammer after it has been fashioned.

PLATE A term, now obsolete in non-specialist usage, referring to hammer-wrought gold or silver. Not to be confused with *Sheffield plate* or *electroplate*.

PLIQUE-À-JOUR ENAMELLING *See* Appendix I, page 232.

POMANDER A small box, usually more-or-less spherical, containing perfumes and/or spices and carried suspended round the neck or from the girdle. cf. vinaigrette.

PORRINGER (POTTAGER, POTTINGER) A term about which a certain amount of confusion has arisen in modern times. Silver-collectors in England apply it to what is here defined as a *caudle-cup*, and those in the United States to a flat shallow bowl with one, or more rarely two, short flat handles or ears set at right angles to the rim. There seems to be no doubt that the American usage is the correct one, since the English herald Randle Holme describes and illustrates such a bowl as a 'pottinger' in his *Academie of Armory*, of which the first volume was published in 1688 (Vol.II, 1905, pp. 4–5). It was used for serving soup or broth. Porringers are now commonly called *bleeding-bowls* in England, in the belief that they were used by surgeons when letting blood for medicinal reasons. This was clearly not their primary purpose, but Randle Holme (Vol.I, p.438) describes and illustrates a miniature one, which he calls a chirurgeon's 'Blood Porrenger', to hold one or two ounces of blood. Some examples of normal size are marked inside with a scale formed of concentric rings, presumably for this purpose.

POSSET-POT A cup for posset, a drink made of hot milk curdled with wine, ale, etc. Probably the same as a *caudle-cup*.

POT-À-OILLE A round tureen used in France for the serving of a ragout of game, meat and vegetables.

POTATO-RING *See* dish-ring.

PURITAN SPOON A seventeenth-century spoon with a thick, narrow, parallel-sided stem with the top cut off at right angles.

PYX A medieval term, from the Latin *pyxis*, originally applied to any box or container, it came to refer particularly to the small box in which the sacramental wafers for the *Eucharist* are kept. The annual *assaying* of the coinage known as *The Trial of the Pyx*, which is still carried out by the London Goldsmiths' Company, derives its name from the box in which the samples of coinage were kept.

PYXIS (A) A cylindrical box with a lid, for cosmetics or trinkets.

QUAICH A Scottish drinking-vessel, for spirits or wine, comprising a low footed bowl with two lug-like handles set at right angles to the rim. Many examples are of wood, but are frequently mounted in silver.

RAISING *See* Appendix I, page 229.

RAT-TAIL SPOON A spoon with a tapering rib – resembling a rat's tail – running down the back of the bowl from where it joins the stem.

RECUSANT PLATE A recusant was a Roman Catholic who refused to conform to the English sixteenth- and seventeenth-century laws banning the practice of his religion and requiring attendance at Anglican services. Special plate – notably *chalices* – was made for use at secret services of the Mass, constructed so that it could be easily concealed.

REEDING Narrow parallel mouldings resembling long stylized reeds.

RELIQUARY A container, usually of precious metal, for the display of a relic of a sacred or sanctified person.

RENAISSANCE The artistic and cultural revolution produced by the renewal of interest in the art and literature of Ancient Rome that started in Italy in the fourteenth century and eventually affected the whole of Europe.

REPOUSSÉ *See* embossing.

RHYTON (A) Drinking-horn, often in the form of an animal, or animal's head.

RINCEAU French term for a spiral leaf decoration.

ROCK CRYSTAL A transparent, colourless variety of quartz, capable of being carved and polished.

ROCOCO (French: *rocaille*) The light and elegant decorative style that succeeded, and was a reaction against, the baroque style. It made much use of asymmetry, S-shaped scrolls, rock-like motifs (*rocailles*), grotesques, including *chinoiseries*, and bright clear colours combined with much gold and silver.

ROUNDEL A small circular panel, plate or medallion, usually decorative.

SALVER A flat dish, at first on a trumpet-shaped central foot, later on three or more small feet beneath the rim, by which time it had become, in effect, what would now be called a tray. Also originally called a *waiter*, a term now confined, artificially, to a small salver.

SCONCE A wall candelabrum, supporting one or more candles, with a back reflector that also serves as a wall-plate.

SEAL-TOP SPOON A spoon with a short baluster-shaped *finial* surmounted by a horizontal flat disc, resembling a seal, at the top of the stem.

SHEFFIELD PLATE *See* Appendix I, page 225–6.

SILVER-GILT Silver gilded all over.

SINKING *See* die-stamping.

SITULA A bucket-shaped vessel, Roman in origin, usually for consecrated water for liturgical use. It was used in the West until the early Middle Ages.

SKYPHOS (A) A deep drinking-cup with two handles.

SLIP-TOP SPOON A form of spoon used from the late Middle Ages until the mid-seventeenth century with a narrow stem cut off diagonally at the top.

SOY-FRAME A cruet-frame for small bottles of sauce. cf. cruet.

SPINNING *See* Appendix I, page 230.

STANDING On a tall foot, as in *standing-cup*, *standing-paten*, *standing-mazer*, etc.

STANDISH An inkstand.

STEEPLE-CUP A type of early-seventeenth-century English *standing-cup* with a cover surmounted by a steeple-shaped *finial*.

STIRRUP-CUP A cup for taking a drink, usually of spirits, on horseback before going out hunting, and introduced as a distinctive type in the 1760s. Designed so that it cannot stand, it usually takes the form of the head of an animal of the chase, that of a fox being the most popular.

STRAPWORK Ornament consisting of interlaced bands or straps.

STRAWBERRY-DISH A term applied to a whole group of shallow, circular or, more rarely, oval dessert-dishes with flat bottoms and fluted upcurved sides. It is not certain that all were used for strawberries.

SURTOUT-À-TABLE Term used in France (and in England) to describe an elaborate centrepiece for the dinner-table. cf. epergne.

SWAG A festoon of cloth.

TANKARD A drinking-vessel, originally used for wine as well as beer and ale, similar to a *mug*, but with a hinged cover.

TAPER-STAND (WAX-JACK, BOUGIE-BOX) A stand for a long wax taper, which is coiled round a reel or a vertical spindle accompanied by a scissor-like clamp. The upper end of the taper is held in this last and it can be drawn up through it as it burns down. The *bougie-box* is a version comprising a cylindrical box with a central hole in its lid – like a string-box – through which the end of a taper coiled inside is passed.

TAPERSTICK A miniature candlestick designed to take a taper.

TASTEVIN *See* wine-taster.

TAZZA The Italian word for cup, applied in England and America since the nineteenth-century to a drinking-cup or dish with a flat circular bowl and a tall, central foot.

THURIBLE *See* censer.

TOASTED-CHEESE DISH A flat, oblong dish with a straight wooden handle at the back and a cover hinged on the same side, for cooking and serving toasted-cheese. The cover both protects the hand and reflects heat onto the cheese.

TREMBLEUSE French term for a silver frame to hold a porcelain chocolate- or tea-cup, usually *en suite* with a silver saucer.

TRIFID SPOON A form of spoon popular in the late-seventeenth and early-eighteenth centuries with the spatulate end of the flat stem shaped to three short points.

TROY WEIGHT A system of weights used for precious metals, with a pound of twelve ounces.

VERROTERIE CLOISONNÉE (Latin: *opus inclusorum*) A French term for a type of late-Antique and early-medieval cloisonné decoration in which plaques of red glass or garnet are set in compartments.

VINAIGRETTE A small decorative container, carried on the person, for a sponge soaked in aromatic vinegar held under a pierced inner lid. Examples can be box-shaped or take some fanciful form. cf. pomander.

WAGER-CUP A type of cup originating in seventeenth-century Germany or Holland, incorporating an additional small bowl suspended in a pivot. To win the wager both had to be drained without setting the cup down. Examples often take the form of a female figure who holds the smaller bowl above her head and whose skirts form the larger bowl.

WAITER *See* salver.

WAVY-END SPOON A type of spoon used in the period around 1700 with the spatulate end of the flat stem shaped to an incurved rounded triangle. Also called *dog-nose*.

WAX-JACK *See* taper-stand.

WELCOME-CUP (German: *Willkommbecher*) A special cup kept by many craft-guilds, especially in Germany and Scandinavia, for drinking a welcome to new members. Some German families kept a *Willkommbecher* to pledge guests.

WINE-CISTERN A large bowl, on feet, which could be filled with water (and ice) for cooling bottles of wine in the room where it was served, and also for washing the drinking- and serving-vessels. cf. ice-pail.

WINE-COOLER *See* ice-bucket, wine-cistern.

WINE-FOUNTAIN A large urn, often made *en suite* with a *wine-cistern*, with one or more taps, resembling a much-enlarged coffee- or tea-urn. It was used both for water for washing the drinking- and serving-vessels, and for the service of wine.

WINE-LABEL *See* bottle-ticket.

WINE-TASTER (French: *tastevin*) A small, saucer-shaped bowl, with or without a small handle at the side, used for tasting and examining wine to assess its quality.

· INDEX ·

Numbers in italics refer to captions of illustrations

A

B

E

F

G

· ACKNOWLEDGEMENTS ·

Museums and Art Galleries
The Warden and Fellows of All Souls College, Oxford, 65 (bequest of Mrs Catherine Griffith); Archaeological Museum, Plovdiv, 13, 19 bottom; Archaeological Museum, Thessaloniki, 14 right, 15, 16, 17; Ashmolean Museum, Oxford, 74 right; Bibliothèque Nationale, Paris, 26, 49 bottom; by courtesy of The Trustees of The British Museum, London, 24–5, 29 left, 31, 46 right, 61 left, 63 bottom right (on loan from The Vicar and Parochial Church Council, Lacock), 77, 84 (Waddesdon Bequest), 89, 126; The Brooklyn Museum, New York, 190 top (gift of The Estate of May S. Kelley); Trustees of The Chatsworth Settlement, 1, 2–3, 4–5, 6, 104 bottom, 105 left, 111, 115 bottom; Conques Abbey Museum, 48 right; The Cleveland Museum of Art, 128 right (purchase, Leonard C. Hanna, Jr. Bequest); Dumbarton Oaks Collection, Washington, 35; Field Museum of Natural History, Chicago, 20; Frisian Museum, Leeuwarden, 97 bottom (on loan from the board of the Popta Almshouse, Marssum); Germanisches Nationalmuseum, Nuremberg, 79, 203; The J. Paul Getty Museum, Malibu, 128 left; Groeningemuseum, Bruges, 70; Collection of The State Museums of the Moscow Kremlin, 90 left, 92 left, 121; Kunstgewerbemuseum, Berlin, 80, 92 right; Kunsthistorisches Museum, Vienna, 24 bottom, 43 top, 63 bottom left, 64 left, 72; Kunstindustrimuseet, Copenhagen, 186; Kunstindustrimuseet, Oslo, 165 bottom, 185; Los Angeles County Museum of Art/Mr and Mrs Arthur Gilbert, 73; The Metropolitan Museum of Art, New York, 8 (gift of J. Pierpont Morgan), 18 top and 21 (Rogers Fund), 22 bottom (Fletcher Fund), 32 right (The Cloisters Collection), 32 left and 88 (gift of J. Pierpont Morgan), 94 (Rogers Fund), 140 (gift of Mr and Mrs Charles Wrightsman), 147 top (bequest of A.T. Clearwater), 193 (gift of Mrs Winthrop Atwell); Minneapolis Institute of Arts, 81 (James Ford Bell Family Foundation Fund, The M.R. Schweitzer Fund and The Christina N. and Swan J. Turnblad Memorial Fund), 191 (lent by the family of John Booth Cooley); Musée Bouilhet-Christofle, Saint-Denis, 172; Musée d'Art et d'Histoire, Geneva, 86 top; Musée des Antiquités Nationales, Saint-Germain-en-Laye, 19 top; Musée des Arts Décoratifs, Paris, 171; Musée Nissim de Camondo, Paris, 143 right; Musées de Sens, 43 bottom; Musées Royaux d'Art et d'Histoire, Brussels, 48 left; Museo Archeologico, Florence, 12; Museo degli Argenti, Florence, 71 left; Museo dell'Opera del Duomo, Orvieto, 60; Museo dell'Opera del Duomo, Siena, 110; Museo di Villa Giulia, Rome, 11; Museo Nazionale, Naples, 18 bottom, 23; Museu Nacional de Arte Antiga, Lisbon, 62; Museum of Fine Arts, Boston, 10 bottom (Francis Bartlett Donation), 27 right (Helen and Alice Coburn Fund); The Museum of London, 27 left; National Archaeological Museum, Athens, 22 top; National Gallery of Art, Washington, 45 (Widener Collection); National Gallery of Canada, Ottawa, 155 top; National Hermitage Museum, Leningrad, 14 left, 33; National Museum, Bucharest, 29 right; National Museum of Ireland, Dublin, 42 top, 151 right; Nationalmuseum, Stockholm, 154 left; National Museum of Wales, Cardiff, 42 bottom (reproduced by Gracious Permission of Her Majesty The Queen), 76 top; Nationalmuseet, Copenhagen, 57; Österreichisches Museum Für Angewandte Kunst, Vienna, 177, 198 top; The Pierpont Morgan Library, New York, 55 top right; Real Academia de la Historia, Madrid, 30 right; Residenzmuseum, Munich, 75, 78 right, 86 bottom, 100; Réunion des Musées Nationaux, Paris, 24 top, 36, 39, 44, 74 left, 98 bottom, 103, 119 top (© CNMHS/SPADEM); Rijksmuseum, Amsterdam, 85, 96, 97 top, 173; Römermuseum, Augst, 30 left; Royal Ontario Museum, Toronto, 195; The St Louis Art Museum, 188 right (bequest of The Harry Edison Foundation); Schatzkammer, Vienna, 46 top left; Schweizerisches Landesmuseum, Zurich, 118; Smithsonian Institution, Washington, 190 bottom, 194; Staatliche Kunstsammlungen, Kassel, 106; Staatliche Museen Preussischer Kulturbesitz, Berlin, 80 left, 92 right; Staatsbibliothek, Munich, 50; Capitolo di S. Pietro in Vaticano, Rome, 80 right; by courtesy of The Trustees of The Victoria and Albert Museum, London, 10 top, 58, 92 bottom, 93, 104 top, 109, 113, 114, 122, 134 left, 142, 148, 156, 158 right, 159, 160, 162 bottom, 164, 166, 169, 179, 183, 192, 205 top, 207 bottom, 217; The Walters Art Gallery, Baltimore, 153; Yale University Art Gallery, New Haven, 123 (The Mabel Brady Garvan Collection), 155 bottom.

We would like to thank the following for lending us their materials: A.C.L., Brussels, 52, 54 top, 55 top left; Archivio IGDA, 11, 12; Bavaria-Verlag, Gauting, 49 top; Friedrich Becker, Düsseldorf, 222; Lee Boltin Picture Library, New York, 13, 19 bottom; J.H. Bourdon-Smith Ltd., London, 150 top; Viky Calliora, 29 Voukourestion, 136 Athens, 14 right, 15, 16, 17; Christie, Manson & Woods Ltd., London, 68, 129, 130, 143 left, 145, 151 left, 152 bottom, 170, 188 left; Collection of Mr and Mrs Cotton, Guernsey, 216 top; Crown Copyright, reproduced with the permission of The Controller of HMSO, 98 top, 105 right; Crown Copyright, reproduced by Gracious Permission of Her Majesty the Queen, 135 top, 162 top; Prudence Cuming Associates Ltd., London, 108, 112; The Design Council, London, 203; Collection of The Duke of Buccleuch and Queensberry, K.T., Boughton House, Kettering, 115 top; by kind permission of His Grace The Duke of Marlborough, 131, 137; Edimedia, Paris/Roger Guillemot, 64 right; Arline Fisch, San Diego, 214 top; L. Garner Collection, London, 198 bottom, 199, 200, 201, 202, 204 top, 205 bottom, 206 top, 208, 209, 210, 211; Garrard & Co. Ltd., London, 150 bottom; Giraudon, Paris, 48 right, 55 bottom; Hancocks & Co. (Jewellers) Ltd., 165 top; Hirmer Fotoarchiv, Munich, 38, 53; Brand Inglis, London, 135 bottom, 138, 139 left, 146; Georg Jensen, Copenhagen, 215; Stanley Lechtzin, Melrose Park, Pennsylvania, 224 left; Grant Macdonald, London, 224 right; Novosti Press Agency, London 92 left; Okehampton Town Council, 117; Olle Ohlsson, Stockholm, 223 bottom; Collection of H.R.H. Princess Juliana of The Netherlands, 107; private collection, London, 139 right, 147 bottom; Rheinisches Bildarchiv, Cologne, 47; The Royal Collections, Stockholm, 99, 144 bottom, 184; Sabattini S.p.a., Bregnano, 223 top; Scala, Florence, 40, 60, 61 right, 71 left; Sotheby, Parke Bernet & Co., London, 76 bottom, 124, 144 top, 149, 152 top, 154 right, 158 left, 168, 174, 176, 178, 180, 181; Thyssen-Bornemisza Collection, Lugano, 101, 119 bottom; Vaap, Moscow, 14 left, 33, 121; Robert Welch, Chipping Campden, 219; The Worshipful Company of Goldsmiths, London, 161, 196, 204 bottom, 206 bottom, 207 top, 212, 216 bottom, 218, 220 top, 221.

We would also like to thank these photographers for their help: Beedle & Cooper, Northampton, 115 top; Sheldon Collins (Metropolitan Museum, New York), 90 left; Simon De Courcy-Wheeler, London, 1, 2–3, 4–5, 6, 111, 161, 196, 204 bottom, 212, 216 bottom, 220 top, 221; Hilda Deecke, Berlin, 80 left; Lucinda Douglas-Menzies, 216 top; Umicini Giovanni, Padua, 69; Grassi, Siena, 110; Ian Haigh, 220 bottom; Marie Ann Haller, Südstadt, 46 top left; R. Leducq, Maubeuge, 56; Ann Münchow, Aachen, 41, 46 bottom, 51; R. Pedicini, Naples, 18 bottom, 23; Joe Rock, Edinburgh, 91; N. Terebenin, Moscow, 33; Thomas Photos, Oxford, 65; C. Valkenburg, Brussels, 48 left; H. Vanhaelewyn, Bruges, 70.